中国高速动车组概论

（中英双语）

主　编　黄　超　彭文菁
副主编　蔡　磊　何洲红　余水平
主　审　朱金凤　郭　毅

西南交通大学出版社
·成都·

图书在版编目（CIP）数据

中国高速动车组概论：中英双语 / 黄超，彭文菁主编. —成都：西南交通大学出版社，2023.6
ISBN 978-7-5643-9328-1

Ⅰ. ①中… Ⅱ. ①黄… ②彭… Ⅲ. ①高速动车 – 概论 – 英语 – 高等职业教育 – 教材 Ⅳ. ①U266

中国国家版本馆 CIP 数据核字（2023）第 101211 号

Zhongguo Gaosu Dongchezu Gailun (Zhongying Shuangyu)
中国高速动车组概论（中英双语）

主　编／黄　超　彭文菁	责任编辑／张文越
	封面设计／吴　兵

西南交通大学出版社出版发行
（四川省成都市金牛区二环路北一段 111 号西南交通大学创新大厦 21 楼　610031）
发行部电话：028-87600564　028-87600533
网址：http://www.xnjdcbs.com
印刷：四川森林印务有限责任公司

成品尺寸　185 mm×260 mm
印张　18.75　　字数　523 千
版次　2023 年 6 月第 1 版　　印次　2023 年 6 月第 1 次

书号　ISBN 978-7-5643-9328-1
定价　49.00 元

课件咨询电话：028-81435775
图书如有印装质量问题　本社负责退换
版权所有　盗版必究　举报电话：028-87600562

前　言

随着高速铁路快速发展，截至 2023 年初，我国高铁运营总里程达到 4.2 万公里，居世界第一，占全球的 2/3 以上。如今，高铁已经成为我国在国际舞台上一张亮丽的名片。

作为高铁核心的高速动车组是集当今世界先进的计算机技术、微电子技术、遥感与自控技术、新型材料技术、现代制造技术、空气动力学技术等现代科学技术为一体的系统工程的产物。

为切实提高中国高铁国际影响力，让国际学生，尤其是"一带一路"国家学生了解我们中国高速动车组发展情况和技术，我们编写了《中国高速动车组概论》(中英双语)国际教材。

本书满足动车组检修专业国际留学生的学习需求，为他们后续的动车组专业课程的学习打下基础。本教材还可用作动车组检修技术专业学生和铁道车辆技术专业学生的"专业英语"课程的教材，以及"动车组概论"课程的教材。

本教材注重突出动车组的基本结构组成、基本工作原理，还图文并茂、深入浅出地介绍动车组知识，便于读者理解，同时力求教学内容的全面性、系统性、时代性、实用性兼具，以满足高职院校的教学需求。

本教材由武汉铁路职业技术学院的黄超、彭文菁任主编，蔡磊、何洲红、余水平任副主编，邓命、孙亦冰、何丽娟任参编，朱金凤任英文部分主审、昆明铁道职业技术学院的郭毅任中文部分主审。

各章编写的分工分别是：武汉铁路职业技术学院的黄超编写了第四章中文部分和第六章中、英文部分，彭文菁编写了第十章的中、英文部分，何洲红编写了第七章的中、英文部分和第三章的英文部分，蔡磊编写了第二章的中、英文部分和第三章的中文部分，余水平编写了第八章的中、英文部分，孙亦冰编写了第一章的中、英文部分和第四章的英文部分，邓命编写了第五章中、英文部分，何丽娟编写了第九章的中、英文部分，全书由黄超统稿。

编　者
2022 年 8 月

目 录

1 概 述 ·· 1
   1.1 国外高速铁路的发展 ·· 1
   1.2 我国高速铁路的发展 ·· 1
   1.3 高速铁路的特点 ·· 2
   1.4 高速铁路的定义 ·· 4
   1.5 动车组的定义与分类 ·· 4
   1.6 动车组动力配置方式的特点与选择 ································· 6

2 高速动车组车体 ·· 8
   2.1 车体的用途 ·· 8
   2.2 车体基本组成及技术特点 ··· 8
   2.3 动车组的外形尺寸 ··· 9
   2.4 动车组的车体结构 ··· 10

3 动车组的车钩 ·· 17
   3.1 自动车钩 ··· 18
   3.2 半永久车钩 ··· 23
   3.3 过渡车钩 ··· 26

4 转向架 ··· 28
   4.1 转向架构架 ··· 30
   4.2 带有轴箱的轮对 ··· 31
   4.3 轴 箱 ·· 33
   4.4 一系弹簧悬挂 ·· 34
   4.5 二系弹簧悬挂 ·· 35

4.6　摇　枕 …………………………………………………………… 37
　　4.7　转向架牵引装置 ………………………………………………… 38
　　4.8　转向架上安装的制动部件 ……………………………………… 38
　　4.9　减振器 …………………………………………………………… 39
　　4.10　轮缘润滑 ………………………………………………………… 40
　　4.11　撒砂系统 ………………………………………………………… 40

5　动车组牵引系统 ………………………………………………………… 42
　　5.1　组成及作用 ……………………………………………………… 42
　　5.2　受电弓 …………………………………………………………… 43
　　5.3　牵引变压器 ……………………………………………………… 45
　　5.4　牵引变流器 ……………………………………………………… 46
　　5.5　牵引电机 ………………………………………………………… 56
　　5.6　真空断路器 ……………………………………………………… 57

6　动车组制动系统 ………………………………………………………… 59
　　6.1　主要制动类型 …………………………………………………… 59
　　6.2　动车组制动系统介绍 …………………………………………… 60
　　6.3　动车组制动系统工作原理 ……………………………………… 62
　　6.4　盘形制动装置 …………………………………………………… 67
　　6.5　防滑保护 ………………………………………………………… 70
　　6.6　供风系统 ………………………………………………………… 71

7　辅助供电系统 …………………………………………………………… 78
　　7.1　系统组成与工作原理 …………………………………………… 78
　　7.2　辅助变流器 ……………………………………………………… 79
　　7.3　充电机+蓄电池 ………………………………………………… 83
　　7.4　配电系统 ………………………………………………………… 86

8　动车组网络控制技术 …………………………………………………… 88
　　8.1　概述 ……………………………………………………………… 88
　　8.2　动车组网络控制系统组成 ……………………………………… 89
　　8.3　动车组网络控制系统原理 ……………………………………… 92
　　8.4　动车组网络的系统功能 ………………………………………… 99

9 空气调节系统 ··· 104
9.1 空气调节系统概述 ··· 104
9.2 空气调节装置工作原理 ··· 106
9.3 空气调节单元机组 ··· 110

10 高速动车组服务系统 ·· 119
10.1 旅客信息系统 ·· 119
10.2 照明系统 ·· 122
10.3 厨房设施和设备 ·· 125
10.4 给水装置 ·· 130
10.5 卫生系统 ·· 132

参考文献 ··· 134

Contents

Chapter 1　Outline Introduction ········· 136

　1.1　Development of foreign high-speed railway ········· 136

　1.2　Development of high-speed railway in china ········· 137

　1.3　Characteristics of high-speed railway ········· 137

　1.4　Definition of high-speed railway ········· 140

　1.5　Definition and classification of EMU ········· 140

　1.6　Characteristics and selection of EMU power configuration mode ········· 142

Chapter 2　High-Speed Car Body ········· 145

　2.1　The Usage of the EMU Car body ········· 145

　2.2　The primary structure and technical characteristics of the EMU car body ········· 145

　2.3　The shape and size of the EMU ········· 147

　2.4　The body structure of the EMU ········· 147

Chapter 3　Couplers of EMU ········· 155

　3.1　Automatic coupler ········· 156

　3.2　Semi-permanent couplers ········· 162

　3.3　Coupler adapter ········· 165

Chapter 4　Bogies ········· 167

　4.1　Bogie frame ········· 170

　4.2　Wheelset with axle box ········· 171

　4.3　Axle box ········· 173

　4.4　Primary suspension ········· 173

　4.5　Secondary suspension ········· 174

　4.6　Bolster ········· 177

　4.7　Traction system of the Bogie ········· 177

  4.8 Bogie mounted brake components ··· 178
  4.9 Damper ··· 179
  4.10 Wheel flange lubrication ··· 180
  4.11 Sanding system ··· 180

Chapter 5 The traction system of EMU ··· 182

  5.1 Composition and function ··· 182
  5.2 Pantograph ··· 183
  5.3 Traction transformer ··· 186
  5.4 Traction converter ··· 187
  5.5 Traction motor ··· 199
  5.6 Vacuum breaker ··· 199

Chapter 6 Brake System ··· 202

  6.1 Main types of brake system ··· 202
  6.2 Introduction to brake system of EMU train ··· 204
  6.3 Working principles of brake system for EMU ··· 206
  6.4 Brake calliper unit ··· 211
  6.5 The wheel slip protection (WSP) ··· 216
  6.6 Air supply system ··· 217

Chapter 7 Auxiliary power supply system ··· 224

  7.1 Composition and operation principle of auxiliary power supply system ··· 224
  7.2 Auxiliary converter ··· 225
  7.3 Charger and battery ··· 230
  7.4 The power distribution system ··· 233

Chapter 8 EMU Network Control Technology ··· 235

  8.1 Overview ··· 235
  8.2 EMU network control system composition ··· 236
  8.3 EMU network control system principle ··· 238

  8.4 System functions of EMU network ·· 248

Chapter 9 HVAC System ·· 253

  9.1 Overview ·· 253

  9.2 Principles of HVAC system ·· 256

  9.3 The HVAC unit ·· 260

Chapter 10 High-Speed EMU Service System ·· 270

  10.1 Passenger information system ·· 270

  10.2 Lighting system ·· 274

  10.3 Kitchen facilities and equipment ·· 277

  10.4 Water supply device ·· 282

  10.5 Health tsystem ·· 284

参考文献 ·· 288

1 概 述

随着科技的快速发展及人们生活节奏的加快，为满足人们对交通工具现代化的需要，高速铁路应运而生并逐步成为当今世界铁路发展的普遍趋势。

1.1 国外高速铁路的发展

自 1825 年英国修建了世界上第一条铁路后，铁路这一交通工具便在世界各国迅速发展，对当时社会经济文化的发展与繁荣起到了极大的推动作用。

日本是世界上第一个建成实用性高速铁路的国家。1964 年 10 月 1 日，日本东海道新干线开通，最高运营速度达到 210 km/h。东海道新干线取得了良好的经济效益和社会效益，新干线更是被誉为"日本经济起飞的脊梁"。

世界高速铁路建设共经历过三次高潮。

（1）20 世纪 60 年代至 80 年代末期——高速铁路建设的第一次高潮。

1964—1990 年，建设并投入运营的高速铁路有：日本的上越、东北、山阳和东海道新干线；法国的大西洋 TGV 线，东南 TGV 线；德国的汉诺威—威尔茨堡高速新线；意大利的罗马 - 佛罗伦萨线。

（2）20 世纪 80 年代末至 90 年代中期——高速铁路建设的第二次高潮。

20 世纪 80 年代末，世界各国对高速铁路的高度关注和研究重视，酝酿了高速铁路的第二次建设高潮。第二次建设高峰形成于 20 世纪 90 年代的欧洲。1991 年，瑞典开通了 X2000 型号的摆式列车；1992 年，西班牙引进德国、法国的技术，建成了马德里—塞维利亚高速铁路线；1994 年，英国和法国，通过英吉利海峡隧道连接在一起，这是第一条高速铁路国际连接线；1997 年，从巴黎开出的"欧洲之星"，又将德国、荷兰、比利时、法国连接在一起。

（3）20 世纪 90 年代中期至今——高速铁路建设的第三次高潮。

20 世纪 90 年代中期，形成了高速铁路建设研究的第三次高潮。这次高潮波及到大洋洲、北美洲、亚洲以及整个欧洲。

1.2 我国高速铁路的发展

我国高速铁路较世界发达国家起步较晚，但自 21 世纪以来得到迅速发展，其发展速度之快、建设规模之大、运输能力之巨，可谓世界第一。

20 世纪 90 年代中期，我国铁路面临速度慢、运能不足的局面，难以满足人们出行需要。自 1997 年到 2007 年的 10 年间，我国铁路先后进行了六次大规模提速，建立了完整的技术理论体系和成熟的技术措施，为我国高速铁路建设和运营管理提供了强有力的技术支撑。

2004年1月，国务院批准了《铁路中长期发展规划》（简称《规划》），提出了跨越式发展思路，确定了我国铁路发展的蓝图。同年，我国开始着手引进国外高速铁路相关技术。经过不断学习、研发、创新，我国已经系统掌握了高速列车系列核心关键技术，形成自主知识产权技术体系和标准体系，高速铁路的建设和运用技术达到国际领先水平。

2021年，国务院发布《"十四五"现代综合交通运输体系发展规划》，在高铁方面提出的发展目标为：到2025年，主要采用250千米及以上速度标准的高速铁路网对50万人口以上城市覆盖率达到95%，普速铁路瓶颈路段基本消除。7条首都放射线、11条北南纵线、18条东西横线，以及地区环线、并行线、联络线等组成的国家高速公路网的主线基本贯通，普通公路质量进一步提高。

在综合交通运输发展的铁路主要指标方面，铁路营业里程将从2020年的14.6万千米发展为2025年的16.5万千米；其中高速铁路营业里程将从2020年的3.8万千米发展为2025年的5万千米。

1.3 高速铁路的特点

高速铁路出现后，之所以在世界各国受到普遍欢迎并得以快速发展，决非偶然。这不仅是由于高速铁路克服了普通铁路速度低等缺点，与目前高速公路的汽车运输和中长途的航空运输相比较，高速铁路具有下列优势。

1. 安全性好

安全始终是人们选择出行交通运输方式的首要因素。有资料表明，在各国交通运输中，铁路、公路、民航运输的事故率（每百万人千米的伤亡人数）之比大致为1∶24∶0.8。由于高速铁路普遍采用线路的全封闭和运行控制的自动化，且有一系列完善的安全保障体系，故其安全可靠性大大高于其他交通工具。

2. 运输能力大

高速铁路保留了普通铁路大众运输工具的基本特征。有专家分析计算：高速铁路动车组的最小行车间隔可达4 min，列车密度可达20列/h，若每列车载客人数按800人计算，扣除线路维修时间（4 h/d），则每天可开行高速列车400列，输送旅客32万人，年均单向输送将达到1.17亿人。而4车道高速公路，单向每小时可通过汽车1250辆，每天也按20小时计算，可通过25 000辆，如大轿车占20%，每车平均乘坐40人，小轿车占80%，每车乘坐2人，年均单向输送能力为8700万人。目前，最大的飞机可载客300～400人，两地飞行按单向每天20架次计算，每天运输旅客为6000～8000人。

3. 速度快

速度快是高速铁路技术的核心，也是其主要技术经济优势所在。迄今，高速铁路是陆上运行距离最长、运行速度最高的交通运输方式之一。

4. 能耗低

据统计资料显示，各种交通运输工具平均每人千米的能耗：飞机：2998.8 J，小轿车：3309.6 J，高速公路公共汽车：583.8 J，高速铁路：571.2 J。除此之外，汽车、飞机均使用的是不可再生的一次能源——汽油或柴油（现代新型节能汽车尚未批量投入运用），而高速铁路使用的是二次能源——电力。随着水电、太阳能、风能和核电等新型能源的推广和发展，高速铁路在能源消耗方面的优势还将更加突出。这也是在当今石油能源紧张的情况下，世界各国选择发展高速铁路的重要原因之一。

5. 污染轻

环境保护是当今关系人类生存发展的全球性紧迫问题，而交通运输与生态环境密切相关。当前，交通运输对环境的污染主要是废气和噪声。据统计，在旅客运输中，各种交通运输工具一氧化碳等有害物质的换算排放量，公路为 0.902 kg/人，铁路为 0.109 kg/人，客机为 635 kg/h。由于高速铁路实现了电气化和集便器等设施设备，使铁路基本消除了粉尘、油烟和其他废气（物）对环境的污染。另外，在噪声污染方面，日本曾以航空运输每千人千米产生的噪声为 1，则大轿车为 0.2，高速铁路仅为 0.1。

6. 占地少

复线铁路占地宽度为 13.7 m，一条 4 车道高速公路占地宽度为 26 m，飞机航道虽然不占用土地，但一个大型机场占地相当于 1000 km 复线铁路的占地面积。

7. 造价低

工程造价的高低在一定程度上是制约某种交通运输方式迅速发展的重要因素之一。高速铁路的工程造价虽然大大高于普通铁路，但并不比修建一条高速公路或民航机场的建设费用高。据法国资料，法国高速铁路基础设施造价要比 4 车道的高速公路节约 17%。TGV 高速列车平均每座席的造价仅相当于短途飞机每座席造价的 1/10。

8. 舒适度高

随着人们物质生活水平的不断提高，出行舒适状况已成为人们选择出行交通方式的重要依据之一。高速铁路线路平顺、稳定、曲线半径大，列车运行平稳，振动和摆动幅度都很小，速度快。由于采用新型材料，动车内宽敞明亮，设施先进，装备齐全，乘坐舒适，活动半径大，旅客在途中占有的活动空间大大高于汽车和飞机。

9. 效益好

高速公路的日常交通堵塞和事故频发给各国国民经济带来了巨大经济损失，也严重影响了社会的和谐稳定。欧洲共同体国家每年用于处理高速公路堵塞和公路交通事故的费用分别占国民生产总值的 2.9%和 2.5%。而修建高速铁路的直接经济效益却是非常明显。据统计，日本东海道新干线 1964 年投入运营，1966 年就开始盈利，1971 年就收回了全部投资。法国

TGV东南线1983年全线通车，1984年开始盈利，运营10年投资全部收回。我国高速铁路的建设主要集中在目前运能十分紧张、人口密度大、经济发展快的大中城市间，因此，其投资回收周期可望更短。

1.4 高速铁路的定义

高速铁路是一个具有国际性和时代性的概念，定义相当广泛。我国高速铁路定义为新建设计开行250 km/h及以上的动车组列车，初期运营速度不少于200 km/h的铁路。

铁路速列车运行速度度的分类一般规定为：速度100~120 km/h称为常速；速度120~160 km/h称为中速；速度160~200 km/h称为准高速或快速；速度200~400 km/h称为高速；速度400 km/h以上称为超高速。

1.5 动车组的定义与分类

1.5.1 动车组的基本概念

由若干动力车和拖车或全部由动力车长期固定连挂在一起的车组称为动车组。动车组的基本组成单元称为动力单元。每个动力单元由不同数量的动车及拖车组成。整列动车可根据需要由若干个动力单元组成。动车组的两端都带有司机室，可在线路上往复运行。动车组具有较强的灵活性和适用性，既可以通过对动拖车比例的调整来适应不同速度等级的运行需要，又可以通过对编组的调整来满足不同运量的需要（见图1-1）。

图1-1 我国"和谐号"高速列车实物图

1.5.2 高速动车组的分类

按照不同的标准和方式，动车组可以有多种不同的分类，主要可归纳为以下几类。

1. 按速度等级分类

（1）准高速动车组：运行速度为 160～200 km/h。
（2）高速动车组：运行速度为 200～400 km/h。
（3）超高速动车组：运行速度为 400 km/h 以上。

我国城际铁路一般采用准高速动车组，跨越多个城市以及跨省的一般为高速动车组。

2. 按牵引动力类型分类

（1）电力动车组：由于电力牵引具有牵引功率大、轴重轻、经济性好、利于环保等优点，因此，尽管电力牵引具有较大的初始投资，但目前 80%以上的高速动车组都采用了电力牵引。

（2）内燃动车组：内燃牵引高速动车组由于其投资少、见效快、灵活性好等优点，常常用于尚未电气化的高速铁路区段，或者作为发展高速铁路建设的一种过渡牵引形式。

（3）磁悬浮动车组：磁悬浮列车是一种全新的交通运输工具，它与传统的列车有着截然不同的特点，它是利用电磁系统产生的吸引力（或排斥力）将列车托起（或抬起），使整个列车悬浮在导轨上，并利用电磁力进行导向，利用直线电机将电能直接转换为推进力，推动列车高速前进。磁悬浮列车由于轮轨不接触，没有摩擦轮轨阻力，因而适于超高速运行，速度可达到 500 km/h；且安全性好，利于环保，占地面积小，运行平稳。

除上海龙阳路站至上海浦东国际机场站的上海磁浮示范运营线，中国高速动车组一般为电力动车组。

3. 按动力配置方式分类

1）动力集中型高速动车组

动力集中型高速动车组是将动力车挂在两端，中间是拖车编组的动车组。

2）动力分散型高速动车组

动力分散型高速动车组是指一定数量的动力车和拖车组成单元，再编组形成的动车组。

4. 按转向架连接方式分类

1）独立式高速动车组

独立式高速动车组即为传统的车辆与转向架的连接方式，每节车辆的车体都置于两台转向架上，车辆与车辆之间用密封式车钩相连接，列车解体后车辆可独立行走。

2）铰接式高速动车组

铰接式高速动车组是将车辆的车体之间用弹性铰相连接，并放置在一个共用的转向架上，因此，每节车辆不能从列车上分解下来独立行走。

按照动力配置和转向架连接方式组合，可以将高速动车组分为 4 种类型，如图 1-2 所示。

我国一般采用独立式高速动车组。

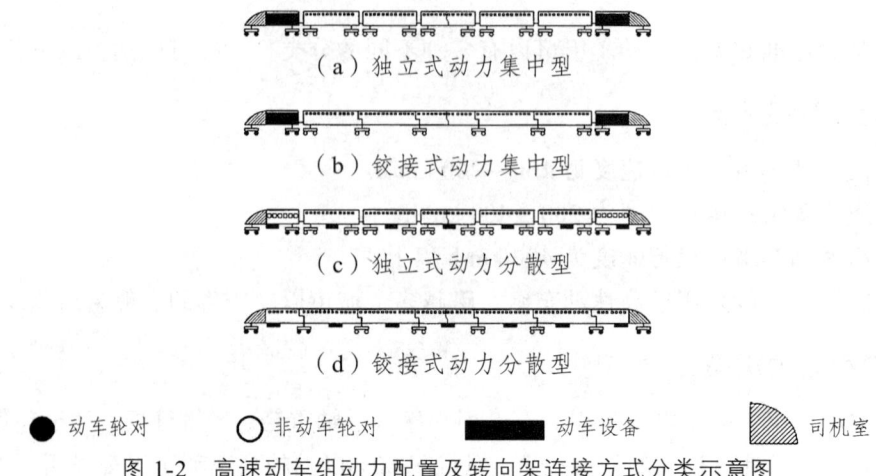

● 动车轮对　　○ 非动车轮对　　■ 动车设备　　◤ 司机室

图 1-2　高速动车组动力配置及转向架连接方式分类示意图

1.6　动车组动力配置方式的特点与选择

如前所述，高速动车组动力配置有两种方式，即动力集中型和动力分散型。两种形式的产生、发展都有其自身的历史原因和环境条件。

1.6.1　动力集中型

动力集中型高速动车组最早由欧洲发展起来，是传统机车牵引的延伸和发展。

动力集中型高速动车组的牵引力是由集中在动力车的动力轮对提供的。因此，它带来了两个值得注意的问题：一是动力轴的轴重必须足够大，以能够提供所需的牵引力；二是动力轴的轴重不能太大，否则在高速运行时会产生过大的轮轨力，损坏钢轨和线路。

1. 动力集中型高速动车组的优点

（1）由于与传统的机车牵引列车相似，因此，可以按照传统习惯对车辆进行运行管理和维修管理。

（2）便于维修。机械设备和电气设备在运用中便于进行监测和技术保养。

（3）舒适性好。由于机械和电气设备都集中在动力车中，与载客拖车相隔离，因此，载客车厢内振动小、噪声低、舒适性好。

（4）方便摘挂。能够方便列车由高速线进入既有线，甚至可更换内燃机车使列车直接进入非电气化铁路区段。

2. 动力集中型高速动车组的缺点

（1）载客量小。由于动力车不能载客且占用编组，因此，相对减少了载客量。

（2）动力车轴重较重，难以降低。

（3）制动欠佳。动力车的制动能力受黏着系数的限制，需要拖车分担部分制动功率。

（4）动力车大的黏着牵引力与车轮轴重要求形成矛盾。

1.6.2 动力分散型

动力分散型高速动车组是由日本首先研制出来的。它是在传统的城市轨道交通列车基础上发展、延伸出来的。

1. 动力分散型高速动车组的优点

（1）载客量大。由于动力装置和各种电气设备分散布置在各节车辆中，因此，各个车辆均能载客，从而增加了列车的载客量。

（2）轴重较轻。同样，由于动力装置和牵引电机等设备的质量和功率分散在各节车辆上，因此，较易实现了高速列车减轻轴重的需求。

（3）制动较好。

（4）因牵引力分散在各个动力车轮上，可解决高速列车大牵引力与轴重限制间的矛盾。

2. 动力分散型动车组的缺点

（1）舒适度有所降低。由于动力装置是吊装在各车辆下部，运行中的振动和噪声会影响车厢内旅客的舒适度，且目前技术上彻底解决隔振降噪尚有一定难度。

（2）分散的动力设备的故障率较高。

（3）只能分单元编组，不能驶入非电化区段运行，且与传统的运营、维修管理体制不配套，必须建立一套新的维修管理体系。

2 高速动车组车体

2.1 车体的用途

车辆供乘客乘坐的部分称为车体。它的用途主要表现在以下方面：
（1）用来安装各种电气设备和机械设备，并保护车体内各种设备不受雨、雪、风沙的侵袭。
（2）是供旅客乘坐场所和乘务人员操纵、维修、保养机车的场所。
（3）承受垂向力：承受车体内各种设备的重量，并经支承装置传给转向架以至钢轨。
（4）传递纵向力：接受转向架传来的牵引力、制动力，并传给设在车体两端的牵引缓冲装置，以便牵引列车运行或实行制动。
（5）传递横向力：在运行时，车辆要承受各种横向力的作用，如离心力、风力等。

2.2 车体基本组成及技术特点

2.2.1 基本组成

车体是动车组的主要承载体。一般来说，车体结构的主要部件包括：底架、侧墙、车顶、端墙及头车的司机室结构等。

动车组车体可分为两种形式，即头车车体和中间车体。两头车车体结构基本相同，各中间车体结构也大体相同，都采用大型中空铝合金挤压型材焊接而成，其车体结构是由底架、侧墙、车顶、端墙、司机室、裙板结构等组成的筒型整体承载焊接结构，可以承受垂直、纵向、横向、扭转等复杂载荷。司机室前端的下方设有排障器，排障器距轨面高度为150 mm，为固定式高度，不可调节。为便于将车体顶起，在车体底架上设4个顶车位。

2.2.2 动车组车体的技术特点

动车组有以下几个技术特点：
（1）车体的外形具有良好的流线型设计，以减小列车高速运行时产生的空气阻力和附加阻力。
（2）车体具有良好的气密性，以提高和改善旅客乘坐的舒适度。
（3）车体具有良好的轻量化设计指标，以降低列车在运行过程中的能量消耗。
动车组的车体轻量化主要体现在两个方面：一是车体材料采用了具有密度低、强度高、焊接性能好、挤压加工性能好、耐腐蚀性好等特性征的铝合金材料；二是车体结构采用了铝合金筒形整体承载结构。

动车组车体承载结构采用车体全长的大型中空铝合金挤压型材组焊接而成的筒型整体承载结构，这种结构形式也称为双壳结构。双壳结构相对于单壳结构而言，车体质量稍重。但是中空型材具有截面刚度高的特性，可以提高车体结构整体刚度；同时可以去掉单壳结构中必须使用的加强材料，因此可以减少车体结构零件的数量。另外，由于过度追求车体轻量化将会对车体结构的安全性和旅客乘坐舒适性带来不利影响，因此，近年来，随着人们对乘坐舒适度的要求越来越高，车体结构不仅仅是追求轻量化，而是要合理地控制车体结构的质量。动车组的车体采用双壳结构，可适当地增加车体的质量从而改善车辆的舒适性。双壳结构型材带有中空腔，CRH2 型动车组车体承载结构如图 2-1 所示。

图 2-1 双壳车体结构型材

动车组体现了车辆整体轻量化的设计理念。其在车辆轻量化方面的考虑是十分细致的，除了主体结构外，在车内设备装饰材料以及车辆地板上的单线和地板上下的屏蔽线都采用了轻量化电线，以利于车体的轻量化。

2.3 动车组的外形尺寸

以 CRH2 型动车组为例，动车组两头车长 25 700 mm、中间车长 25 000 mm、总长 201.4 m、车宽 3380 mm、车高 3700 mm。CRH2 型动车组车体质量见表 2-1，车体的主要技术参数见表 2-2。

表 2-1 CRH2 型动车组各车辆车体质量表

整列编组车型	T1c	M2	M1	T2	T_{1k}	M2	M1s	T2c
车体质量/kg	7643	7947	7821	7831	8373	7822	8042	7185

表 2-2 CRH2型动车组车体主要技术参数

车体长度	25 700 mm	头车
	25 000 mm	中间车
车体最大宽度	3380 mm	
车体最大高度（距轨面）	3700 mm	
车门处地板面距轨面高度	1300 mm	
车厢天花板高度	2277 mm	
轨距	1435 mm	
转向架中心距	17 500 mm	
固定轴距	2500 mm	
车轮轮径	860 mm	
车钩距轨面高度	1000 mm	
车体弯曲固有频率（整备状态下）	≥10 Hz	

2.4 动车组的车体结构

以CRH2型动车组为例，车体结构主要分为头车车体和中间车车体两种，主要由底架、侧墙、车顶、端墙、车体附件（车下设备舱、前罩开闭装置、和前头排障装置）等组成（头车车体还包括司机室头部结构）。两个头车的车体结构基本相同，如图2-2所示，各中间车车体结构也大体相同，如图2-3所示，其车体结构都是采用大型中空铝合金挤压型材焊接而成的筒型整体承载结构，可以承受垂直、纵向、横向以及扭转等复杂载荷。

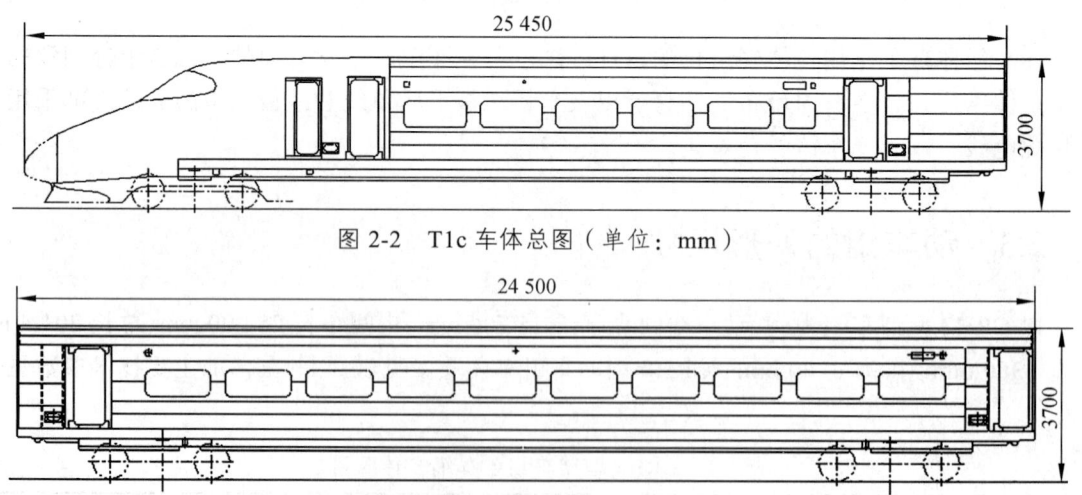

图 2-2 T1c 车体总图（单位：mm）

图 2-3 M1 车体总图（单位：mm）

2.4.1 底架组成

动车组车体底架分为头车底架和中间车底架。头车底架由车身底架和车头底架两部分组成，T1c 车底如图 2-4 所示。中间车底架只有车身底架，底架组成包括支持车体重量且与转向架相接的枕梁；传达前后方向力的侧梁、端梁、中梁；支持客室设备和乘客等并吊装地板下设备的横梁。如图 2-5 所示。

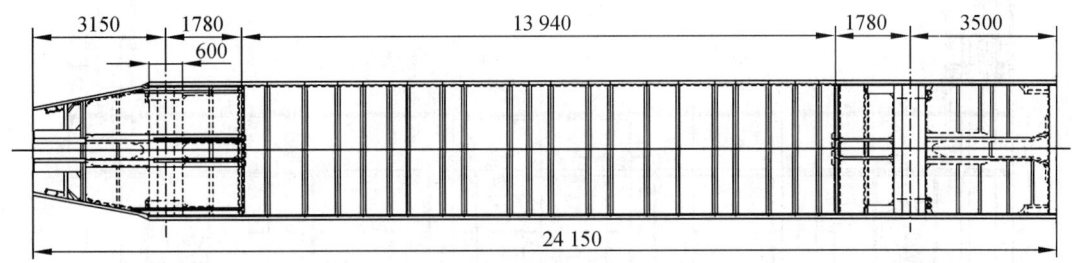

图 2-4　T1c 车体底架图（单位：mm）

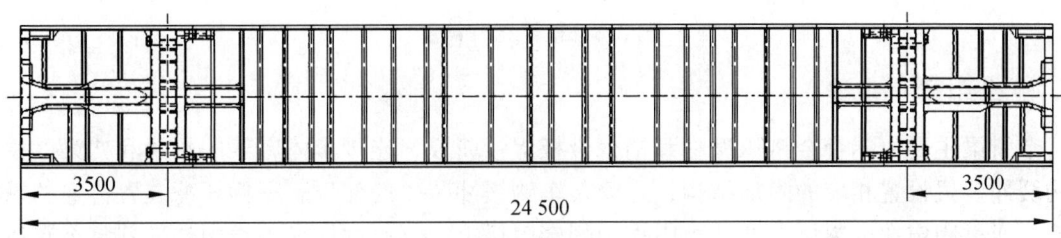

图 2-5　M1 车体底架图（单位：mm）

1. 侧梁和端梁

侧梁是位于底架地板下左右两侧的纵向梁，采用通长铝合金挤压型材拼焊而成，是底架与侧架连接成筒体的关键部件，能够支承车体负载、地板下设备负荷，为一体式结构或组装式结构。端梁是位于底架两端的横向梁，由铝合金挤压型材和铝合金板焊接而成。

2. 枕　梁

枕梁采用厚壁中空型材，构成宽 800 mm、高 200 mm 的箱形，具有抗扭和抗弯曲的高度刚性。枕梁在转向架中心上和侧梁联结，有安装转向架的相应结构，能够支承车体的负荷，并且避免从转向架传来的振动直接传到地板。枕梁外侧设置顶车座，便于救援和维修时顶车作业。枕梁结构简图如图 2-6 所示。

3. 横　梁

横梁是为支承安装地板下设备以及支承地板而在两侧梁或侧梁和中梁间的横向梁。横梁上面作为气密地板，使用由带加强肋的铝板整体成型的大型型材，在前后位转向架之间作为地板托和风道托有向上的加强肋结构，在车端部为确保风道断面积用向下的加强肋结构，地板托和风道托均用焊接。此外在厕所和洗面室下部考虑配管为无加强肋的气密地板。横梁需要有安装设备、支承地板所需的强度，在大质量设备安装处，要有设备安装座和补强措施。在横梁上设有配管贯通孔，与横梁及地板下设备安装螺栓孔相对应的位置，应留有足够的尺寸空间，确保地板下挡板拆装作业不受影响。

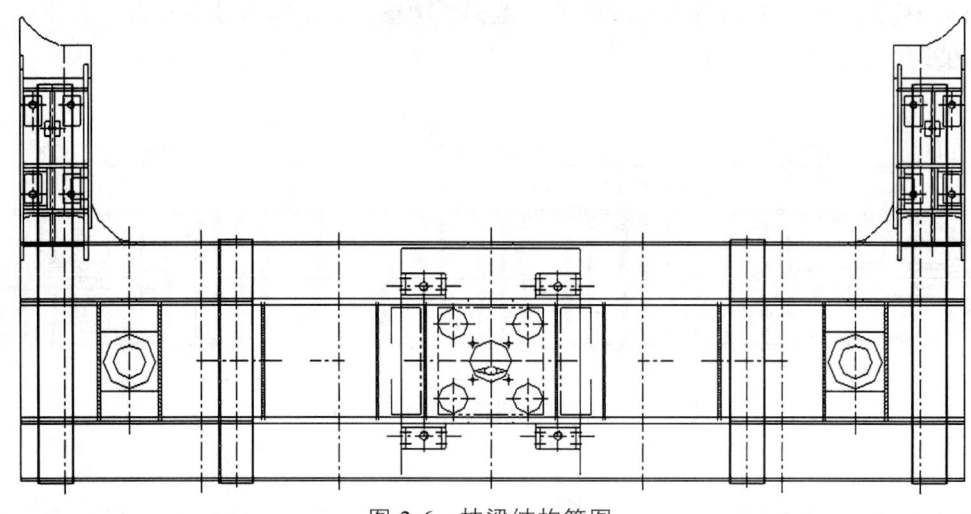

图 2-6　枕梁结构简图

4. 牵引梁（中梁）

牵引梁主要由铝合金挤压型材和铝合金板焊接而成，连接车体底架的端梁和枕梁，并为车钩缓冲装置设置相应的附加结构，是安装车钩缓冲装置的部位。车钩缓冲装置传递的纵向载荷，通过固定在牵引梁上的从板座作用到牵引梁上，再通过枕梁等结构传递到整个车体结构，实现整体承载。从板座与牵引梁采用铆钉连接，并在车钩装置对应的牵引梁相应部位进行局部加强。牵引梁结构简图如图 2-7 所示。

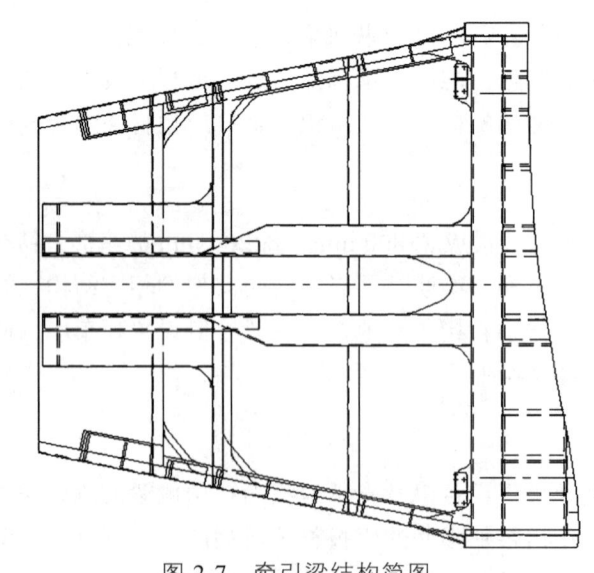

图 2-7　牵引梁结构简图

5. 地板承板

在底架上面安装地板承板,以支承地板结构,增强底架强度、刚度,保持车内气密性结构。地板承板是在车体纵向延长的型材,作为特殊地板结构部分是平面也可以。

6. 前头部底架

前头部底架是适合头部形状的弯曲侧梁、中梁和补强横梁的结构。前头部底架要有支承前头部端墙、前头排障器、缓冲装置、车钩、缓冲器等相应的结构。

2.4.2 端 墙

头车的车体一侧带有端墙,中间车两侧均带有端墙。端墙结构主要是由端墙力柱、横梁和车顶拱组成,根据车辆端部有无卫生间和洗脸间的布置主要分为分体式和整体式两种,端墙的结构形式如图 2-8 所示。

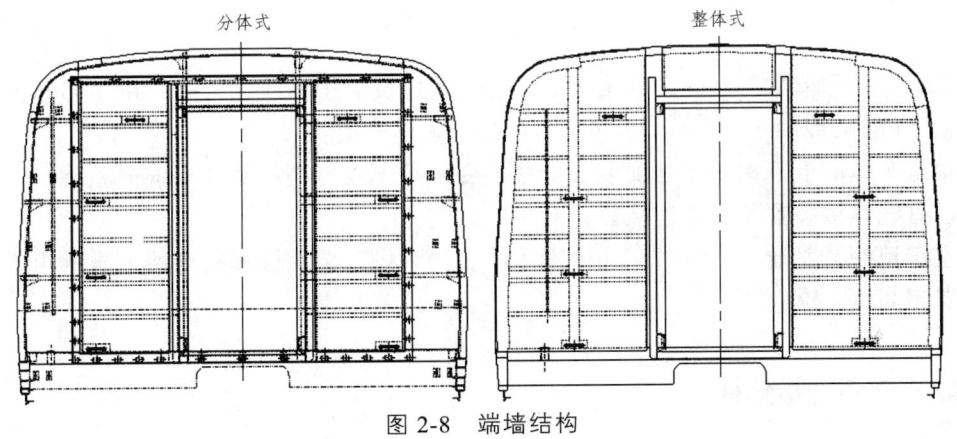

图 2-8 端墙结构

车端内部结构主要是由端墙力柱、横梁和车顶拱组成(如图 2-9 所示),在中间车连接部分的端墙设有贯通道、外折棚、车端减震器、特高压电缆配线,同时具有安装换气用新鲜空气出入口等设备的相应结构。

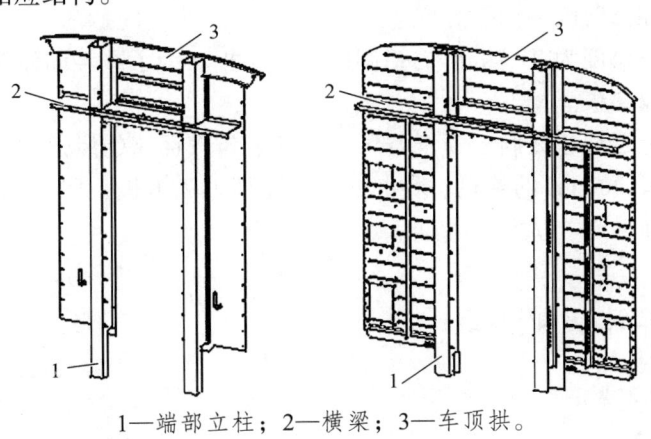

1—端部立柱;2—横梁;3—车顶拱。

图 2-9 车端结构

2.4.3 车顶结构

车顶由大型中空挤压型材构成（如图2-10所示），省略了纵向梁。型材相互间的焊接为沿车体长度方向的连续焊接，但与侧墙的结合部位，车内侧采用点固焊接，车外侧采用连续焊接。

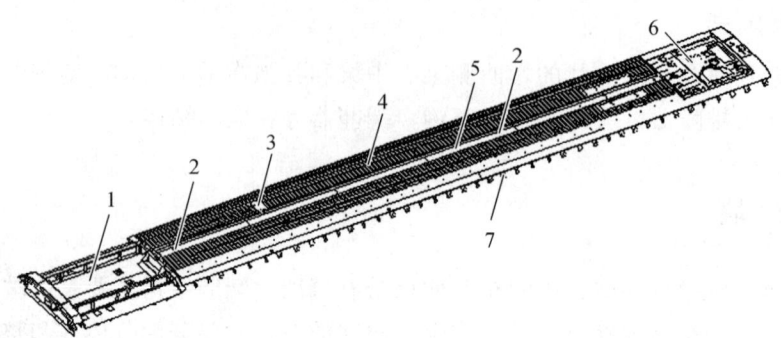

1—通风单元位置；2—安装天线位置；3—高压电缆引入口；4—带纹路车顶板；
5—平滑车顶板；6—车顶高压板；7—车顶拱。

图 2-10　车顶结构

1号车和0号车车顶上设置有无线电信号天线以及防护无线电天线，在7号车前位上，设置电视、FM 天线。

车顶是车体的上部构件，是安装受电弓、受电弓罩及特高压联通电缆的基础，并在车端部有高压母线连接装置及安装连接装置的相应结构。

客室车顶棚，普通车、软席车均由通用的中央顶棚、侧顶棚和行李架上板所组成。在车顶上设置超高压电缆。

2.4.4 客室地板结构

地板对客室内的负荷有足够的强度，并从地板下、地板中间考虑有足够隔音结构。地板结构为下部气密地板和上部蜂巢状地板组成的双层结构，在地板中有空调风道和座位配线的空间。

气密层地板为大型压型材料和地板托的焊接结构。在联结端墙的车端部处，为确保地板内风道的空间而将加强肋改为向下方向。

上部地板使用总厚度为 21.7 mm 的铝制蜂窝夹层板，为了减轻固体传播噪声，地板的衬垫使用难燃性的橡胶垫板。

在气密地板和上层地板之间，新鲜空气、空调、排气回路的风道均按钢轨方向布置，在气密地板上粘贴有厚 20 mm 的绝热材料。此外，座椅埋入地板，用 M12 的六角螺栓固定在螺栓孔内。

2.4.5 车头排障装置和裙板

1. 排障装置的结构

在司机室的前端设置主排障器，如图2-11所示。排障装置的作用是排除运行中线路上障碍物，缓和在障碍物冲撞时车辆承受的冲击力，防止轨道结构的异物引起列车脱轨，排障器具有运行除雪结构，在排雪板下部还设有辅助排障装置。缓冲器是 5 片铝板合成的多层结构，位于排雪板的后方，通过变形吸收冲击能量。

图 2-11　主排障器

排障装置主要由排障器和缓冲装置构成，安装在前头底架的下面。有的排障装置安装在最前位转向架构架上，轨道排障器使用螺栓接头固定在转向架构架上，轨道排障器的下部是一块可调节的板，用螺栓接头紧固至轨道排障器臂上，排障装置的结构如图 2-12 所示。

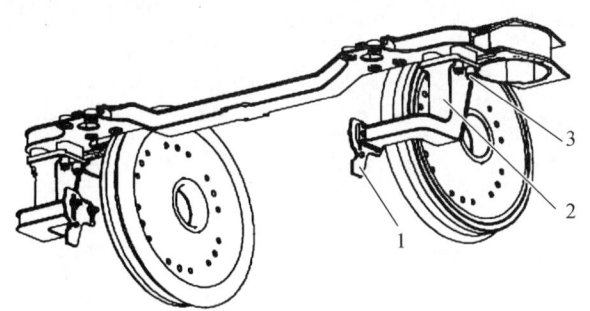

1—轨道排障器；2—轨道排障器臂；3—螺栓接头 M20（螺丝钉，垫片和管子）。

图 2-12　轨道排障器结构

2. 排障能力

1）排障板的排障能力

当列车以 200 km/h 行走时，可以排除高 250 mm、质量 100 kg 以下的障碍物。静态强度可满足 137 kN 的要求。排障板距轨道面的高度固定在 150 mm 以上。

2）排雪能力（包括排雪犁、排石器）

当列车以 240 km/h 行走时，以能够抵抗 182 kN 以上的排雪阻力为基准。

3. 裙　板

1）转向架裙板

转向架部分为了减低噪声而设置了裙板。下端距轨道面 550 mm，以对检修不产生障碍为范围。考虑到装卸问题，将裙板分割为二部分。如图 2-13 所示。

图 2-13 转向架裙板

2）车端部裙板

在车端部设置了使用大型型材制作的裙板。在裙板上装有各种地板下装置的检查盖和为了从轨道上乘车的踏脚件等。

3 动车组的车钩

在铁道车辆的两端都有车钩,车钩将一节车厢连接到另一节车厢,或将动车组列车连接到另一节车厢。通常,动车组列车中的车钩分为两大类,分别是自动密接式车钩和半永久车钩。

自动密接式车钩位于动车组列车的两端(参考图3-1),它将列车与另一辆动车组列车或机车连接起来。

图 3-1 自动车钩实物图

自动密接式车钩的连挂无须人工,可以自动完成,它还有紧密、稳定、牢靠的优点。自动密接式车钩还有空气管路连接器和电器连接器,可以自动实现空气管路和电器线路的制动连接和断开。此外,通过设计的枢轴布置,它允许水平和垂直轨道变化。

半永久车钩连接 EMU 列车中的两个相邻车辆。车钩的操作(连挂和解钩)只能手动完成。牵引和压缩载荷通过两个半永久车钩(A 和 B)从一辆车传递到另一辆车如图3-2所示。

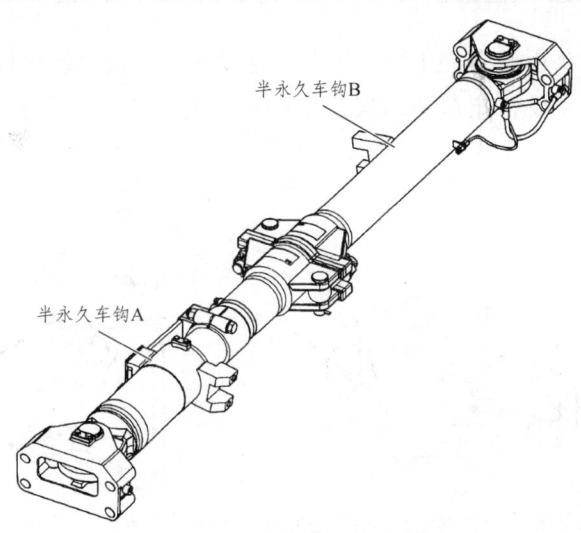

图 3-2 两个半永久车钩

3.1 自动车钩

车钩的前部设计成凸锥和凹锥形状,这样,当被连挂在一起时具有自动的对正和对中功能。牵引和冲击载荷经缓冲器缓和后传递到枢轴支座上。

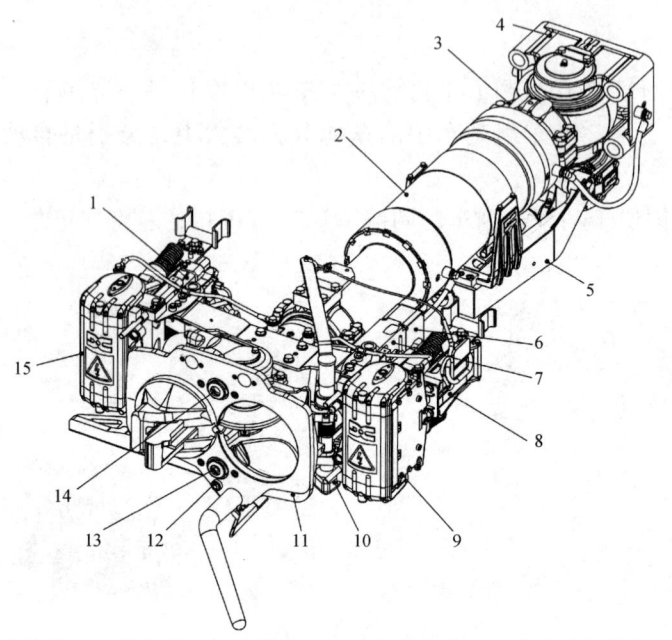

1—右侧电气车钩激活器;2—缓冲器;3—套筒接头;4—枢轴支座;5—支撑对中装置;6—加热接线盒;
7—气动系统;8—左侧电气连接器激活器;9—左侧电气连接器;10—手动解钩装置;
11—自动密接式车钩钩头;12—UC 阀门;13—MRP 风管连接器;
14—BP 风管连接器;15—右侧电气连接器。

图 3-3 自动车钩装置组成

3.1.1 钩头

自动密接式车钩钩头由弹簧、主销、锁杆、触发器、钩板、连接杆组成,如图 3-4 所示。钩头前部的面板能主要承受冲击载荷,拉伸载荷由连接杆和锁板传递,防护罩用来防止连接杆和锁板锈蚀。

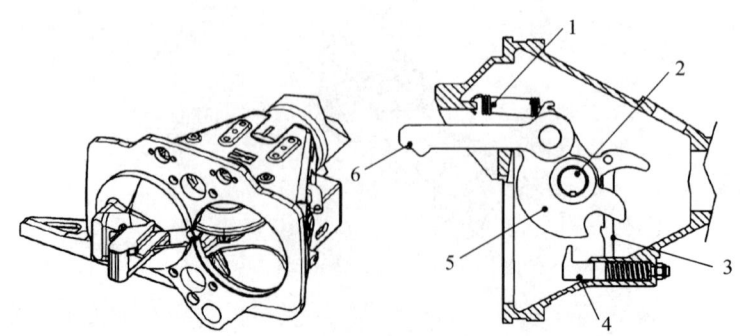

1—弹簧;2—主销;3—锁杆;4—触发器;5—钩板;6—连接杆。

图 3-4 自动密接式车钩钩头结构图

1. 车钩连挂作用原理

如图 3-5 所示的是两个准备连挂的自动车钩,这是待连挂车钩的通常状态。

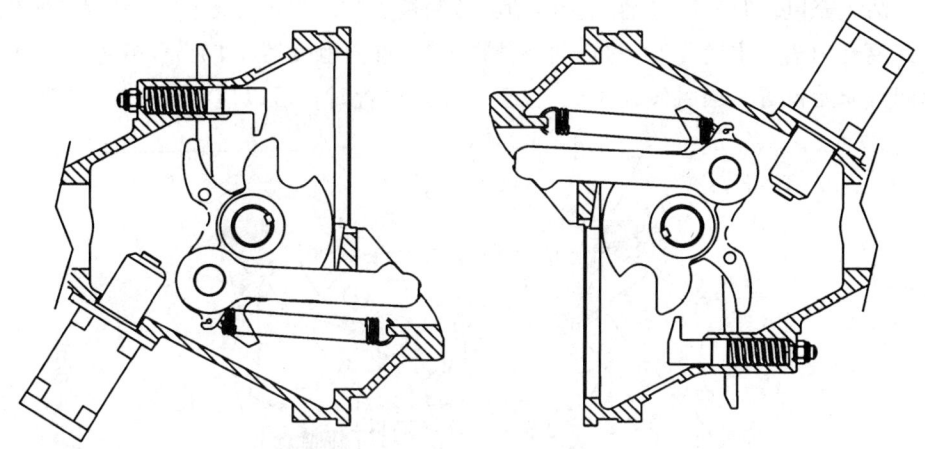

图 3-5　待挂位置的自动车钩

图 3-6 所示的是两个处于闭锁位置的自动车钩。当两个车钩相互靠近时,啮合车钩的连接杆(6)进入对面车钩的转动构板(5)的槽内。同样,对面车钩的连接杆(6)也进入啮合车钩的转动构板(5)的槽内。

连挂过程中,一车钩的连接杆(6)将压下对面车钩的触发器(4)。当压下触发器(4)时,锁杆(3)上移,导致主销(2)被释放。主销释放后,拉力弹簧(1)将使钩板(5)转动,以完成联挂过程。

就在联挂完成之后,连接杆和钩板会形成一个平行四边形,它将拉力经由主销传递至车钩主体。在此平行四边形位置,两个车钩头会形成一个刚性、紧密且无间隙的牢固连接。

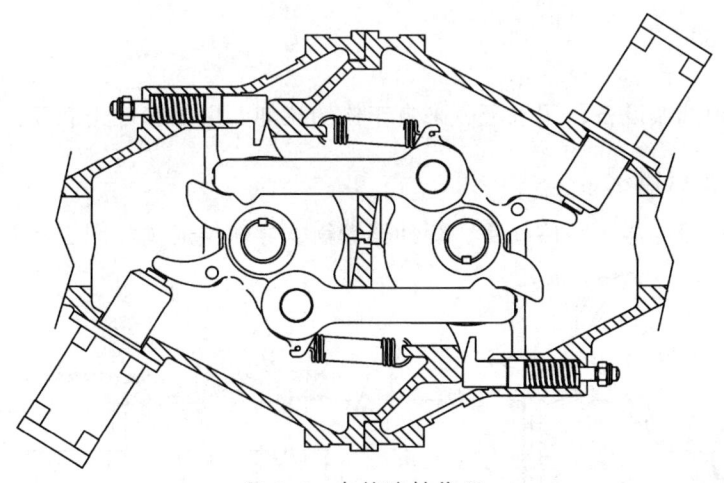

图 3-6　车钩连挂位置

2. 解钩作用原理

解钩操作是指将两节连挂的车辆分开,解钩通常有两种方法。

1）自动（遥控）解钩

参见图 3-7，首先从司机室发出解钩指令信号，激活位于机械车钩侧面的解钩气缸。在解钩气缸被激活（充风）时，气缸活塞会推动旋转钩板（5）。当钩板（5）旋转时，主销（2）将随之转动并离开销槽。主销（2）的转动将锁杆（3）推向触发器（4）。当车钩分开时，触发器（4）将返回其原始位置。当触发器（4）位于其原始位置时，可以使锁杆（3）挂到锁头上。

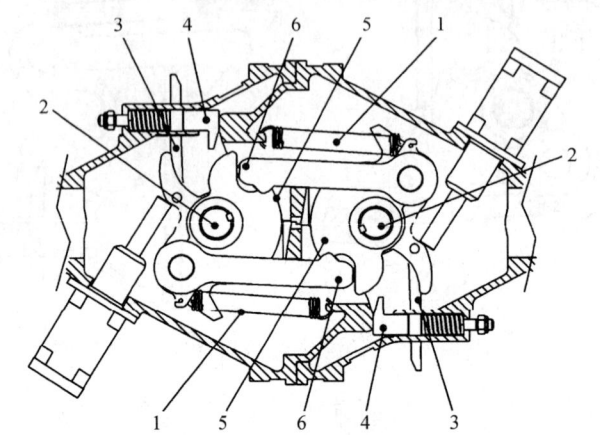

1—弹簧；2—主销；3—锁杆；4—触发器；5—钩板；6—连接杆。

图 3-7　车钩开锁位置

2）手动解钩

手动解钩可以通过机械车钩旁边的解钩手把完成。解钩手把被连接至机械车钩内的旋转钩板上，拉动解钩手柄转动机械车钩内的钩板，车钩就被分解开。当两车辆分开后，这个解钩弹簧和机械车钩中的弹簧将会返回其解钩时的位置。

3.1.2　缓冲器

缓冲器是一种减振设备，用来吸收来自车钩的拉伸、压缩和冲击载荷。

3.1.2.1　缓冲器概况

缓冲器由液压缓冲器、摩擦弹簧、缓冲器管筒、导轨组成（如图 3-8 所示）。

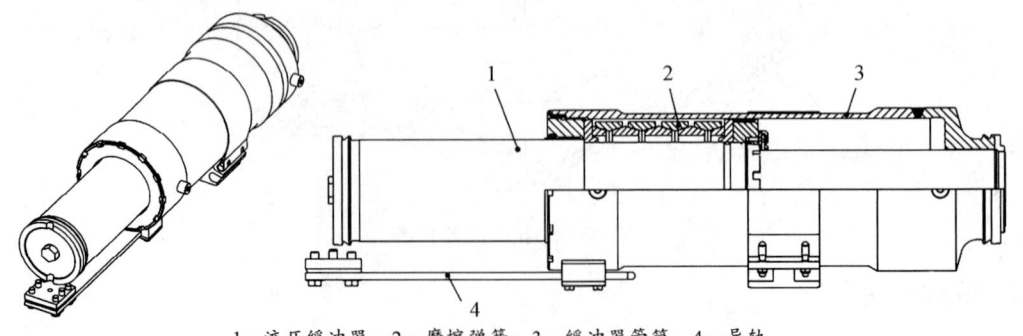

1—液压缓冲器；2—摩擦弹簧；3—缓冲器管筒；4—导轨。

图 3-8　缓冲器

缓冲和牵引载荷由机械车钩经摩擦弹簧（2）传递至车辆。弹簧（2）吸收载荷并将其传递至液压缓冲器（1），然后再传递至固定在车辆底架上的枢轴支座。固定在缓冲器管筒（3）底部的导轨（4）可防止缓冲器在缓冲管内转动，进而防止自动车钩转动。

3.1.2.2 工作原理

液压减振器在压缩和牵引载荷下的各位置参见图 3-9。

A. 处于正常位置的缓冲器（无缓冲和牵引载荷）；
B. 处于缓冲过程的缓冲器（最大行程）；
C. 处于牵引过程的缓冲器（最大行程）。

液压缓冲器是一个气液型减振器，负责吸收主要的缓冲载荷。当缓冲器承受缓冲载荷时，其工作行程为 200 mm（参见图 2-9，位置 B）。安装在前端套筒接头上的指示器在达到满行程之前会削减 8 mm，以表示缓冲器承受了最大冲击载荷。当缓冲器承受牵引载荷时，其工作行程为 30 mm（参见图 3-9，位置 C）。摩擦弹簧吸收主要的牵引力。

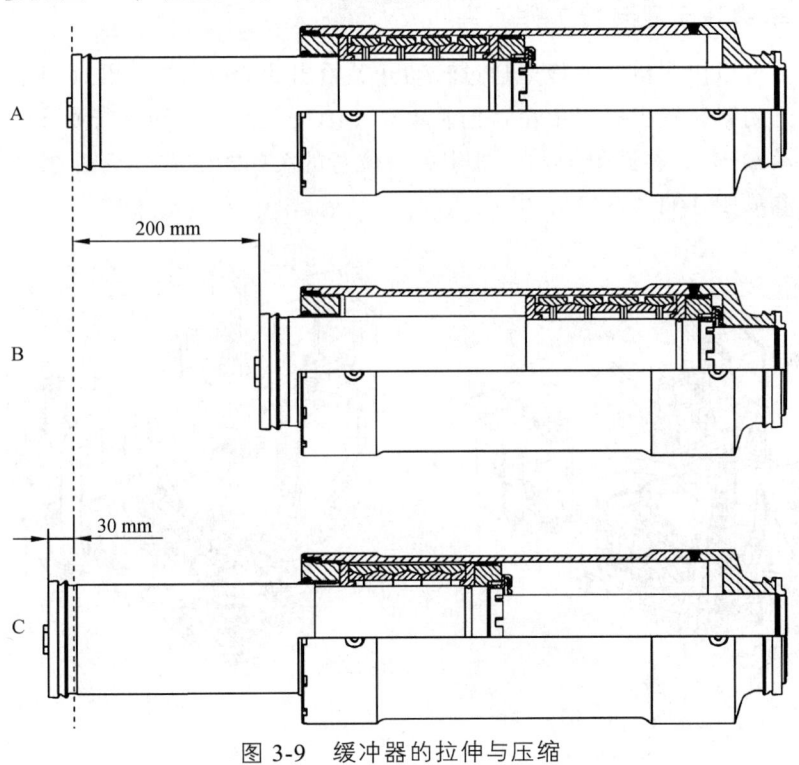

图 3-9 缓冲器的拉伸与压缩

3.1.3 车钩开闭罩装置

车钩开闭罩装置（参见图 3-10），包括罩盖、车组接口、罩盖接口以及罩盖控制单元等。

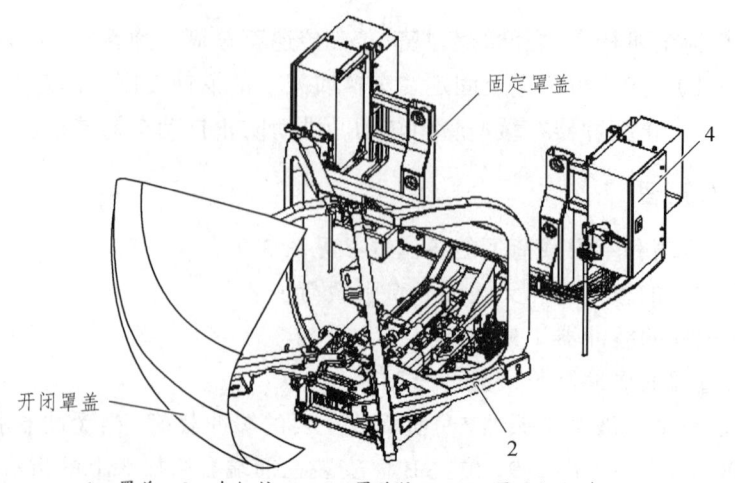

1—罩盖；2—车组接口；3—罩盖接口；4—罩盖控制单元。

图 3-10 开闭罩装置结构组成

3.1.3.1 车钩开闭罩装置工作原理

开闭罩装置可以由司机台面板上通过转动开关给出的 OPEN/CLOSE（开启/关闭）命令进行自动操作。开闭罩装置也可以由箱盖控制单元（HCU）内的按钮进行操作，在电源故障时也可以采用手动操作。（参见图 3-11，处于关闭位置的关闭罩装置参见图 3-11（A），处于开启位置的箱则参见图 3-11（B））

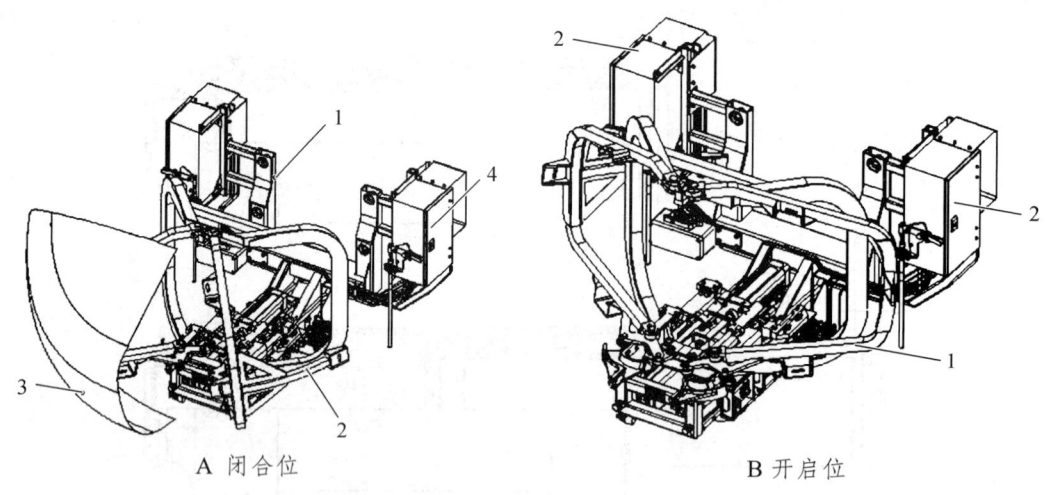

图 3-11

3.1.3.2 车钩开闭罩控制单元（HCU）

动车组接口上装有 2 个车钩开闭罩控制单元（HCU）。每个车钩开闭罩单元包含有用于开闭罩控制的不同组件（参见图 3-12）。右侧单元包含电气设备，左侧单元则包含气动设备。

两个单元都有可拆式盖板，从而可以操作按钮（1）以进行开闭罩机构的控制（解锁、开启和关闭）。两个单元各有一条接线（4），在车组压缩空气系统故障时用于外部供风。三通阀（3）可进行内部与外部供风间的切换。如果未连接外部供风，系统将进行排气，以便进行手动操作。此外，左侧单元还有一个可拔取的钥匙（2），用于隔离电源和风源，以便安全地对开闭罩机构进行作业。

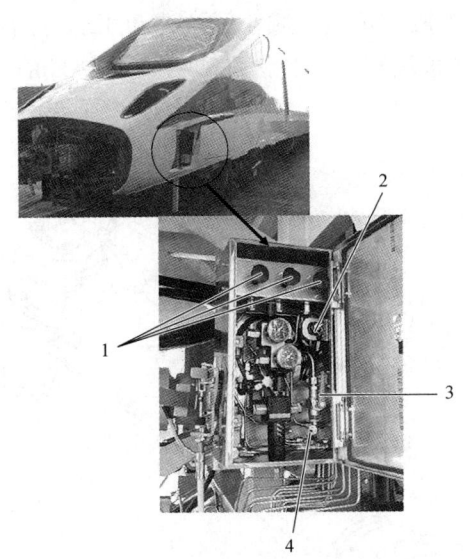

1—按钮（本地控制）；2—可拔钥匙；3—三通阀；4—外部供风接线。
图 3-12　箱盖控制单元

3.2　半永久车钩

3.2.1　半永久车钩的类型和结构

半永久车钩有两种类型：A 型半永久车钩和 B 型半永久车钩。图 3-13 所示的是 A 型半永久车钩，主要由车钩头、缓冲器、缓冲器支架、导轨组成。

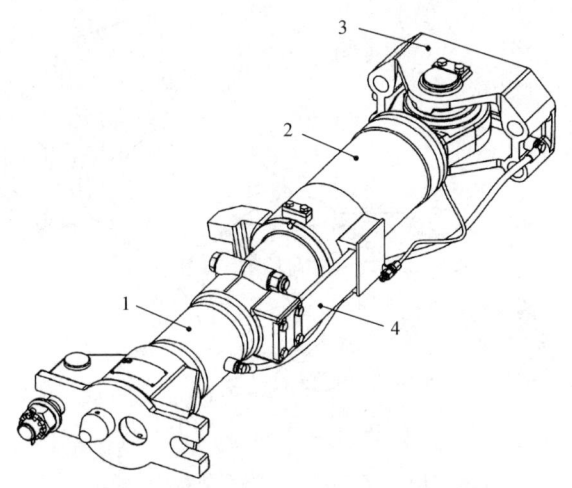

1—车钩头；2—缓冲器；3—支承架；4—导轨。
图 3-13　A 型半永久车钩

A 型半永久车钩通过一个支承架安装在车辆上。缓冲器缓和 A 型半永久车钩在运行期间压缩或拉伸载荷并吸收冲击能力。导轨（4）可以防止液压缓冲器（2）在缓冲管内转动，从而防止车钩头转动。球状的橡胶支承装置减小了拉伸和压缩时的冲击，延长了枢轴的寿命。

图 3-14 所示的是 B 型半永久车钩，其钩头和 A 型是一样的，但 B 型是直接焊接在钩体上形成了一个刚性的管筒。

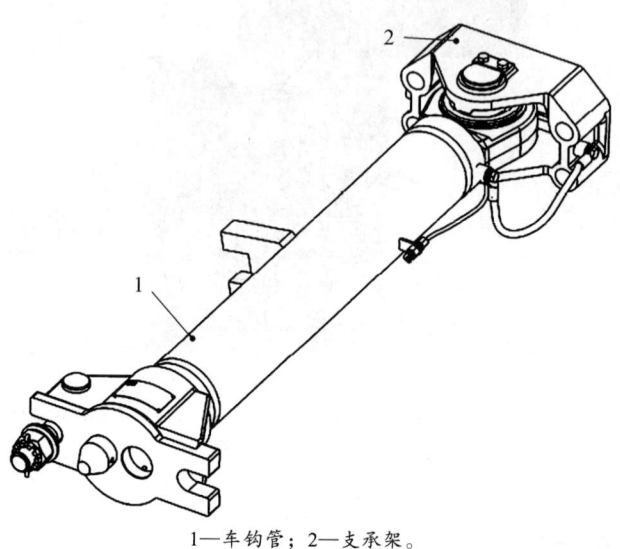

1—车钩管；2—支承架。

图 3-14　B 型半永久车钩

车钩钩头的结构如图 3-15 所示，压缩和冲击载荷经由特殊设计的钩头接触面传递到支承座。对于 A 型半永久车钩，牵引力通过有孔螺杆传动缓冲器，再到车体底架；而对于 B 型半永久车钩，牵引力通过刚性的管筒直接传递到车体底架。

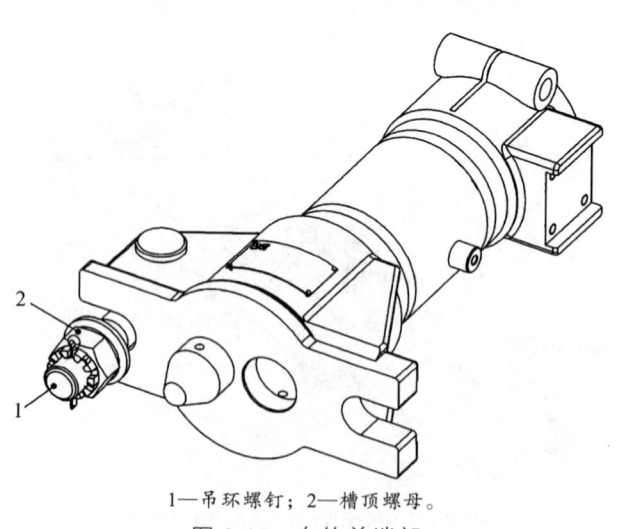

1—吊环螺钉；2—槽顶螺母。

图 3-15　车钩前端部

3.2.2 车钩的连挂和解钩

车钩的连挂和解钩完全通过带孔螺杆和有槽螺母手动完成。A 型半永久车钩在一节车的车端，而另外一节车的车端为 B 型半永久车钩。两车钩的连挂和解钩都只能通过人工手动完成。图 3-16 所示的是准备连挂的两个车钩（分别为 A 型和 B 型），两个有孔螺杆从车钩端面上被转开，以防造成损坏。

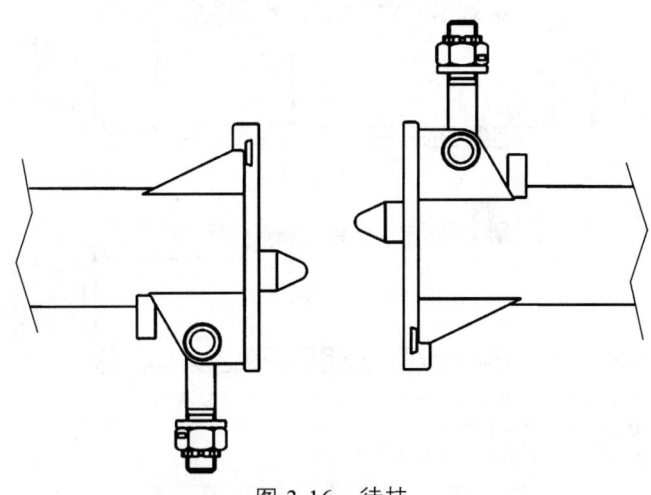

图 3-16　待挂

当两个车钩端面接触在一起时，螺杆安装好，并用螺母在另一个车钩的凸缘背面紧固，这就形成了两个动车组车辆的持久的连挂（如图 3-17 所示）。

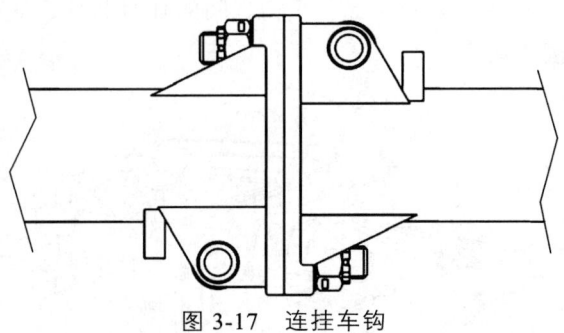

图 3-17　连挂车钩

3.2.3 半永久车钩缓冲器

A 型半永久车钩的缓冲器用来吸收冲击能量，它吸收从钩头来的拉伸和压缩载荷。A 型半永久车钩的缓冲器和自动车钩的缓冲器的结构一样，唯一的不同是缓冲器的行程。图 3-18 显示了 A 型半永久车钩的缓冲器的行程。

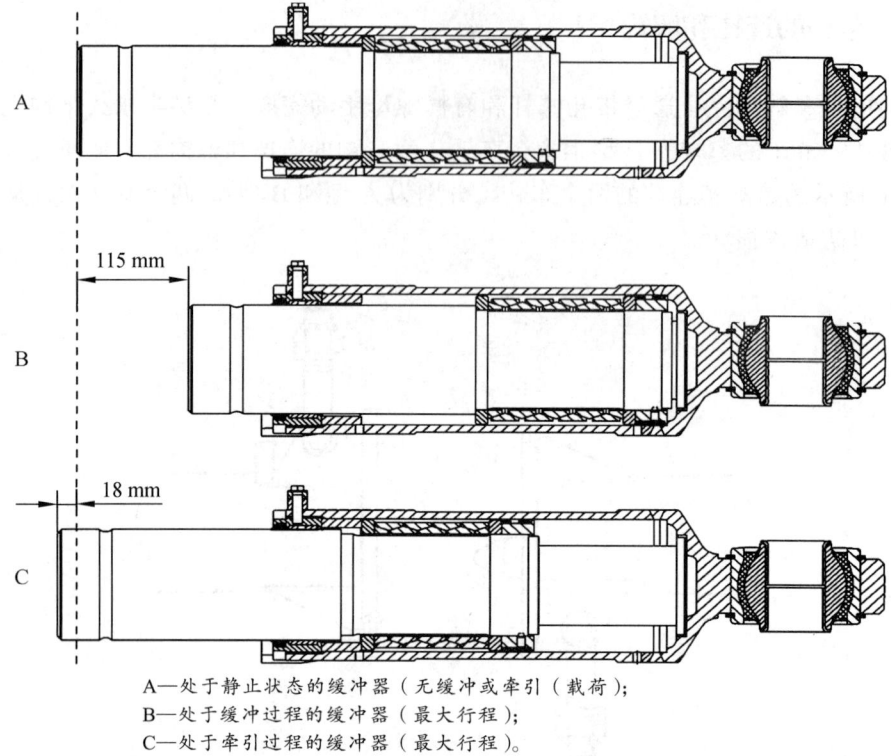

A—处于静止状态的缓冲器（无缓冲或牵引（载荷）；
B—处于缓冲过程的缓冲器（最大行程）；
C—处于牵引过程的缓冲器（最大行程）。

图 3-18 A 型半永久车钩的缓冲器

3.3 过渡车钩

过渡车钩用于普通非密接式车钩与自动车钩之间的临时联挂，其结构参见图 3-19，主要有：密接式钩头、非密接式钩头。

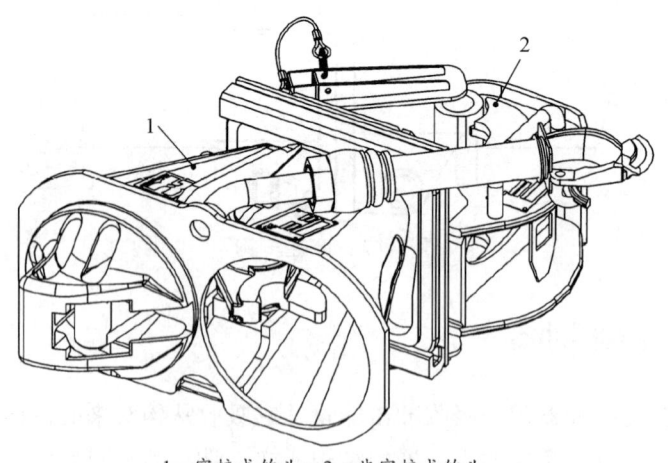

1—密接式钩头；2—非密接式钩头。
图 3-19 过渡车钩

3.3.1 密接式钩头部分

密接式钩头如图 3-20 所示,它用于与动车组的自动车钩相啮合。

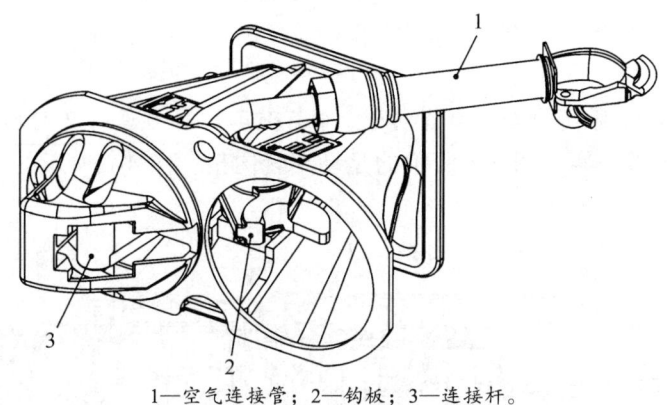

1—空气连接管;2—钩板;3—连接杆。
图 3.20 密接式钩头

3.3.2 非密接式钩头部分

非密接式钩头是一种特殊的设计类型(参看图 3-21),它能够与列车上安装的中国 13 和 15 号关节式车钩进行连挂。

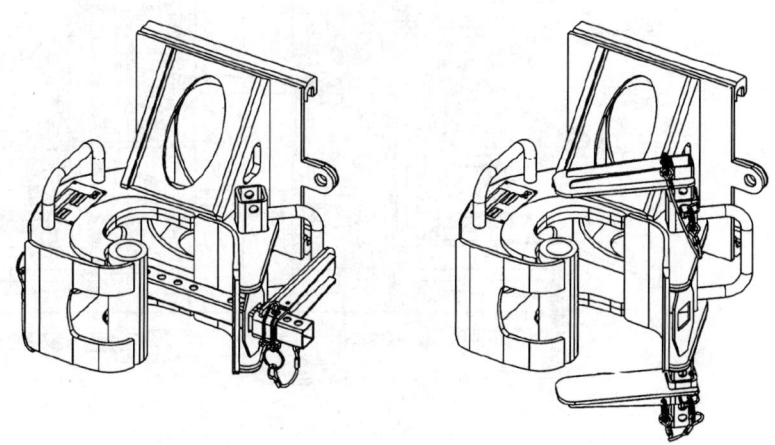

图 3-21 非密接式钩头

4 转向架

动车组通常为 8 节编组列车，4 节动车、4 节拖车，每节车有 2 台转向架。转向架可分为动车转向架和拖车转向架。图 4-1 所示的是动车转向架，图 4-2 所示的是拖车转向架。

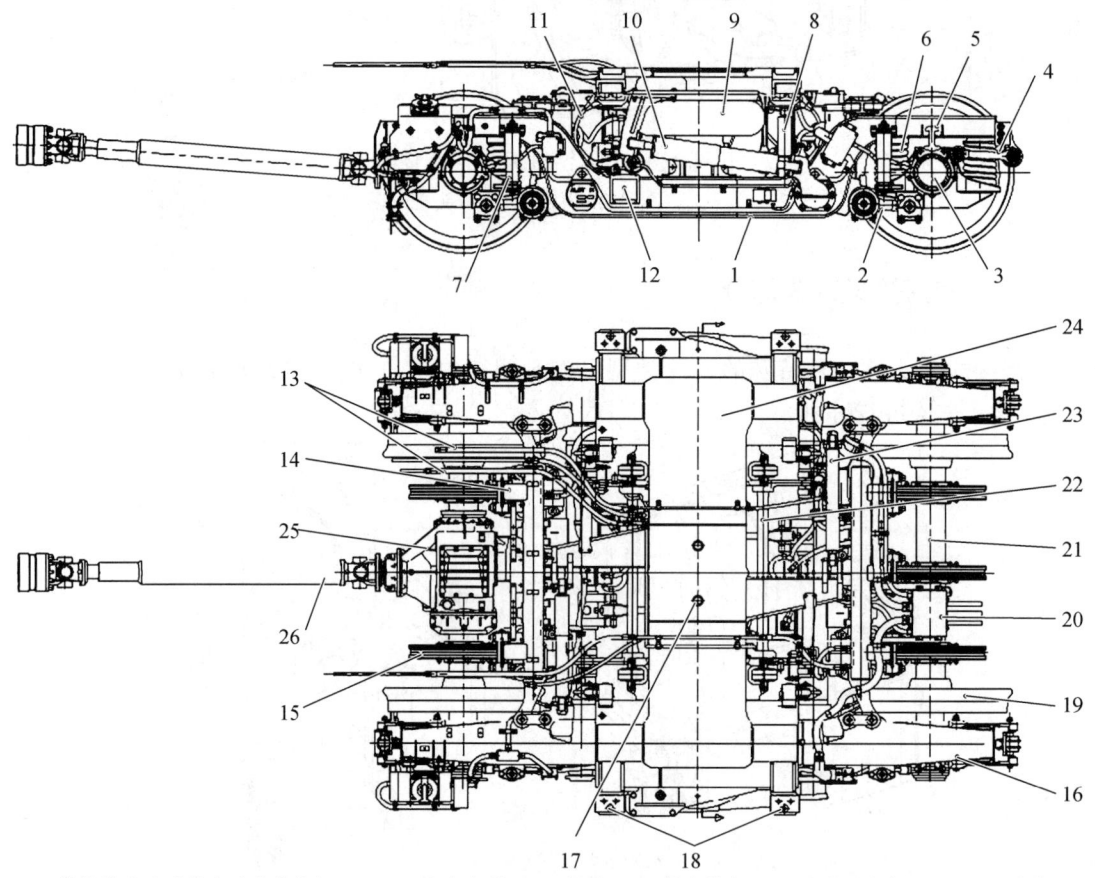

1—带轮缘系统的整个动力转向架 1；2—下部杆组件；3—轴箱；4—整个推杆；5—垂向止挡杆；6—螺旋弹簧；7——系垂向减振器；8—二系垂向减振器；9—空气弹簧；10—抗蛇行减振器；11—二系垂向止挡；12—制动指示器；13—气动连接；14—制动钳；15—制动盘；16—转向架构架；17—摇枕挡；18—支撑；19—整体车轮；20—电气端箱；21—轴；22—抗侧滚扭力杆装置；23—横向减振器；24—车体-转向架摇枕；25—齿轮箱；26—万向轴。

图 4-1 动车转向架

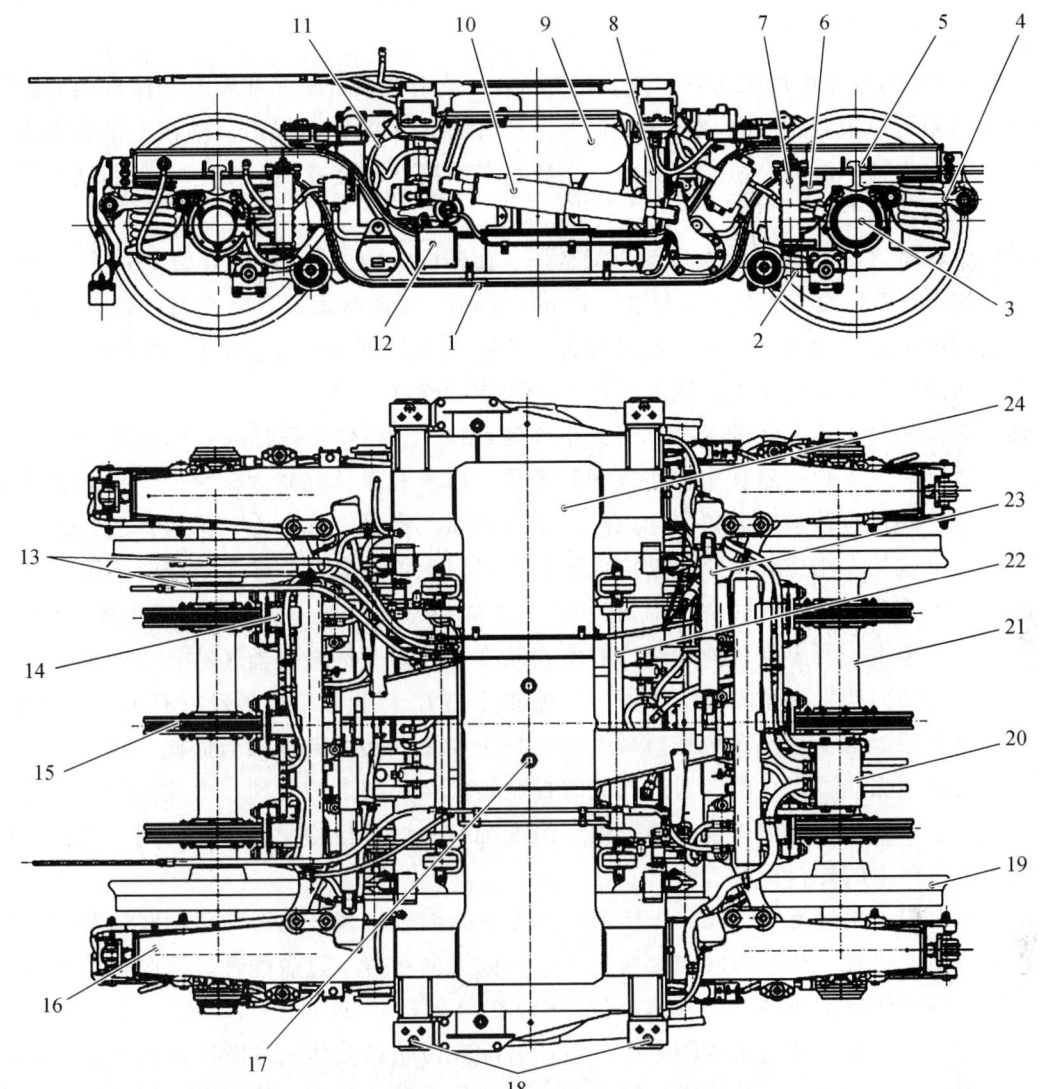

1—非动力转向架；2—下部杆装置；3—轴箱；4—推杆；5—垂向止挡杆；6—螺旋弹簧；7—一系垂向减振器；
8—二系垂向减振器；9—空气弹簧；10—抗蛇行减振器；11—二系垂向止挡；12—制动指示器；
13—气动连接；14—制动钳；15—制动盘；16—转向架构架；17—摇枕挡；18—支撑；
19—整体车轮；20—电气端箱；21—轴；22—抗侧滚杆装置；
23—横向减振器；24—车体-转向架摇枕。

图 4-2 拖车转向架

转向架通过摇枕（24）支撑整个车体结构。转向架和车体结构通过在转向架上的支座（18）进行连接。摇枕（24）有一个箱状结构，用以设置 2 个辅助风缸，用于二系弹簧悬挂空气弹簧系统。

"Z"型牵引系统将牵引力和制动力由转向架传递至车体。"H"型转向架构架（16）由合金钢制成，适于高速运行。转向架构架（16）由下部杆组件（2）和整个推杆（4）连接至 4 个轴箱（3）。

轮对包括 2 个整体式车轮（19）和 1 个车轴（21）。车轮（19）与轴（21）采用过盈方式配合。

轴箱（3）的本体由球墨铸铁制成。轴箱（3）采用带预装配筒和聚酰胺保持架的圆锥滚子轴承。轴箱可以吸收由于铁轨与车轮间相互作用而增大的轴向推力。轴箱上带有集成式传感器，用以检测轴承温度、速度、防滑等参数。在轴箱上还装有一个接地/牵引回流设备，用以构成电流回流通路。

转向架各轴之间的悬挂称为一系弹簧悬挂。在转向架中，2组螺旋弹簧（6）被牢固地置于弹簧支座上，而弹簧支座是整个轴箱（3）的一部分。垂向减振器（7）平行于螺旋弹簧（6），用于在运行中抑制转向架的跳动。通过设置在不同高度的下部杆装置（2）和推杆（4）将轴箱固定在转向架构架（16）上。这些杆件两端均有弹性联轴节。

转向架构架与车体之间的悬挂称为二系弹簧悬挂。二系弹簧悬挂的空气弹簧（9）可以提高乘行舒适度。二系弹簧悬挂中的空气弹簧系统可以吸收车体与转向架之间的垂向和横向载荷。高度调整阀（载荷检测装置）用以控制空气弹簧的操作。如果空气弹簧被放气，则一个与空气弹簧串联的专用橡胶垫（辅助应急弹簧）可以承担此载荷，使车辆能够不限速运行。

除二系弹簧悬挂系统中的空气弹簧（9）组件以外，转向架还提供如下减振器：

每台转向架上平行于空气弹簧组件对角安装2个二系垂向减振器（8），以便抑制运行时的振动。每台转向架上对角安装2个横向减振器（23），以吸收横向振动，有助于通过曲线。

每台转向架上有2个减振抗蛇行减振器（10）安装在转向架构架与摇枕（24）之间。这些减振抗蛇行减振器可以在高速通过曲线时控制转向架小幅度的转动。由此消除了轨道上横向力对车轮造成的过度磨损。仅在第一列车组上配有一个蛇行检测传感器，用于监测在转向架构架水平方向上的蛇行运动。

动力由牵引电机经万向轴（26）传递至车轮，万向轴一端经由转矩限制联轴节（安全联轴节）与牵引电机轴（在动力转向架底架上沿纵向方向布置）过盈配合。万向轴的另一端连接至安装在动力转向架车轴上的减速齿轮箱中（25）。

齿轮箱（25）安装在电机轴的中心，包括装配在齿轮箱箱体内的减速齿轮装置，并通过法兰联轴器与万向轴相连。减速齿轮箱配有一个油位表和若干电气传感器，用以确定油位。在车站停车的时间足够将各相关信息传输至TCMS（列车控制与信息系统）。

安全联轴节是一个连接装置，其一端连接牵引电机轴，另一端连接万向轴。此联轴节具有转矩设定装置。通过调整液压压力，可以将转矩卸载极限设置为所需的数值。当预设转矩超过规定限值时，剪切环将开放，释放联轴节中的油压，之后安全联轴节发生滑动。该过程将在数毫秒内完成。在压力释放之后，联轴节可在轴上空转。

转向架构架与车体-转向架摇枕（24）之间连接有2个抗侧滚扭力杆装置（22）。该抗侧滚扭力杆装置包括一个抗侧滚扭力杆，该杆由2个吊架通过弹性铰链支撑。抗侧滚扭力杆系统可以防止车体在转向架上侧滚。

4.1 转向架构架

参看图4-3，转向架构架是一个H形结构的非合金钢构架。H形钢构架由2根实心纵梁和与之相连接的管状横梁构成。纵梁由金属板焊接而成。管状横梁由轧制而成。

转向架构架包括预装的和需后期机加工的托架，用以装设转向架的其他各个部件。带有预制托架的转向架构架已进行应力消解，以释放焊接过程中形成的应力。构架在焊接和应力消解工序之后被机器加工至精确的尺寸。转向架构架置于一系弹簧悬挂装置的螺旋弹簧上。

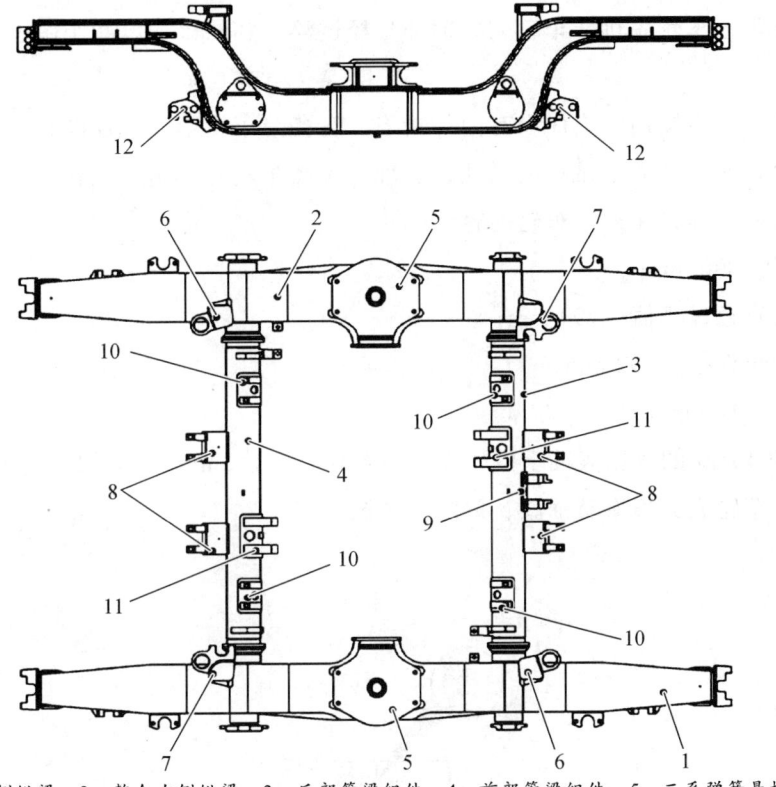

1—整个左侧纵梁；2—整个右侧纵梁；3—后部管梁组件；4—前部管梁组件；5—二系弹簧悬挂支架；
6—制动器管梁支架；7—横向减振器支架；8—制动横梁支架；9—齿轮箱吊杆支架；
10—抗侧滚扭力杆支架；11—牵引杆支架；12—轴箱紧固支架。

图 4-3　转向架构架

4.2　带有轴箱的轮对

每台转向架均包含 2 个带有轴箱的轮对。每个轮对都是一个由牵引电机驱动的转动部件，牵引电机是通过万向轴驱动车辆的转向架的。整个转向架组件通过一系悬挂的螺旋弹簧缓冲安装于轴箱及轮对上。转向架轮对通过一系弹簧悬挂承载车体重量。每个轮对最大承载 17 t 的轴载荷。

4.2.1　车　轮

参见图 4-4，车轮是由 R8T 钢制成的整体式车轮。它是一个直径为 890 mm 的合金钢整体式圆形组件。在机加工操作之前，须对车轮轮辋横截面上样本采样以进行拉力试验、化学分析、冲击试验、硬度试验，还要进行残余应力方向、微结构、晶粒大小和超声探伤检查。车轮为机加工部件，其中心处有一个直径 192 mm 的机加工孔，用以与轴进行过盈配合。车轮被设计用以承受疲劳载荷、垂直载荷、横向载荷和高速运转。

车轮工作部位的踏面是具有一定半径的锥形滚动面，可在通过轨道曲线时起到差速器的作用。轮缘可阻止车轮脱轨。车轮的轮辋部分经过淬火和回火，以减小由于摩擦造成的磨损和破裂。

车轮要经过超声探伤，确保没有内部缺陷。轮孔与车轮踏面直径同心。在轮毂的外径处有一个通向轮孔的直径为 5 mm 的通孔，从轴上拆卸车轮时可用此通孔进行注油。正常工作条件下该孔由一个螺钉保护。车轮的容许尺寸：

新轮轮径：890 mm；

车轮运用直径最小值：794 mm；

轮毂的最小外径：192 mm；

轮毂宽度：180 mm。

直径为 794 mm 的车轮表面上的一个宽 6 mm、半径 2 mm 的机加工槽（3）示出了车轮的运用极限。车轮表面喷涂有油漆，以防止锈蚀。

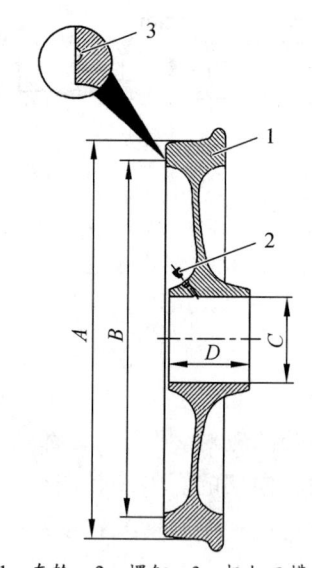

1—车轮；2—螺钉；3—机加工槽。

图 4-4　车轮

4.2.2　轴

轴由合金钢锻造材料制成。它是一个机加工部件，如图 4-5 所示。轴的各个安装座须通过磨削加工最终完成。车轴须进行超声探伤,以避免内部缺陷。锻造成形的轴须采样,经过化学分析、拉力试验、弹性试验、转动弯曲疲劳试验、微观检查和超声探伤,以确保轴的质量。

它采用磨削精加工,以安装轮对和轴箱部件。它包括经过磨削的制动盘座、轮座和轴箱轴承座。轴的两个端面上的锥形孔中可紧固端板,以完全锁定整个轴箱轴承。在非动力轴的中心处,有一个直径为 65 mm 的通孔,用于插进探针进行定期的超声检测。

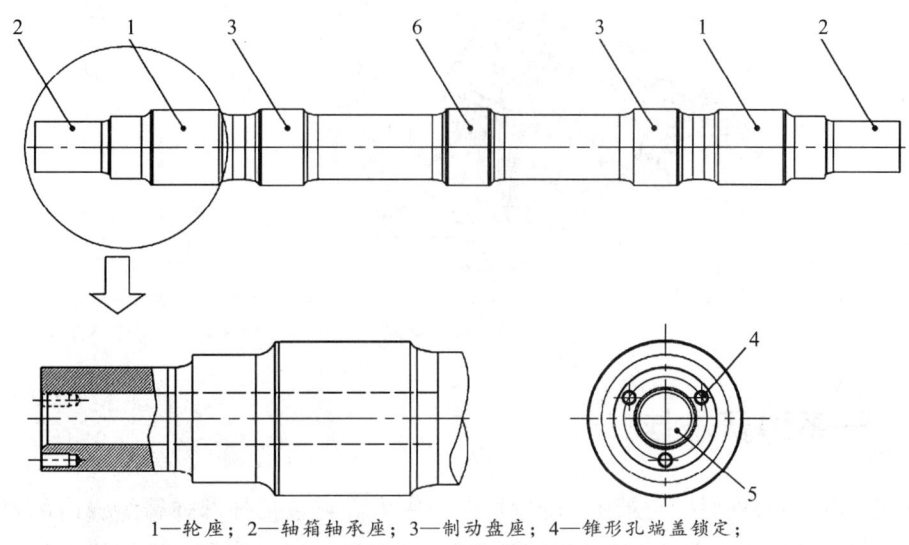

1—轮座;2—轴箱轴承座;3—制动盘座;4—锥形孔端盖锁定;
5—65 mm 直径孔;6—制动盘座(中心)。

图 4-5 车轴

4.3 轴 箱

参见图 4-6,轴箱体由球墨铸铁制成,是机加工部件。其中心有一个机加工孔,用以安装圆锥滚子轴承。轴箱体的两端有圆形环,以安装螺旋弹簧。

轴箱端面有锥形孔,用以紧固中间前盖(左侧)。中间前盖上配有速度和温度传感器。带有轴承组件的轴箱安装在轴的两端。一系弹簧悬挂螺旋弹簧置于轴箱上,由它来承载转向架载荷。这些轴承采用压入配合装配到轴上。锥形轴承单元一端由端盖压紧定位,被安装在轴上。轴承由润滑脂润滑,在轴箱上装有一个回流装置。中间前盖和端盖上带有 O 形环,以防润滑脂泄漏。所有端盖紧固件均采用力矩扳手紧固。

轴箱还配有以下装置:
- 轴承温度传感器(BTS);
- 用于防滑装置的速度传感器(BCU);
- 速度传感器(LKJ);
- 速度传感器(ATP);
- 接地回流装置(ECR)或牵引电流装置(TCR)。

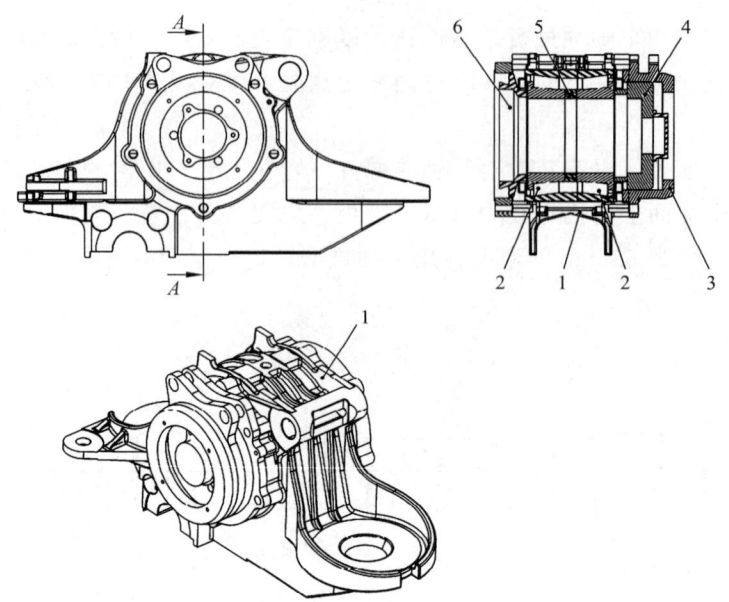

1—轴箱；2—锥形轴承；3—中间前盖（左侧）；4—端盖；5—垫圈；6—轴。

图 4-6 轴箱

4.4 一系弹簧悬挂

参见图 4-7，一系弹簧悬挂用于传递垂向作用力。它包括外部弹簧组、内部弹簧组和垂向减振器。外部和内部弹簧组包括外部和内部螺旋弹簧，这些弹簧由圆弹簧钢丝制成，经过了疲劳试验。外弹簧直径为 29.5 mm，内弹簧的直径为 20 mm。这些弹簧作用于转向架构架与轴箱之间。一系弹簧悬挂包括每个轴箱上的 2 组弹簧组和 1 个垂向减振器。

在轴箱与转向架构架之间连接有一个下部杆组件。下部杆经连接块以螺钉连接至轴箱。整个推杆组件以螺栓紧固件连接至轴箱顶部和转向架构架。这些杆中的弹性联轴节可引导轴箱进行统一的悬挂。

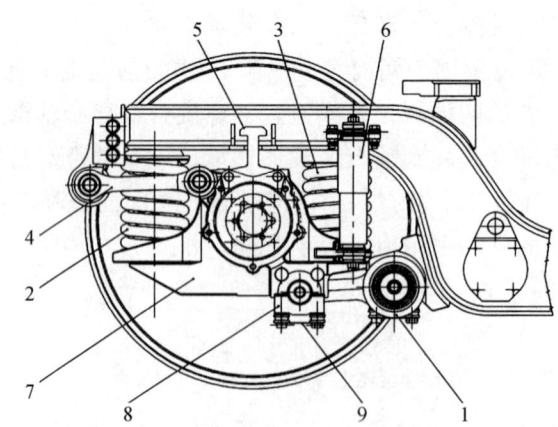

1—下部杆组件；2—外部弹簧组；3—内部弹簧组；4—整个推杆；5—垂向止挡连杆；6—减振器；7—轴箱；8—连接杆挡块；9—用于螺钉的板。

图 4-7 一系弹簧悬挂

轴箱上安装有一个垂向止挡连杆。它用于控制"空载"情况下的转向架构架高度。除螺旋弹簧之外，在转向架构架上还为一系弹簧悬挂安装了减振器，用以在列车运动中减小车辆振动，吸收弹性阻尼。

4.5 二系弹簧悬挂

参见图 4-8，二系弹簧悬挂可吸收转向架与车体之间的垂向和横向载荷，从而确保乘客的乘行舒适度。其通过每台转向架上的 2 个空气弹簧装置（1）、垂向减振器（6）、横向减振器（7）和抗蛇行减振器（4）吸收动载荷。它们均安装在车体转向架摇枕与转向架之间。二系弹簧悬挂可通过每台转向架上的高度调整阀确保动车组高度恒定。

二系弹簧悬挂包括空气弹簧组件、垂向减振器、横向减振器等组成部分。

当空气弹簧本身或空气弹簧的供风有问题时，车体将下降到应急弹簧上，这时只有应急弹簧起作用。在这种情况下，车组必须较低的速度运行，以确保乘客的安全性和舒适度。

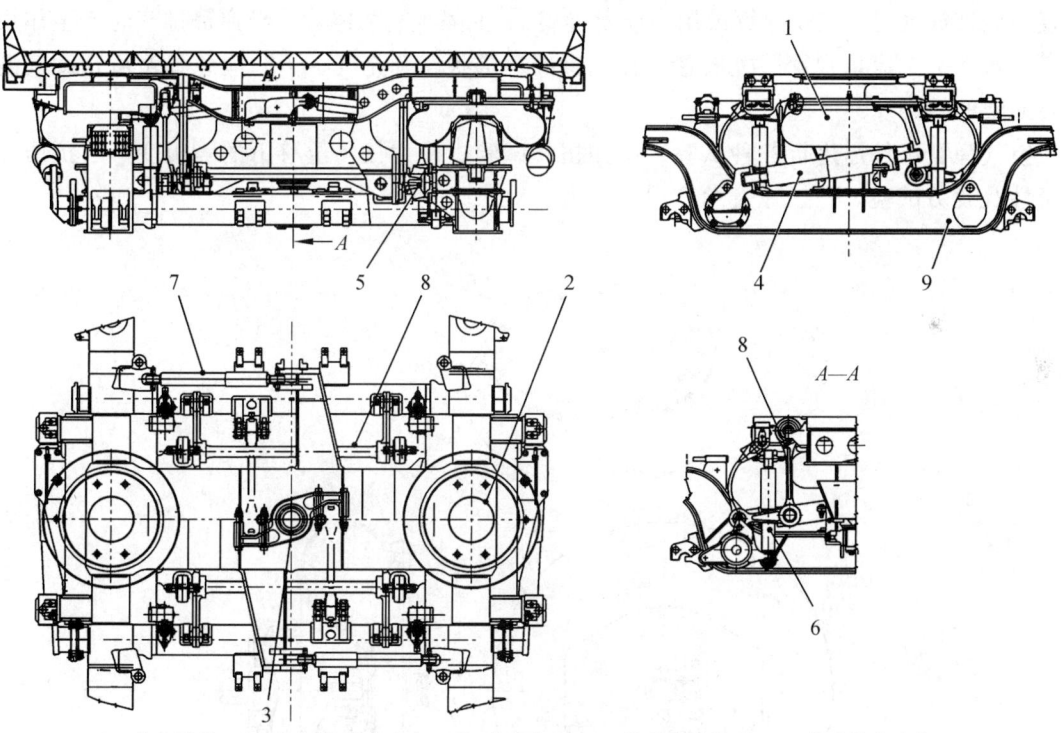

1—空气弹簧；2—转向架-车体连杆；3—牵引系统；4—抗蛇行减振器；5—横向橡胶止挡；
6—垂向减振器；7—横向减振器；8—抗侧滚扭力杆；9—转向架构架。

图 4-8 二系悬挂装置

4.5.1 空气弹簧组件

每台转向架上有 2 个空气弹簧组件。参见图 4-9，2 个空气弹簧通过一个双平衡阀连接，主供风经高度调整阀送入空气弹簧，2 个串联的辅助风缸用来加强空气弹簧系统。

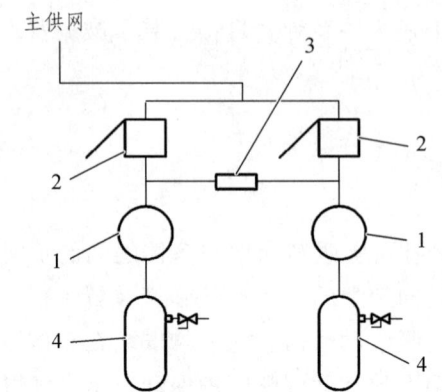

1—空气弹簧；2—高度调整阀；3—双平衡阀；4—辅助风缸。

图 4-9 供风管路示意图

参见图 4-10，空气弹簧装置包括空气弹簧隔板、与空气弹簧串联布置的锥形橡胶弹簧（当空气弹簧被放气时，橡胶弹簧被用作应急弹簧）、上隔板、摩擦片（当弹簧排气时产生作用）。空气弹簧和一个应急弹簧层叠放置，在气囊的正常状态（充气）下，应急弹簧可帮助气囊实现转向架的转动。

空气弹簧组件需进行各种试验，例如扭转试验、最大径向位移下的隔板变形、抗压性、气密性及疲劳试验。空气弹簧的破裂压力为 2 MPa。

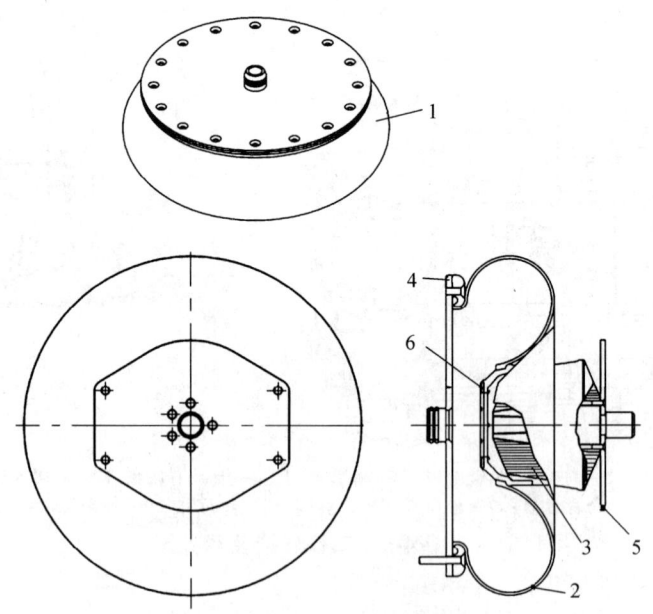

1—空气弹簧装置；2—空气弹簧隔板；3—锥形橡胶弹簧（应急弹簧）；
4—上隔板；5—下板；6—摩擦片。

图 4-10 空气弹簧装置

4.5.2 空气悬挂控制系统

空气悬挂控制系统可实现对车辆的空气弹簧气囊的充气和排气。它还可以在车辆载荷情况下控制车体的高度。

空气悬挂装置允许弹簧相对于站台乘车高度进行有限的调整。为此,空气悬挂控制设计用于在任何车辆载荷工况下保持车体下方的空气弹簧气囊保持在一个恒定的高度。实现此功能的装置是一个高度调整阀(3),它通过连杆的预置长度(设定点)与瞬时弹簧高度(实际值)之间的差来对气囊进行充气、排气或关断,从而确保气囊的高度不变。

4.6 摇 枕

摇枕(图4-11)是车体与转向架之间的一个中间部件。每台转向架有一个摇枕,它置于二系弹簧悬挂弹簧上。车体在车体支撑托架的4个角以螺栓紧固件连接至转向架摇枕。摇枕设有一个箱体结构,以容纳二系弹簧悬挂空气弹簧的气动系统所需的2个辅助风缸。它将车辆载荷经二系弹簧悬挂传递至转向架。

二系弹簧悬挂减振器和抗侧滚扭力杆吊架也连接至摇枕。它有一个枢轴销用以装配牵引平衡器。摇枕的两端均有可作用于横向止挡的面板。摇枕配有用于车体连接的支撑托架。

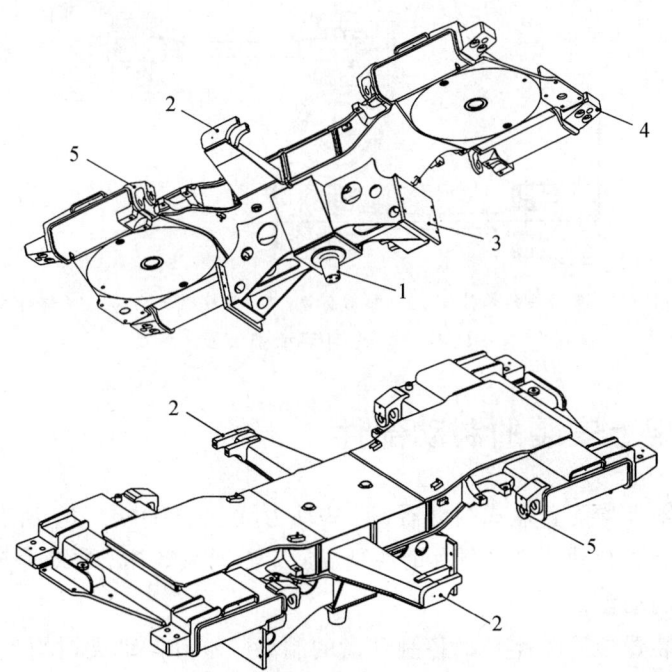

1—枢轴销;2—外部支架;3—用于横向止挡的面板;4—车体支撑托架;5—支架垂直辅助挡块。

图 4-11 转向架摇枕

4.7 转向架牵引装置

参见图 4-12,转向架的牵引装置用连杆将摇枕连接至转向架构架。此系统安装在转向架的中心。每台转向架有一个牵引装置,包括牵引杆、整个平衡器、牵引杆接头。它将转向架的纵向力传递至车体。摇枕的中心有一个枢轴,牵引系统平衡器由垫片和锥形套管配以 3 个螺钉装配至枢轴销上。平衡器的两端均以螺钉及螺母与牵引杆接头相连。带有连接件的牵引杆以螺栓连接至转向架构架托架。

牵引杆接头包括一个销钉、一个圆柱和一个接头,它可实现牵引系统中的球面运动。这些连接件被装配在牵引杆上,后者上有一个 103 mm 的孔;销钉上有 2 个直径为 25 mm 的孔。牵引杆用于将整个平衡器连接到转向架上。弹性联轴节须经过强度增强、几何尺寸、机械载荷等方面的检测,以及静态硬度试验。

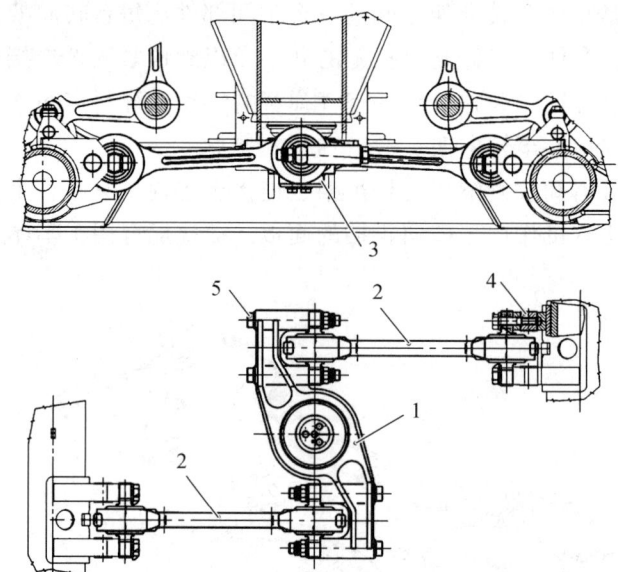

1—整个平衡器;2—带接头的牵引杆;3—锥形套管;4—圆柱螺母 M24;5—螺钉 M24×220。

图 4-12 转向架牵引装置

4.8 转向架上安装的制动部件

动车组在所有轴上均配有盘式制动器,在非动力轴上配有电制动。所有轴均配有 640 mm 直径的车轴安装的盘式制动器,它们由钢铁制成,无需通风散热。非动力轴上有 3 个制动盘,在动力轴上有 2 个制动盘。

转向架的制动装置参见图 4-13,各制动盘的制动气缸和制动夹钳均为常规类型,带有内置式闸片间隙自动调整装置。带停放制动器的制动气缸和制动钳为整体弹簧式。制动闸片为烧结型,按照 600 ℃ 的最高允许温度和 30 mm 的最大磨损量来设计。

制动设备安装在 2 个制动横梁上,这些横梁安装在转向架构架上。各制动气缸均通过管路连接至制动控制系统。制动缸充气由位于所有车辆底架上的制动控制单元控制。

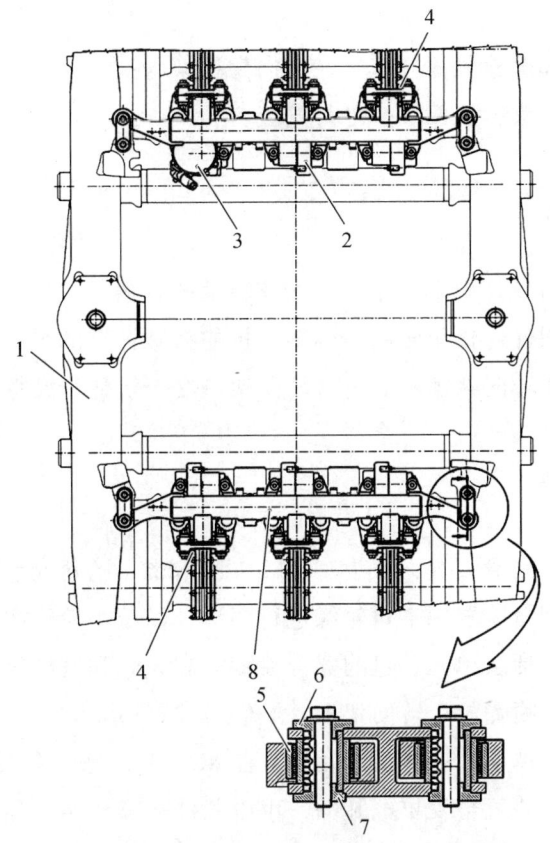

1—非动力转向架；2—制动钳单元（常规）；3—制动钳单元（停放制动）；4—烧结型制动闸片；
5—制动横梁的上部弹性衬套；6—制动横梁紧固衬套；
7—制动横梁紧固衬套；8—制动横梁。

图 4-13　转向架制动装置

4.9　减振器

4.9.1　垂向减振器

一系弹簧悬挂的垂向减振器设置在转向架构架与轴箱之间。它可以吸收车辆的冲击和振动。减振器的一端由 2 个弹性联轴节固定在一块钢板上。该钢板被固定在转向架构架的支架上。减振器的另一端以 2 个弹性联轴节固定在轴箱上，各联轴节用螺母紧固。每台转向架的一系悬挂装置有 4 个减振器。

二系悬挂装置的垂向减振器安装在转向架构架的支撑托架和摇枕的托架上。每台转向架上的二系弹簧悬挂装有 2 个垂向减振器，它可以吸收车辆的振动和冲击，其两端均有安装接头，且两接头相互垂直。

4.9.2 横向减振器

横向减振器由托架和螺栓紧固件安装在转向架构架与摇枕之间,用以吸收车体的横向振动。减振器的两端均有接头,且两接头平行安装。

4.9.3 抗蛇行减振器

抗蛇行减振器是专门设计用于控制小幅正弦转动的减振器。抗蛇行减振器的一端由一个支撑托架和若干螺栓紧固件连接至转向架构架。抗蛇行减振器的另一端由一个支撑托架和若干螺栓紧固件连接至车体转向架摇枕。每台转向架有 2 个抗蛇行减振器。

4.10 轮缘润滑

在车组上装设有轮缘润滑装置,在头车(Mc1 和 Mc2)的每台前转向架的轮轴上设有一个轮缘润滑装置。轮缘润滑装置用来对轮缘进行润滑,以减小轮缘的磨损。润滑剂经轮缘流至钢轨。轮缘润滑装置包括泵单元、过滤器、喷嘴、软风管和润滑软管。泵单元及其他部件位于车体上,只有管路和喷嘴位于转向架上。

一列动车组有 2 个泵单元,一个泵单元安装在 Mc1 上,另一个泵单元则安装在 Mc2 上。在车组运行时,电子控制装置会发出电脉冲,由电脉冲来操作相应运行方向的电磁阀。当车组以 Mc1 车的方向运动时,泵会向位于 Mc1 轴左轮和右轮前方的喷嘴供油,而此时 Mc2 上的另一个泵单元不会工作。当车组以 Mc2 方向运动时,泵会向位于 Mc2 非动力轴左轮和右轮前方的喷嘴供油,而此时 Mc1 上的泵单元不会工作。

根据车组速度,系统以预先规定的时间或空间间隔,并按照车组运行方向被激活。通常每 300 米执行一次润滑循环。润滑油由植物油制成,可生物降解。

4.11 撒砂系统

参见图 4-14,在车辆起动阶段和坡道上时,撒砂操作可以增大车轮踏面与轨道之间的摩擦力。在撒砂操作中,干燥的砂子由喷嘴喷向轨道。砂箱(1)中装有干燥的砂子。

每个动力轴在每个车轮上均配有一个撒砂器。每个砂箱有 2 个压缩空气接入口。一个接入口一直通以连续的气流,使砂子保持干燥,另一个接入口则用于撒砂。当司机手动操作撒砂手柄时,砂子在压缩空气作用下被喷射到轨道上。砂子用电加热。撒砂系统包括砂箱、砂箱盖、砂管加热器、喷嘴、联轴节和支撑托架。

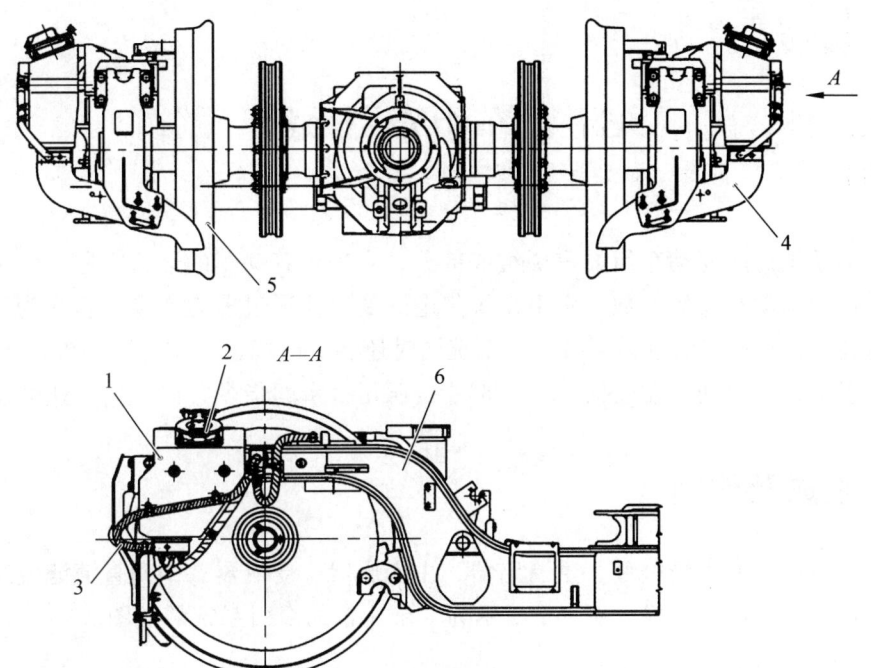

1—砂箱； 2—砂箱盖； 3—螺旋缠绕管； 4—砂喷嘴支架； 5—动力轮对； 6—转向架构架。

图 4-14 砂箱布置图

5 动车组牵引系统

牵引传动系统是高速动车组的重要组成部分,它决定着动车的运行方向、牵引效率、运行速度等一切和运动有关的参数。牵引系统将电网的电能通过电力变换,转化为牵引电机能够接受的电能,驱动列车前进。牵引传动系统同时还要对电机进行控制(电机调速),以便输出适当的牵引力,使得动车在任何环境下都能按照司机室的指令,以规定的速度运行。

5.1 组成及作用

牵引传动系统一般由受电弓、主断路器、主变压器、变流器、中间直流滤波组件,逆变器、牵引电机等几大部分组成。图 5-1 所示为一个完整的牵引系统的框图。

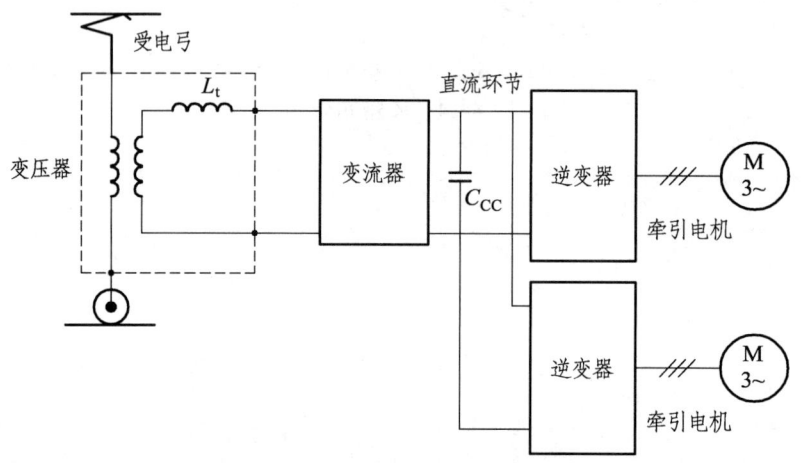

图 5-1 牵引系统基本组成示意图

受电弓的作用是在动车需要能量时,将电网的电能通过受电弓传送到动车上;在动车不需要通电时,受电弓降下,将动车和高压电隔离。通常受电弓都安装在一个带绝缘柱的底座上,以实现安装在车体上的同时,实现高压电和车体之间的隔离。要特别指出的是,运用时,这个绝缘柱一定要保持良好的清洁,否则上面附着的杂质很可能降低绝缘等级,从而发生被高压电击穿的危险。

主断路器的作用是在受电弓升起时,切断或连接主回路和电网的联系。

变压器的作用是将受电弓得到的高压电,变压至电压等级合适的电能,以方便变流器对电能进行控制。变压器的体积和质量都比较大,因此一般都将其安装在拖车上。

变流器的作用是将变压器输送过来的电能,经过稳压、变换后输送给牵引电机。通常变流器由一个前级的脉冲整流器将变压器过来的交流电整流为一个稳定的直流,然后将这个直流电进行逆变,将电能输送给牵引电机。通常情况下,电机由专门的 TCU 控制,结合司机室指令信息和本车的自身情况，如本车自重、坡度等信息，输出适当的牵引力，以实现对动车的恒速或变速牵引。目前，动车变流器都具备再生制动功能，也就是在制动情况下（电制动），变流器还可以反向运行，将制动的能量反馈回电网。牵引电机此时作为发电机运行，吸收动能将其转换为电能。

由于变流器作为能量转换装置，其能耗也相对较大，不可避免地会产生较大的热量，因此，变流器也需要专门的冷却装置。就目前来讲，其冷却方式一般为水冷和风冷结合冷却，也需要专门配置冷却单元对其进行冷却。

5.2 受电弓

受电弓在接触网与电气操作的车辆之间起电气接触作用，它是一种高电压设备，该设备可从 25 kV，50 Hz 交流接触网处得到电能，线路上的钢轨可用作回流导体。受电弓有单臂和双臂两种，我国目前所使用的均为单臂受电弓。

受电弓的设计应该具有最高的操作可靠性和符合要求的接触压力，即使在高速运行工况下也要满足这个要求。

5.2.1 结构和组成

受电弓一般包括底架、阻尼器、升弓装置、紧急降弓装置（ADD）、上臂、下臂、碳滑板、弓架、导向杆等，受电弓总成图参见图 5-2。

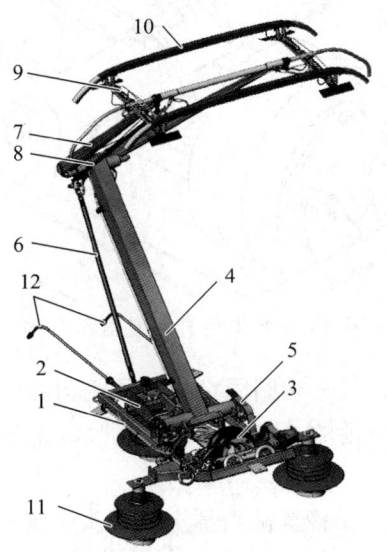

1—底架；2—阻尼器；3—升弓装置；4—下臂；5—弓装配；6—下导杆；7—上臂；
8—上导杆；9—弓头；10—碳滑板；11—绝缘子；12—绝缘软管。
图 5-2 受电弓总体结构图

受电弓底架由钢制成，上臂和下臂由较轻的铝合金材料制成并固定在底架上。如图 5-3 所示整个受电弓安装在三个绝缘子上，并用适当的紧固件进行刚性固定。由于绝缘子易受到污染，且较脆弱，如受异物打击易出现破损，因此绝缘子设计为可单独拆卸结构，便于更换。

绝缘子由陶瓷材料制成。在升弓位置，受电弓的整个结构均可传输电功率，是一个带电导体，而绝缘子的下部就是车体，车体和受电弓之间依靠绝缘子绝缘。因此，绝缘子是受电弓上的安全部件之一。

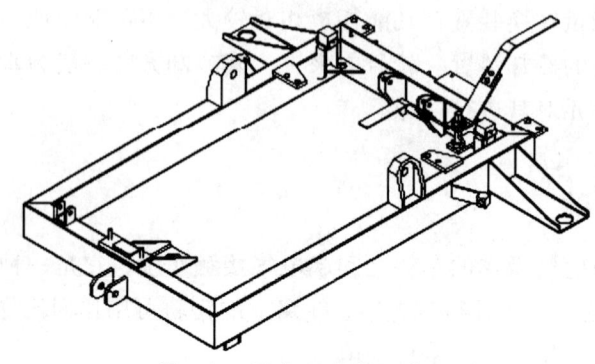

图 5-3 受电弓底架示意图

升弓装置包括气动操作的气囊驱动装置和空气升弓装置。如图 5-4 所示任何时候只要压缩空气通入气囊驱动装置，升弓装置就会运动，向上转动下臂。由此，上臂向上移动，直至弓头接触到接触网。

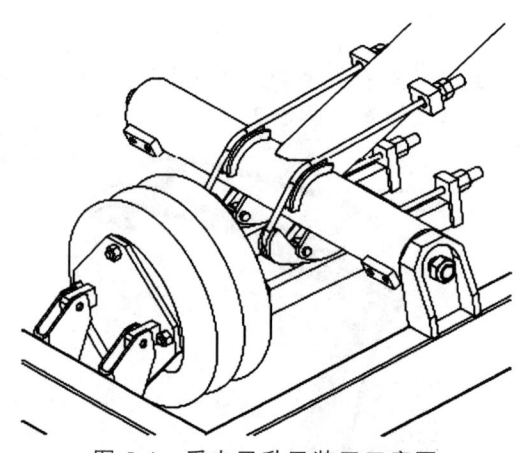

图 5-4 受电弓升弓装置示意图

阻尼器一端固定在底架上，另一端则固定在升弓机构的升弓装置（下臂）中。阻尼器可在升弓和降弓时降低受电弓对车顶的冲击，同时也可吸收由车辆运动和接触网相互接触引起的受电弓振动。

在降下位置，受电弓架在 3 个橡胶减振器上，弓头则置于弓装配上。3 个橡胶减振器承担受电弓的整个结构。弓头被弓装配保持就位。

弓装配形状的设计可确保弓头在降下位置时不会发生任何损坏。只要弓装配固定得当，它就可以防止受电弓的倾斜和弯曲。

下导杆在受电弓升弓和降弓操作中支承下臂。这可以帮助引导下臂就位，以防止倾斜和弯曲。下导杆的一端连接至底架，另一端连接至下臂的顶端部分。

上臂为铝合金制成的空管，设计用以保持弓头就位。

上导杆可将弓头保持水平就位。对它的调整将使弓头准确地水平置于一个平均工作高度上。这样有助于实现 2 个碳滑板的均等或均匀磨损。上导杆由铝合金制成。

弓头包括：托架构架、横向弹簧、弓角、碳滑板、气动软管连接（ADD）。它设计用于承受横向和纵向冲击。此外还可保持对接触网线的恒定接触压力。

弓头由带两个托架的刚性构架组成，托架上装配有碳滑板。该构架悬挂在四个拉簧上并纵向装配在托架内。此外，两个横向弹簧安装在弓头和上臂之间，从而可以确保横向弹动。这种悬挂结构可使碳滑板构架在纵向上能够灵活移动，这样就能够缓冲纵向上的冲击，达到保护碳滑板的目的。

碳滑板的主要材料是人工合成的高强度碳，碳滑板表面必须光滑，以确保集电时不产生火花。自动降弓装置会通过压缩空气来监测滑板的工况。在动车组的受电弓中，碳滑板内充有压缩空气，当碳滑板破裂或者损坏时，自动降弓装置能够检测到受电弓破损从而紧急降弓。

受电弓上装有一个气动提升系统，可确保受电弓正常的动态特性、保持与接触网之间的恒定接触压力。该气动提升系统可实现调整碳滑板与接触网之间的接触压力。

气动提升系统和自动降弓装置可从气路中获得压缩空气。由压缩空气系统操纵的气囊气缸可使受电弓抵住接触网。当压缩空气从气囊驱动装置中排出时，受电弓会受其自身重量影响而下移。

5.3 牵引变压器

变压器的工作原理是利用交流电的互感原理，通过共轭线圈将原边电压感应给副边。通过设计原、副边线圈匝数之比不同，就可以得到需要的输出电压。由于接触网的电压很高，达到 25 kV，这样的电压等级显然是不能够直接引入动车进行牵引供电的。因此，需要通过电压变换装置将来自电网的电压进行降压变换后再对变流器供电。变压器的主要工作原理基本相同，都是利用原、副边绕组通过铁心耦合而传递能量。

但是由于牵引变压器容量很大，而且需安装在高速运动的动车上，因此，要最大程度地减轻质量。例如：CRH2 型车的总重只有不到 3 t 图 5-5 为牵引变压器实物图。

图 5-5 牵引变压器实物图

5.3.1 结构特点

CRH2 型动车组使用的变压器，其绕组为一个原边绕组，三个副边绕组（两个牵引绕组和一个辅助绕组。其绕组如图 5-6 所示。

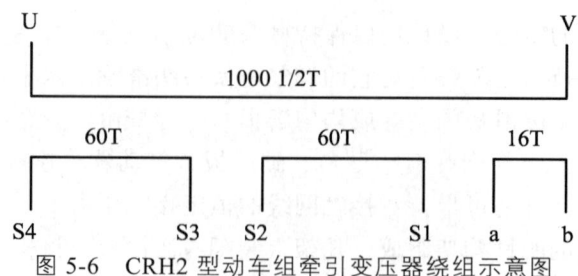

图 5-6 CRH2 型动车组牵引变压器绕组示意图

其结构特点为：

（1）二次绕组为 2 个独立绕组，每个绕组与一台牵引变流装置连接，使二次绕组具有高电抗和弱耦合性，确保牵引变换装置具有稳定运行的特性。另外，为对应于每个二次绕组的增容，一次绕组配置了 2 个并联结构的线圈。

（2）为了减轻质量，一次线圈采用了铝质线圈。

（3）一次绕组接地侧、二次绕组侧及三次绕组侧的绝缘套管采用了耐热环氧树脂将 11 根铜质中心导线注塑一体成形的端子板，相对于三次绕组侧的一端子使用并引出了 2 根中心导线。

5.3.2 内部结构和组装

变压器具有壳式变压器结构，油箱分为上下两部分。在组装变压器内部器件时，首先按规格将绕组卷成板状形，在各绕组之间设置绝缘物及油隙后按规定尺寸进行层叠。

该绕组群垂直设置在下部油箱底板上，将铁心形成额缘状层叠在板状绕组群的外周及内侧直至所定的高度。此时的铁心应层叠在设有下部油箱上缘的法兰盘上。

5.4 牵引变流器

5.4.1 概　述

牵引变流器是动车运行的关键设备，也是动车组关键技术之一。其工作原理：利用新型的半导体功率器件（如绝缘栅双极晶体管或智能功率模块等），采用先进的 PWM 脉冲宽度调制技术，对电能进行智能控制，以实现对牵引电机的输出功率进行精确控制。

牵引变流器的外型和内部结构图如图 5-7 所示。

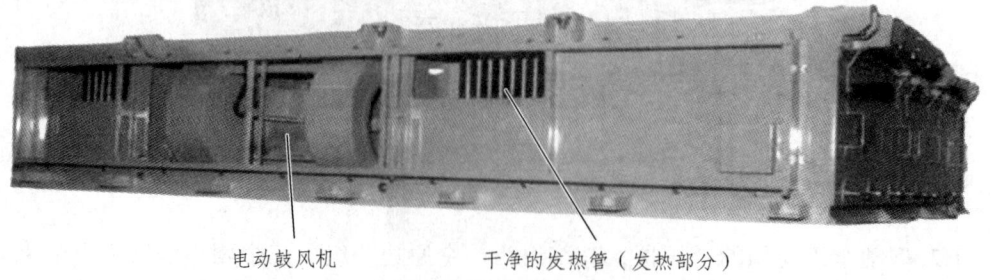

图 5-7　CRH2 型动车组牵引变流器外形实物图

由于动车从交流电网获得的电源为单相交流电,而牵引电机一般为三相交流电机,因此,变流器通常采用一个前级的交-直环节,将单相交流电整流为中间直流,然后再通过 PWM 逆变器将其逆变为三相交流,输出给交流电机,以实现对其的基本控制。在动车的牵引变流器设计中,还采用了先进的四象限技术,即:当动车处于牵引状态时,变流器可以将电网的电能输送给牵引电机;而在动车处于制动工况时,牵引电机变为发电机状态运行,变流器将牵引电机发出的电能反馈至交流电网。目前,我国运行的所有动车变流器都具备再生制动功能。

由于牵引变流器也是一个能量转换设备,因此也需要专门对其额外的配置冷却设备对其进行散热。通常牵引变流器使用水冷和强迫风冷相结合的方式进行冷却。

5.4.2 结 构

由上节介绍可知,牵引变流器包含一个前级的交-直环节和一个 PWM 逆变器。由于考虑到能量需要双向流动,因此,前级的这个交-直环节通常用一个四象限整流器。对于不同的动车而言,这个四象限变流器的结构也有所不同。传统四象限变流器结构如图 5-8 所示,是由四个功率开关组成的桥式电路,即每一个桥臂上有一个功率器件(绝缘栅双极晶体管或智能功率模块),每个功率器件上反并联一个二极管以用于能量的双向传输和电路必要的续流。而由于动车所用的牵引变流器功率相对较大,电压等级也相对较高,因此对这个脉冲整流器的处理上就有不同的方案。这几种方案中,如图 5-9 所示,有 CRH2 型车的带二极管钳位的三电平变换器方案,CRH5 型车的双整流器并联的方案,还有 CRH3 型车的单桥臂双管并联方案。从设计思路上看,CRH2 型车的三电平变换器能够降低单管的压降,从而可以提高系统容量,在相同的中间直流电压下,减低单管压降。并且采取三电平输出,二次谐波含量低,这样就可以省去体积和重量都相对较大的二次谐波滤波器,减轻了变流器的体积和重量。而采取双整流器并联的方案,可以输出较小的纹波,有利于中间直流的稳压。采用双管并联的方案,能够提高系统的容量,可以使用耐压更高的开关管,从而降低直流损耗。目前我国动车所用的几种方案的选择都和主电路的选择有关,各有特色。

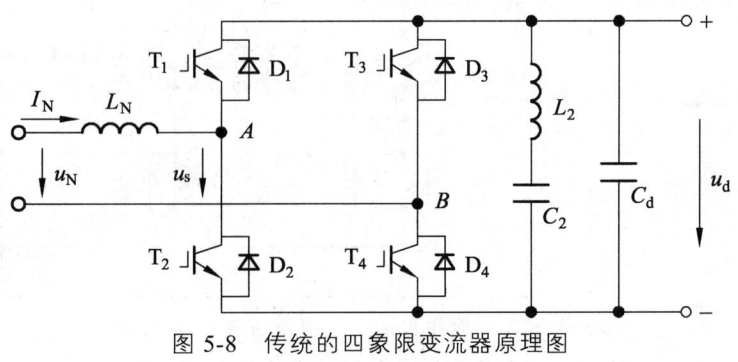

图 5-8 传统的四象限变流器原理图

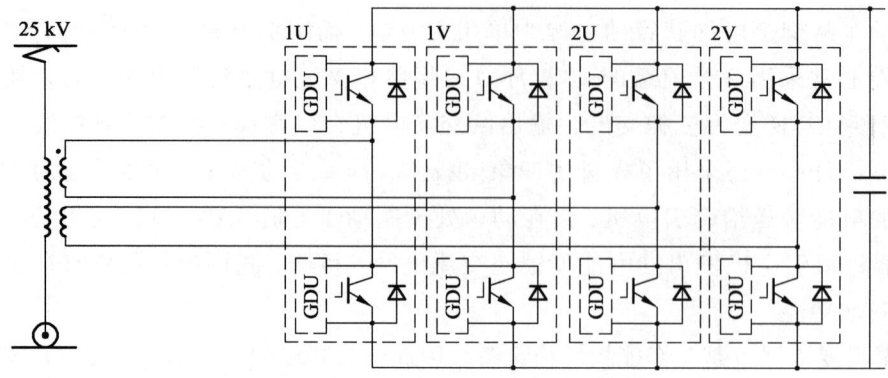

（a）采取双变流器并联方案的脉冲变流器

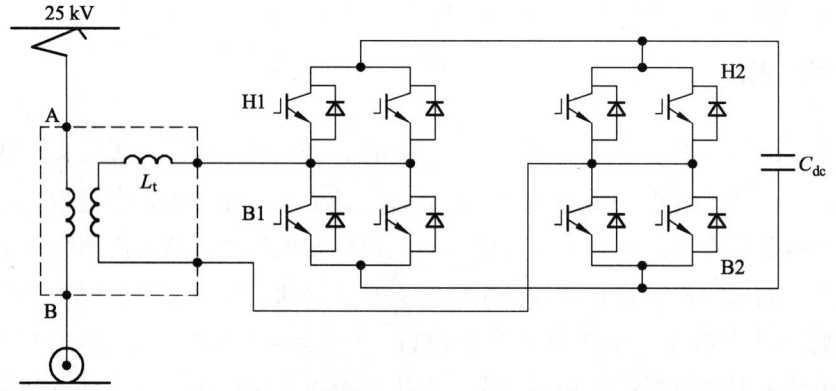

（b）采取单桥臂双管并联方案的脉冲变流器

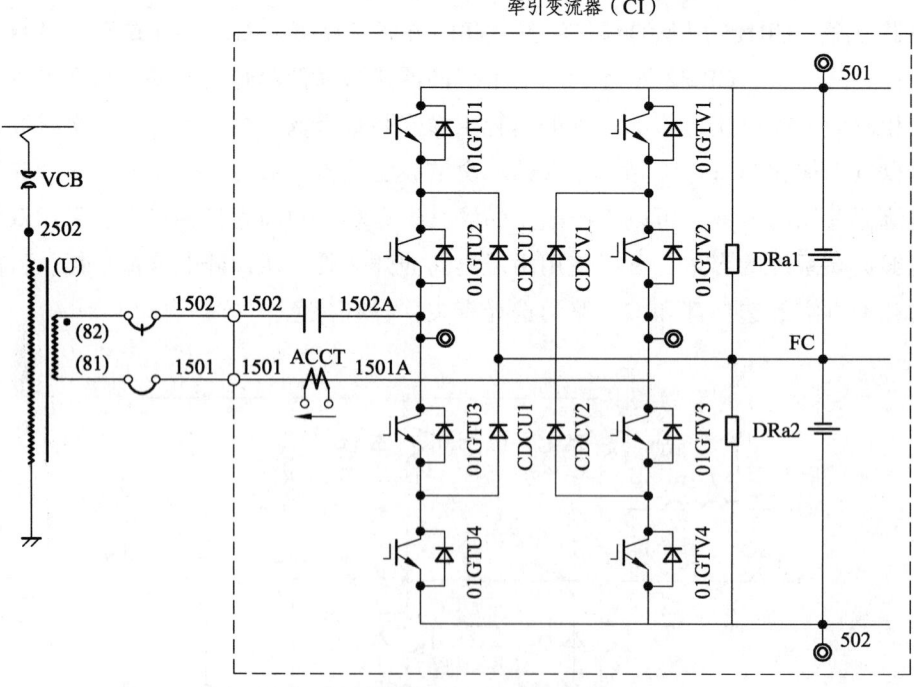

（c）采用二极管钳位的三电平脉冲整流器电路

图 5-9　三种不同方式的脉冲整流器电路原理图

由于动车组结构紧凑，其对各部分空间要求比较严格，因此，牵引变流器的结构也要求尽可能紧凑。无论是何种型号的动车，均把牵引变流器作为一个单独的模块进行封装，各电路元件之间的距离要求尽可能地近，这样才能满足动车空间的要求。

在结构上，日系动车和欧系动车间最显著的区别在于：欧系动车的主牵引系统中，一般都包括了辅助供电系统，其牵引变流器中包含辅助逆变器，它们安装在一起，封装在一个变流器箱内，采取集中逆变和集中散热的方式；而日系动车组的主牵引系统中，仅从主变压器上抽出一个辅助抽头，然后单独构成一套辅助供电系统，主牵引系统和辅助变流系统是分开的。

产生这种结构上的差异是因为，在整车的供电系统的设计中，欧系动车将主牵引系统和辅助供电系统均设计成具有统一供电母线的供电系统，即分为高压母线，中压母线和低压母线。而变流器则作为供电系统的源头，统一向这些母线提供稳定的输出。因此其在设计时将辅助供电系统也设计在主变流器内，直接从主变流器的中间直流处获得辅助供电系统的能量，然后再输出给中低压母线，辅助负载均从中低压母线上获得电能。而日系动车组将辅助供电系统作为一个专门的部分从主牵引系统中分开。主变流器上专门设计了一个辅助绕组以给辅助系统提供电能。而辅助系统则专门设计一个辅助变流器，针对车内不同的负载，辅助变流器输出多路不同制式的电压，给不同的负载供电。

这两种结构上的区别，导致了其工作原理和性能上也产生了很大的差异。

由于日系的辅助供电系统直接从牵引变压器的辅助绕组供电，因此在列车运行时，当主断路器断开（过分相），或接触网暂时无电的情况下，辅助供电系统就处于失电状态，如果列车频繁地过分相，则会导致辅助系统频繁地启动和停止。

而欧系动车组的情况则不同，由于其辅助供电系统和主变流器是做在一起的，辅助供电系统从主变流器的中间直流处获得电能，而主变流器具备再生制动功能。因此，当动车在运行中，即使当主断路器断开，或者接触网短时无电的情况下，辅助供电系统依然能从中间主变流器的中间直流处获得电能。这样辅助供电系统就能一直平稳工作了。

5.4.3 工作原理

变流器工作原理如图5-10所示，前面已经知道，变流器工作时，主变压器送来高压电后，由四象限变流器将其变为稳定的中间直流电，PWM逆变器从中间直流环节处获取电能，逆变出三相交流电后，驱动牵引电机运行。下面就分别介绍其中的两个主要部分，四象限变流器和PWM逆变器的工作原理。以CRH3型车的单桥臂双管并联方案为例来说明。

如图5-11所示，每个桥臂配有两个并联IGBT，以增加同一桥臂的承载电流的容量，每个IGBT内置一个反并联二极管。在下文的描述中，将以DH1、DH2、DB1、DB2代指与IGBT H1、H2、B1、B2等相关联的二极管。

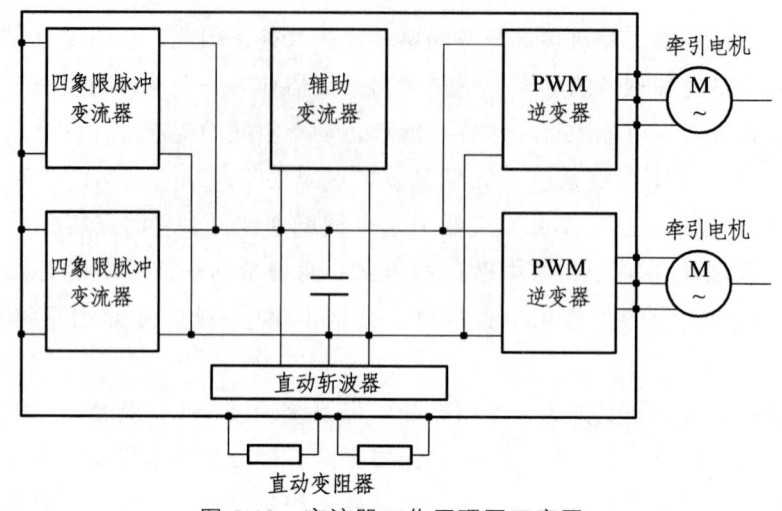

图 5-10　变流器工作原理图示意图

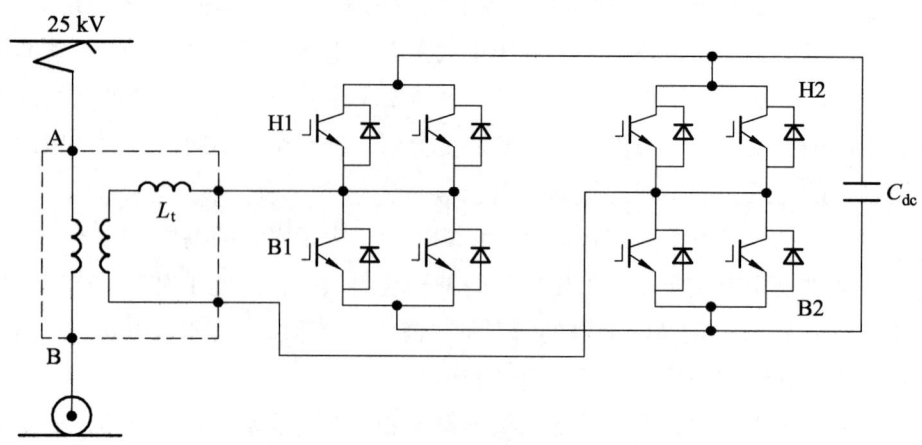

图 5-11　四象限变流器工作原理图

而四象限变流器可以工作在牵引和制动两种工况,现在就这两种不同的工况来分别介绍其工作原理。

1. 牵引工况

当工作在牵引工况时,四象限变流器相当于执行一个"整流器"的功能,在载波固定频率为 250 Hz 且占空比可变(PWM 调制)情况下,采用某个逻辑(下文将进行具体分析)控制四象限变流器。因此,假如变压器端子 A 和 B 上存在线电压的正极性半波,可在某段时间(T_{ON})内对某个元件(如 H2)进行控制。DH1 和 H2 导通时的电路图如图 5-12 所示:

实际上,可通过 H2 和 DH1 使变压器短路,且电感器"Lt"以线性增大电流运行,更精确来讲,它可积聚特定能量。紧急情况下,电子牵引调节装置可控制 H2 (T_{OFF})的关闭,由"Lt"积聚的能量通过二极管 DH1-DB2 传送至输出滤波器(由电容器"Cdc"表示),如图 5-13 所示:

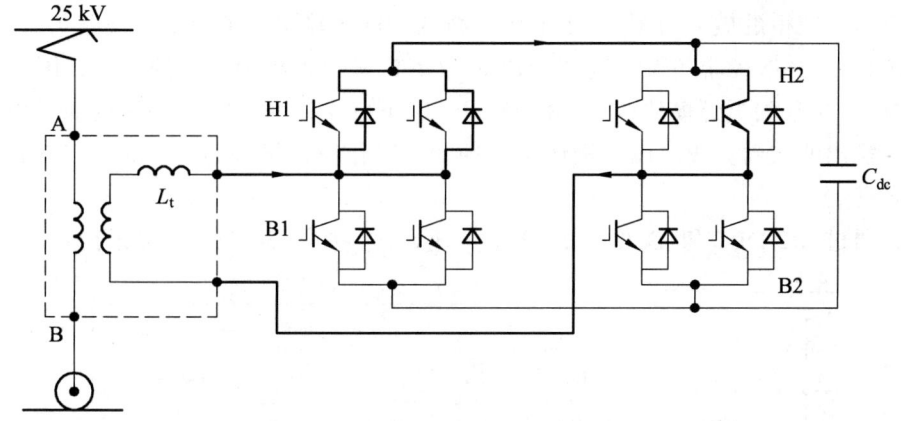

图 5-12 DH1 和 H2 导通时电路图

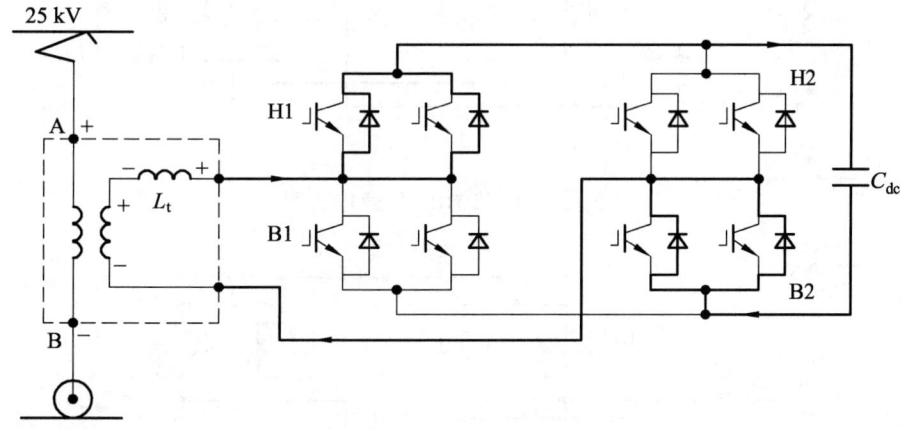

图 5-13 DH1 和 DB2 导通时电路图

主变压器输出端子上存在的电压（进而流经滤波电容器），由变压器次级电压和电感器"Lt"的自动感应电压的矢量之和构成。因此，IGBT 中 T_{ON} 适当调整明显改变，确切来讲，由"Lt"积聚的能量和输出滤波器上存在的整流电压值改变。通过传导 DB1 和二极管 DB2 完成之后的循环 T_{ON} - T_{OFF}。B1 和 DB2 导通时的电路图如图 5-14 所示。

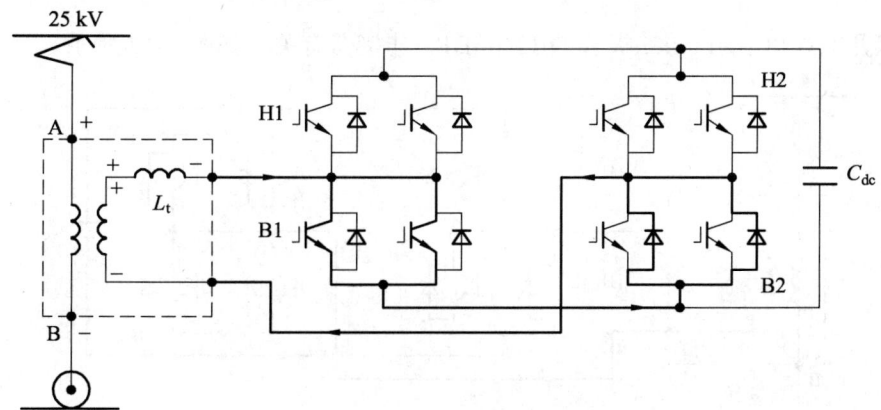

图 5-14 B1 和 DB2 导通时电路图

主变压器上获得的效果与图 5-22 上所分析的相同（输出端子上出现短路），但是通过不同的 IGBT-DIODI 连接器获得。这便于耗散 IGBT 开关过程中产生的热量，因为两个相关 IGBT 设在两个单独的电源模块内。DB1 关闭情况下(T_{OFF})，由"Lt"积聚的能量以相同的模式被传输至输出滤波器。线电压负极性半波期间，工作原理保持不变，除非与其它电源组件的电流传导有关。

例如，通过 B2-DB1 和 DH2 H1 交替实现导通，如图 5-15、5-16 所示。

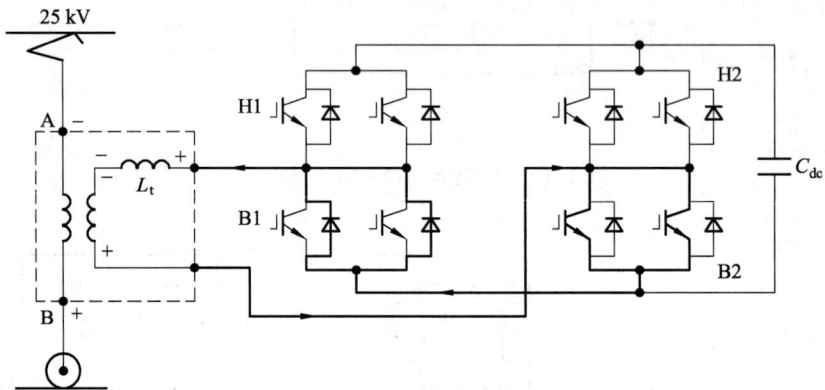

图 5-15　B2 和 DB1 导通电路图

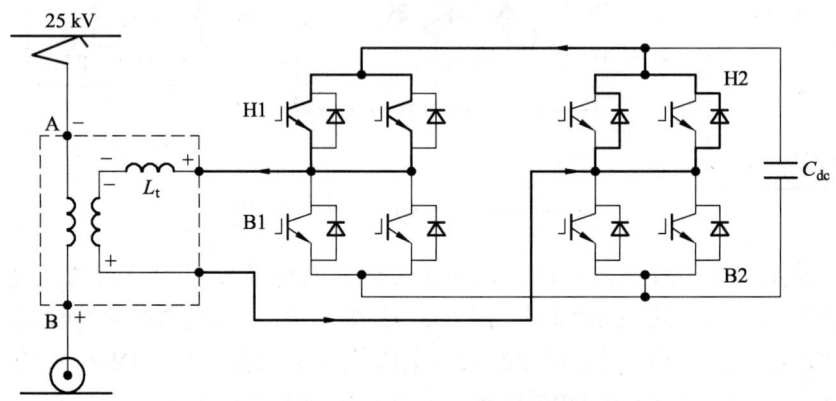

图 5-16　DH1 和 DH2 导通电路图

而在禁用阶段(T_{OFF})，与二极管 DH2 和 DB1 连接器有关，如图 5-17 所示。

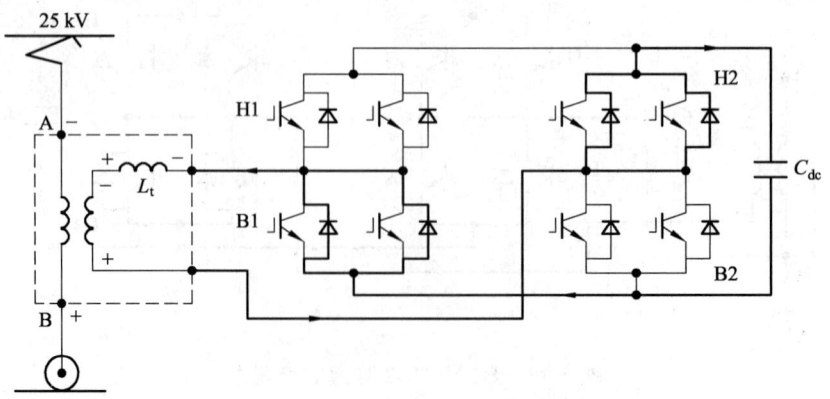

图 5-17　DH2 和 DB1 导通电路图

产生 PWM 的方式为：逻辑方式按以下方式构成三角形波（载波）具有固定频率和振幅 (f= 1350 Hz)，由一个正弦波（调制）分割，该正弦波频率为 50Hz（与线电压相同）、振幅和相位均可变。载波与调制波的交叉点处产生 PWM，如图 5-18 所示。

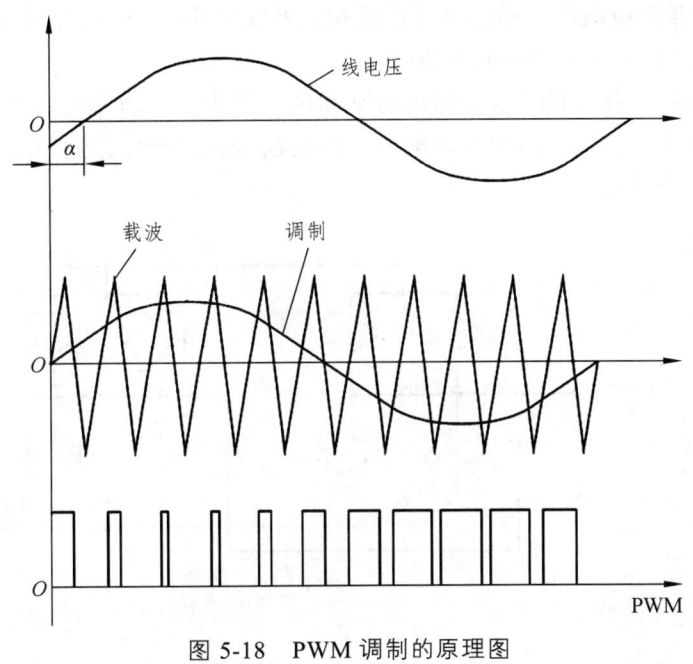

图 5-18　PWM 调制的原理图

2. 制动工况

当四象限变流器工作在制动工况时，在执行电制动阶段，能量回收可通过将能量从四个象限(Cdc)输出内的滤波电容器传输至主牵引变压器的次级来实现。所有这些与 25 kV 线路上存在的电压和上述次级绕组上电压之间的相位紧密相关。另外，此情况下，功率变压器分散电感的重要结果应在高值时实现。假设 25 kV 线压上存在正极性半波，然后要将能量从电容器传输至"Cdc"滤波器（参见图 5-19）至主变压器的次级，需要连接器 H1 和 B2 引入传导：

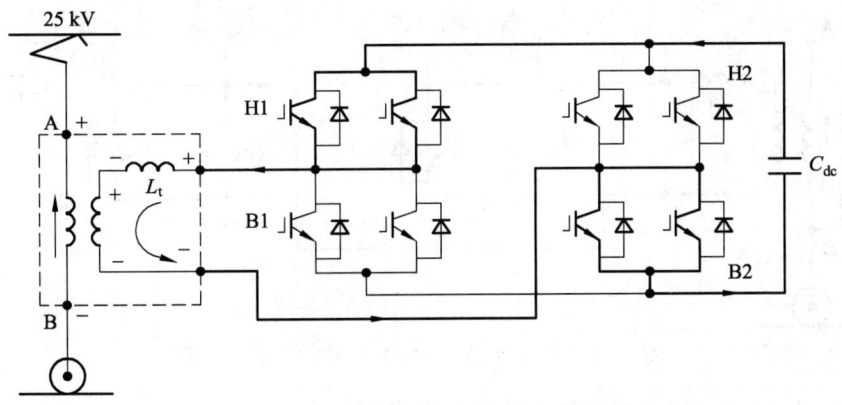

图 5-19　制动阶段时 H1 和 B2 导通电路图

此阶段可注意到两个重要现象：

（1）"Lt"电感器的电流正增长（上升），很明显，流经功率变压器次级绕组的电流也一样。

（2）功率变压器初级绕组上感应电流形成相位及线电压，甚至允许变压器用作发电机（与线路相关），然后向其发送预设强度电流。

通过上述 IGBT 连接器的 T_{ON}，然后至某相位，该相位下功率变压器的次级传输端子发生短路，这样可减少同一变压器的循环电流。以便执行关闭操作，例如关闭 IGBT B2，然后电流会流经至下一个网孔。

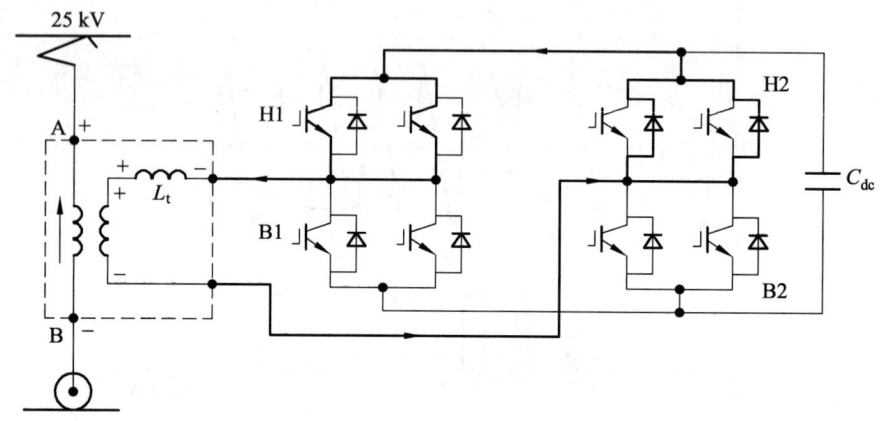

图 5-20 制动阶段时 H1 和 DH2 导通电路图

在此阶段，如图 "Lt" 电感器用作发电机，且如变压器内的电流保持同一方向，将产生一个负增长。该阶段后，将产生另一个 T_{ON}，如图 5-20 中所示。后一个 T_{OFF}（变压器次级绕组短路）将可轻松关闭 H1。

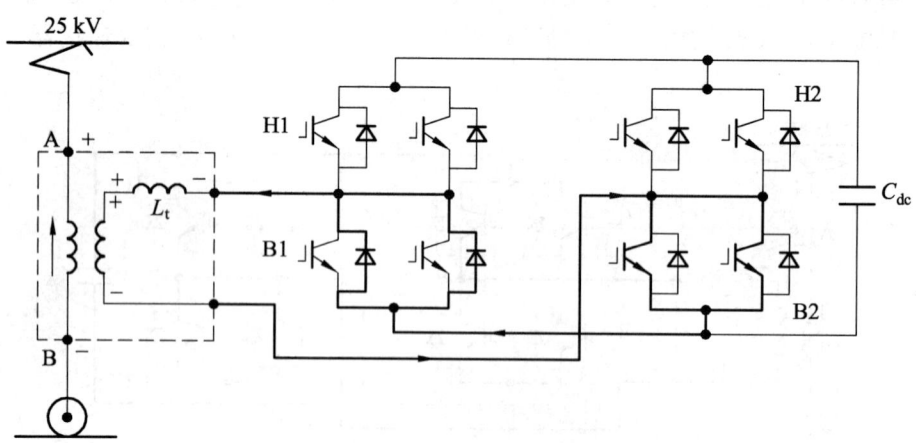

图 5-21 制动阶段时 DB1 和 B2 导通电路图

如图 5-21 所示，电流呈现负增长，然而所不同的是 H1 及 B2 交替导通以便进行散热。通过适当调制 T_{ON} 和 T_{OFF}，可向高压线路输送预设振幅的电流。当高压线路存在负极性半波时，4个象限内斩波器的运行总体上保持不变，除IGBT被引导的顺序不同之外。实际上，在T_{ON}期间，连接器H2-B1将被控制；T_{OFF}期间，H2-DH1和H1-DB2连接器将交替传导。列车上2台驱动装置故障情况下，IGBT的换向频率将由250 Hz降至83 Hz，因此线路的"拾取"频率应为332 Hz，以优化谐波和驱动装置发射的干扰。

以上就是脉冲整流器的工作原理。

对于目前几种车型来讲，除了CRH2型动车组的逆变器结构为三电平以外，其它几车型的逆变器主电路基本相同，都是三相桥式全桥逆变器，其结构如图5-22所示：

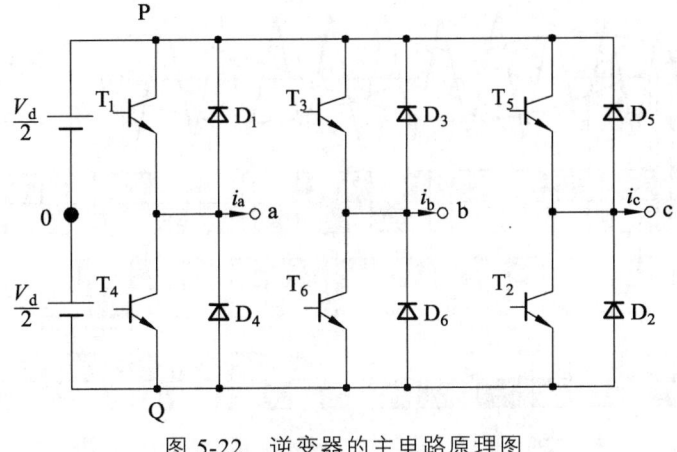

图 5-22 逆变器的主电路原理图

现以图5-23为例，说明逆变器工作的原理。

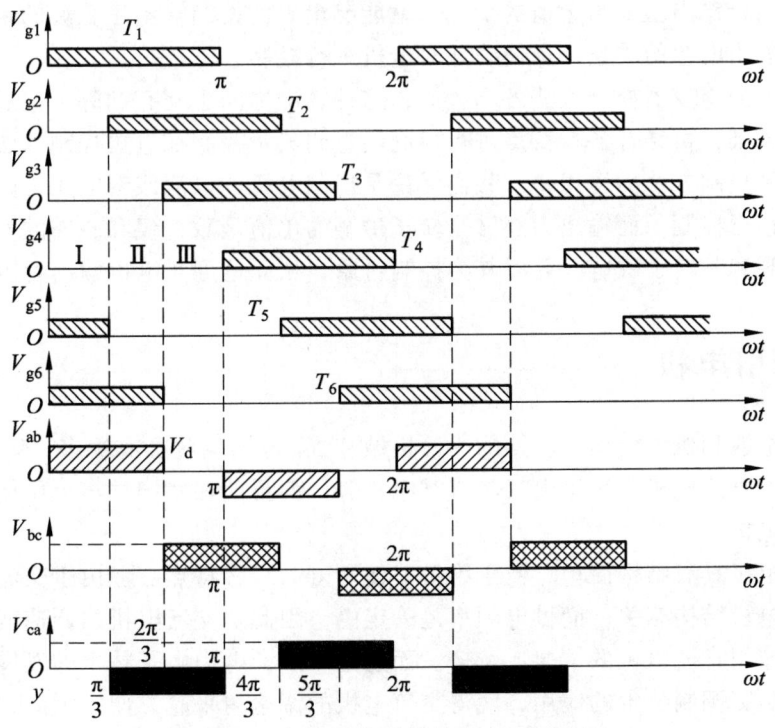

图 5-23 方波逆变器的输出电压示意图

如图 5-23 所示，在图 5-22 所示的逆变器中，只需要将每只 IGBT 的开关信号由下图所给顺序依次给出，即 T1 至 T6 依次相隔 120 度导通，每次导通 180 度角，就能得到如图所示的线电压 V_{ab}、V_{bc}、V_{ca}，这样就可以得到一个交流的方波输出了。

但在负载是交流电机的情况下，方波电压的输出脉动很大，而且不能对电机的转矩进行控制，因此不能适应动车的需求，所以采用了 PWM 调制的办法，即用一个频率较高的载波（通常为三角波）和我们需要的正弦波（调制波）相叠加，从而产生一系列的脉宽，由此来得到每只开关管的开关信号。详细情况如图 5-24 所示：

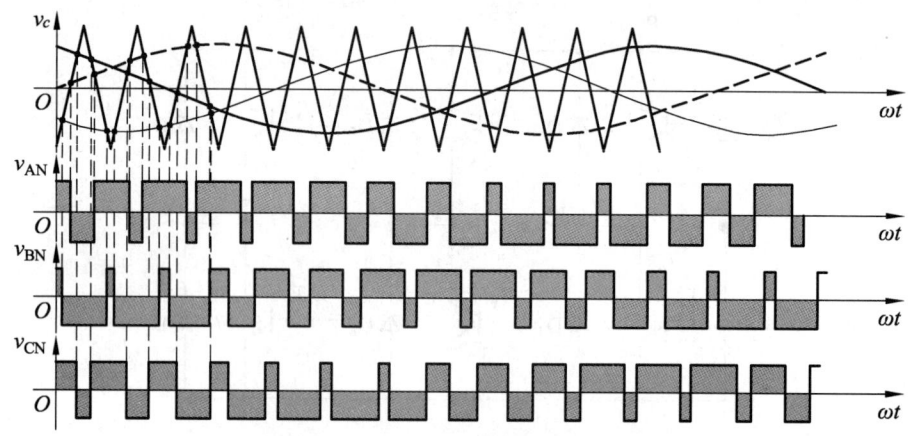

图 5-24 正弦波调制的 PWM 脉宽调制法示意图

这样得到的输出电压就很接近正弦波了。如果对调制波的生成再经过适当的控制，加上合适的算法，结合输出值和给定值的变化，就能够精确的控制输出正弦波的频率和幅值，从而大大的提高输出电源的质量，更精确地对电机进行控制。

目前动车上的逆变器控制方法各不相同，这种算法之间也互有利弊，但通常都以空间矢量控制算法为基础，再结合各自特点进行控制。空间矢量控制在电机控制算法里也叫做直接转矩控制，这种控制方法的思想是，我们无论是控制电机的电流或者电压，归根结底都是要对其输出力矩进行控制，而输出力矩又是转子磁链的单值函数，仅和磁链的变化有关。既然如此，就直接观测其转子磁链，并以其为控制对象，从而达到对电机输出力矩的精确控制。

5.5 牵引电机

电机是将电能和机械能相互转换的一种机械装置。电机的种类有很多，有交流异步电机、交流同步电机、直流电机、步进电机、直线电机等。而目前在我国动车上所使用的牵引电机均为交流异步电机。

交流异步电机具有结构简单、便于维护、使用寿命长等特点。但由于交流电机的转速仅和供电频率、电机结构有关，而供电频率是一定的，因此对交流电机的调速就特别困难，故在机车牵引领域用直流电机的情况比较多。而这些年来，电力电子技术的发展，尤其是变频技术的出现、脉宽调制技术的应用，使得交流电机的调速越来越方便，因此，交流异步电机的应用越来越广，已经广泛应用于机车牵引、大中型水电站等领域。

动车用的牵引电机结构均比较简单，一般由转子、定子、转子轴承、外罩、引出线等组成。

5.6 真空断路器

真空断路器（VCB）是一种高压电气开关装置，安装真空断路器的目的，在于当主高压器二次侧以后的电路发生故障时，能迅速、安全、确切地切断过电流。同时，它也是平常开闭主回路一种开关，它兼有断路器和开关两种功能，VCB外形图如图5-25所示。

图 5-25　VCB 的外型图

这种真空断路器在被封闭的真空容器中配置动静触头、通过动静触头，利用真空中有较高的耐绝缘能力和电弧扩散作用来断开电流。VCB一般配置在车顶部。

5.6.1　VCB 的结构及性能参数

VCB由以下基本元件组成：
（1）支架：安装各功能组件的架体。
（2）真空灭弧室：实现电路的关合与开断功能的熄弧元件。
（3）导电回路：与灭弧室的动端及静端连接构成电流通道。
（4）传动机构：把操动机构的运动传输至灭弧室，实现灭弧室的合、分闸操作。
（5）绝缘支撑：绝缘支持件将各功能元件，架接起来满足断路器的绝缘要求。
（6）操动机构：断路器合、分间的动力驱动装置。
对于VCB来说，我们一般对其性能有如下要求：
（1）非常高的绝缘等级。
（2）对气候条件的敏感度低。
（3）尺寸小。
（4）断开能力强。
（5）吸合时间短。

(6)使用寿命长。

(7)维护工作量少。

5.6.2 工作原理

当总风压力足够的情况下,电磁阀接到"VCB 合"的指令后,电磁阀动作,允许总风管的压缩空气进入高压气缸。利用压缩空气的压力将连接机构顶起,通过机械杠杆的力量将高压回路的主接触点联通。同时,当高压气缸的金属活塞被顶起后,在高压气缸的顶部设置有一个保持线圈,利用保持线圈将活塞紧紧得吸住,以产生一个接触压力,使得主触点保持紧密接触状态。当主触点紧密接触后,电磁阀吸合,释放掉动作 VCB 的压缩空气。

VCB 的断开过程比较简单,当其接到"VCB 断开"的指令后,保搞压气缸内的保持线圈失电、在弹簧的作用下通过机械杠杆的作用将高压触点断开。

6 动车组制动系统

6.1 主要制动类型

让列车减速或停车叫制动。制动系统就是让列车制动的设备。运动的车辆有动能，消散动能才能让列车减速或停车。有一定速度的运动车体，它的动能是质量与速度平方的乘积。对于高速动车组，工程技术人员采用多种方法来消散其动能以便让它安全地停车，它们是摩擦制动和动力制动。摩擦制动可分为两个子类：自动式空气制动和电控的空气制动。

6.1.1 自动式空气制动机

图6-1展示了最简单的自动式空气制动机的结构组成。

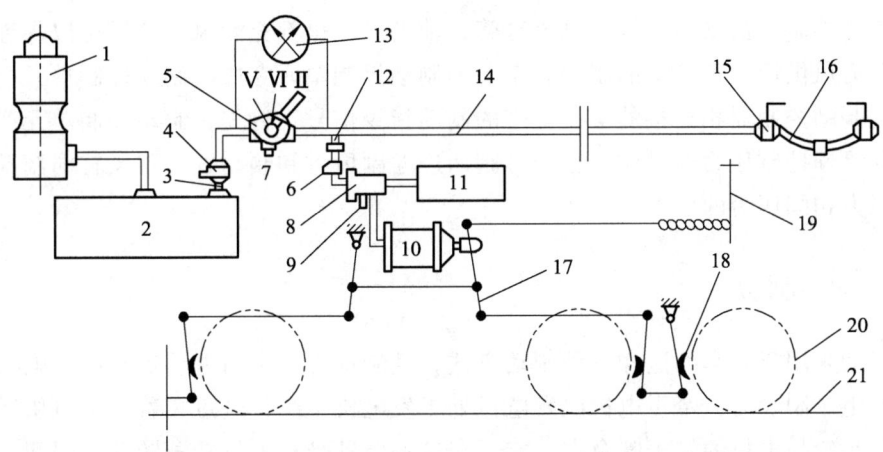

1—空气压缩机；2—总风缸；3—总风缸管；4—给风阀；5—自动制动阀；6—远心集尘器；7—自阀排风嘴；8—车辆制动阀；9—车辆制动阀排风嘴；10—制动缸；11—副风缸；12—截断塞门；13—双针风表；14—制动管；15—折角塞门；16—制动软管；17—基础制动装置；18—闸瓦；19—人力手制动机；20—车轮；21—钢轨。

图6-1 自动式空气制动机示意简图

首先，由电动机驱动的空气压缩机将压缩空气充入到总风缸，直到总风缸达到最高压力（900 kPa）后停机。当司机将自动制动阀手柄置于缓解位时，总风缸内的高压力压缩空气将充入到制动管。这样制动管压力升高，车辆制动阀动作，从而联通副风缸和制动管，制动管的压缩空气冲入到副风缸，直至副风缸压力升至定压（600 kPa）。同时，车辆制动阀连通制动缸到排大气嘴的通路，使制动缸内的压缩空气排大气。随着压缩空气的排出，制动缸活塞将在其缓解弹簧作用下复位，并带动基础制动装置使闸瓦不再与车轮接触。这时，列车缓解。同时副风缸也充满风以备下一次制动。

当司机将自动制动阀手柄置于常用制动位时，制动管中的压缩空气排出，其压力降低，车辆制动阀随即动作，连通副风缸和制动缸。这样，副风缸的高压力压缩空气充入到制动缸，制动缸活塞因压缩空气与大气的压差而克服缓解弹簧的弹力被推向外侧，活塞杆伸出，并通过基础制动装置使闸瓦贴近并压紧车轮踏面，产生制动作用。

制动管贯通整列车，车辆间通过柔软的制动软管连接。制动软管连接器须分开才能再分解列车。通过制动管中压缩空气压力的变化来控制列车中每一节车的制动和缓解，司机仅需通过机车上的自动制动阀来控制制动管中压力空气压力的变化，就能轻易地控制整列车的制动和缓解。

6.1.2 电空制动机

纯空气制动机要依赖压缩空气压力信号在制动管中的传输来实现制动控制，压力信号触发制动作用先是从列车队的前部车辆开始，沿着列车传递，直到最后面车辆。从前部车辆开始产生作用到最后面车辆产生作用，可以觉察到明显的时间延时。它不能运用于高速动车组，只能用作动车组的备用制动装置。

实际上作为标准装备应用到动车组上的是电空制动机，电空制动机用与司机制动控制器相连的电线来控制。沿整列车设有总风缸管，辅助风缸也都充满风，这样可以保证每节车都有充足的压力风供给。每节车的制动有车上的制动控制单元完成，制动控制单元受控于上面说的与司机制动控制器相连接的电线传来的制动指令信号。首先，制动控制单元产生一个预控制压力，该预控制压力通过作用于中继阀而连通副风缸和制动缸，副风缸向制动缸中充入与预控制压力相同压力的压缩空气。

6.1.3 动力制动

动力制动是用于列车的这样一种制动方式，其制动力由牵引电动机按照发电机的形式重新连线来产生。制动时，牵引电机以发电机处于发电机工况，这意味着牵引电机转动受到阻碍。动车的车轮与电机的转子啮合在一起，车轮的转动带动电机转子转动，因而在发电机工况下产生了制动力。

在制动时，列车的动能可以被转换成电能，并被传输至接触网供附近其他列车使用，这就是再生制动。但如果附近没有其他列车来消耗这些再生出来的电能，接触网就不能吸收这些电能，列车就只能通过其自身所装设的热电阻来消耗掉这些多余的电能。这就是电阻制动。

6.2 动车组制动系统介绍

动车组列车的制动系统是通过使用两种不同的制动系统来实现：电.空制动和动力制动，并用自动空气制动作为备用。电动空气制动系统和动力制动系统由微处理器控制，具有各种制动控制功能，能控制和诊断制动过程中所涉及的除了停放制动装置之外的各种相关设备。带分配阀的自动空气制动机用于常用制动设备出现故障时的救援，该系统为纯空气型，完全独立于常用制动系统，该系统通过基于微处理器的电子控制单元进行控制。

6.2.1 常用制动

司机室的制动手柄通过列车线发出制动信号给各节车的制动控制单元，制动控制单元产生动力制动指令和电空制动指令以产生动力制动和电空制动。施加常用制动时，动力制动先施加，然后是电空制动。

对于动车车轴，通过调节器励磁的电空阀会切除电空制动。当施加最大常用制动时，动车会施加最大动力制动，对拖车施加电空制动，以确保达到列车对制动力的需求。在低速（10 km/h）时以及在动力制动失效时，电空制动会因联锁的电空阀的失磁而激活。通常情况下，电空制动只是在动力制动达到最大值后才能施加在拖车的车轴上。常用制动施加时，牵引是被切除的。

6.2.2 紧急制动

在紧急制动情形下，牵引装置和动力制动都会被切除，自动式空气制动机因制动管通大气而施加最大制动力。紧急制动可以由以下情形触发：

（1）制动操纵杆置紧急制动位。在此位，安全环路开路，所有的车辆均施加最大空气制动力。

（2）压司机室的紧急制动按钮。

（3）安全装置（信息设备）。

（4）安全回路在非正常状态下被切断。

（5）乘客报警。

当司机室的紧急制动按钮被压下，贯穿列车的紧急制动环路被断开，制动管也由每个端部车辆的紧急阀排大气，这样分配阀施加最大制动力。

是由自动式空气制动机（而不是电空制动机）确保紧急制动的施加。在紧急制动时，安全回路的开路切除了动力制动，也让备用制动的电磁阀消磁，从而隔离开制动管，以防止其被再充气。

6.2.3 客室紧急制动

每节车辆都配备了客室紧急制动，该装置包括每个车厢中的两个制动手柄。乘客操作制动手柄会将制动管中的空气排放到大气中。司机可以关闭该设备的操作。当客室紧急制动被激活时，会发生以下动作：

（1）在驾驶室内向驾驶员发出视觉和蜂鸣器信号。

（2）驾驶室紧急制动面板的电磁阀断电，导致紧急制动。

（3）备用制动装置的阀门断电，以防止制动管的重新充气。当司机重置客室紧急制动时，可以取消客室紧急制动的作用。

6.2.4 备用制动

当电子制动控制单元失效或是处于救援时,列车可以以间接式空气制动方式继续运行。这时的制动是由制动管中的空气压力来控制,制动管空气压强由安装在司机工作台上的自动制动阀来控制,该制动阀通过备用制动的手动控制杆操控来产生作用。

在每节车上,分配阀会根据制动管的减压量产生一个制动压力信号,该信号控制中继阀以产生制动作用。在投入备用制动时,电空制动被切除。制动管上的压力开关和备用制动控制阀的微动开关切除了牵引力。

6.2.5 停放制动

列车上装有以弹簧力为动力的停放制动装置,它由制动风缸提供所需压力风。它可满足30%坡度下的安全停车要求,设有手动缓解装置。

在司机室中,通过按压按钮,可以将停放制动应用到列车和重联的列车上(在多列车重联的情况下)。停车制动施加或缓解由司机室内按钮操控,并由压力开关检测,其状态可显示在司机的操作台上。在列车运行时,停放制动应被切除。

在停放制动缸旁设置有手动缓解手柄。通过颜色指示停放制动的施加和缓解的状态。红色(中间有黑色斑点)表示施加停车制动,绿色表示缓解停放制动。

6.3 动车组制动系统工作原理

图 6-2 说明了制动系统的配置和工作原理。

基于微处理器的电子制动控制单元(EBCU)(B01)执行本车制动控制功能。BCU 用于接收和转换制动需求信号以及来自列车组的其他信号,以控制电空制动系统。微处理器功能还包括故障诊断和故障指示,以便于维护和操作。

用于摩擦制动系统操作的压缩空气由主风缸(MR)提供。MR 中的压力风由连接至牵引联锁控制电路的压力开关监控。如果主风缸管中的压力水平不足,此压力开关可防止列车开动。压缩空气通过单向阀(B04)进入容量为 125 L 的制动设备的辅助制动储风缸(B05)。该制动设备(B04 和 B05)位于制动架(B08)中。在 MR 压力风漏泄的情况下,单向阀(B04)确保在辅助制动器储液罐(B05)中保留气压,以便使摩擦制动产生制动作用。

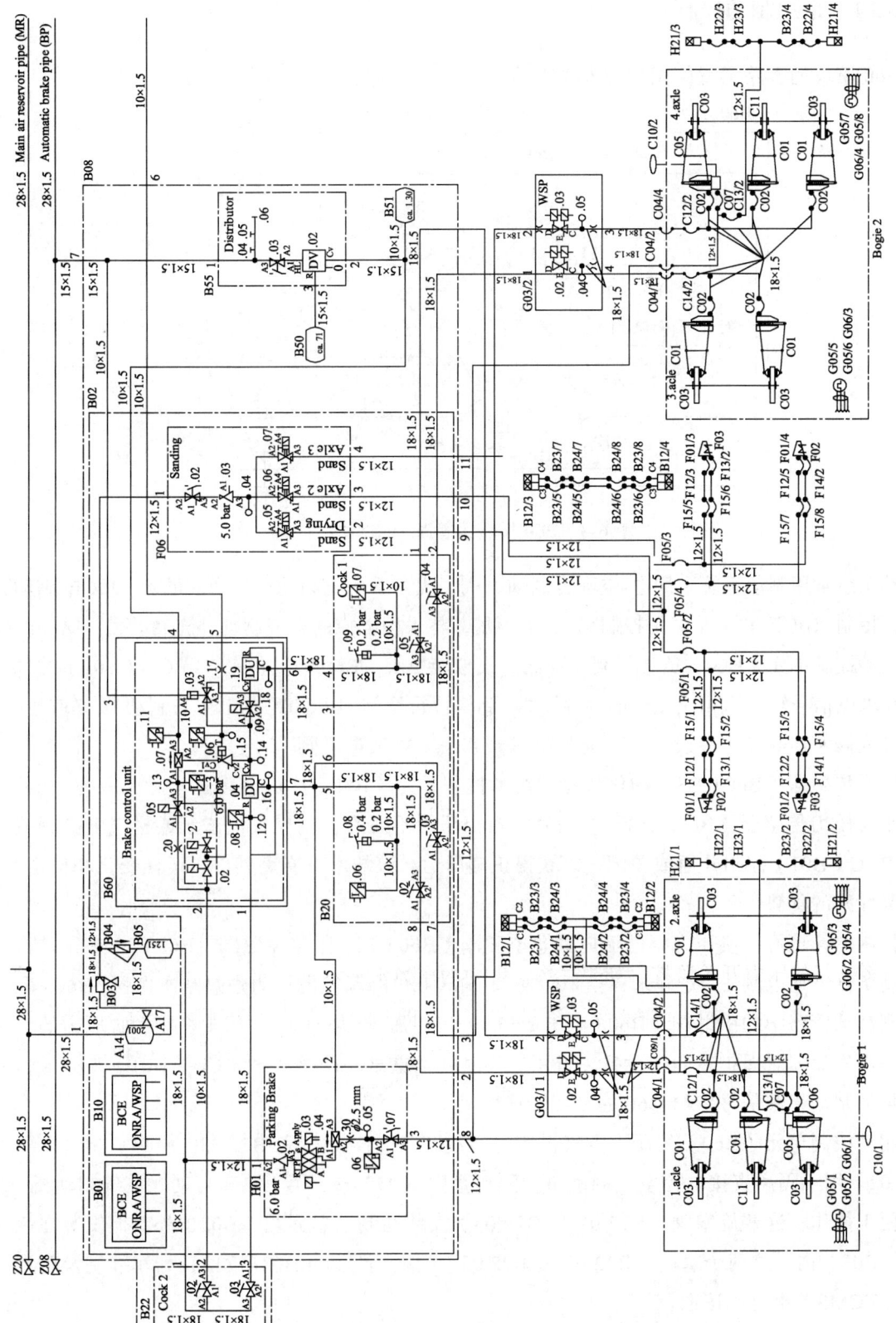

图 6-2 动车组制动系统管路示意简图

6.3.1 常用制动控制

B60 模块的管路示意简图如图 6-3 所示。

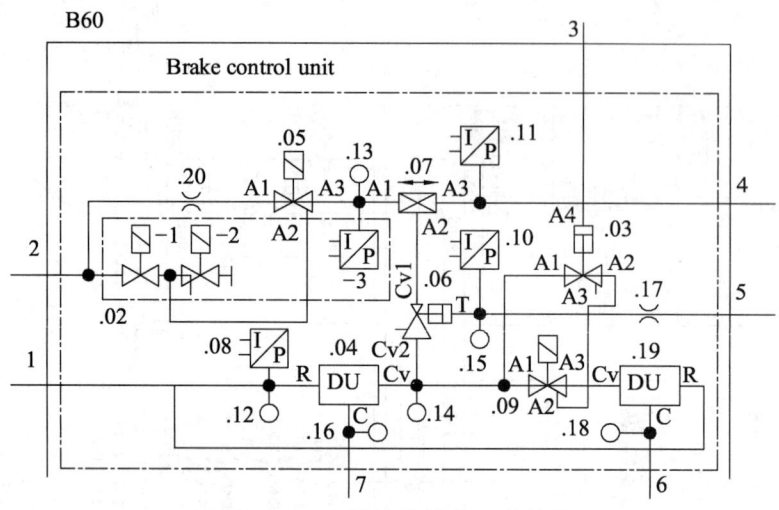

图 6-3　B60 模块的管路示意简图

动车组常用制动系统采用电-空联合制动方式，优先采用电制动（动力制动）。如果电制动力（其控制取决于 TCU（牵引控制单元））不足，将采用电控的空气制动补充制动力。电控的空气制动控制单元（B60）负责气制动控制。模拟转换阀（B60.02）将来自 BCU（B01）的气制动需求电信号转换为相应比例的预控压力。到模拟转换阀（B60.02）的信号为制动/缓解信号。模拟转换阀（B60.02）装设有一个充气电磁阀和一个排气电磁阀。

压力传感器（B60.02-3）的信号指示制动控制单元（B60）中的制动缸实际压力的大小。如果来自压力传感器（B60.02-3）的信号与指令压力不匹配，则充气电磁阀或排气电磁阀就会由 BCU（B01）控制开通或关闭，以获得正确压力。该技术具有高精度、线性变化和稳定、可重复性好的优势。

控制单元也可控制压力空气流向紧急电磁阀（B60.05）。紧急电磁阀（B60.05）在正常行车制动条件下通电励磁，允许来自模拟转换阀（B60.02）的预控制压力通过空重车阀（B60.06）输入到制动管路中的中继阀（B60.04 和 B60.19）。限压阀（B60.06）用于在制动缸压力的传感设备产生故障时保护转向架设备。常用制动时，空重车的调整通过 BCU（B01）来完成，然后再把制动指令信号传给 B60 的模拟转换阀。

制动控制单元（B60）的压力空气供应可通过塞门（B22.02 和 B22.03）隔离。排气塞门（B22.02）用于隔离直接电控空气制动机，隔离塞门（B22.03）用于隔离自动式空气制动机。为了便于操作，这些旋塞阀（B22.02 和 B22.03）安装在制动单元箱（B02）外，但安装在制动架（B08）内。这两个塞门（B22.02 和 B22.03）的电信号由 EBCU 读取，列车控制及监控系统（TCMS）也可以读取。

6.3.2 备用制动装置

如果直通电空制动系统出现故障或是处于救援模式，列车组将使用备用制动系统，即自动式空气制动系统。备用制动系统由系统中制动管的压力变化来控制，该压力由安装在驾驶台上的FB11（D02）型的司机自动制动阀控制。制动管也可以通过救援机车或救援列车组进行控制。

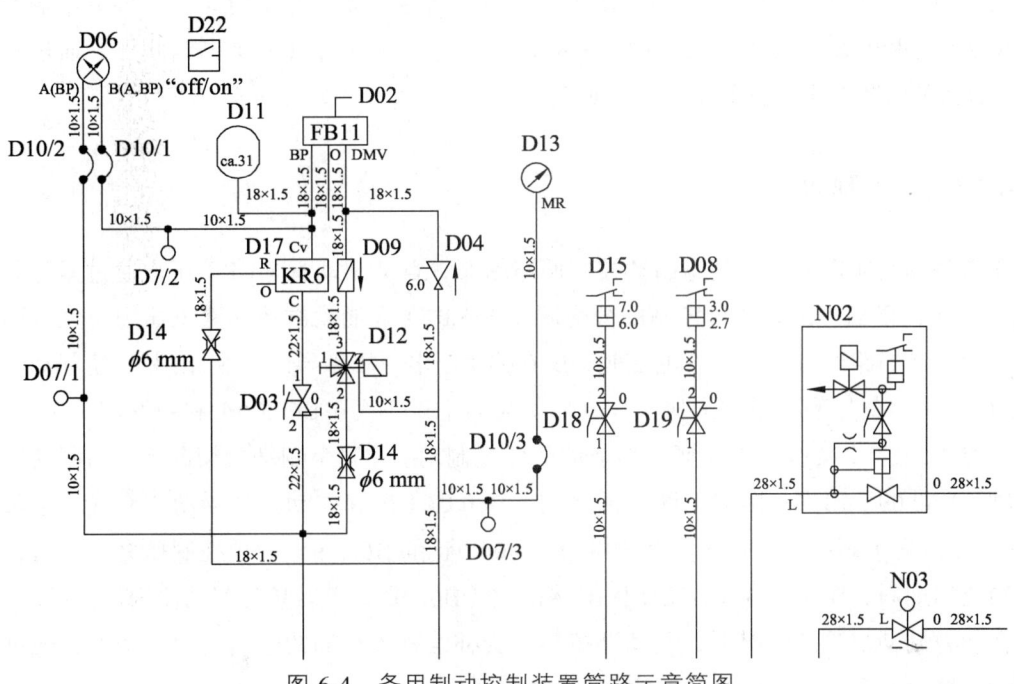

图 6-4 备用制动控制装置管路示意简图

备用制动控制系统是一种产生制动的机械装置，用于装设直通式电空制动系统车辆的辅助制动。在救援操作期间，如果直通式电空制动系统不可用，该备用制动系统也可以作为自动式空气制动机使用。通过司机制动系统，列车制动式空气制动系统中制动管中的压力在激活后充风至定压，因此，列车组的间接作用式的自动式空气制动机也可以作为救援时的另一个常用制动来进行施加。

直接作用分配阀（B55.02）缓解时的设置为 600 kPa 的 BP（制动管）定压。列车组制动控制时通过牵引/制动控制器（TBC）（D01）完成。TBC（D01）产生制动电信号，电信号通过离散导线或总线系统在列车组中传输。制动信号被传输到每辆车上，以使直通式电空制动装置产生制动。因此，不要制动管中的压力保持在大于制动管定压，并在列车自动式空气制动机产生制动来停车或是紧急制动时，制动管需减压。因此，紧急制动阀（N02）也与备用的自动式空气制动机的制动管相连以控制制动管的减压。

备用制动系统在正常操作中能实现以下基本功能：
（1）通过安装在司机控制台中的"切断"开关（D22）实现隔离。在 TBC（D01）正常运行模式下，只要列车不是施加自动式空气制动机制动停车或紧急制动，隔离电磁阀（D12）和紧急阀（N02）就会通电。这样，总风缸中压缩空气从减压阀（D04）、单向阀（D09）和流量节流阀（D16）充入自动式空气制动机的制动管。

（2）减压阀（D04）调节备用的自动式空气制动系统制动管的定压。流量节流阀（D16）限制充风速度，以确保间接作用的空气制动机的可靠作用。

当 TBC（D01）或其他紧急和自动车列停车设备激发紧急制动时，车列各节车辆的紧急阀（N02）均断电，自动式空气制动机的制动管通过一个大排气口排出。此外，通过隔离电磁阀（D12）的断电来防止制动管压力回升。

6.3.3 紧急制动

在紧急制动应用期间，紧急制动控制回路断开，自动制动管（BP）压力通过紧急制动阀（N02）排出。随后，通过 BP 控制的分配阀（B55.02）向制动缸快速充入压力空气。同时，紧急制动控制回路断开后，紧急电磁阀（B60.05）断电（故障导向安全原则），使制动供风风缸（B05）的空气压力通过双向阀（B60.07）流向空重车阀（B60.06）和中继阀（B60.04 和 B60.19），从而产生具有空重车调整功能的的紧急制动。在紧急制动的情况下，当制动缸分级联锁阀（B60.09）出现故障时，旁通活塞阀（B60.03）确保向动车的制动缸充气。空重车阀（B60.06）根据车辆载重的气压限制中继阀（B60.04 和 B60.19）的预控制压力。同时，在紧急制动应用期间，BCU（B01）还使模拟转换阀（B60.02）产生紧急制动压力。

在动力制动切除的情况下，气动摩擦制动会补偿相关车辆的电制动力，例如：通过打开相关制动缸分级联锁阀（B60.09）或增加制动缸压力。

可通过制动缸充风管路中带有电气开关（B20.02、B20.03、B20.04 和 B20.05）的塞门手动隔离，以隔离制动控制单元（B60），从而隔离各个轴的制动，并缓解制动缸（例如：在模拟转换阀 B60.02 或紧急电磁 B60.05 发生故障时）。

6.3.4 制动指示

列车信息与控制系统从压力开关（B20.08 和 B20.09）读取有关制动装置（制动/缓解）状态的信息。该制动设备安装于制动箱（B02）内。驾驶室内配备了一个双针压力表（D06），用于指示预控制压力和空气制动机的制动管压力。双针压力表（B11）显示驾驶室内动车和拖车的制动缸压力。压力表（D13）用于指示主风缸压力。上述所有仪表（D06、B11 和 D13）均配有照明设备（电源电压为 24 VDC）。

为方便制动装置的目测检查，制动指示器（B12）安装在转向架外侧两侧，制动装置缓解时显示绿色标志，制动时则显示的红色标志。停车制动器指示器（H21）也用于指示停放制动缸内的压力。

6.4 盘形制动装置

6.4.1 概况

列车在所有车轴上都配备了盘形制动装置，每个轴上都配备了直径 640 mm 的固定在轴上的制动盘，制动盘由钢制成，不需通风散热。通常拖车轴上有 3 个制动盘，动车轴上有 2 个。

盘形制动装置是制动卡钳和制动缸的组合，当制动闸片和制动盘磨损时能够自动调整间隙。用于常用制动的盘形制动装置有一个制动缸。每个盘形制动装置的制动缸和卡钳都不要，带有传统类型的内置闸片间隙自动调节器。因此，在缓解位位置，制动盘和制动片之间的间隙几乎保持不变，以确保平稳运行。刹车片为烧结型，其设计的最大允许温度为 600 °C，最大磨损为 30 mm。

盘形制动装置安装在转向架的两个制动横梁上。这些横梁安装在转向架构架的制动横梁支架的上。制动缸通常通过气路管道连接的产生作用的制动系统。

制动缸的供气由位于各车辆底架内的制动控制单元控制。

6.4.2 盘形制动装置的结构

盘形制动装置既可用于常用制动器，也可用于停放制动。用于常用制动的盘形制动装置没有弹簧储能器，而用于常用制动和停放制动的盘形制动装置的制动缸装设有一个弹簧储能器。弹簧储能器用于并在没有压缩空气的情况下的制动和确保停放车辆的制动。

盘型制动装置主要由制动缸、制动夹钳和带快速弹簧锁锁紧的制动闸片托组成。

制动卡钳装置通过三点紧固装置固定在转向架上。三点紧固装置包括作为拉杆一部分的支点支架和两个吊架，每个吊架用两个用螺栓铰接上制动闸片托。拉杆通过支点支座悬挂在转向架上，其螺栓位于锥形轴套中。螺栓由两个法兰轴套、两个垫圈和和锁紧螺母安装在转向架上。吊架用螺栓安装在转向架上。销接头和弹性锥形轴套允许制动夹钳装置根据轮对的轴向移动进行调整。

制动卡钳是一个预装配构件。它由两个在拉杆上铰接的扭转刚性制动杠杆组成。制动闸片托安装在制动杠杆的一端。制动杠杆的另一端有用于支撑制动缸的枢轴螺钉的螺孔。

停放制动可在驾驶室中操作。弹簧储能器具有手动缓解装置以在紧急情况下手动缓解停车制动。

常用制动时，制动缸充风，并使制动闸片夹紧制动盘。当制动闸片夹紧制动盘时，就形成了制动力。

制动缸排气可使常用制动缓解，制动缸中的复位弹簧将制动缸活塞杆推送至缓解位置。弹簧储能器充风可缓解停放制动器，当弹簧储能器弹簧被压紧时，制动缸活塞杆处于缓解位置。在没有充入压力风的情况下，也可以通过手动缓解装置人工手动缓解停放制动。

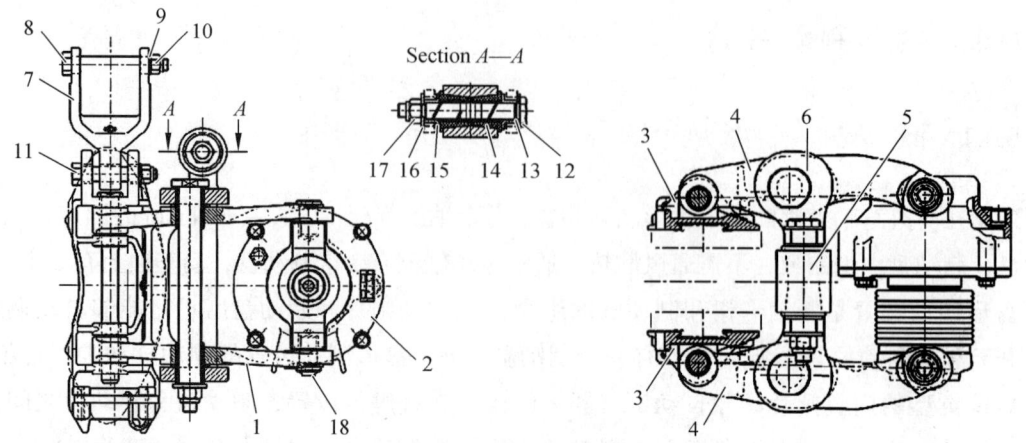

1—制动夹钳；2—制动缸体；3—制动闸片托；4—制动杠杆；5—支点支座；6—拉杆；7—吊架；
8—螺栓；9—垫片；10、17—锁紧螺母；11、12—螺栓；13—垫圈；14—锥形轴套；
15—法兰轴套；16—垫圈； 18—枢轴螺钉。

图 6-5 盘型制动装置组成图

6.4.3 制动缸

具有闸片间隙自动调整功能的制动缸用于动车组的摩擦式空气制动。制动缸小巧紧凑，适合安装在盘形制动装置中以驱动制动夹钳。这一制动缸的特点在于其整体式、制动力控制的闸片间隙调节机构，该机构为单向闸片间隙调节器。在制动过程中，间隙调节器会快速自动修正因磨损而增加的制动片间隙。因此，该间隙在整个间隙调整范围内将保持不变，活塞行程也就基本恒定，压力空气消耗量低，无需手动调整。

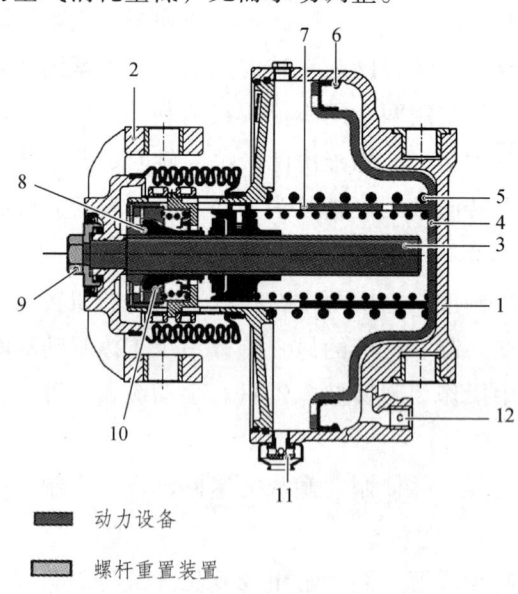

■ 动力设备

▨ 螺杆重置装置

■ 闸调器

1—制动缸；2—支架；3—螺杆；4—活塞；5—缓解弹簧；6—密封圈；7—活塞杆；8—齿轮联轴器；
9—夹紧螺母；10—锥形联轴器；11—通气限孔；12—充气孔。

图 6-6 制动缸

气缸体为铝合金压铸一次成型,为活塞运行提供了一个光滑内壁表面、活塞与缸壁密贴性好和耐磨性好,活塞由带自润滑的密封圈密封.这保证了较长的使用寿命,同时具有最小的泄漏和最高的可靠性。即使是在缓解时,闸片间隙调整器也由一个正作用齿形联轴器可靠锁定。制动缸有放水功能,缓解时,活塞前部气缸室通过位于最低点的通气限孔与大气连通。

6.4.3.1 制动缸工作过程

制动开始后,输送至制动缸的压缩空气被转换为活塞力。该力通过活塞杆和锥形离合器传递到螺杆,当气缸排气时,锥形离合器通过缓解弹簧使缓解弹簧复位。

6.4.3.2 闸片间隙自动调整器

单向闸片间隙自动调整器是自动调整的。在制动磨损而导致制动片间隙过大时,闸片间隙自动调整器可以自动将间隙调小。

6.4.4 带弹簧储能器的制动缸

制动缸由制动缸和弹簧储能缸组成,制动缸具有单向闸片间隙自动调整器。弹簧储能器与制动缸成直角布置。

弹簧驱动气缸的主要部件是活塞和压缩弹簧。压缩弹簧的力通过活塞、螺杆和空心筒作用在楔块上,并通过制动缸传递到制动夹钳的连杆。

在正常工作时,弹簧储能器用压缩空气缓解,但必要时也可以用手快速释放。在弹簧储能器最小缓解压力作用下,手动缓解的弹簧储能器将自动重新激活。

手动缓解装置位于弹簧储能器上,可手动操作。当弹簧储能器没有缓解压力风时,它用于缓解停放制动。手动缓解装置使压缩弹簧伸长,直到活塞碰到气缸底部,弹簧力不再通过螺杆作用在楔块上。制动缸的螺杆通过制动缸的缓解弹簧同时被缩回到缓解位置。

带有弹簧储能器的制动缸具有以下优点:

① 不需要既复杂又浪费空间的手制动装置。

② 由于弹簧储能器是气动驱动的,动车组整个弹簧储能器可以通过驾驶室集中操作。

③ 弹簧储能器通过制动缸作用于制动夹钳,可以产生恒定的制动力,因为后者带有自动松紧调节机构。

④ 增加了制动器故障时的安全性。在紧急情况下,可以使用驾驶台集中控制的弹簧储能器安全地施加制动。

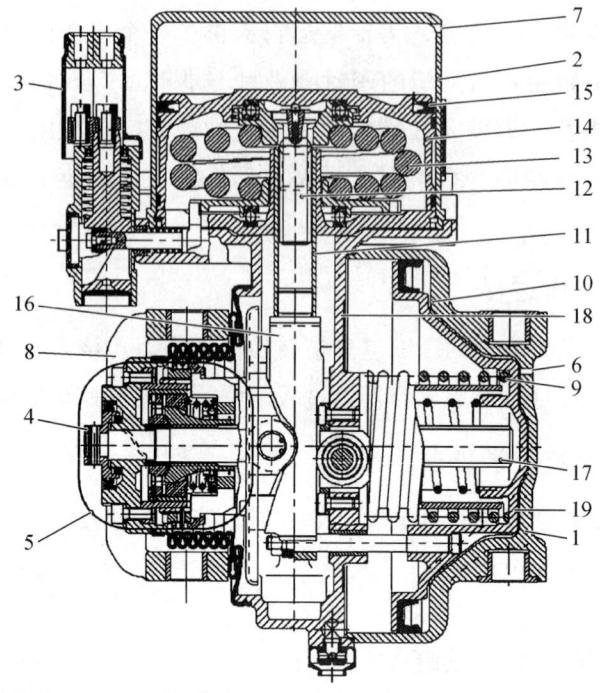

1—制动缸；2—弹簧储能器；3—人工缓解装置；4—螺杆复位装置；5—闸片间隙自动调整器；6—充气孔；8—支架；9—缓解弹簧；10—密封圈；11—空心筒；12—传动螺杆；13—压缩弹簧；14—储能器活塞；15—密封圈；16—楔块；17—螺杆；18—制动缸体；19—制动缸活塞。

图 6-7　带弹簧储能器的制动缸

6.5　防滑保护

基于微处理器的车轮滑动控制系统由速度传感器、测速齿轮、控制单元和防滑阀组成，如图 6-8 所示。

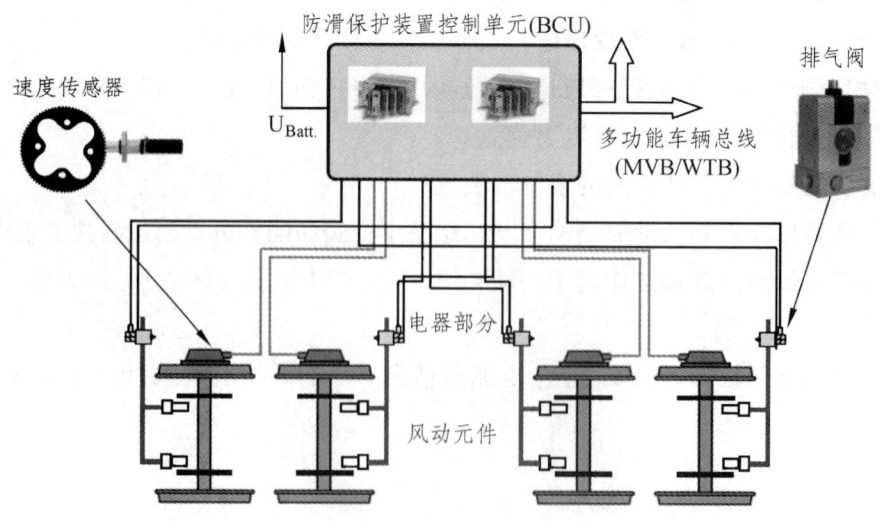

图 6-8　防滑保护系统

车轮防滑保护（WSP）系统安装在每辆车上，有两个用于 WSP 功能的电子控制单元 EBCU1（B01）和 EBCU2（B10），包括防滑阀和集成在车辆轴箱中的单通道速度传感器及测速齿轮。每个轮轴都配备了两个速度传感器。这些速度传感器的信号反馈给两个独立的 EBCU。每个防滑阀由两个控制向制动缸充气的线圈和两个控制制动缸排气的线圈组成，由两个独立的 EBCUs 控制。

WSP 功能还包括检测车轴抱死（DNRA）功能。DNRA 功能检测车轴抱死，并将每个抱死车轴作为故障信息显示出来。如果车轴的速度信号低于某个极限速度值，则会测定该轴抱死。该极限速度值取决于 DNRA 功能的当前参考速度。例如，对于约 200 km/h 的参考速度，极限速度值约为 100 km/h。如果某个轴上的单个速度传感器发生故障，DNRA 仍能在该轴正常工作。如果防滑阀的控制中存在开路或短路，则电子控制单元会持续进行防滑保护。

基于微处理器的车轮滑动控制系统构成一个闭环控制。首先，速度传感器在没有接触的情况下检测车轮的转速，并向控制单元发送一个成比例的频率信号，该信号指示车辆的速度。控制单元评估来自所有车辆的所有速度传感器的频率。如果减速度超过限值，它将生成信号，使防滑阀（G03.02 和 G03）能够排放制动缸压力空气。控制回路根据瞬时轮轨黏着情况来调整制动缸压力，使其处于最优的车轮保持在不打滑的制动力范围内。这样，控制单元确保产生最大可能的制动力。

6.6　供风系统

动车组列车的送风系统由主送风单元和辅助送风单元组成。

6.6.1　主供风装置

动车组列车通常有两个安装在车厢地板下的主供气装置（A01）。每个供气装置包含一台 SL22（A01.01）螺杆式主压缩机和一台双室空气干燥器（A01.04）。压缩机电机由车载电源的 440 V，60 Hz 3 交流母线供电。主压缩机连接到双筒干燥器和带有防冻装置的冷凝液收集器（A15）。来自供气装置的空气被输送至列车主风缸管（MRP），该管道通过软管连接至相邻车厢。MRP 管道用于为所有车辆提供高压力压缩空气。

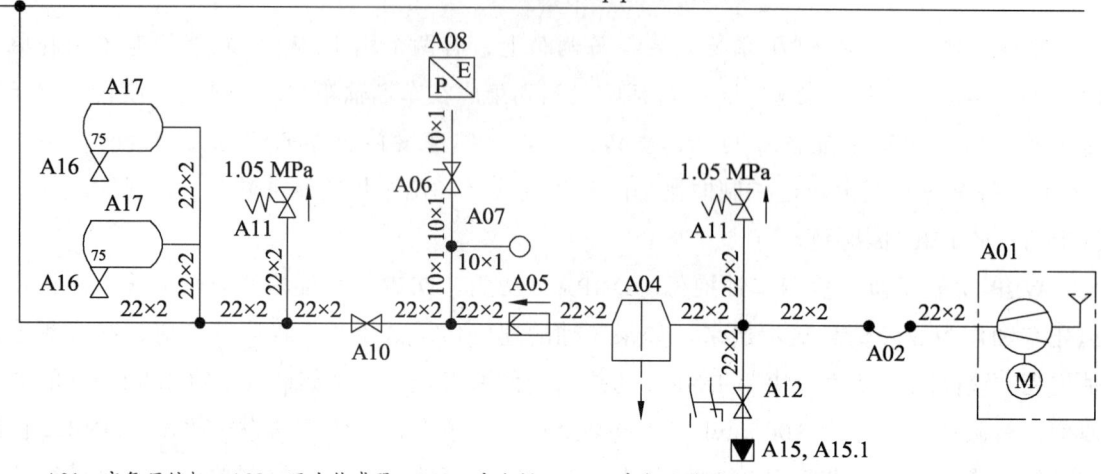

A01—空气压缩机；A08—压力传感器；A03—安全阀；A04—空气干燥器；A17—主风缸；A11—安全阀；
A15—外部压力空气供应；A05—空气滤清器；A07—测试配件。

图 6-9　供风系统管路简图

6.6.1.1　主压缩机

主压缩机通常为螺杆式。图 6-10 展示了主压缩机的结构。

图 6-10　螺杆式空气压缩机实物图

1）主压缩机工作原理

旋转螺杆压缩机使用两个啮合的螺旋螺杆（称为转子）来压缩气体（参见图 6-11）。在湿式润滑螺杆压缩机中，润滑油填塞了转子接触面之间的空间，既提高了转子间的密封，又能平滑传递主动转子和从动转子之间的机械能。气体从吸入侧进入，并随着螺钉旋转流过螺纹内空间。啮合的转子迫使气体流经压缩机，使气体从螺杆末端排出。

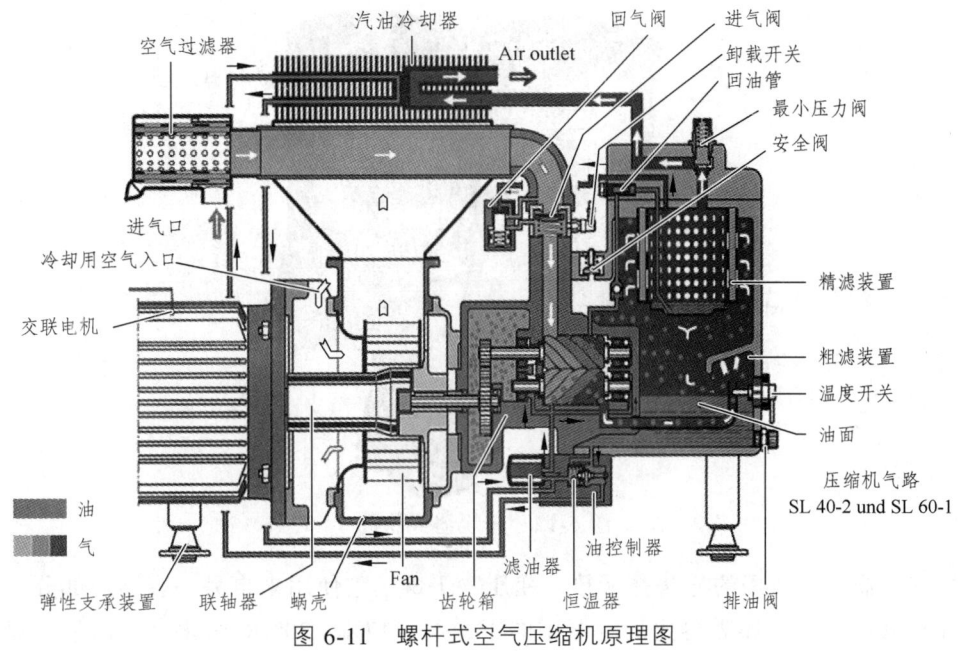

图 6-11 螺杆式空气压缩机原理图

该机构的有效性取决于螺旋转子之间以及转子与压缩腔之间的精确配合。然而，一些泄漏是不可避免的，必须使用高转速来最小化泄漏流量，提高有效流量的占比。

2）主压缩机的控制

压缩机控制设备确定两台主压缩机中的一台为首选主压缩机。如果首选压缩机无法工作，则首选压缩机将被其他可用压缩机替换。如果首选压缩机的运行时间在 1 h 内超过 50%，则首选压缩机也将被其他可用压缩机替代。如果 MRP 平均值小于 850 kPa，则启动一台压缩机；如果平均 MRP 值小于 830 kPa，则启动第二台压缩机。

在一个 8 节车厢的列车组内，两个压缩机依次打开，以避免对电源产生冲击。如果 8 节车厢动车组的电力可用性降低到最低限度，则受此影响的 8 节车厢列车组中的一台压缩机将被激活。当列车运行中，且 MRP 水平低于 700 kPa 时，列车上所有可用的两台压缩机都会运行，这样就减少了 MRP 压力升至 1000 kPa 风压所需的时间。

6.6.1.2 空气干燥器（如图 6-12 所示）

压缩空气通过一个带有两个"塔"的压力容器，其中填充了活性氧化铝、硅胶、分子筛或其他干燥剂材料。处理后压力空气的相对湿度小于 35%，可满足 – 40 °C 时使用要求。

这种干燥剂材料通过吸附作用从压缩空气中吸水。当水附着在干燥剂上时，干燥剂"基体"就饱和了。干燥器根据标准 NEMA 循环定时切换干燥塔，一旦该循环完成，系统的压缩空气通过简单地吹掉黏附在干燥剂上的水来纯化饱和的干燥剂。

干燥室内干燥剂的作用是使压缩空气的的压力露点达到空气中水蒸气无论怎样都不会凝结的水平，或尽可能多地从压缩空气中去除水分。

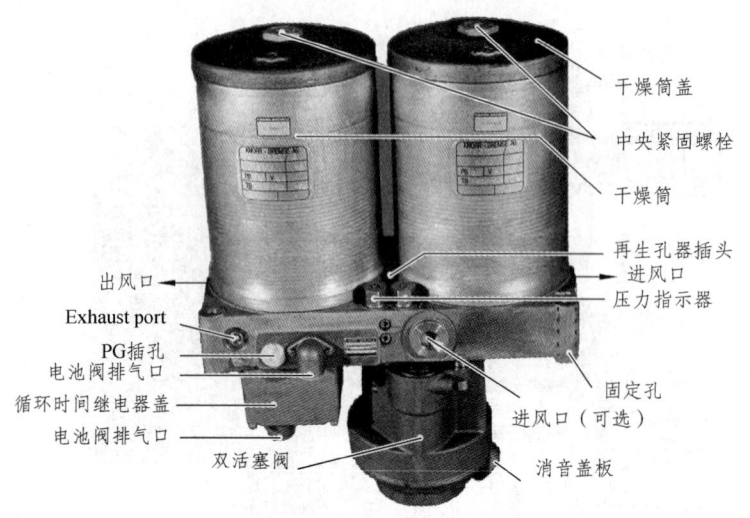

图 6-12 干燥器实物图

干燥剂容器再生所用的方法是无热"变压"干燥，它使用来自另一容器的部分干燥的压缩空气在较低压力下干燥需再生的容器中的干燥剂。17%~20%的净化率。通常，双室干燥器的一个室处于吸附状态，另一个室处于再生状态。它们吸附和再生功能的交替转换由电子转换控制，周期约为 120 s。排水阀处还有一个电加热器以防止结冰；在排放口处装有消声器。

6.6.1.3 安全阀

主供气装置中安装了两个结构相同的安全阀，一个设置为 1.05 MPa，另一个设置为 1.2 MPa，以保护供风系统以及压缩机。

6.6.1.4 油过滤器

压缩空气经滤油器处理后，含油量小于 0.1 mg/m³，应每隔一段时间将滤油器中的油排出。

压缩机的耗油量在很大程度上取决于压缩机类型、油的性质及其运行条件，因此不是恒定的。特别是在高工作温度下，高达 50%的压缩机机油消耗随风吹过空气干燥器，这部分机油几乎完全由滤油器吸附。

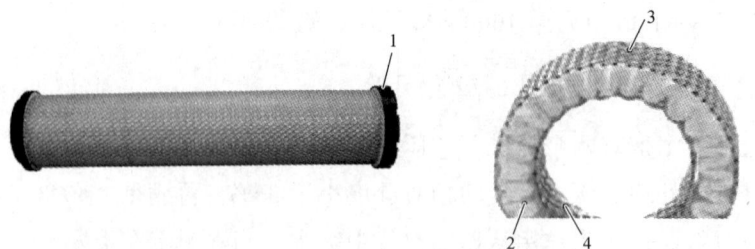

1—塑料盖；2—玻璃纤维层；3—外支撑层；4—内支撑层。

图 6-13 油过滤器

6.6.2 辅助供气装置

如果 MRP 较低，辅助供气装置将向升弓风缸充入压缩空气，其组成如图 6-14 所示。

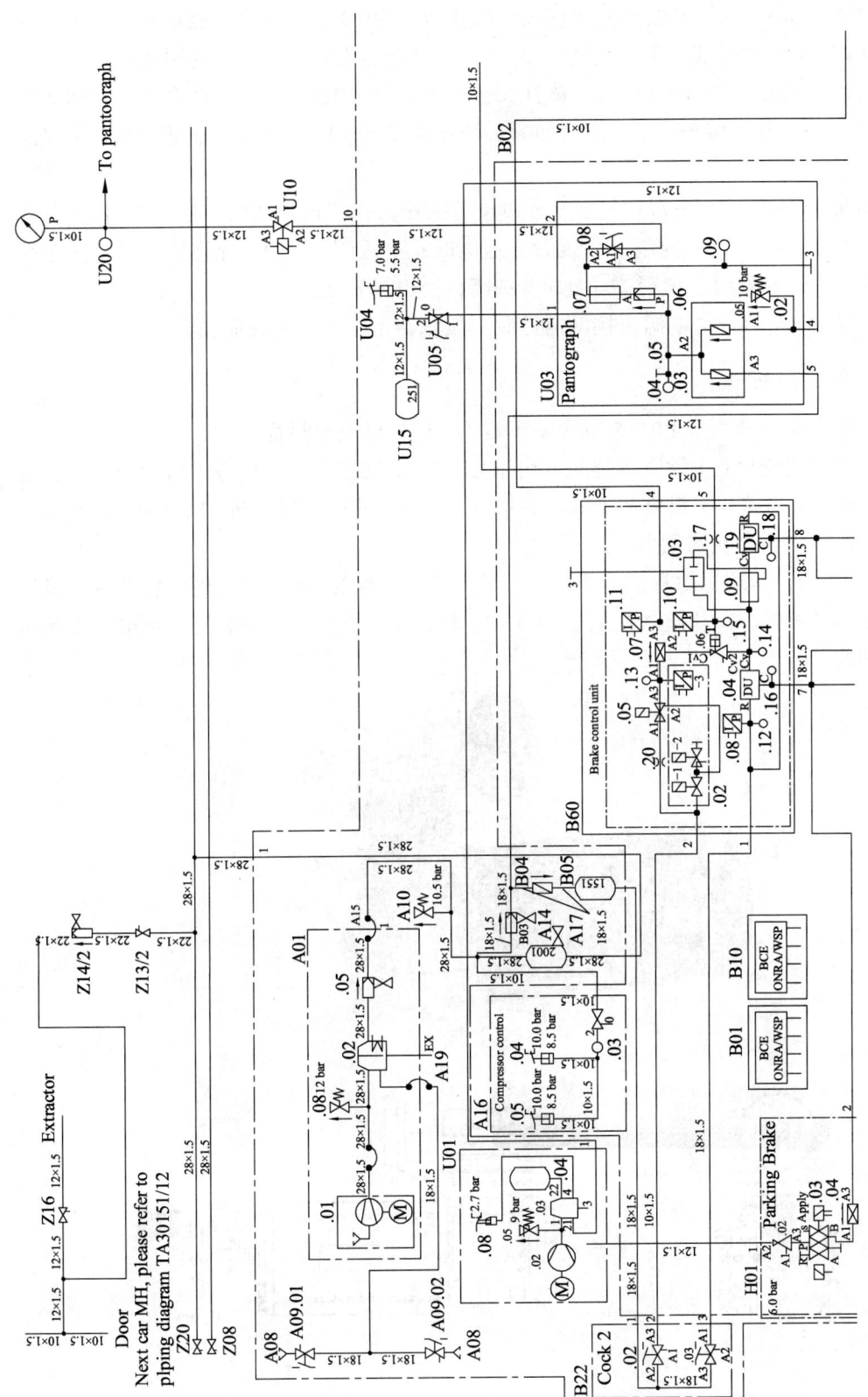

图 6-14 辅助供气装置管路示意简图

受电弓模块（U03）用于控制和监控辅助供风装置（U01）和受流器（受电弓）压缩空气的供给。单向阀（U03.03）防止压缩空气流回主风缸或自动式空气制动机的制动管。

主风缸管由压力开关（U04）监控，该开关位于制动架（B08）中，集成在辅助供风装置（U01）中。如果空气压力降至压力开关（U04）的下限以下，用于升弓的辅助压缩机将接通工作。

通过止回阀（U03.03），来自主风缸管或制动管的压力空气被输送到容量为25 L的升弓风缸（U15）。电磁阀（U10）控制升弓装置。通电时，电磁阀（U10）允许压力风将受电弓升高到减压阀上方。断电时，电磁阀（U10）关闭，受电弓管通大气。

辅助供风装置（U01）的电源由接触器控制，接触器由压力开关控制。

6.6.2.1 辅助压缩机

安装于车厢底架上的两台LP115型辅助压缩机一般伴随受电弓而设置。

如果主风缸未充满风（主供风系统的可用压力不足），则辅助压缩机将为启动列车的受电弓、主断路器和车顶隔离开关提供所需的压力空气。辅助压缩机可以通过110 V DC车辆蓄电池独立供电，而不需要接触网供电。

如图6-15所示，压缩机由直流电机驱动，该电机的供电为24 V直流电。辅助压缩机组是一种单级压缩压缩机，采用模块化的、紧凑式结构，由自支撑法兰安装。直流电机直接与压缩机曲轴相连。

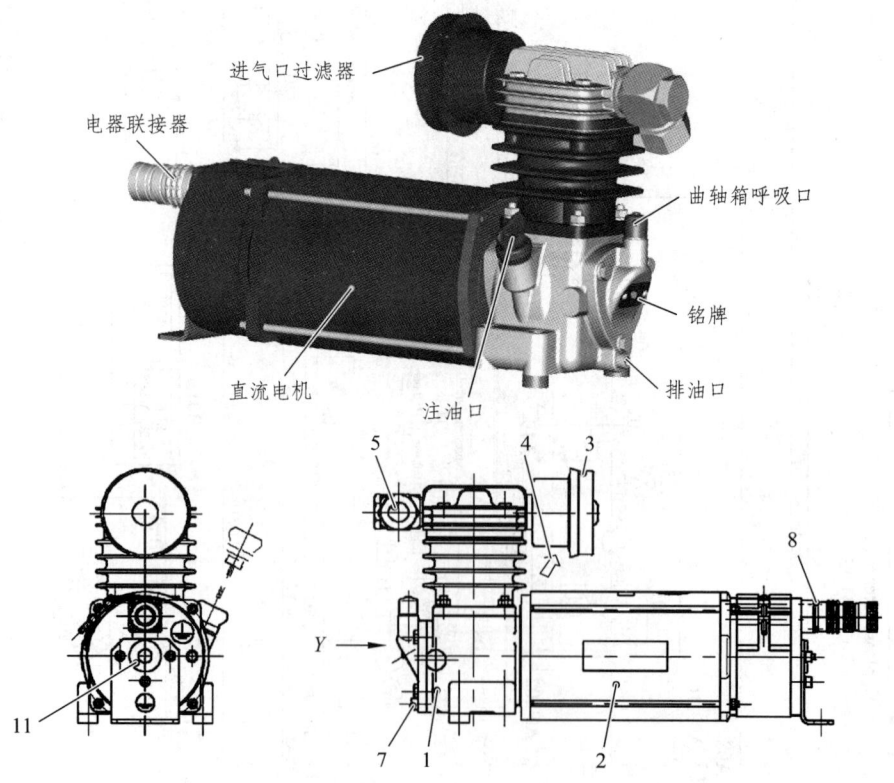

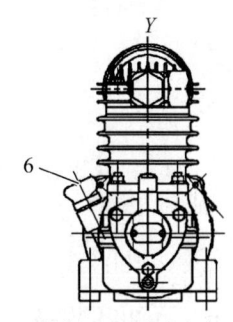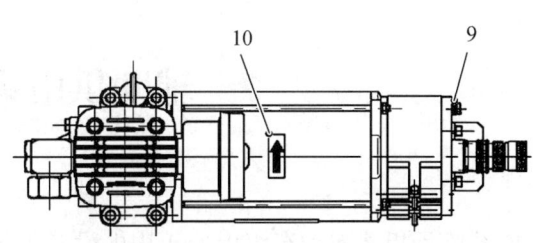

1—压缩机；2—直流电机；3—干式空气过滤器；4—进气口；5—排气口；6—注油孔；7—排油口；
8—接头；9—接地；10—顺时针旋转标记；11—窥望口。

图 6-15 辅助电动压缩机组

6.6.2.2 辅助压缩机的控制

辅助压缩机由 CCU 启用，而后由 TC02/TC07 车辆中的制动控制模块（B02）进行控制。在列车通电启动情况下，当辅助空气压力低于 550 kPa 的下限值时，辅助压缩机会启动。驾驶员的 MMI 屏上将显示信息，显示辅助压缩机需要激活。列车激活时，如果需要辅助压缩机提供升弓所需的空气压力，则需要更长的时间，但列车启动程序本身没有改变。当升弓风缸的风压高于 800 kPa 的停止极限值时，辅助压缩机断电停机。如果超过最大允许运行时间 10 min，则会关闭 90 min。

7 辅助供电系统

辅助供电系统承担着向动车组中低压用电设备提供电能的任务。按电压规格，辅助供电系统分为三相交流中压供电和直流低压供电两个子系统。

为保证动车组牵引、制动等系统的正常运行，车上设有各种必需的辅助电机，包括各冷却用风机、变压器冷却用油泵、变流器冷却用水泵，以及为制动、受电弓等气动装置提供风源的空气压缩机等。此外，为保证良好、舒适的乘车环境和工作环境，车上还设置了空调、电热器、通风机、冰箱、电开水器等电器，这些都需要三相交流中压电源。同时，动车组的网络控制管理系统、照明等则需要直流低压电源提供不间断电能。

交直流辅助电源与上述必需的辅助电气设备之间，依赖贯穿全列的辅助供电配线及遍布各车厢的配电柜，联成闭合回路，完成电能转换。这些配线及配电柜就是辅助供电系统的配电部分。

7.1 系统组成与工作原理

动车组一般由2个对称布局的动力单元组合而成，即（M+T+M+T）+（T+M+T+M）。辅助供电系统的电能输入来自牵引供电系统，但动车组辅助变流器独立于牵引变流器，每个动力单元有1个单辅助变流器和1个双辅助变流器，分别安装在两个拖车上，其工作原理如图7-1所示。

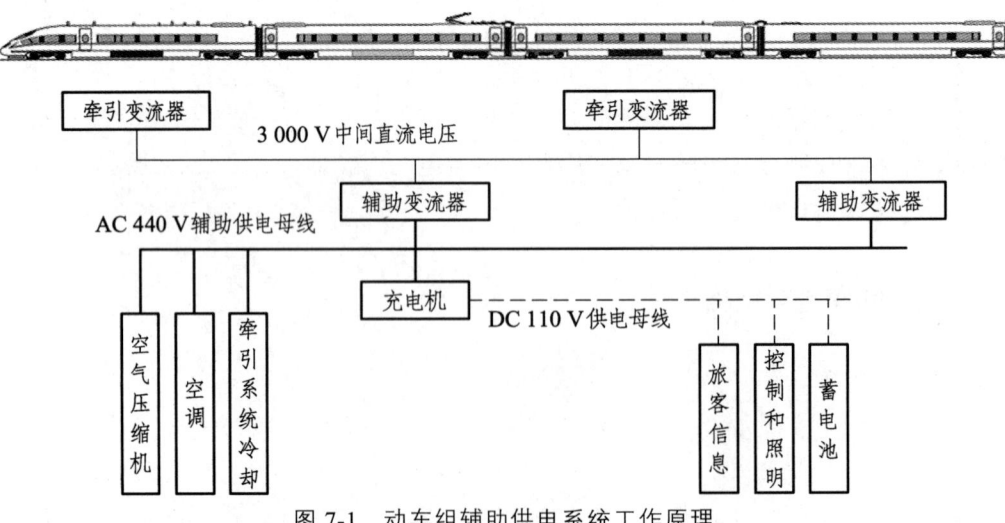

图7-1 动车组辅助供电系统工作原理

位于两个拖车的组辅助变流器,将来自牵引变流器中间环节的 DC 3000 V,变换为 3ϕAC 440 V 向 AC 440 V 母线并网供电,保证各车空气压缩机、空调和牵引系统冷却使用;接着 3ϕAC 440 V 由充电机变换为 DC 110 V 供旅客信息、控制和照明等使用,同时向蓄电池充电。其技术参数见表 7-1

表 7-1 动车组辅助供电系统主要技术参数

辅助变流器	数量	每列车 2 个单变流器,2 个双变流器
	容量	160 kV·A
	电路结构	直-交型
		滤波电容器+PWM+变压器、EMC 滤波器
	输入	DC 3000 V(牵引变流器中间电压)
	输出	3ϕAC(440±5%)V (60±1%)Hz
蓄电池充电机	数量	每列车 2 个
	容量	60 kW
	输入	辅助变流器输出的三相交流电
	输出	DC110 V+(25%,−30%)

7.2 辅助变流器

三相交流中压供电子系统,采用辅助变流器生成 3ϕAC 380 V,50 Hz 交流电压,为动车组上牵引电机的冷却风机、牵引变流器的冷却风机、主变压器的油泵和空气压缩机等供电。辅助变流器根据输入侧的不同,主电路可分为交-直-交型和直-交型;根据输出的不同,可分为恒压恒频 CVCF 和变压变频 VVVF;根据主电路电平级数的不同,可分为两电平和三电平。动车组辅助变流器一般为恒压恒频 CVCF 逆变器。

三电平辅助变流器的特点是可降低开关器件的耐压等级,输出波形较好,谐波较少,但采用的器件较多,控制方式也较复杂。因此,随着电力电子器件的发展,结构和控制均简单的两电平辅助变流器占据了主流地位。

7.2.1 辅助变流器结构组成

辅助变流器输入来自牵引变流器的中间电路 DC 3000 V,辅助变流器进行处理后输出为 3ϕAC 440 V,60 Hz。CRH3 与 CRH380B 型动车组所有辅助变流器同时向一根通达全列(8 辆)车的 3ϕAC 440 V,60 Hz 的母线供电,各辅助变流器分别通过母线进行同步。

母线在列车工作期间处于耦合状态。万一发生故障,可以打开双辅助变流器的耦合接触器，从而将各单元隔离开。

辅助变流器包括开关、保护部件、各种监控设备和电源模块。外壳采用模块式设计，这些模块、保护装置以及电源模块均可以使用专用工具，快速进行更换。

图 7-2 表示了动车组单辅助变流器的主要部件及位置，图 7-3 表示了动车组单辅助变流器安装板的构成。

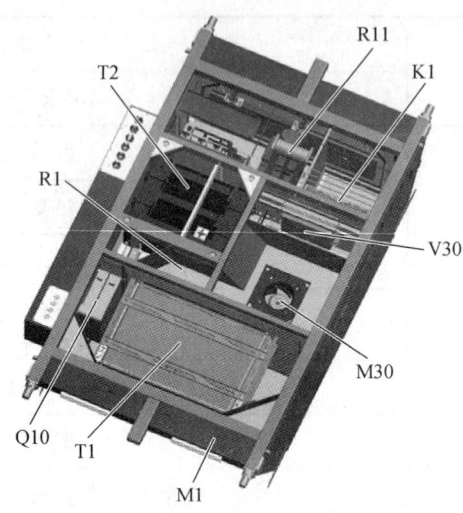

图 7-2　CRH3 和 CRH380B 型动车组单辅助变流器的主要部件及位置

图 7-2 中，K1 Sibcos-M2500 为主控制器，M1 为内置风扇，M30 为主风扇，Q10 为耦合断路器，R1 为滤波扼流圈，R11 为预充电电阻，T1 为脉冲调宽逆变器，T2 为变压器，V30 为电容。

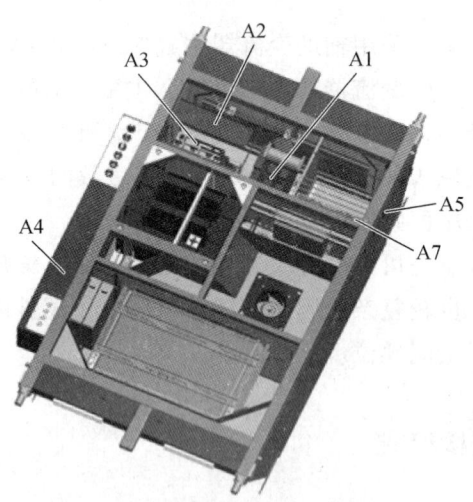

图 7-3　CRH3 和 CRH380B 型动车组单辅助变流器的安装板

图 7-3 中，A1 为主接触器及预充电接触器的安装板，A2 为 3AC 电压探测安装板，A3 为外部供电接触器及输出熔断器安装板，A4 为滤波电容器安装板，A5 为变压器安装板，A7 为接触器安装板。

动车组单辅助变流器采用强制风冷，如图 7-4 所示。

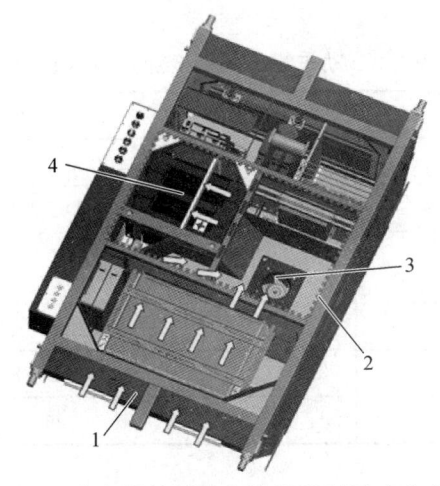

图 7-4 动车组单辅助变流器强制风冷主气流

图 7-4 中，1 为空气过滤器，2 为隔板，3 为主风扇 M30，4 为底盖板上的排风口。空气由安装在外壳前部的两个双喷嘴护栅导入，然后被引导通过伸到导气管中的电源模块的散热片[T1]，主风扇[M30]将冷风吹到中间的隔室。冷风通过变压器[T2]，最后通过位于底部的两个排风口护栅排出。

冷却系统的设计是使主风扇保持尽可能低的转速，这样就能在保持最佳通风和冷却效果的前提下将污垢程度、噪声水平以及风扇工作时间降到最低。

主风扇由主控制器 Sibcos-M2500[2K1] [3K1]根据温度进行控制。各模块将散热器的温度报告给控制器，控制器对温度进行监控，并依据温度情况直接打开或关闭主风扇。风扇控制可以实现充分的自主工作，不需要外部进行干涉。

内置风扇[M1]保证内部的空气循环。这些模块连续工作，它们与系统控制器一起打开或关闭。图 7-5 标出了内置风扇在外壳上的位置和内部气流的方向。

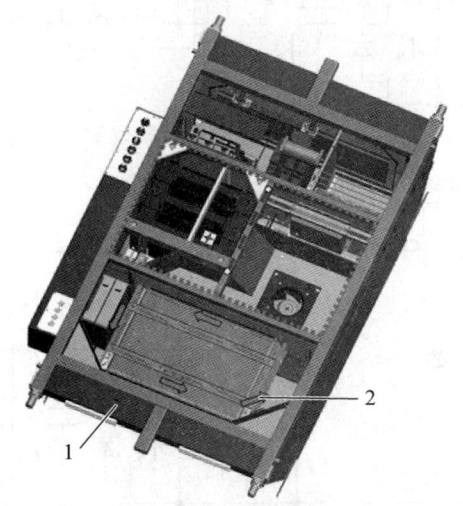

图 7-5 动车组单辅助变流器强制风冷内部气流

图 7-5 中，1 为铰链板上的内置风扇[M1]，2 为内部气流。表 7-2 是动车组单辅助变流器主要技术参数。

表 7-2　动车组单辅助变流器技术参数

序号	内容	参数
1	容量	2×160 kV·A （cosϕ=0.9）
2	输入电压	约 DC 2700~3600 V
3	输出电压	3AC 440 V （停车条件下的机车准备：345 V） （60±1）Hz（停车条件下的机车准备：47 Hz）
4	散热方式	强制风冷方式
5	外形尺寸	1886 mm×2978 mm×699.5 mm
6	质量	约 1450 kg

7.2.2　辅助变流器电路

辅助变流器的主电路属于直-交型。直-交型辅助变流器是从直流电网或直接从牵引变流器的中间直流环节取电，由逆变器实现直流电到三相交流电的转换。直-交型辅助变流器在机车、动车组、城市轨道车辆等场合得到了越来越广泛的应用。

由于输入电压较高，为保证输出辅助电气设备所要求的电压等级，一般需要增加降压设备。有两种方式，一种是先逆变，再通过三相降压变压器将较高的交流电压降到所要求的电压等级；另一种是先通过降压电路将直流输入电压降低到合适的值，再进行逆变。

图 7-6 和图 7-7 分别给出了两种辅助变流器的电路结构。

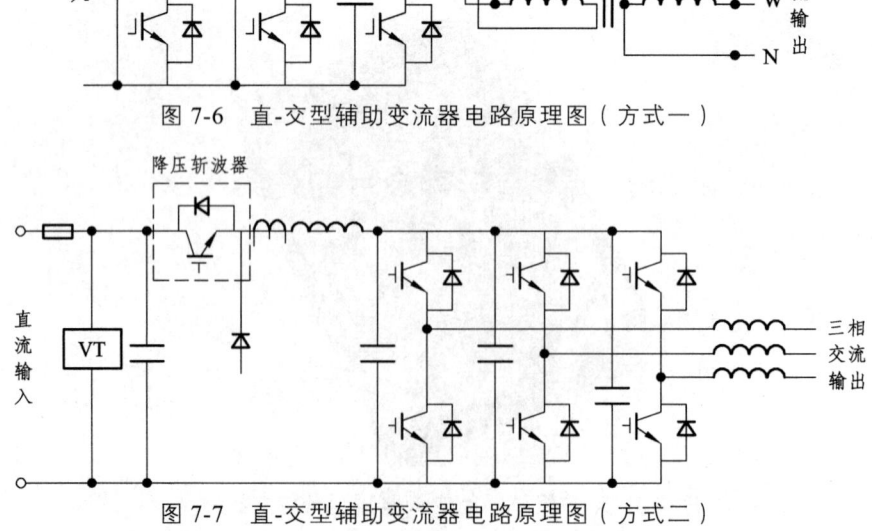

图 7-6　直-交型辅助变流器电路原理图（方式一）

图 7-7　直-交型辅助变流器电路原理图（方式二）

为得到品质良好的三相交流电源，通常需要增加滤波环节。在方式一中，三相电抗器/电容器滤波或三相 *LC* 滤波器可放置在逆变器和降压变压器之间，也可放置在变压器之后。方式二中，则将滤波器放置在逆变器输出之后。

方式一中，△-Y 型变压器不仅实现降压的功能，还实现了高压输入电源回路和负载回路之间的相互隔离。此电路的特点是开关元器件数量少、控制较为简单，缺点是输出三相电压易受直流输入电压的影响，且当直流输入电压较高时逆变器开关元件的耐压要求高，成本较高。因此，该方案比较适用于由牵引变流器中间直流环节供电场合。

方式二中，可采取不同的电路实现降压。最简单的是单管降压斩波器，如图 7-7 所示。它有以下特点：(1) 通过降压斩波的闭环控制保持逆变器输入电压的恒定，从而消除输入电压的波动对三相逆变器输出的影响。(2) 整个电路中仅需一只大功率高压 IGBT 元件，逆变器则可选择较低电压级别的 IGBT 元件，以降低设备成本。但是这种方式没有实现输入电压与输出电压之间的隔离，故同时还应设置针对降压斩波器失去控制后对逆变器和负载等进行保护的保护电路。

7.3 充电机+蓄电池

直流供电子系统为列车照明和控制系统供电（含应急供电），其电压等级常为 DC 110 V。CRH5 型动车组采用了 DC 24 V，虽然省去了 110 V 到 24 V 的变换，但直流母线电压低，发挥同样功率时电流大，所用的线缆粗、损耗大，且抗干扰能力差。

直流电源采用充电机+蓄电池组合模式。正常运行时由充电机为直流负载供电，并给蓄电池浮充电；电网没电时由蓄电池供给直流负载。为了避免蓄电池过度放电而导致动车组控制系统瘫痪，通常对直流负载实施能级管理——自动缩减供电，保证直接影响安全的重要负载的用电。

7.3.1 充电机

7.3.1.1 充电机组成

每个牵引单元配置 1 台动车组充电机，悬挂于 4 车、5 车车下。BC 由 3ϕAC 440 V，60 Hz 母线供电，变换为 DC 110 V，给电池和其他直流负载供电，DC 110 V 母线全列贯通。

充电机包括开关和保护部分，还有很多监视装置和功率模块，如图 7-8、图 7-9、图 7-10 所示。

箱体及部件采用模块化设计，无需特殊工具就能把模块、保护装置和功率模块很快地分开。正常情况下，充电机直接与 D-ACU 的输出连接，获得 3ϕAC 440 V，60 Hz 电源，输出 60 kW。当列车控制单元通过 MVB 发送开机命令，如果 DC 110 V 外接电源断开、输入电压正常、充电机没有故障的三项条件满足，此时充电机正常启动。

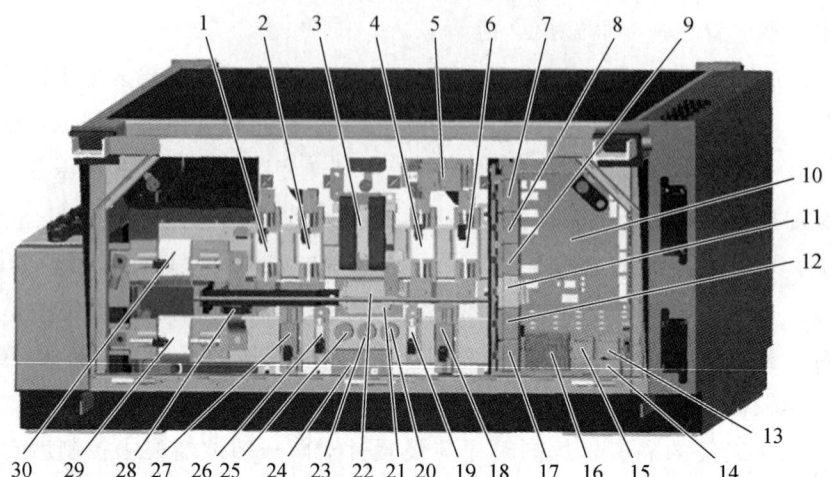

1—熔断器 F4；2—熔断器 F10；3—接触器 Q1；4—熔断器 F3；5—固定架 A2；6—BK 熔断器 F9；7—电压传感器 T6；8—输出电压传感器 T20；9—输出电压传感器 T23；10—主控制器 K1；11—DC 110 V 接地故障检测 T22；12—输入电压传感器 T4；13—风机 A1-Q15；14—马达保护开关风机 A1-F15；15—接触器 A1-Q12；16—熔断器 A1-F1 to A1-F8；17—输入电压传感器 T3；18—BN2 熔断器 F11；19—BD 熔断器 F7；20—EMC 电磁兼容 V25；21—NTC 电阻；22—去耦二极管 R20；23—EMC 滤波电容 V26；24—BN2/BS2 接触器 Q2；25—EMC 滤波电容 V27；26—BD 熔断器 F8；27—BN2 熔断器 F12；28—电池电流传感器 T24；29—熔断器 F1；30—熔断器 F2。

图 7-8 动车组充电机开关设备和控制器件的布局

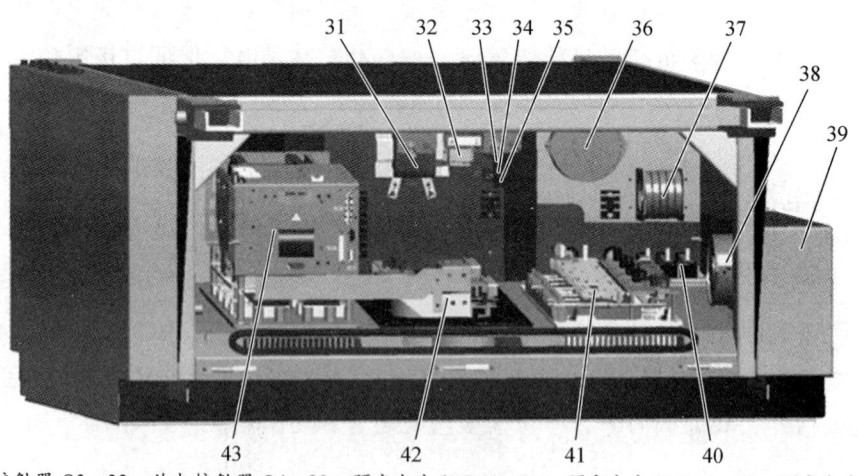

31—输入接触器 Q3；32—放电接触器 Q4；33—预充电电阻 R11；34—预充电电阻 R12；35—预充电电阻 R13；36—内部风机 M2；37—铁环圈 V4；38—内部风机 M3；39—电容座 A4；40—接线柱 A5；41—充电机模块 T2；42—安装板 A3；43—充电机模块 T1。

图 7-9 动车组充电机的模块布局

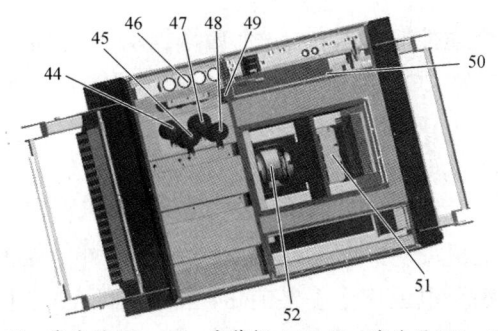

44—滤波器 R4；45—滤波器 R2；46—安装板 A4；47—滤波器 R3；48—滤波器 R1；
49—电流传感器 T21；50—铁心 V11；51—输入滤波 R5；52—主风机 M1。

图 7-10　动车组充电机无底盖中间柜体部分布局

外接电源情况下，充电机由外接电源插座提供 3ϕAC 380 V，50 Hz 电源，输出 36 kW。"停车整备"情况下，充电机由 ACU 提供 3ϕAC 345 V，47 Hz 电源，输出 36 kW。图 7-11 为 CRH3 与 CRH380B 型动车组充电机功率模块简图。

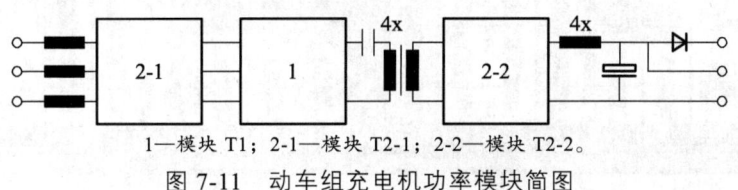

1—模块 T1；2-1—模块 T2-1；2-2—模块 T2-2。

图 7-11　动车组充电机功率模块简图

模块 T1，即可控高频变换器。模块 T2 包括 1 个输入整流器和 4 个输出整流器。

模块电路中安装若干传感器，电流传感器用来检测器件电流和负载电流，电压传感器检测输出电压，蓄电池的电压、电流和温度被记录下来。

主控制器 K1 装入功能强大的控制程序，指挥充电模块 T1、T2 和高频变压器 4X 把三相交流输入电压（440 V/60 Hz）变成电隔离的直流 110 V 输出电压，向电池充电同时给直流负载供电。主控制器 K1 还能根据温度等实时数据对蓄电池充电电压进行调控，以符合温度补偿特性。

7.3.1.2　充电机控制系统

图 7-12 为动车组充电机控制系统简图。

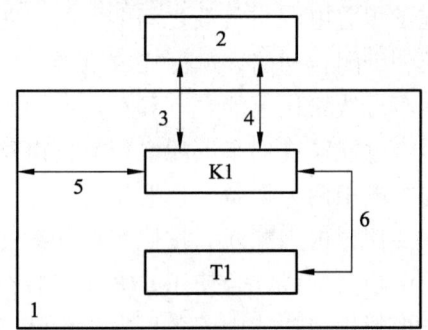

1—充电机；2—中心控制单元；3—二进制输入输出；4—MVB 总线；5—RS232 系列接口；
6—CAN 总线；K1—主控制单元；T1—功率模块。

图 7-12　动车组充电机控制系统简图

充电机控制系统由一个主控制器 K1、一个功率模块 T1 组成。K1 用来监控 BC，具有更高级的功能，它通过 MVB 为 CCU 提供信号。BC 控制系统内部通信采用 CAN 总线。

7.3.2 蓄电池

动车组蓄电池组与充电机配对，每个牵引单元配置 1 组，悬挂于 4 车、5 车车下。电池组由 2 个电池座盘组成，每个电池座盘上装有 84 节串联的 FNC 1502 HR*型单体电池，如图 7-13 所示。

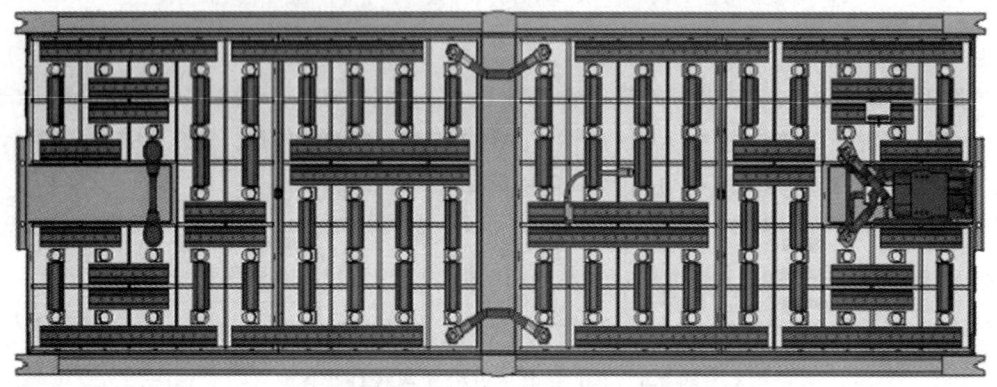

图 7-13 动车组蓄电池组外观

单体电池的互连使电池组的标称电压达到 100.8 V，容量为 $2 \times 160 \mathrm{A \cdot h}$，最大放电电流达 545A，电池类型为 NiCd。

当列车在无网压时，DC 100.8 V 蓄电池系统能够使列车内部照明、外部照明、紧急通风、车载安全设备、广播、通信系统等辅助设备在停车计划规定的时间内保持运行。

单体电池的装配方式能够确保 100.8 V 电池组的爬电间隙规范符合 DIN EN 50272-2 和 IEC50124 标准的要求。

7.4 配电系统

配电系统在辅助供电系统承担着电源与负载之间电气桥梁的作用，是将供电装置、用电设备以及控制保护设备等联成一个闭合回路，从而完成电能的输送、分配和转换。

辅助电源启动后，先向本车母线输送电能，车和车之间通过车端电力连接器使供电母线贯穿全列，每个车厢分线装置将电能输送到车上配电柜，再由配电柜分配到各种负载。

配电系统主要包括配线与配电柜两大设备。按照用途划分，车体配线有电力、广播、网络控制三大类，我们在这里主要探讨电力配线；按照车体配线在车辆中所在的部位，又可分为车内和车下配线两部分。配电柜与配线配合使用，大多安装在车内，方便动车组机械师操作与检修。配线的布置、配电柜的构造功能由于各厂家的设计习惯与制造工艺，存在很大差异，它们数量庞杂、电压等级多，几乎遍布车体的各个部位。

另外，由于动车组电气控制逻辑是通过低压电气系统控制中压和高压电气系统，同时中压电气系统为高压电气系统的辅助设备供电，实际上低压、中压和高压电气系统的关联度很高。以动车组的启动过程为例，顺次经历三个阶段：

第一阶段，低压直流系统启动。主要有照明设备、网络控制系统与两级设备，还有受电弓、主断路器传统控制电路。该阶段发生于升弓合闸前，由车载蓄电池供电。

第二阶段，中压交流系统启动。主要有牵引通风机、制动空气压缩机等牵引制动辅助装置和客室空调机组，为列车运行做好准备工作。此阶段发生于升弓合闸之后，牵引主电路除电机变流器和牵引电机外均投入工作，从牵引变流器中间直流环节取电的辅助变流器启动，并网到中压交流母线上为上述设备供电。与此同时，充电机陆续启动，直流母线转由充电机供电，蓄电池也从放电状态转为充电状态。

第三阶段，高压牵引系统启动。由司机在行车信号给定的条件下，启动牵引电机，列车运行。

8 动车组网络控制技术

8.1 概 述

8.1.1 动车组网络控制系统的目的

动车网络控制系统（以下简称 TCMS）通过贯穿列车的总线实现信息传输，对车辆运行和车载设备动作的相关信息进行集中管理，为司机和乘务员的操作提供有效指导，为设备的维护保养和乘客的服务提供支持。TCMS 系统具有信息传输、逻辑控制、画面显示、故障诊断和用户支持的五大功能。CRH3 型动车组是中国高速动车组中的典型代表，本文以 CRH3 型动车组为例介绍动车组网络控制技术。

8.1.2 缩写术语（表 8-1）

表 8-1 动车组网络控制系统术语缩写

缩写术语	描述
TCMS	列车控制和管理系统
ACU	辅助变流器单元
BCU	制动控制单元
CC	车辆控制
CCU	中央控制单元
CI/O	输入/输出设备
DC	司机室
DS	门
DMI	ATP 显示器
MMI	司机显示器
ET	以太网
FAS/SD	火警系统/烟雾探测器
GW	网关
RP	中继器
KLIP	SIBAS KLIP 设备
HVAC	采暖、通风和空调控制装置
MVB	多功能车辆总线

续表

缩写术语	描述
OL	操作杆
TCU	牵引控制单元
TR	列车无线电
WC	厕所
WTB	绞式列车总线

8.2 动车组网络控制系统组成

以 CRH3 型动车组为例，每列动车组的网络中通包括网关 GW、中央控制单元 CCU、牵引控制单元 TCU、制动控制单元 BCU、辅助控制单元 ACU、以及充电机单元 BC、空调控制单元 HVAC、门控制单元、旅客信息中央控制器 PIS—STC、人机显示接口 MMI、分布式输入输出站 SIBAS KLI 等设备。这些智能设备通过列车总线 WTB 或车辆总线 MVB 连接到动车组网络上。

动车组网络图结构如图 8-1～图 8-6 所示。

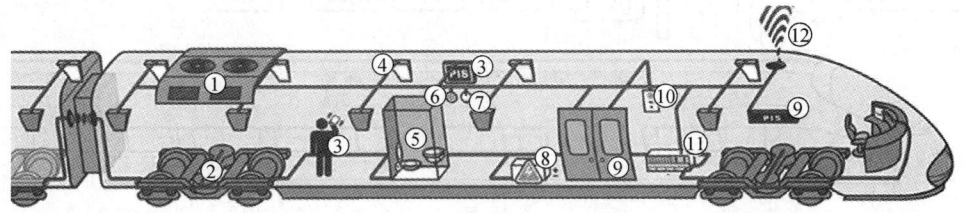

图 8-1 动车组网络布线图

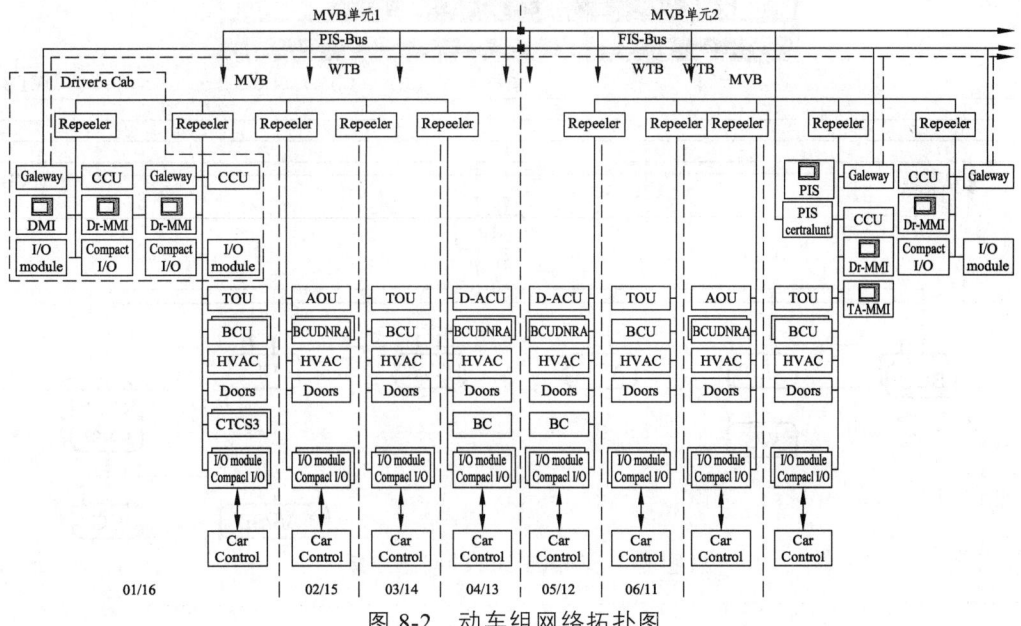

图 8-2 动车组网络拓扑图

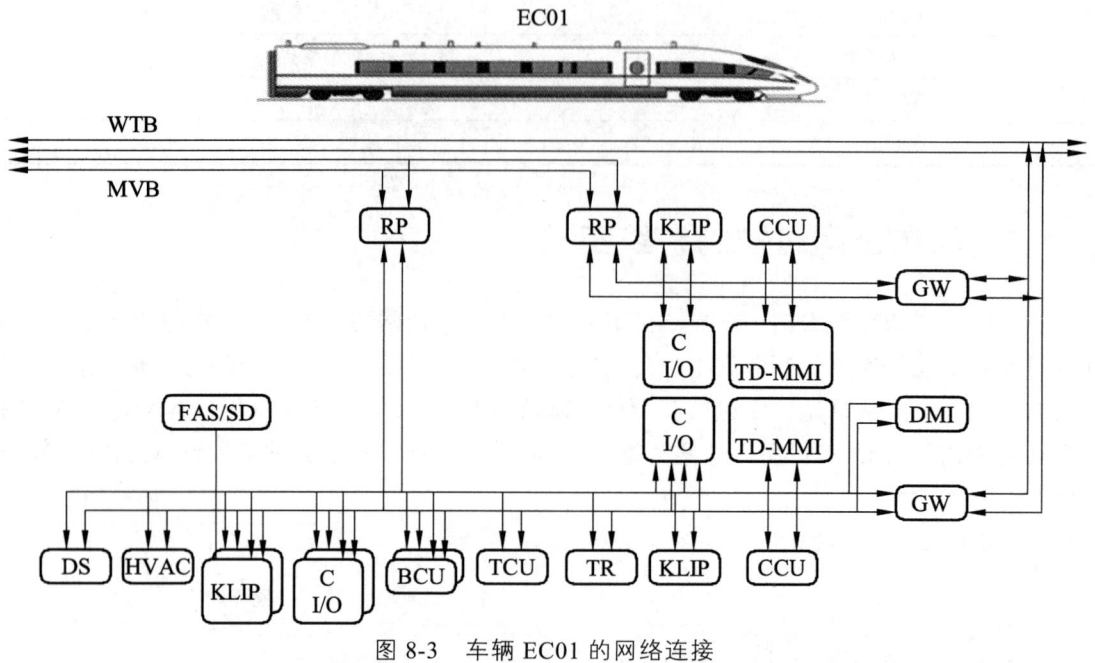

图 8-3 车辆 EC01 的网络连接

图 8-4 车辆 TC02 的网络连接

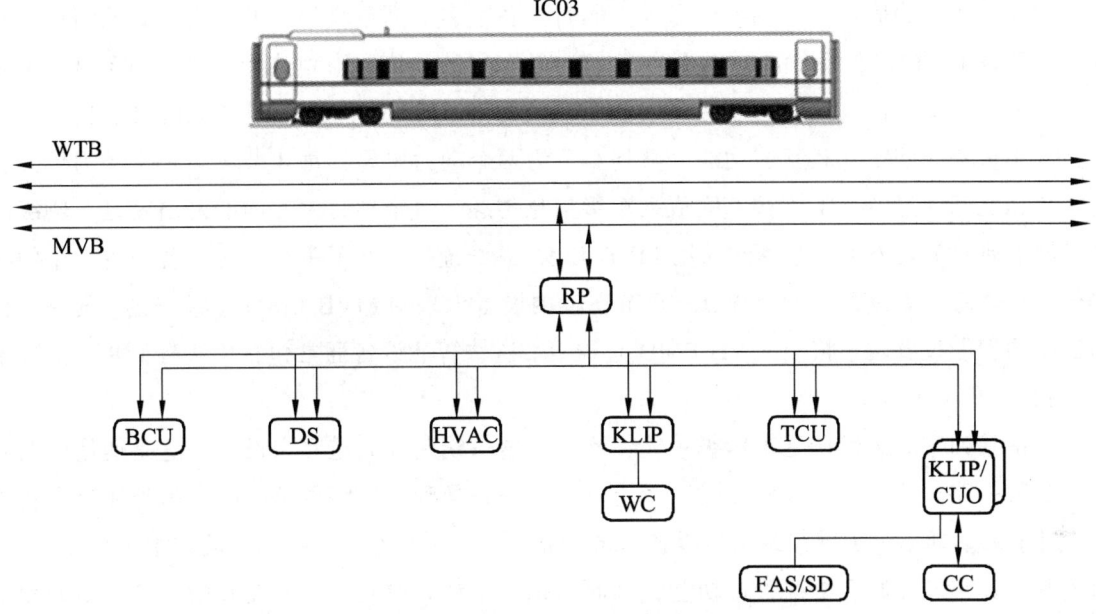

图 8-5　车辆 IC03 的网络连接

图 8-6　车辆 BC04 的网络连接

8.3 动车组网络控制系统原理

一列动车组为固定的 8 辆编组形式，同时具备最多 2 列重联编组的能力，其网络控制系统采用符合 IEC61375 标准的 TCN 网络协议。动车组的通信网络划分为 2 级：列车级网络和车辆级网络。TCN 网关连接列车级网络和车辆级网络。列车级网络采用 WTB 总线贯穿全车，并且承担重联时网络互联互通功能。整列车分为两个动力单元，每 4 节车为一个动力单元。两个单元之间通过 WTB 连接，完成列车级信息传递。每个动力单元内的网络就是车辆级网络。每个动力单元内不同车辆间采用 MVB-EMD 总线连接，除了头车和尾车各设置 2 个中继器外，其余每节车设置一个中继器；每节车辆内设备也采用 MVB-EMD 总线连接，同一车辆内部不同智能设备均连接至 MVB-EMD 总线上。这些智能设备通常包括中央控制单元、显示器、TCU 和 ACU 等。

不论是列车级总线还是车辆级总线，均采用通信线路双通道冗余设计，这是通信线路冗余。当某一路通信线路出现故障时，系统可以自动切换到另一路通信线路。另外还有设备冗余，对于采集动车组关键控制信号设备一般配备两个，互为冗余。例如网关和中央控制单元，由于其兼具车辆控制和总线管理功能，因此在每一个动力单元中对网关及中央控制单元做了热备冗余配置。对于 WTB 总线，中央控制单元通过底层协议芯片的竞争机制自动选取其中一个为主设备，其他中央控制单元从设备，实时监视当前主设备的工作状态。当主中央控制单元出现故障时，备用中央控制单元将接管主中央控制单元的职责，行使 WTB 总线管理和控制功能。主权的切换为自动切换方式，不需要人工干预，并且主权的切换不会导致列车控制功能的中断和故障。对于 MVB 总线，每个动力单元为一个独立的 MVB 网络，在每个 MVB 网络内部的总线管理、冗余和切换机制与 WTB 一致。

一列 8 辆编组的动车组由两个动力单元构成，每个动力单元为一个 MVB（多功能车辆总线）网段，每个 MVB 采用了主链-分支结构，每辆车都设中继器，将一个基本单元内的 MVB 分成了多个分支。这样即使出现了某个子系统设备网络通信故障，最多只影响网络与本辆车中子系统的通信，不致影响整个基本单元的网络通信。

网络控制系统采用分布式控制技术，即分布采集及执行，中央集中控制与管理的模式。由牵引控制单元 TCU、制动控制单元 BCU、充电机控制单元 BC、辅助变流器控制单元 ACU、车门控制单元 DCU、火灾检测和烟雾报警控制单元 FAS/SD、智能显示单元等组成，通过 MVB 总线或 WTB 总线和中央控制单元 CCU 进行通信。

8.3.1 多功能车辆总线 MVB

MVB 是专为铁路列车（车辆）内设备互联而开发的可靠性高和实时性强现场总线，MVB 有 3 种传输介质，它们分别是 ESD、EMD、OGF，一个 MVB 网络结构应包括一个或多个

MVB 总线段，MVB 特点是：

（1）电气短距离介质 ESD。ESD 是依照 RS485 标准的差分传输导线对，在无需电气隔离的情况下在 20 m 的传输距离内最大可支持到 32 个设备。若使用电气隔离，则传输距离可更远。

（2）电气中距离介质 EMD。由屏蔽双绞线组成的电气中距离介质，在 200 m 的传输距离内最大可支持 32 个设备，允许使用变压器作电气隔离，如图 8-7 所示。

（3）光纤介质 OGF。通过星形耦合器汇出，传输距离可达 2.0 km，主要用于较为苛刻的环境。

（4）采用 8 位的循环冗余校验方式。

（5）物理层支持三种传输介质，通过本身两个通道进行冗余，重要的 I/O 采用双份，冗余切换过程将在尽量短的时间内进行。

（6）设置总线控制，网络拓扑可为总线型、星型或混合型。

（7）数据链路层支持三种基本的数据传输模式：过程数据、消息数据、监督数据。

（8）传输波特率为 1.5 Mb/s，信号采用双向 L 型差分曼彻斯特编码。

不同的网络（EMD）终点需要配置专用的终端器，如图 8-8 所示。

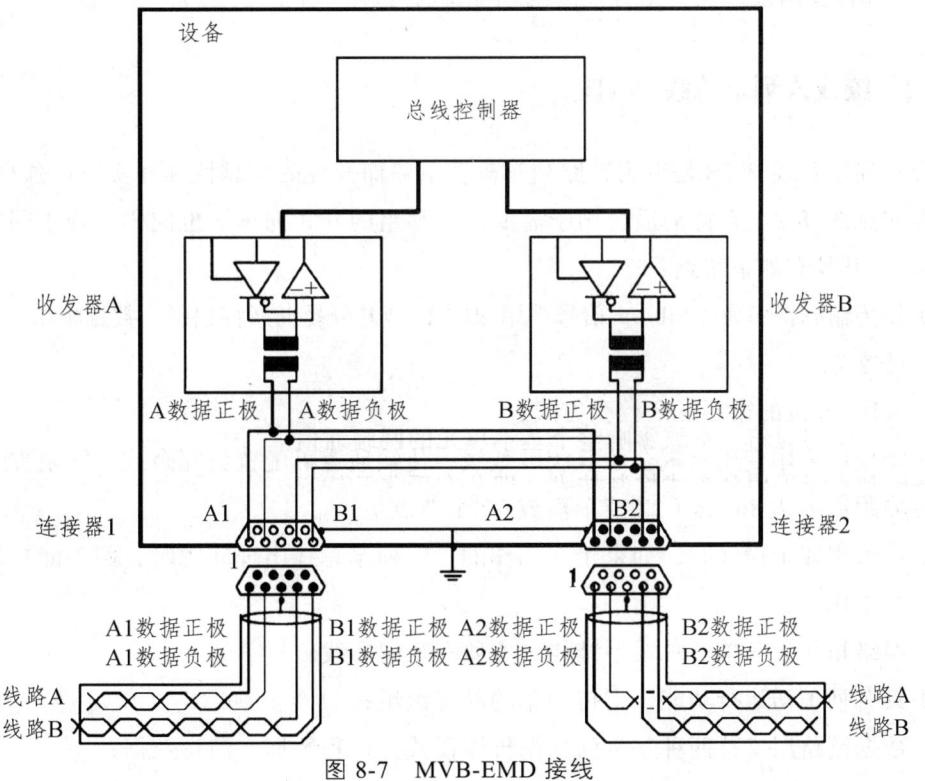

图 8-7　MVB-EMD 接线

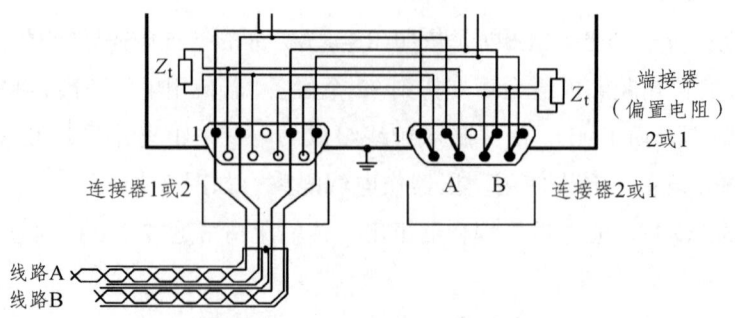

图 8-8 MVB-EMD 网络终端

动车组的车厢级通信网络采用 MVB 车辆总线，它的拓扑结构是固定的，不能动态改变，一个牵引单元内 4 辆车一起构成一个 MVB 网段。通信采用中距离传输介质即屏蔽双绞线，在车厢内分为两路冗余布线。

一个 MVB 网段内采用构架式的网络结构，即每辆车形成一个 MVB 分支网通过中继器与一个牵引单元的 MVB 主干网相连接，这种结构的优点是一个 MVB 分支网故障时不致影响其他车辆的 MVB 分支网通信。在端车上由于冗余的原因有两个 MVB 分段，分别通过两个中继器接入整个 MVB 网段，在每个分段的两端都接有终端电阻（120 Ω）。

8.3.2 绞线式列车总线 WTB

绞线式列车总线 WTB 是专为铁路列车车辆重联而开发的可靠性高和实时性强现场总线，其连接方式见图 8-9。它特别适合用于需要动态编组的开式列车（也同样适合于固定编组的闭式列车），其具有如下特点：

（1）其传输波特率为 1 Mb/s，信号采用双向 L 型差分曼彻斯特编码，数据帧格式为高级数据链路控制格式；

（2）采用 16 位的循环冗余校验方式；

（3）物理层采用变压器耦合的双绞屏蔽线，传输通道可配置为冗余或非冗余方式，不需中继器传输距离可达 860 m（22 节车辆或 32 个节点）；

（4）当采用冗余设计时，如果正在工作的一组列车总线出现问题时，网关能自动控制切换到另一组工作；

（5）网络拓扑为简单的总线型结构，方便车辆间布线；

（6）具有列车初运行功能，支持列车的动态编组；

（7）数据链路层支持两种基本的数据传输模式：过程数据、消息数据；

（8）WTB 通过本身两个通道进行冗余，重要的 I/O 采用双份，冗余切换过程将在尽量短的时间内进行。

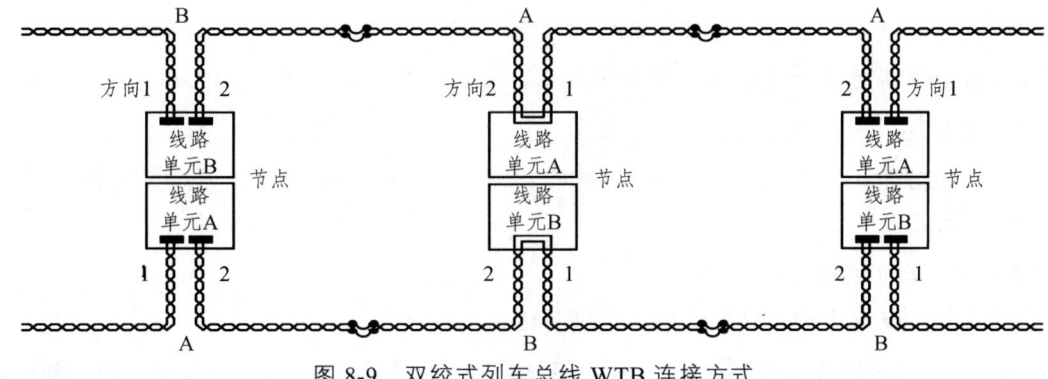

图 8-9 双绞式列车总线 WTB 连接方式

列车总结 WTB 的作用就是连接两个动力单元，以便两个动力单元之间能进行必要的列车级数据交换。完成列车级网 WTB 和车辆级网 MVB 之间数据交换的基础是 TCN 网关，它负责 WTB 和 MVB 两个总线之间的数据转换和路由任务。每个动力单元有两个网关，位于端车（即 1 车和 8 车）的司机室右柜中，分别集成在两个中央控制单元（CCU）内，互为冗余，但只有在作为主的中央控制单元中的网关才参与 WTB 和 MVB 通信。从中央控制单元中网关接通电源但不激活。

在动车组联挂和解编时，通过 WTB 能够动态识别网络终端和网络拓扑的特点，实现 WTB 节点动态地址分配，自动完成列车级的相关配置。在配置完成时，所有列车总线设备都获得一个明确的列车通信网络地址（即每个动力单元中被激活的网关地址）。

8.3.3 中央控制单元 CCU

即每辆端车的司机室内，都各有两个中央控制装置（CCU），它们位于两个不同的基本单元内（每 4 节车厢为一个基本单元），同一车厢内的两个 CCU 互为冗余。其中头车一个 CCU 在主方式下工作，尾车的另一个 CCU 在从方式下工作。在司机室占用端的 CCU 叫作列车主 CCU，除了进行主 CCU 的工作外，它还负责整个列车的的网络控制。其他基本单元的主 CCU 称为被引导主 CCU。

每个基本单元的主 CCU 负责本单元内的车辆控制。它从车辆总线 MVB 和列车总线 WTB（通过其附属网关）读取命令和信息，并向列车总线 WTB 和车辆总线 MVB 发送控制信号和反馈信息。

中央控制单元 CCU 的任务有：

（1）对主断路器和受电弓控制。

（2）牵引控制单元（TCU）的牵引设置点的生成。

（3）变压器保护。

（4）车载电源控制。

（5）前端自动车钩和开闭机构控制。

（6）针对各种装置的更高级命令和控制预置值的生成，例如车门、HVAC、照明等。

（7）安全环、火警系统和转向架诊断监视。

（8）通过分布式输入/输出站（SIBAS®-KLIP，MVB-Compact I/O）完成数字和模拟信号输入和输出控制。

（9）整备运行控制。

（10）CCU 设备诊断，列车总线和车辆总线通信诊断。

（11）通过附属网关连接到列车总线（WTB），对动车组和联挂列车进行配置确定和检测。

（12）从 CCU 运行和主 CCU 相同的程序，然而没有主动的过程控制。从 CCU 监视主 CCU 的状态，并做好在主 CCU 发生故障时接过主 CCU 工作的准备。在 CCU 发生主-从转换时不但 CCU 的 MVB 接口配置变换，而且它们的附属网关也要转换。原因就是只有主 CCU 内的网关才能激活，因此由于网关的转换，同时就会触发列车总线（WTB）的初运行。

8.3.4 分布式输入输出站

在动车组中有两种类型的输入输出站，一种是输入输出点数固定不变的，并且结构非常紧凑的紧凑式输入输出站，另一种是输入输出模块可随输入输出通道数量的增减而变化的智能外围终端 SIBAS®-KLIP。其中紧凑式输入输出站有两种类型：一种是用于采集司机室内专用信号的 MVB-Compact I/O，例如，来自按钮、开关、指示器、断路器、编码插头和主控制器的信号；另一种用于采集 PT100 温度传感器信号。

SIBAS®-KLIP 主要由 AS318 模块、总线模块、输入/输出模块、电源模块组成。AS318 是 SIBAS®-KLIP 与 MVB 的接口模块，总线模块是其内部通信的桥梁；输入输出模块可以提供 16 位数字量的输入，8 位数字量的输出或 16 位的数字量输出，8 位的继电器输出，4 通道的模拟输入（±10 V、±20 mA、Pt100），2 通道的模拟输出（±10 V / ±20 mA），电源模块用来将车上的 110 V 电压转换为 24 V 电压。

8.3.5 中继器 MVB-Repeater

MVB-Repeater 本身并不具有与 MVB 总线其他设备进行信息交互的能力，它只是延长 MVB 总线的通信距离。在 CRH3 动车组中共有 10 个中继器，其中两个端车内各有 2 个，其他车内各有 1 个。MVB 中继器除具有信号转发、放大、整形作用外，同时还具有故障隔离作用。一旦某个车的 MVB 分支网络或设备通信出现故障，可以方便地进行故障隔离，不影响其他车 MVB 总线的正常通信。

8.3.6 人机接口设备 MMI

司机和列车乘务员的 MMI 是动车组车厢网络设备中主要与人进行交互信息的设备。一方面 MMI 接收来自 MVB 上的信息,经过处理后通过显示界面将必要的信息显示给相关人员;另一方面操作者可操作 MMI,把自己的意图和信息输入到 MMI 中,经 MMI 处理后,将有关信息存储到本身的存储系统中或是传到 MVB 网络上。

8.3.7 牵引控制单元 TCU

在 CRH3 动车组中共有 2 个基本单元(每 4 节车厢构成一个基本单元),在每一个基本单元中有两个动力单元。4 个牵引变流器分别位于两个端车以及 3 车和 6 车车下,在每个牵引变流器中都有一个牵引控制单元。4 个牵引电动机并联提供牵引。每个牵引变流器主要由两个四象限斩波器(4QC)、一个带有串联谐振电路的中间电压电路、一个制动斩波器(BC)和一个脉冲宽度调制变频器(PWMI)构成。中间电源回路给列车供电模块提供电源,列车供电模块位于牵引逆变器箱外部,它给列车辅助供电系统和车载设备(包括牵引系统的辅助设备,如泵、风扇等)供电。TCU 负责在正常牵引模式、自动速度控制模式、紧急牵引模式下生成和分配牵引力控制指令,并对牵引系统部件进行保护。

8.3.8 制动控制单元 BCU

在 CRH3 动车组中,每个车都有一个制动控制单元,出于冗余的考虑,如果端车 BCU 的一个模块故障,另一个模块可替代其部分功能。在拖车内的 BCU 也有冗余功能,可以在其中一个模块故障的情况下由另一个模块带替其部分功能。

每节车内的制动控制单元都可执行各自子系统内的控制和诊断,即对自己所在车辆的制动系统进行控制和诊断,其中包括防滑功能。在端车内的 BCU 除管理本车制动系统的控制和诊断外,还担负着本牵引单元内的制动管理任务。当承担本牵引单元内的制动管理的 BCU 作为列车主控单元时,还担负着列车的制动管理任务。

8.3.9 电池充电机控制单元 BC

CRH3 动车组上共有两个电池充电机,分别位于餐车和一等车,电池充电机控制系统就位于充电机中。电池充电机的输入电源为 3 相 AC 440 V,60 Hz,输出为直流 110 V,是动车组 110 V 负载的供电电源。它有两个主要控制模块,一个是充电机的核心控制模块,同时还负责和车辆总线 MVB 进行通信,另一个是主要用于充电的功率模块。

8.3.10 辅助变流器控制单元 ACU

每节动车都有一个辅助变流器。其电源输入与牵引变流器的中间电路相连。输入电压标示为 DC 3000 V。辅助变流器有两种：一种是单辅助变流器，位于 2 车和 7 车两个变压器车车下；一种是双辅助变流器，分别位于 4 车和 5 车车下。辅助变流器的输入来自于牵引变流器的中间直流环节输出。

所有辅助变流器同时为一根贯通整列列车的 3AC 440 V，60 Hz 的总线供电。总线在列车工作期间处于耦合状态。万一总线发生故障，可以打开双辅助变流器的耦合接触器，从而将各部分隔离开。总线为各节车厢的所有大负载供电。各辅助变流器单独通过 3AC 440 V 60 Hz 总线进行同步。

输出端设置了防空载、短路和过载三种工作模式，且与输入端是电隔离的。输出端不接地，且在输出变压器的二次侧装有永久接地故障检测装置（用于诊断目的）。辅助变流器由其中心控制系统对其进行控制和诊断，在双辅助变流器中有两个辅助变流器的中心控制系统，分别为各自的逆变器单元工作，这两个控制系统之间通过 MVB 进行连接，并最终连到车辆总线 MVB 上。

8.3.11 车门控制单元 DCU

CRH3 中除餐车外（餐车没有外门），每辆车的几个外门中都存在一个连接到车辆总线 MVB 上的主车门控制单元，其他外门的门控制单元通过 CAN 总线和其联系，然后由该主车门控制单元和车辆总线 MVB 通信。读入传感器和执行机构的信息并诊断，监测门联锁装置，接收相应的速度信号执行安全锁闭。

8.3.12 空气调节装置 HVAC 控制单元

CRH3 在每辆车上都有一个 HVAC 控制单元，并且都通过车辆总线 MVB 连接到列车通信和控制系统中。可通过操作司机室的司机 MMI 和餐车的列车乘务员 MMI 实现（制冷制热除湿等）空调系统的基本功能。

8.3.13 卫生间控制系统 WC

CRH3 动车组中的卫生间控制系统，除了控制本子系统内部的电气元件完成卫生间相应的功能外，还要通过已定义的输入输出信号与列车网络控制系统进行通信，为列车乘务人员和维护人员进行故障检查、诊断和维护提供支持。

在带有两个卫生间的车辆中，有一卫生间作为主，负责与列车网络控制系统交互信息。

作为主的卫生间本身没有与 MVB 直接通信的能力，它通过 SIBAS®-KLIP 连接到列车通信网络上，主要是一些二进制的状态信息要反馈到列车网络控制系统，然后这些信息可以在列车员 HMI 上显示出来。这些信息主要是：卫生间的错误信息、净水箱空故障信息、污水箱满 95%故障信息、卫生设施的加热系统温度过高、紧急呼叫信息。

8.3.14　旅客信息系统的控制器（PIS-STC）

旅客信息系统（PIS）用于旅客视听信息、列车人员通信和旅客娱乐。其系统控制器 PIS-STC 是整个信息系统 PIS 的控制核心，也是 PIS 与列车控制网络连接的桥梁。它负责处理来自 MVB 总线、PIS 中的设备，以及属于该系统的 GSM 天线、GPS 天线、FM 天线等设备传来的信息，处理后发出相应控制指令或相关信息到相应目标处。同时在 STC 内有掉电保持功能的存储器，可以存储重要的操作数据，同时也使得 PIS 在电源出现故障以后可自动恢复到之前的一个状态。PIS-STC 在管理旅客信息子系统的同时，还要与列车控制系统进行通信。

8.3.15　火灾报警和烟雾探测系统 FAS/SD

火灾报警和烟雾探测系统主要由烟探测控制器、光电感烟探测器和线性热探测器等设备以及相应的电缆组成。其中烟探测控制器和光电感烟探测器通过 CAN 总线连接起来并形成一个回路。

该结构的优点就是当回路中有一处中断时，CAN 总线仍然能正常通信，提高了系统的可靠性和安全性。在每个车的火灾报警和烟雾报警系统中都有一个线性热探测器，它位于辅助变流器或者牵引变流器中，并通过专门的导线与其中的一个光电感烟探测器相连，当线性热探测器所测位置处温度超过设定值时，会将与之连接的两根导线短路，这样与该线性热探测器相连的光电感烟探测器就会察觉，然后通过 CAN 总线传递相应的信息给烟探测控制器。每个光电感烟探测器都可生成警报信号、故障信号及准备就绪信号，此外还可提供维护和诊断信息，它们的电源均由烟探测控制器提供。光电感烟探测器电源均由烟探测控制器提供，该探测器分布于驾驶室、控制柜、PIS 柜、卫生间中。

8.4　动车组网络的系统功能

动车组网络控制系统主要采用列车分布式网络通信和控制系统（DTECS 平台），DTECS 平台是专为轨道车辆的控制和通信设计的一套车载计算机系统，主要完成轨道车辆的通信管理、功能控制、故障诊断、信息显示和事件记录等功能。由若干个 DTECS 平台的模块构建的网络控制系统,称为 TCMS 系统。

TCMS 系统具有如下几个特点:

(1) 总线传输,减少硬连线,减轻车辆质量;

(2) 对车辆运行状态信息和车载设备状态信息进行集中管理,提高列车信息化程度,支撑司机工作;

(3) 实现车上检查自动化,减轻维修保养工作;

(4) 集成旅客信息系统功能,支持乘客服务。

DTECS 网络控制系统采用模块化设计,特别适合轨道交通车辆的车载网络控制系统,并使得系统的构成十分灵活,不但减少了系统布线距离,而且十分容易扩展。动车组网络控制系统主要参照了以下标准:

EN 50121-3-2:2000 机车车辆电气设备电磁兼容性试验及其限值;

IEC 60571:1998 铁道机车车辆电子装置;

IEC 61375:2007 列车通信网络;

UIC 556:1999 列车总线上的信息传送。

8.4.1 通信功能

实现 IEC 61375 和 UIC 556 规定的网络通信协议,为网络上的车载设备提供信息交互通道。

8.4.2 控制功能

基于网络通信功能,完成对包括牵引系统、辅助供电系统、制动系统、门控系统、空调系统、照明系统、旅客信息系统等在内的整车系统的逻辑控制、状态监视、故障诊断等功能。控制功能主要包括以下内容:

(1) 网络控制系统具有对基本单元内车辆网络的管理功能,具有对列车级总线和车辆级总线及设备通信状态的诊断功能。当检测出总线或网络设备通信故障时将产生报警信息,中央控制单元(含网关)冗余热备;当中央控制单元故障或中央控制单元所在的网段故障时,从控中央控制单元自动切换为主控,使对动车组管理功能不受影响。

(2) 网络控制系统具有列车级和单元级控制和监视功能,即实现对动车组或本牵引单元的控制和监视。在牵引单元内,能够控制和监视牵引、制动、辅助变流器、车门、空调等各功能子系统。当牵引单元为主控牵引单元时,评估整列车的输入操作,发布列车控制指令,监视子系统反馈状态,实现对整列动车组的控制与诊断。

（3）网络控制系统具备对牵引系统的控制功能与接口。从列车级控制考虑在正常牵引模式、自动速度控制模式、紧急牵引模式下牵引力控制指令的生成和分配，同时根据对整车运行情况的监视，采用牵引封锁、功率限制等控制策略实现对以上模式下的牵引系统部件的保护。

（4）网络控制系统对紧急制动环路、停放制动环路、制动缓解环路、转向架监视环路、乘客紧急制动环路、司机警惕装置的监控和诊断，生成牵引封锁、最大常用制动或紧急制动指令、停放制动指令并在全列发布。

（5）网络控制系统具备与辅助变流器的通信接口，根据辅助系统的工作模式和工作状态，自动完成辅助系统设备的故障切换、冗余管理，实现动态负载分配和能量管理，实现对整列车所有交流负载（包括空气压缩机、牵引系统冷却泵和风机、牵引变压器冷却泵和风扇、空调及其他设备）和直流负载的投入、切除控制。并对列车交流供电、直流供电、交流负载运行、直流负载运行的状态监控和诊断。

（6）网络控制系统具备与车门控制器的通信接口，实现全列车门的释放、开门、关门、锁闭的控制和状态监视，并实现车门与牵引的联锁。

（7）网络控制系统具备与空调控制器的通信接口，实现全列车空调控制指令发布以及状态监视，并与空调控制器一起配合完成能量管理。具备在火灾情况下的空调紧急关闭功能。

（8）网络控制系统具有火灾报警监视功能，能够集中显示火灾报警环路状态和火灾报警部位，具有火警环路自动测试功能。

（9）网络控制系统具有对全列车内部照明和外部照明的控制和状态监控功能。内部照明具有全部照明和紧急照明工作模式。

（10）网络控制系统具有司机室辅助设备（撒砂、轮缘润滑、前风挡加热等）的控制与监视。

（11）网络控制系统具有与列车运行控制系统车载设备之间的信息传输接口，当列车超过规定速度运行时将通过制动系统自动减速运行。

（12）网络控制系统具备恒速运行控制功能和手动设定点功能用于速度调节，所需的速度由设定点控制装置定义，司机可通过人机界面或恒速手柄等方式激活恒速运行模式，网络控制系统可以自动调节牵引力或制动力来满足给定的速度要求。恒速功能应提供重联、调车和洗车时的速度控制模式。

（13）网络控制系统具备整备运行模式，列车停运后通过启动整备运行模式，使动车组根据重返运营时间自动完成系统检测和车内温度调节。在整备模式可以执行高压、牵引、制动、空调、火警系统的自动测试并报告检测故障，在整备运行模式下通过控制空调照明负载达到节能目的，并能够在任一时间退出该模式重返运营。

（14）除整备运行模式外，网络控制系统还具备紧急牵引模式、换端操作模式、拖拽模式等多种运行模式，以满足实际运营的各种需求。

（15）网络控制系统提供重联和解编控制功能，与机械和电气重联接口相配合，完成重联和解编模式下的列车重新配置功能，满足两列 8 辆编组动车组不同司机操纵端各种组合方式的重联控制功能。使用 WTB 总线实现重联，并实现 2 列重联编组，编组间可采用头尾、尾尾、尾头等连挂形式。每个编组节点同时作用于 WTB 总线上，为实现重联控制功能，依次实现编组数量的识别、重联位置识别、非重联端识别、主控编组识别、激活编组识别、行驶方向识别，最终构建重联编组拓扑。重联后网络控制系统的控制和诊断功能不受列车编组变化的影响。

（16）网络控制系统对重要的子系统及设备进行状态监视和诊断，通过过程数据或消息数据进行传输。具有快速和可靠的排除故障以及故障隔离能力，动车组诊断系统故障不影响动车组的正常运行。

（17）网络控制系统对转向架安全相关状态进行监视、故障诊断及保护，包括：转向架横向稳定性监视、非旋转轴监视、轮对轴温、牵引电机轴承温度、齿轮箱轴承温度监视。具备预警、报警和自动限速的功能。

（18）网络控制系统重要设备如中央控制单元和人机接口显示屏具备冗余和自动切换功能。

8.4.3　监控显示功能

该系统能对动车组和各个重要部件的性能进行实时监测和报警，确保动车组运行安全。系统的监测信息一般包括制动系统工作状态、制动动作情况、车上用电系统状态、车门状态等。通过系统监测能够及时发现事故隐患，以便及时进行维修。监控和诊断数据实时地通过司机显示屏显示，为驾驶员安全驾驶提供支持。

8.4.4　故障诊断与存储功能

网络系统完成车载各部件故障数据的采集、分析、转储和显示。故障信息在司机台上通过显示屏显示，诊断信息能上传到地面维修和服务系统中，供长期的储存和深入的地面分析。

诊断系统能够在动车组运行、维护和维修期间为列车人员（司机、乘务员）和检修人员的维护和检修提供有效的支持。动车组是一个由多个分布式控制单元组成的复杂系统。诊断系统能够确认、评估、报告在所有的操作模式中可能发生的多数故障，包括对其他系统的影响，并可提供操作指南。诊断系统的功能集成在人机界面中。动车组诊断由中央诊断系统和诊断子系统两部分组成。诊断子系统可对牵引、制动等功能进行诊断，并报告可能的故障和单独的功能限制给中央诊断系统，并由中央诊断系统对其进行存储、分类和显示。

故障存储区用于永久存储整个车辆的事件数据（故障数据、环境数据、协议数据），所有系统的数据采集以系统时间作为同步模式。存储的数据便于检修人员作业时参考。故障存储区是一个事件驱动的故障数据存储区。在故障存储区中为每个故障代码保留一个固定的存储区域。对于每一个代码，至少记录第一次故障和最近发生的3次故障。故障存储区分历史故障和当前故障。网络控制系统具备容易接近的便携式设备传输接口和无线信息传输接口，可用便携式设备采集数据和分析，也可根据需要将诊断设备记录的数据以无线方式传送至地面维护基地。

通过司机和乘务员显示器实现人机交互功能，司机和乘务员能实时在线观测整车运行状态，或通过显示器控制相关系统的运行状态。

9 空气调节系统

9.1 空气调节系统概述

空气调节系统对动车组的司机和客室空气进行处理,一般由 2 个司机室空气调节单元机组和 8 个客室空气调节单元机组构成(一个客室一个空气调节单元)。动车组 HVAC 单元机组根据其用途可以分为客室空气调节单元机组和司机室空气调节单元机组两种,这两种结构基本相同,我们以客室空气调节单元机组为例介绍其结构和作用。客室空气调节单元机组总体结构如图 9-1 所示。

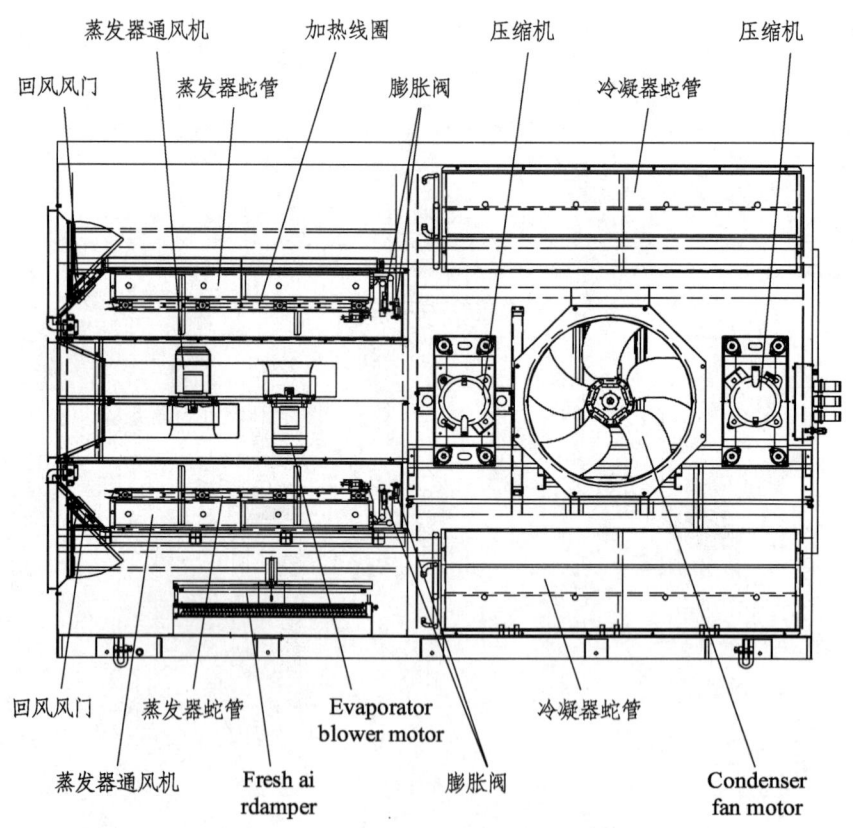

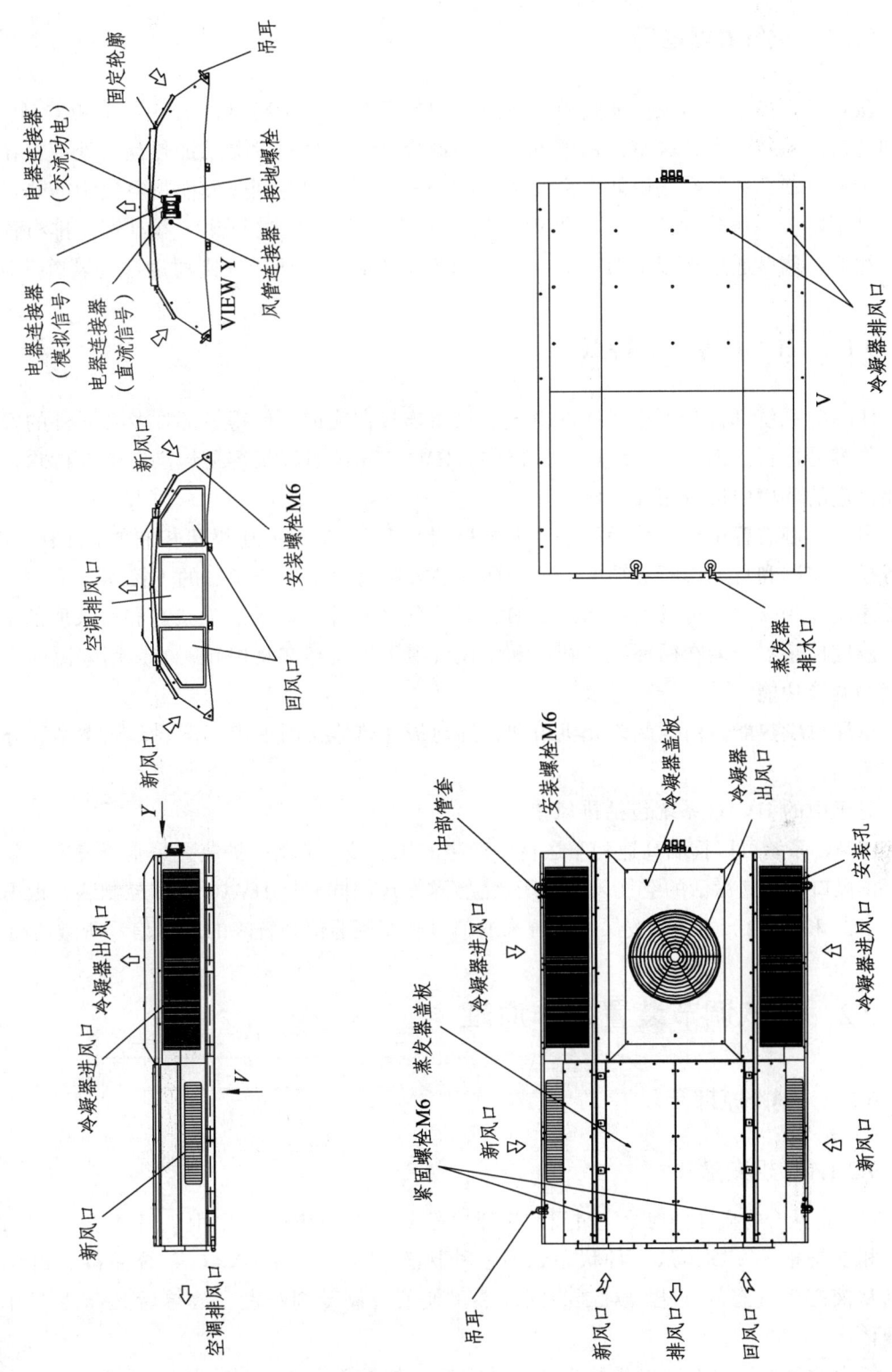

图 9-1　客室 HVAC 单元机组主要部件布置图

9.1.1 空气处理过程

从新风口吸入的新风体通过单元蒸发器内的两个格栅（新风口）进入 HVAC 单元，新风和通过回风口进入的客室回风的混合，该混合空气经过蒸发器或加热盘管处理：在制冷模式下，来自混合箱的空气由两个离心风扇吹经蒸发器，制冷剂蒸发使得空气中的热量被吸收而温度下降；在供热模式下，待处理空气（回风+新风）经过与蒸发器盘管并排布置的加热盘管加热，然后通过连接于 HVAC 单元的风道送入客室，而废气则通过排气风道排到车外。

9.1.2 HVAC 系统的特点

HVAC 系统部件与列车系统的电气连接由连接器完成，使得各部件及各元件的安装与拆除工作容易进行。因此，在后面的大修中，HVAC 系统可以很容易地从车体上拆除，并在与之相适应的环境中进行相关工作。

电子控制装置位于一端操控平台上的控制面板中，它是基于微机控制的，具有温度调节、运行模式控制和自动诊断等功能。控制面板还安装有一个用于 PC 的连接器，采用该指定应用程序的专用软件就可以查找和诊断 HVAC 系统的故障，显示故障状态和可采取的措施。

温度传感器安装在循环风、新风和供风管道中以及客室及相邻区域，用来协助完成车内温度的调节功能。

车厢总供热能力由空调单元机组和辅助地板加热器共同承担，不同车辆类型其分配方式略有不同。

每车中的 HVAC 系统包括排风单元。

HVAC 系统可以抑制高速列车运行中产生的压力波。基础保护装置是基于设置在新气进风口和排风口能迅速激活的空气风门关闭装置。这些风门同时被 HVAC 电子控制装置根据位于端车（MC1 和 MC2）的压力波保护系统来的信号和车辆通信系统来的隧道信号所激活而关断。

9.2 空气调节装置工作原理

9.2.1 制冷原理

9.2.1.1 相变潜热

状态是某个物质在任何给定时间的物理状态或形式。物质可以以固体、液体或气体形式存在。

相变是指一个物体从一种状态到另一种状态的变化。就 HVAC 系统而言，相变是指制冷剂从液态到气态的变化。对制冷剂加热可使液态制冷剂蒸发，放热后又会使它由蒸气变成液体。

压力的改变可以改变发生状态变化的温度。如果压力低，制冷剂从液态到气态转变的温度就会降低。如果压力增加，制冷剂从气态变到液体的温度就会升高。改变制冷剂的压力可以使系统在同一个温度下利用空气来使制冷剂蒸发或使制冷剂凝结。

状态的改变总是伴随着热量的释放或吸收。当一个物体从固态向液态或从液态向气态转变时，就需要吸收热量。当物体从气态向液态或从液态向固态转变时，会释放热量。

潜热是物体改变状态而温度不变时吸收或释放的热量。温度计无法测量潜热。在物体状态的改变过程中吸收或大量的热，但同时温度并不改变。液体汽化吸收的热量或者蒸气液化放出的热量称为汽化潜热。

从一个区域向另一个区域转移热量最高效的方法是利用潜热。制冷剂液体在车体内蒸发将会吸收大量的热，并将其变成制冷剂蒸气的热能。该蒸气可压缩并在车外冷凝，当它凝结时，它向外边的空气释放出潜热，然后制冷剂液体又被送回到车内并再次吸收热量而蒸发。

9.2.1.2 制冷流程

图 9-2 是 HVAC 系统空调部分的制冷剂流程图。该图显示了制冷剂在系统主要部件中如何流动。注意：系统通过压缩机和膨胀阀被分成了高压力和低压力区，并且通过蒸发器和压缩机被分成气态和液态。制冷剂连续循环地流动：

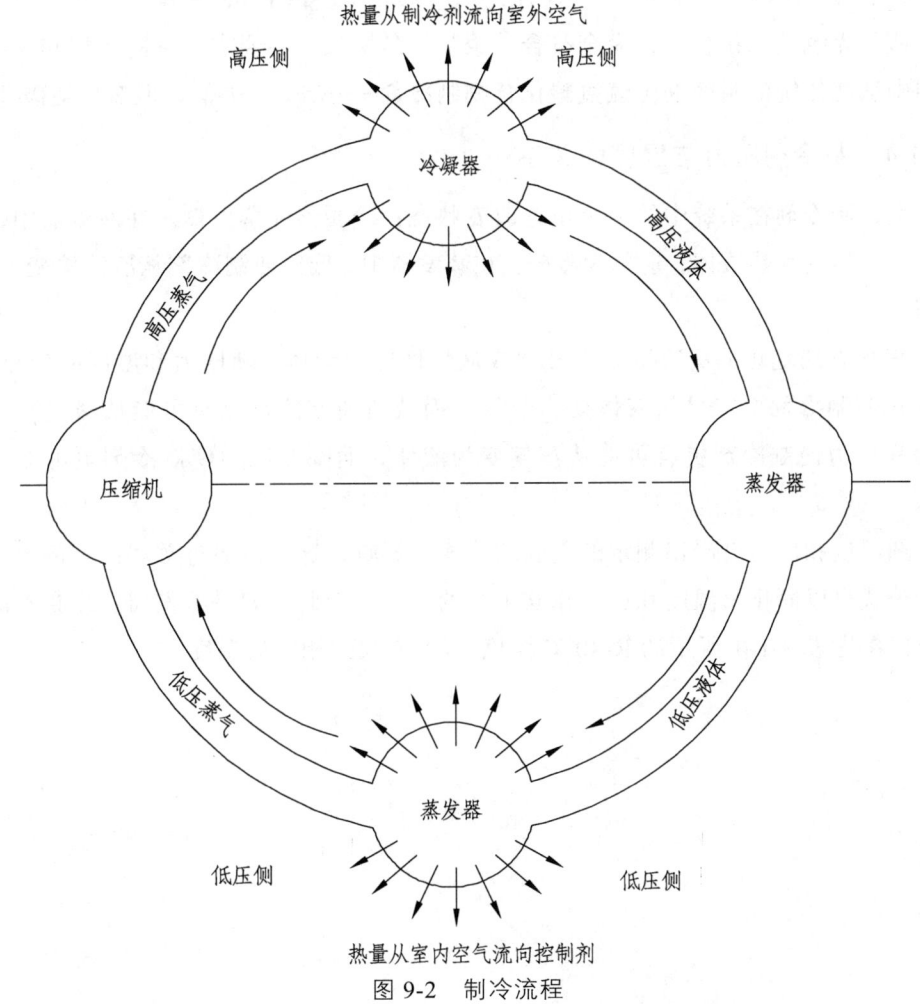

图 9-2 制冷流程

（1）在蒸发器中吸热由液态变为气态；
（2）通过压缩机使压力增高；
（3）在冷凝器中释放热量，由气态变回液态；
（4）在膨胀阀中使液体压力降低。

9.2.1.3 制冷剂

制冷循环是基于这样一个原理，即挥发性液体可在蒸发器部分通过从液体变为气态来吸热。有很多液体可以通过汽化吸热，但其中有些更适合用于制冷是因为它们的物理和化学特点。HVAC 系统中使用的制冷剂（R-407C）应具有以下性质：

- 不易燃、非爆炸性、无毒；
- 稳定（不能和设备中使用的物质结合）；
- 只需要低或中等工作压力；
- 更容易获得。

HVAC 系统使用制冷剂 R-407C（$CH_2F_2/CHF_2CF_3/CH_2FCF_3$），它是一种零 ODP（臭氧损耗潜势）值的无氯碳氟化合物，完全符合《蒙特利尔协议》的要求。它的特性和性能类似于该类应用中那些传统的制冷剂（氯氟碳化合物制冷剂——CFC）类似，但对环境破坏小。

9.2.1.4 制冷剂压力与温度的关系

请注意，制冷剂在系统中的两个位置改变状态：冷凝器和蒸发器。在冷凝器中，高压使制冷剂从热气体变为热液体，这称为冷凝。在蒸发器中，低压使制冷剂从冷液体变为冷气体，这称为蒸发。

制冷剂状态的变化（从液体变为气体或从气体变为液体）随压力和温度的变化而变化。首先，加热使制冷剂更容易从液体变为蒸气，而放热使制冷剂更有可能从蒸气变为液体。其次，提高压力使制冷剂更有可能从蒸气变为液体，而降低压力使制冷剂更可能从液体变为蒸气。

制冷剂温度和压力沿严格测定的曲线的线相互影响，这可以通过关联两者的公式进行预测。这些公式可以简化为温度和压力相互关联的图表。因此，如果蒸发器和冷凝器的压力已知，则可以参考表 9-1 中所示的 R-407C 温度-压力来找到相应的温度。

表 9-1 R-407C（湿蒸气）温度 - 压力

温度 (°C)	温度 (°F)	蒸气压力 (PSI)	温度 (°C)	温度 (°F)	蒸气压力 (PSI)
-31.7	-25	3.6	18.3	65	104.8
-28.9	-20	6.1	21.1	70	115.2
-26.1	-15	8.8	23.9	75	126.2
-23.3	-10	11.9	26.7	80	137.8
-20.5	-5	15.2	29.4	85	150.2
-17.8	0	18.9	32.2	90	163.4
-15	5	22.9	35	95	177.4
-12.2	10	27.3	37.8	100	192.1
-9.4	15	32.0	40.6	105	207.8
-6.7	20	37.2	43.3	110	224.4
-3.9	25	42.7	46.1	115	241.9
-1.1	30	48.7	48.9	120	260.5
1.7	35	55.2	51.7	125	280.1
4.4	40	62.1	54.4	130	300.9
7.2	45	69.5	57.2	135	322.9
10	50	77.5	60	140	346.2
12.8	55	86.0	62.8	145	370.8
15.6	60	95.1	65.5	150	396.9

使用相同的图表，可以根据温度确定任何部件内部的压力。例如，此表允许技师通过读取蒸发器中制冷剂的压力来确定其温度，允许两到三度的温差通过蒸发器金属进行传热，使技师可以通过找到蒸发器压力来确定离开蒸发器的空气的近似温度。

9.2.2 电加热器原理

电加热器根据电阻原理来工作。电阻（单位为Ω）是电的三个主要特性之一，它与电压和经过电路中特定点的电子数（电流或安培数）一起被测量。这些电气特性决定了在电热器线圈中产生热量。

9.2.2.1 电流和电阻

电流被认为是由原子间移动的电子组成的。它以安培（A）为单位测量。引起电子移动的电压力称为电压。允许电子流动的物质称为导体。当电流流过任何类型的导体时，导体材料的自然电阻与之相阻碍。这种电阻是由原子不愿意放弃或接受电子引起的。

利用电压推动电子对抗电阻的一个副作用是产生热量。这种热可以被认为是由于试图通过不情愿原子的电子的摩擦引起的。因此，使用高压推动许多电子通过高电阻导体可以产生大量热量。在许多电路中，热量是多余的，如果不清除，会严重损坏设备。然而，电加热器总成的设计目的是从可用电流中产生尽可能多的热量。

9.2.2.2 电加热器基本结构

电加热器组件是由车载交流电压供电的一个完整电路。电加热器绕组的组件是由金属合金组成的，该金属合金则是由非常不愿意提供电子的原子构成，有很高的电阻。

当电流在电源电压作用下流过加热器线圈时，电子和原子之间的摩擦产生热量，称为电阻热。电阻热使线圈变得非常热。通风机使空气流过线圈上方，盘管的热量在空气通过加热器盘管时传递给空气。然后，暖风送入乘客室。为确保线圈不会过热，线圈电路与通风机系统联锁。因此，除非鼓风机电机运行，否则线圈无法加热。线圈还包含热保护装置：一个过热恒温器和两个过热熔断丝。

9.3 空气调节单元机组

制冷循环如图9-3所示，主要部件在图中亦有标出。

离开蒸发器的低压蒸气流被吸入压缩机（1）。在压缩过程中，蒸气压力增加，温度升高，它们是车内和车外环境温度的函数。经过压缩的蒸汽温度比凝结温度高。位于系统高低压区之间的一个旁路电磁阀（14）根据蒸发器的实际热负载调整压缩机排气量。压缩机在进气管路有一个吸气减振器（13），在输出管道有一个排风减振器（2）和止回阀（3）。止回阀有一个带强制关闭的浮式活塞来确保进入冷凝旋管的制冷剂在停车时不会逆流回压缩机。压缩机排出的高压高温蒸气流经止回阀（3）后，进入冷凝盘管（4）。

制冷剂蒸气从压缩机进入冷凝盘管（4），流向充气阀（6）、干燥过滤器（7）和观察孔/湿度指示器（8）。冷凝盘管和散热片肋片从制冷剂蒸气中吸走热量。当高压高温蒸气经过每个冷凝器的盘管时，外部空气由电动冷凝器风扇吹经盘管和散热片，这样流经冷凝盘管的空气就带走了制冷剂中的热量。这样冷凝器就带走制冷剂由蒸发器从车内吸收的那部分热量。当从蒸气中带走热量时，蒸气经由冷凝风扇冷却凝结，温度降低到所能达到的最低温度。

充气阀用来实现抽真空和重新充注制冷剂等维修操作。

通过湿度观察孔可以检查系统中液体制冷剂的相对干燥值（含湿量），也可通过观察孔检测制冷剂是否过少或过多。这些状况由制冷剂中的可见气泡流来显示，可通过观察孔看到。

观察孔出口的制冷剂液体然后流经液体管路上的电磁阀（9）。这些阀是由微处理器激活，用来控制制冷剂流入两个蒸发器盘管，这样就可实现全冷却或部分冷却的控制。由液体管路电磁阀出来的制冷剂液通过热力膨胀阀（10）引导流入相应的蒸发器盘管。

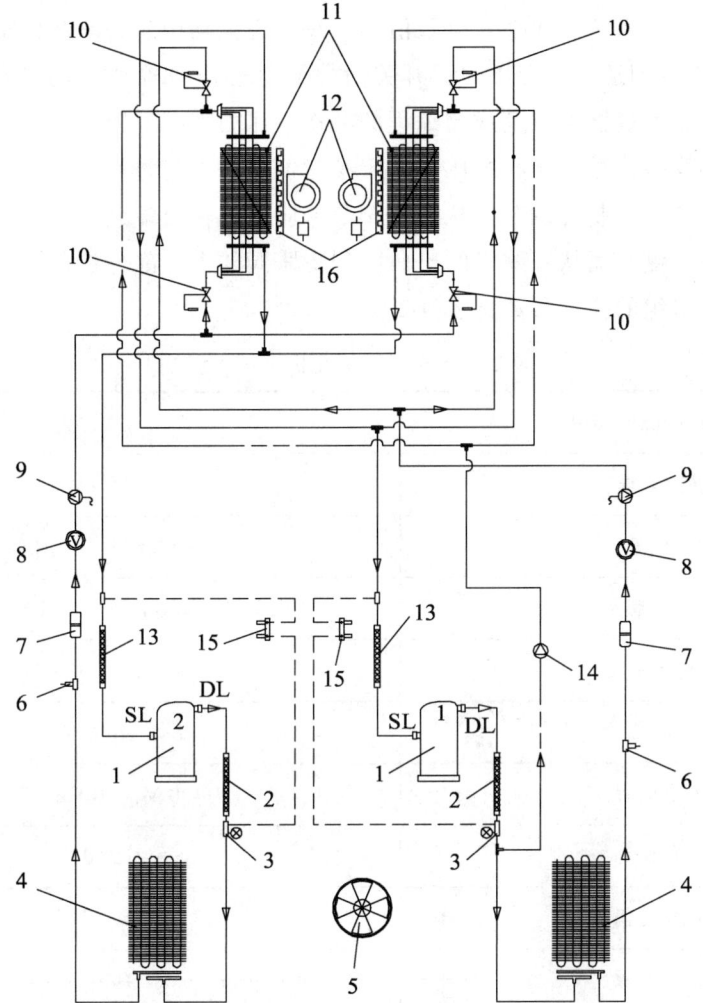

1—压缩机；2—排风减振器；3—止回阀；4—冷凝旋管；5—冷凝器风扇电机；6—充气阀；7—脱水过滤器；
8—湿度观察孔；9—液体管线电磁阀；10—温度调节装置膨胀阀；11—蒸发器旋管；12—蒸发器送风机电机；
13—抽风减振器；14—旁路电磁阀；15—制冷控制器；16—电热器组件。

图 9-3 空气调节单元机组工作原理示意图

热力膨胀阀有两个功能：

a. 降低蒸发器盘管中制冷剂发生相变（蒸发）所需的压力。

b. 调节制冷剂量流入量以产生期望的车内空气冷却效果。这些空气是由蒸发器通风机驱动，流经蒸发器盘管（11）。

液体制冷剂通过膨胀阀进入分配管，并进入蒸发器盘管（11）。分配管确保了制冷剂在蒸发盘管中的平均分配。蒸发器是一个由铜管和铝散热片组成的热交换器。

当膨胀阀调节进入蒸发器的液体制冷剂时，压力迅速降低。快速的压力降和从车内吸收的热量使得低压制冷剂蒸发，同时使车内温度下降。

制冷控制器（15）作用于制冷循环的整个压缩过程中，控制器包括两个压力开关和两个压力传感器。压力开关是当制冷剂压力达到一个高压或低压限值时而被激活的安全设备。这就确保了压缩机和整个系统工作在安全限值内。每个开关均由压力激活，被激活时，开关开路（断开）。当压力返回适当的范围时，开关闭合（接入）。每个开关的打开或闭合状态都送给微处理器，然后微处理器可以完成预编程的动作。压力传感器监测吸风和排风压力并生成一个正比于压力的模拟信号。当吸风压力低于参考值或高压超过参考值时，在达到切断开关限值之前温度控制器进行制冷调节。从温度调节膨胀阀的输出端到压缩机输入端，这个制冷回路部分被称为低压侧，而从压缩机的出口阀到膨胀阀的入口部分被称为高压侧。

空气调节单元机组的技术参数见表 9-2。

表 9-2 空气调节单元机组技术参数

参数	数值
制冷容量（text = 40°）	44 kW
供热容量	29 kW
总风量	4300 m^3/h（±10%）
新风量（制冷）	1 400 m^3/h（±10%）
回风量（制冷）	2900 m^3/h（±10）
制冷剂	R-407C
交流电源	400 V，50 Hz，3 相
电压容许偏差	±10%
频率容许偏差	±5%
直流电源	24 VDC

9.3.1 压缩机

压缩机吸入来自蒸发器盘管的低压冷空气并进行压缩，转变为过热的高压气体。

本单元采用的压缩机是涡旋式，COPELAND 公司的 ZR125-KCE-TFD-522（图 9-4）。该型号压缩机几乎没有可移动零件，没有动态的进气阀、排风阀。此外，其具有极低的振动量和噪声，并对普通制冷系统中常见的液体沉淀物、启动时的液体溢出及碎片和磨屑等引起的应力有很强的耐受能力。

两个压缩机均安装于一个压缩机工作台上。该工作台由四个减振器连接在单元上以消除振动和噪声。

压缩机抽风和排风管道配有软管减振器来减少磨损并降低振动和噪声。抽风管道减振器直径为 35 mm，而排风管的直径则为 Ø22。

制冷控制器安装在压缩机旁。每个压缩机的控制器包括两个高、低压压力开关和两个高、低压传感器。

压力开关属于安全设备,当制冷剂压力降至低于最小(低压)或超过最大(高压)时动作。这样就确保了两个压缩机和系统在安全限值内工作。当压力开关激活时,开关开路(切断);当压力回到允许限值时,开关闭合(切入)。每个开关的开闭状态的信息均会输送给微处理器,然后微处理器就可以按预定程序来执行。

压力传感器感知进风和排风压力并生成一个正比于相应压力的模拟信号。当进风压力低于参考值或高压超出参考值时,在达到开关限值之前先由温度控制器进行调节。

此外,压力控制器组件包括接入口用于和快速压力表连接,也方便维护保养操作。

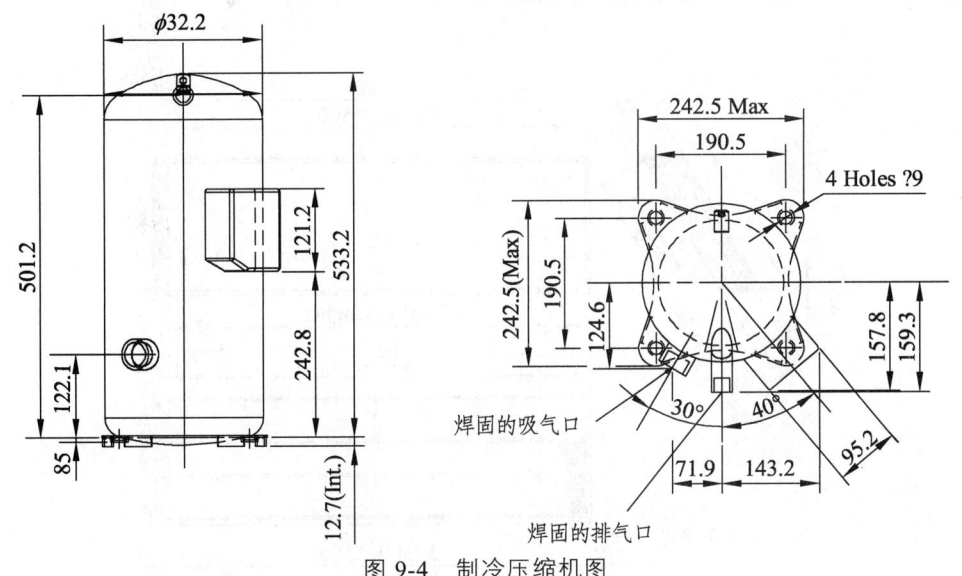

图 9-4 制冷压缩机图

制冷压缩机技术参数如表 9-3 所示。

表 9-3 制冷压缩机技术参数

型号	Copeland ZR125-KCE-TFD-522
类型	涡旋式
制冷剂	R-407C
功率调节类型	热空气旁路
电压	400 V(±10%),3 相
频率	50 Hz(±5%)
油量	3.25 L
油类型	多元酯醇 Copeland 3 MA(32 cSt)
数量	2

9.3.2 冷凝器

9.3.2.1 冷凝盘管

从压缩机出来的高温高压气体流至冷凝盘管。由于制冷剂温度远高于环境气温，在流经盘管时其热量排放到周围空气中。制冷剂蒸气温度显著降低，发生凝结。

每个冷凝盘管是由一组直径 3/8"的并排的铜管组成。铜管等距平行排列并与气流方向垂直，并带有间距 2.5 mm、与管道垂直排列的 0.18 mm 铝散热片。

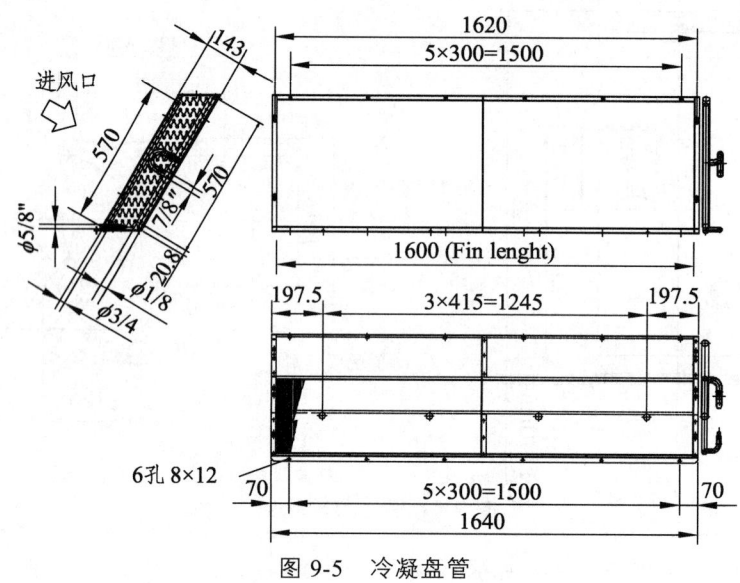

图 9-5 冷凝盘管

冷凝盘管的技术参数如表 9-4 所示。

表 9-4 冷凝盘管技术参数

型号	24T-6F-1600 L
管子、弯管，连接器，集流器	铜
管子直径 φ	3/8"
散热片	铝，0.18 mm 厚
散热片距离	2.5 mm
构架	镀锌钢材板 1 mm 厚
扣件和铆钉	不锈钢
测试压力	30 °C 时，水中 3 MPa
数量	2

9.3.2.2 冷凝风扇及电机组件

为在盘管获得更多热交换表面，风扇将外面周围的空气吹过冷凝盘管。该组件包括一个轴流式风扇，外直径为 750 mm，由 5 个倾角为 37°的叶片组成。风扇由一个 IP-56 保护、F 级绝缘的异步电机（1.8/1.3 kW，AC400 V，3 相，50 Hz）带动。

9.3.3 干燥过滤器

干燥过滤器的目的是滤出管道系统中可能的任何固体颗粒（灰尘、铁锈、焊接微粒等）。它也黏滞制冷回路中难以避免的湿气和酸性物质。

HVAC 单元的每个制冷回路装于冷凝旋管出口处的液体管路上都有一个干燥过滤器。该过滤器由一个实心干燥筒（由硅胶和活性氧化铝混合物组成）和一个金属过滤器组成（参阅图 9-6）。

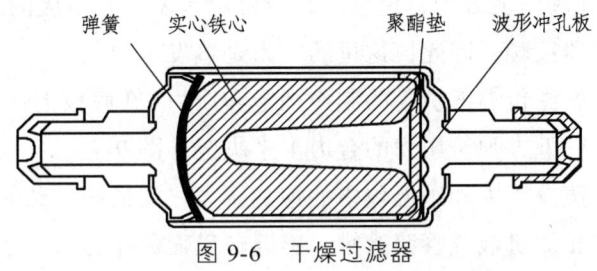

图 9-6 干燥过滤器

9.3.4 蒸发器

9.3.4.1 蒸发器盘管

蒸发器盘管由一组 1/2"直径的铜管组成，带 0.1 mm 厚、间距 2.5 mm 的铝散热片。制冷剂液体流过蒸发盘管，当液体蒸发时，盘管和肋片就被制冷剂冷却，循环的空气在吹入客室前经过蒸发器的盘管和肋片的冷却。

盘管由一个温度调节装置膨胀阀供气。膨胀阀通过蒸发器的毛细管的小分配孔均匀地分配制冷剂，因此制冷剂流经时就会有一个压力降，制冷剂的温度因此而下降。

表 9-5 蒸发器盘管技术参数

型号	10T-4F-1175 L
管子、弯管，连接器，集流器	铜
管子直径 ϕ	1/2"
散热片	铝，0.18 mm 厚
散热片之间的距离	2.5 mm
构架	镀锌钢板，1 mm 厚
扣件和铆钉	不锈钢
测试压力	30° C 时，水中 3 MPa
数量	2

9.3.4.2 蒸发器通风机

冷却处理过的空气由两个包括离心式通风机压入车内。该离心风扇带镀锌板叶片和装于三相单轴电机（400 V， 50 Hz 时 0.75 kW，转速 1，500r/min）上的铸钢轮毂。

9.3.5 热力膨胀阀

热力膨胀阀可使适量的液体流入蒸发盘管，从而使制冷剂在流过出口时得到恰当的蒸发。同时，它也确保了制冷系统高低压侧之间有足够的压差。

为实现这个目的，这个阀须由一个阀体和通过毛细管连接的感温包组成。阀体安装在液体管路上，感温包固定在蒸发器出口上，在吸入管路上。感温包中含有少量制冷剂。感温包内的自由空间、毛细管和阀门上方的自由空间在与感温包温度相对应的压力下充满饱和蒸汽。膜板下方的空间与蒸发器接触，因此，这里的压力是蒸发压力。

阀门的打开程度由感温包温度引起的制冷剂饱和压力（在膜板上侧）和膜板下的压力（蒸发压力与作用于膜板上的下方弹簧压力的合力）来决定（图 9-7）。

因此，蒸发器中的蒸发压力和感温包中的饱和压力之间的压差致使热力膨胀阀动作。由于感温包和蒸发器出口压缩机吸气管路接触，感温包里面的压力取决于吸气管路的温度，这样就可以进行制冷剂流量的控制。

热力膨胀阀设有外平衡管，它连接蒸发器出口，位置靠近感温包的外平衡管是用来补偿分配器和蒸发器盘管引起的压降。液体分配器的作用是均衡地分配到制冷盘管的制冷剂流量。

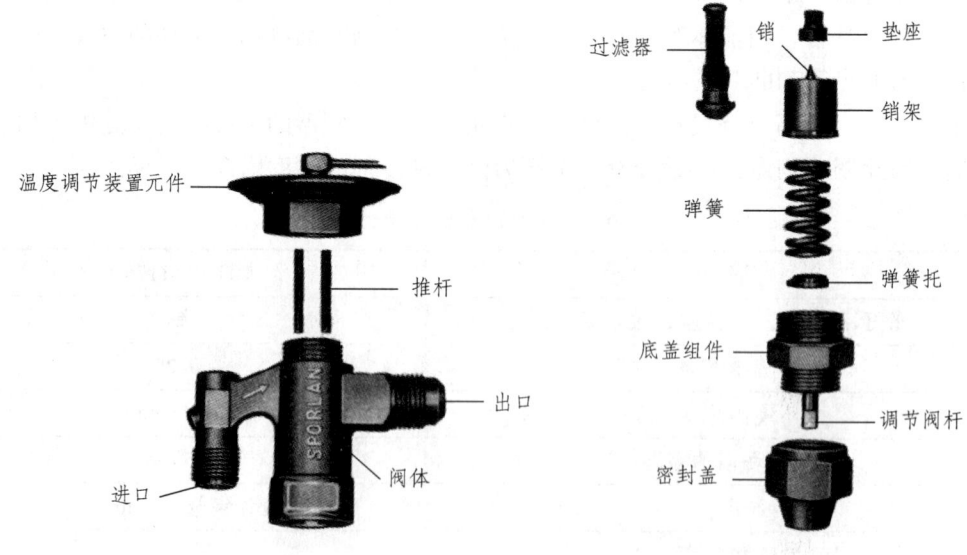

图 9-7　膨胀阀

膨胀阀的技术参数见表 9-6。

表 9-6　膨胀阀技术参数

连接器	1/2" ~ 5/8"，焊接
蒸发温度	－50℃ ~ +10℃
注入气体	由制冷剂再加热控制
均压器	外部
球体的最大温度	100 ℃
最大测试压力	2.8 MPa
数量	4

9.3.6　空气加热器组件

HVAC 单元组件包括两个并联的电热器，它们与蒸发器平行安装，用 29 kW 车顶供热功率供给乘客系统。

每个空气加热器组都由两个安全温度调节装置进行过热保护。第一个调节装置会在温度达到 90 ℃ 时断开加热接触器，当温度降到安全工作限值（69 ℃）时，重新接通。

如果温度达到 125 ℃，第二个安全温度调节装置使空气加热断路器跳闸。HVAC 控制器将会通过 MVB 发送故障信息。

9.3.7　电子电器控制面板

基于微处理器的控制系统可控制所有的常用功能：预处理、通风、制冷、供热，并通过 MVB 接口向列车网络提供信息。

控制面板内安装有各种必需的电气元件（接触器、继电器、断路器等）来控制客室的各种工作模式，而司机室的控制面板内还安装压力波控制系统。

控制器接收不同传感器发送的温度信号并发送需要的指令来触发各种工况下所涉及的元件，以便在给定时间内达到车厢的设定温度。

此外，该电子控制装置还执行其他功能，比如，在一个寄存器中存储压缩机电机工作时间、记录将来用于维护或检查空气调节单元机组工作性能的主要温度值。

存储器中储存的数据可以通过一个带特定软件程序的进行读取或处理，该程序是专门开发用于预防性维护的。

9.3.8 压力波保护系统

客室内强烈的气压变化会给乘客带来不舒服感,压力波保护系统的用途是避免车内强烈的压力变化。该系统由以下部分组成:
- 安装在端车(MC1 和 MC2)前面部分的 4 个压力波传感器,每侧各一个。也即每辆端车两个传感器,每列车共有 4 个。
- 安装在 MC1 和 MC2 车控制面板内的 2 个电子控制板(每列车 2 个控制板)。
- 安装在所有车上的新风进气口和排风口的快速动作风门,以及安装在 HVAC 单元内的排风风门。

压力波传感器电气连接于相应的控制板上。这样,外部压力的任何大的变化都会被压力波控制板存储和处理。控制板还会给排风风门和新气风门机械驱动装置发送一个驱动信号以迅速关闭风门。

压力波控制板生成一个输出信号。该信号经由与所有车组内车辆的排风和新风风门驱动装置连接的列车电线来传输,以便优化响应时间。

10 高速动车组服务系统

动车组服务系统包括旅客信息系统、照明系统、厨房设备、给水装置、卫生系统。旅客信息系统的主要作用是引导旅客顺利抵达目的地，并在旅途中给旅客提供高品质的娱乐性服务；而照明系统则是保证旅客在乘车过程中拥有充足的光源，可以进行阅读、娱乐及其他活动；由于动车组运用的特点，厨房设备一方面强调车上饮食的安全卫生，另一方面由于动车本身行程时间短，快捷也成为重要的技术要求；给水装置则是依据厨房用水、卫生用水及饮用水三大方面对其的组成结构进行介绍；卫生系统重点突出了它与众不同的人性化设施，使动车组卫生系统的优势一目了然。

10.1 旅客信息系统

旅客信息系统（Passenger Information System，简称 PIS），通过声音和视觉信息使旅客在旅途中及时准确地了解旅途相关信息，引导旅客顺利地抵达目的地，同时，使旅客旅途生活更安全、舒适、便利。PIS 从功能可分为：通告与通信子系统，信息显示子系统，影音娱乐子系统。

10.1.1 通告与通信子系统

通告与通信子系统由以下主要部件组成：PIS 控制器（STC）、PIS 人机交互界面（PIS-MMI）、PIS 的车辆控制器（CCT）、内部通信站、防火箱、扬声器、GPS 天线、GSM 天线、UIC 总线、PIS 数据总线等。如图 10-1 所示。

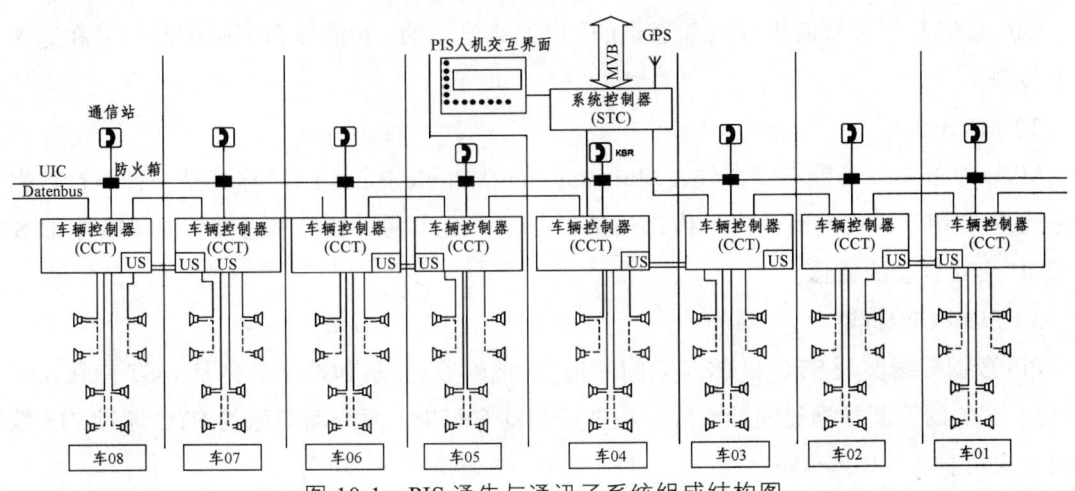

图 10-1 PIS 通告与通讯子系统组成结构图

1. 系统控制器（STC）

STC 是整个信息系统 PIS 的控制核心，也是 PIS 与列车控制网络连接的桥梁。它负责处理来自 MVB 总线、PIS 中的设备，以及属于该系统的 GSM 天线、GPS 天线、FM 天线等设备传来的信息，处理后发出相应控制指令或相关信息到相应目标处。同时，在 STC 内有掉电保持功能的存储器，可存储重要的操作数据，同时也使得 PIS 在电源出现故障时可自动恢复到之前的状态。

2. PIS 的人机交互界面（PIS-MMI）

PIS-MMI 是 PIS 与人实时交流的主要接口，它负责把 PIS 或控制网络传来的的信息反馈给操作人员，同时也把操作人员的要求传给 PIS 系统。

3. PIS 的车辆控制器（CCT）

每个车厢都装有 CCT，并且都能通过唯一的地址经由 PIS 数据总线和 STC 通讯。

4. 内部通讯站、防火箱、扬声器

每节车厢的内部通讯子系统都包含有一个内部通讯站和防火箱及连着扬声器的 CCT，CCT 与防火箱都安装在 PIS 柜中，各车的防火箱都连在 UIC 总线上。

5. GPS 天线、GSM 天线

GPS 天线、GSM 天线接收必要的信号，并传到 STC 中由其进一步处理，GPS 传输的信息保证到达或经过指定的行车位置时触发通告和可能的内容显示，GSM 可以接收数字语音通知(DVA)及广告文字信息给 STC，供其处理。

6. 总线系统

1）UIC 总线

UIC 总线是用来做通告和内部通讯的。内部通讯站的 LF 信号和个别控制信号在这条总线上传输。

2）MVB 总线

MVB 总线是多功能车辆总线（Multifunction Vehicle Bus）的简称，是一种串行数据通信总线，主要用于固定编组的车辆内部通信，是动车组车辆级的控制总线，是 PIS 中的 STC 与 CCU 交互信息的通道。

3）PIS 数据总线

PIS 数据总线实现 STC 和 CCT 之间的通讯。把配置、显示和控制数据从 CCT 传到 STC，同时把 CCT 的诊断数据传输给 STC。在重联的动车组上，两个动车组的 STC 通过 PIS 数据总线交换信息。

通告和通信子系统的功能分为通告和内部通信的基本功能、通告扩展功能。通告和内部通信的基本功能在每个单动车组内都是可用的。重联的动车组中，每个动车组和整列车的基本功能也同样可用。通告的基本功能主要有全列通告、可选通告、某个 CCT 故障时的通告。基本通信功能是通过内部通信站上的拨号键实现各通信站的拨号，在单动车组或重联动车组都可实现。但此功能仅在连接了 CCT 的情况下可用，一旦 CCT 因故障失效，此功能将不可用。

通告扩展功能只能由列车乘务区的内部通信站发起。有三类选择：一是到全部动车组或者相邻的动车组里的扬声器；二是到操作人员所在动车组或者与之联挂的动车组通告车厢的选择；三是到操作人员所在动车组或者与之联挂的动车组通告级别的选择。

10.1.2　信息显示子系统

信息显示子系统的主要功能是向乘客信息显示器、列车侧面目的地显示器传输显示内容及显示指令。乘客信息显示器所显示的内容（停车站向导、新闻、广告等）在地面计算机进行编辑后，存储到 IC 存储卡中。通过司机室 IC 卡读写装置读出，输入到列车信息控制装置中，发出车号信息显示器的显示信息及指令。其组成部分主要有：单色 LED 信息显示器、相关通信总线、GSM 天线、GPS 天线、CCT。如图 10-2 所示。

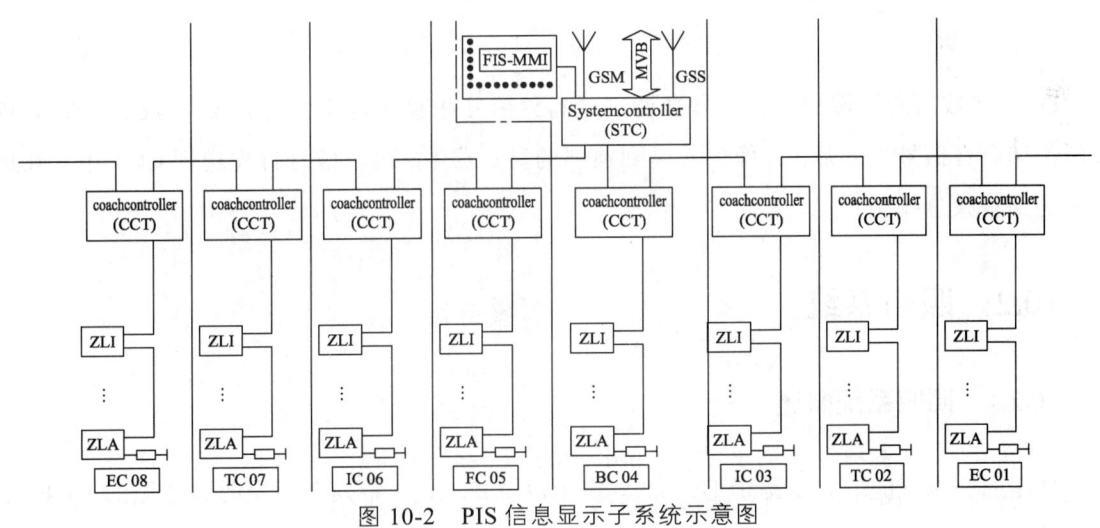

图 10-2　PIS 信息显示子系统示意图

每节车厢的显示系统包含列车外部信息显示、列车内部信息显示、显示总线。显示的控制可分为两种不同的模式，分别是自动显示控制（正常模式）和手工显示控制（仅用在列车内部显示）。

10.1.3 影音娱乐子系统

该系统主要是为了使一等车（FC05）中的乘客更舒适，在旅途中可以进行音乐或视频方面的娱乐。它分为两个子系统：音频系统和视频系统。

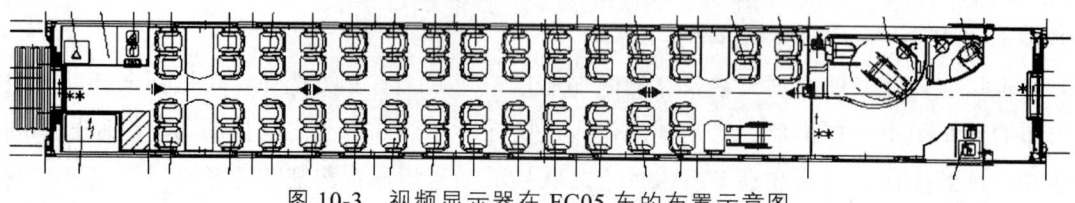

图 10-3　视频显示器在 FC05 车的布置示意图

工作过程如下：

1. 音　频

SCT 将 UKW 无线电接收器或 MP3 播放器的 LF 信号通过音频总线以数字信号形式传输到 CCT 中，并在那里与视频中的声音信号一起经过 PIS-MMI 选择后传到 FC05 车上座椅中的 AEU，并且传到顶部的扬声器中（背景音乐）。

LF 信号是以模拟信号形式从每个 AEU 的耳机中传出去的。每位乘客能够通过键盘单独地改变声音频道和音量。背景音乐的音量仅能由每个动车组的 PIS-MMI 来改变。

2. 视　频

DVD 播放器的影像和声音信号被调制成高频信号并通过同轴线缆被送到 VDR。在 VDR 中影像和声音信号被分开：影像信号送到顶部的显示器中，声音信号首先送到 CCT 中并在那里传送到音频总线。

10.2　照明系统

10.2.1　照明系统概述

列车照明系统的电力来源于 DC110 V 电源以及蓄电池。整列车的照明布置见图 10-4。由图可见，普通照明布置在车顶中部以及侧墙与车顶交接处，这些照明一般采用荧光灯，由 110 V 直流转换成 220 V 交流电。在车内座椅上方还有阅读灯，在餐车采用卤化物灯，这些照明由 110 V 直流转换成 24 V 直流电供电。

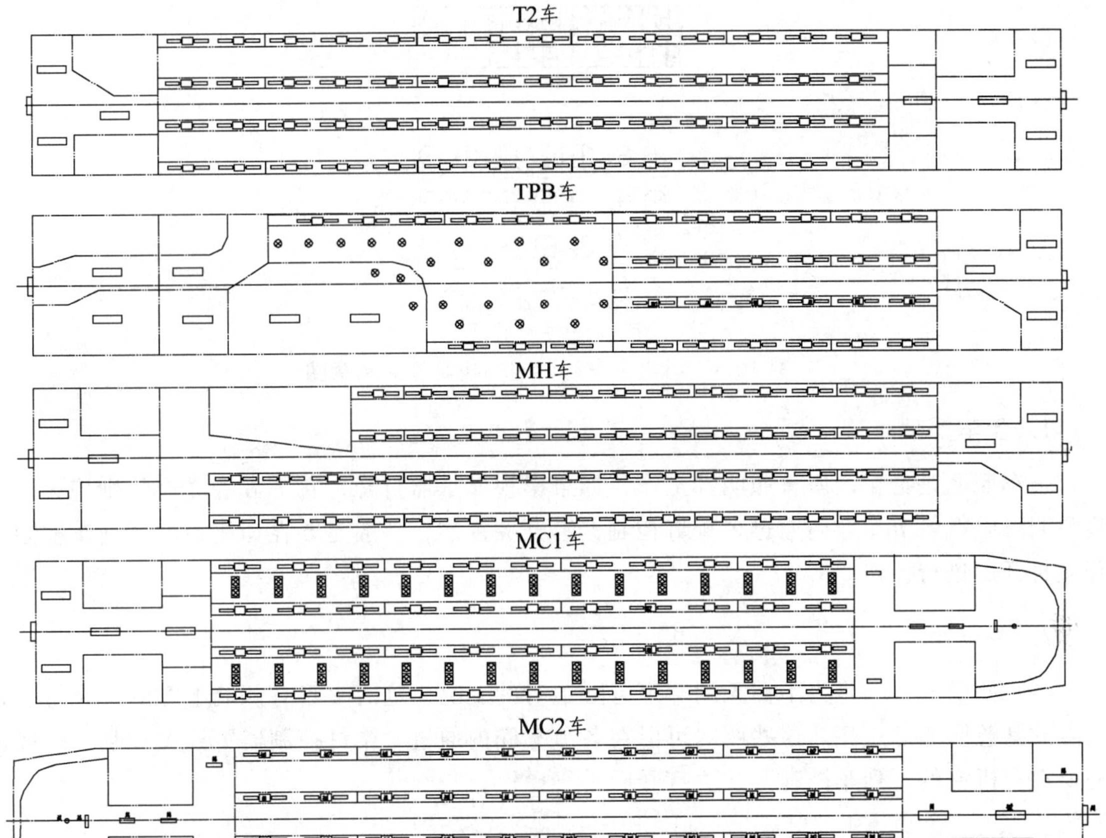

图 10-4 整列车的照明布置结构图

车内照明控制开关根据照明的种类分为全车照明、半车照明、夜晚照明、紧急照明和故障显示等。照明既可以在各节车厢内控制,也可以由司机室控制,如图 10-5 所示。

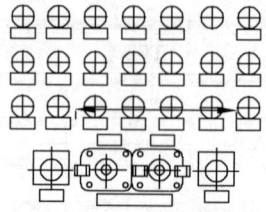

图 10-5 司机室车厢内照明控制开关示意图

1. 全车照明

全车照明是指车内所有照明都工作，如果影视显示器打开，它上方的 2 个灯则熄灭。这些照明可以在各节车厢内通过"全灯控制器"开关控制，一般是要在司机室的"列车控制"开关打开后进行操作。

2. 半车照明

半车照明的目的是为了白天列车穿越隧道时的工况，这时，只有侧墙上方的荧光灯、车顶内的紧急照明灯点亮。这些照明可以在各节车厢内通过"半灯控制器"开关控制，一般也是要在司机室的"列车控制"开关打开后进行操作。

3. 夜晚照明

夜晚照明由乘务员室内的开关控制，这时只有车顶内的紧急照明灯、侧墙和厕所的部分灯点亮。夜晚照明开关不受司机室内的总开关控制。

4. 紧急照明

紧急照明是在紧急状态下自动点亮的，同时，门口及厕所的部分灯也在紧急照明时点亮。

5. 司机室照明

司机室照明由司机操纵台上的"司机室灯控制器"开关控制，位置见图 10-6 中三波段开关，它可以使司机左侧的灯单独亮，也可以使司机室内的 2 个灯都亮。

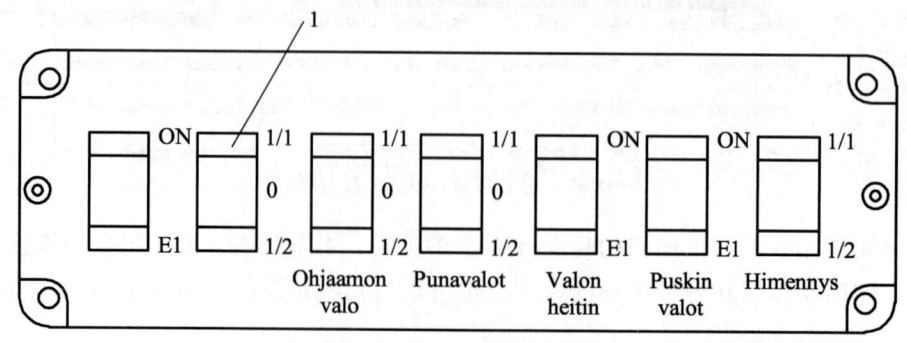

图 10-6 司机室照明控制示意图

6. 关灯操作

车内照明可以由开关"灯光关闭控制"关闭，司机室内可以通过"全灯控制器"开关将整列车的照明关闭。餐车、乘务员室的照明有自己的控制开关。

7. 阅读灯

阅读灯安装在座椅上方的行李架内，开关与灯安装在一起，由乘客自己控制。

8. 餐车照明

在餐车除了有荧光灯以外，还有卤化物灯。这些灯的照明由餐车配电盘单独控制。

10.2.2 照明的维护

一般当照明出现问题时，通常是灯管出现了问题，因此，首先需要更换灯管。当更换灯管不起作用时，可能是电源转换器出现了故障。而对于客室内的阅读灯和餐车内的射灯都采用 24 V 电压的卤化灯；当更换灯管不起作用时，可能是开关出现了故障。

10.3 厨房设施和设备

1. 厨房设施和设备的说明（图 10-7）

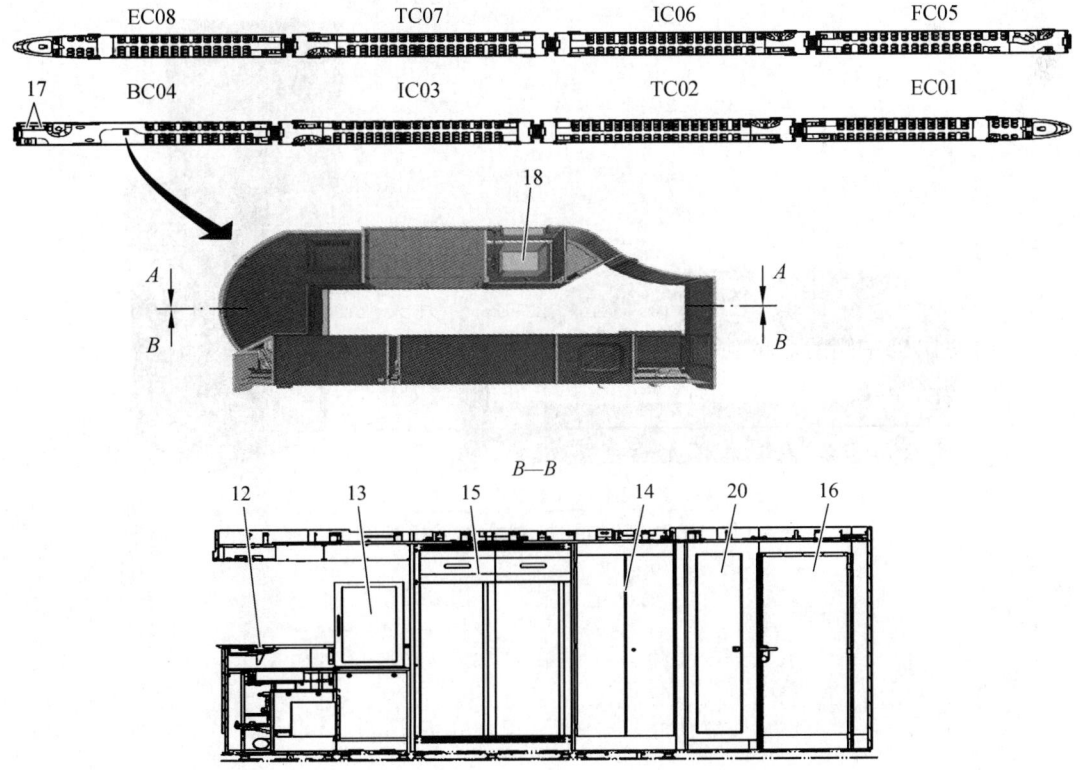

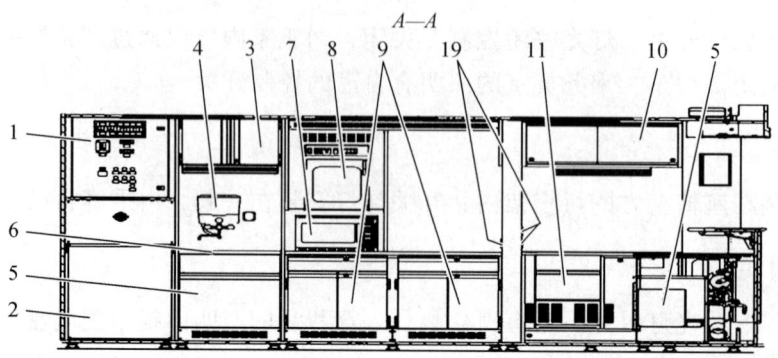

1—控制面板；2—垃圾车；3—壁柜；4—热水锅炉；5—废物抽屉；6—Sink/水槽；7—微波炉；8—蒸锅；9—储存舱；10—壁柜；11—制冰机；12—酒吧台；13—陈列柜；14—热水配送单元；15—冰箱单元；16—入口门；17—厨房仓库；18—热水配送器；19—电源插座；20—存衣柜。

图 10-7　厨房设施及设备结构图

1）门

通过乘客区/酒吧区的门进入厨房工作区。这个门在乘客区/酒吧区一侧有锁，因此，只有利用钥匙才能进入工作区。在工作区一侧没有门锁。

2）厨房单元

（1）废物和控制柜单元，如图10-8所示。

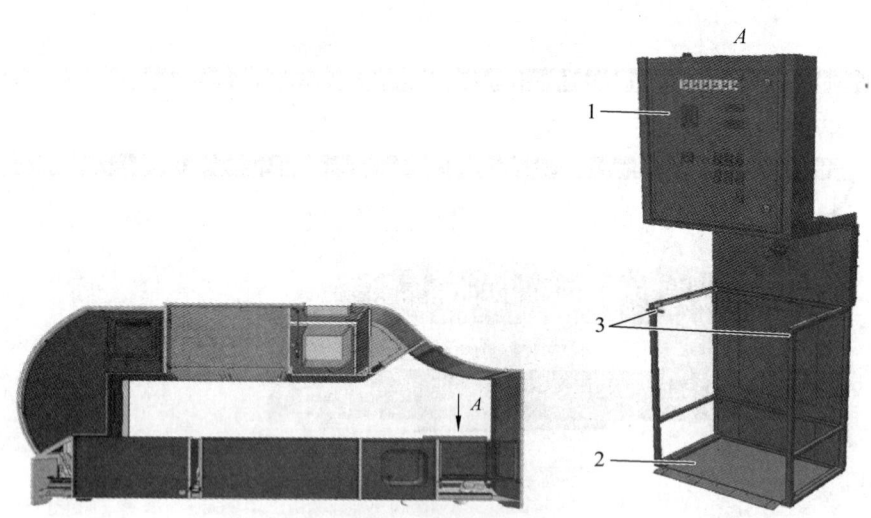

1—控制柜；2—两个垃圾车储存处；3—有锁车柜。

图 10-8　废物和控制柜单元模拟图

（2）水槽单元，如图10-9所示。

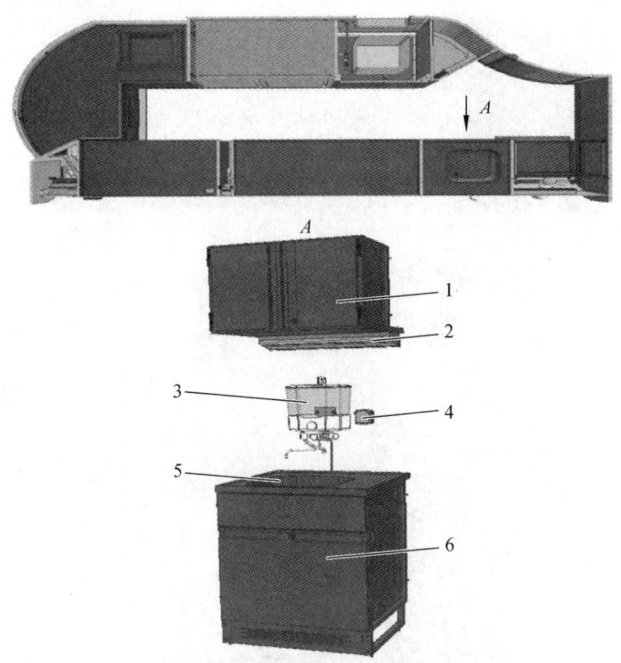

1—壁柜；2—工作区照明灯；3—热水锅炉；4—电源插座；5—水槽；6—废物抽屉
图10-9　水槽单元模拟图

（3）加热单元，如图10-10所示。

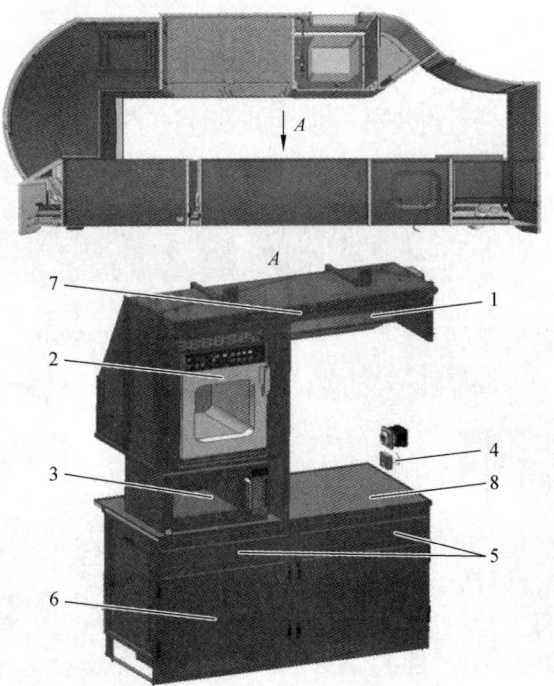

1—工作区照明灯；2—蒸锅；3—微波炉；4—电源插座；5—抽屉；6—储存舱；7—抽油烟机；8—操作台。
图10-10　加热单元模拟图

（4）冷、热饮料单元，如图 10-11 所示。

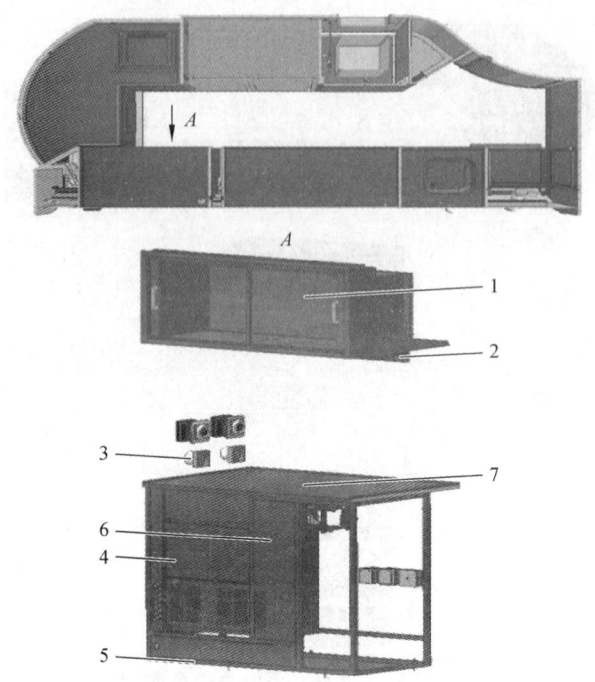

1—壁柜；2—工作区聚光灯；3—电源插座；4—制冰机；5—调节口；6—调节口；7—操作台。

图 10-11　冷、热饮料单元模拟图

（5）柜台单元，如图 10-12 所示。

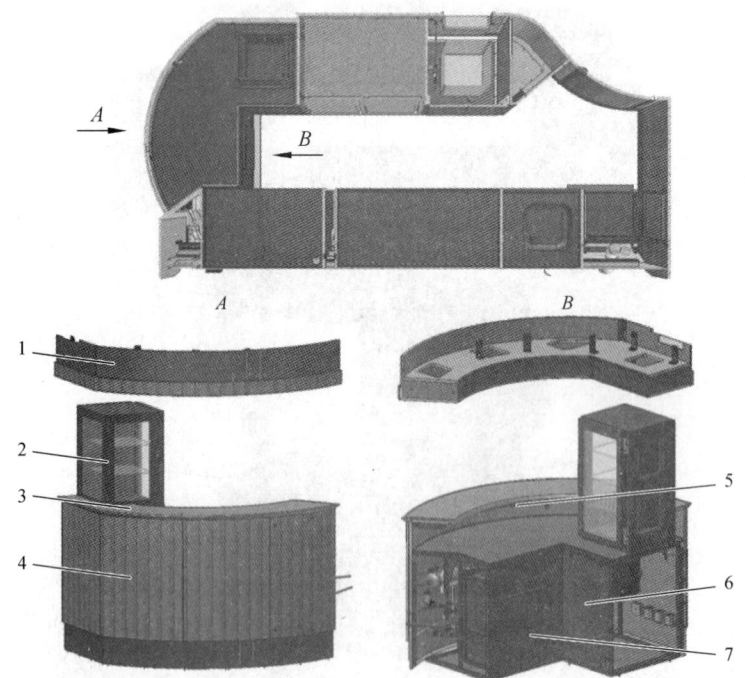

1—柜台上部结构；2—陈列柜；3—酒吧台；4—调节口；5—工作区聚光灯；6—调节口；7—废物抽屉。

图 10-12　柜台单元模拟图

（6）制冷单元，如图 10-13 所示。

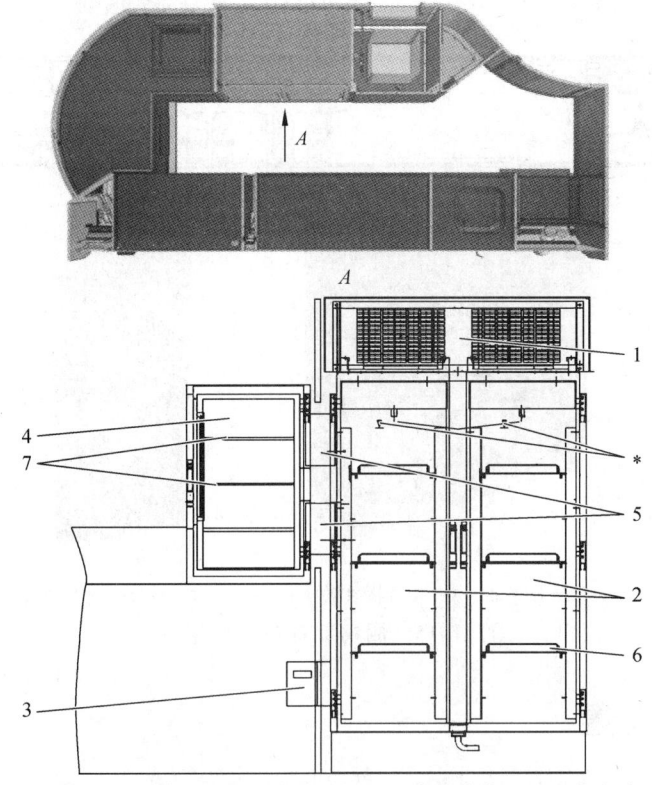

1—冷冻机组；2—冰箱；3—冰箱控制器；4—陈列柜；5—空气导管；6—格架支座；7—玻璃格架。

图 10-13　制冷单元结构图

（7）开水炉单元，如图 10-14 所示。

开水炉单元内装有一个热水面板。该单元利用两个推拉门关闭。用一个插销门锁（方形锁）锁住。

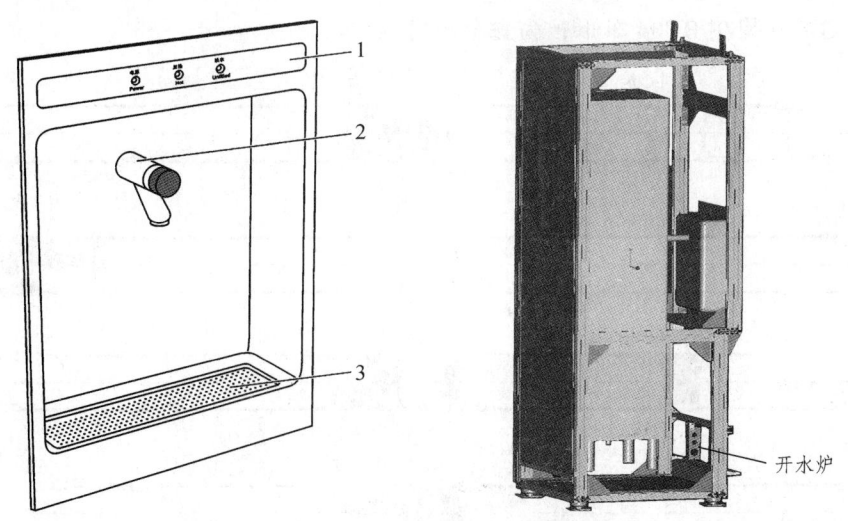

1—指示器板；2—水龙头；3—排水装置。

图 10-14　开水炉单元示意图及模拟图

（8）厨房储存单元，如图 10-15 所示。

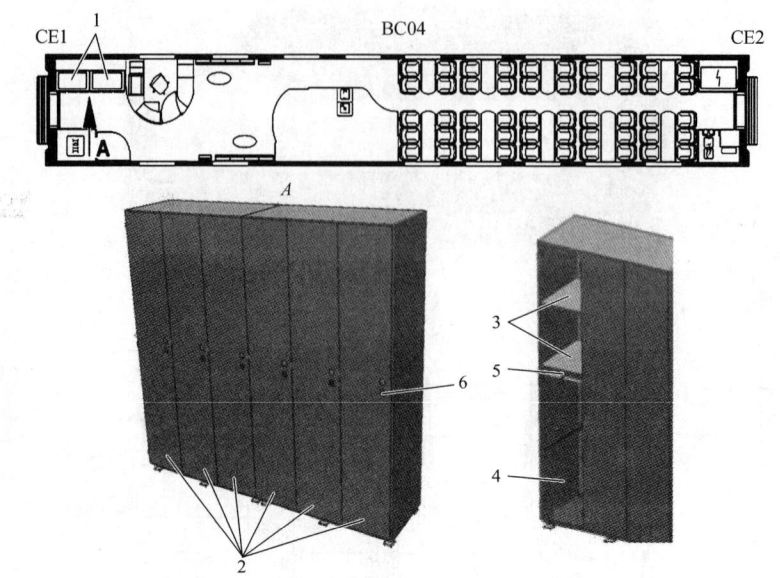

1—厨房储存单元；2—储存柜；3—箱内格架板；4—车进入车柜；5—有锁车柜；6—门锁。

图 10-15　厨房储存单元模拟图

10.4　给水装置

10.4.1　总体布置

一列 8 车厢编组的 CRH3 动车组上卫生设施布置如图 10-16 所示。160 L 净水箱（图中 A）安装在 EC01/08 车顶，为开水炉（图中 F）供水；300 L 净水箱（图中 B）安装在 TC02/07、IC03/06、FC05 车顶，为相应的卫生间（图中 C、E）和开水炉（图中 F）供水；700 L 水箱模块（图中 G）安装在 BC04 车下，为餐车厨房供水。

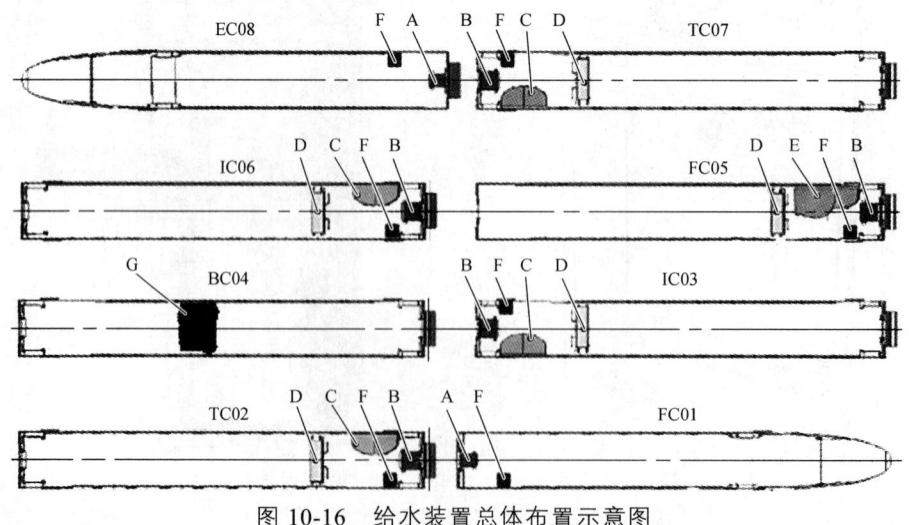

图 10-16　给水装置总体布置示意图

10.4.2 组 成

头车 EC01/08 车给水装置包括 160 L 净水箱、注水管路、供水管路和排水管路（见图 10-17）。

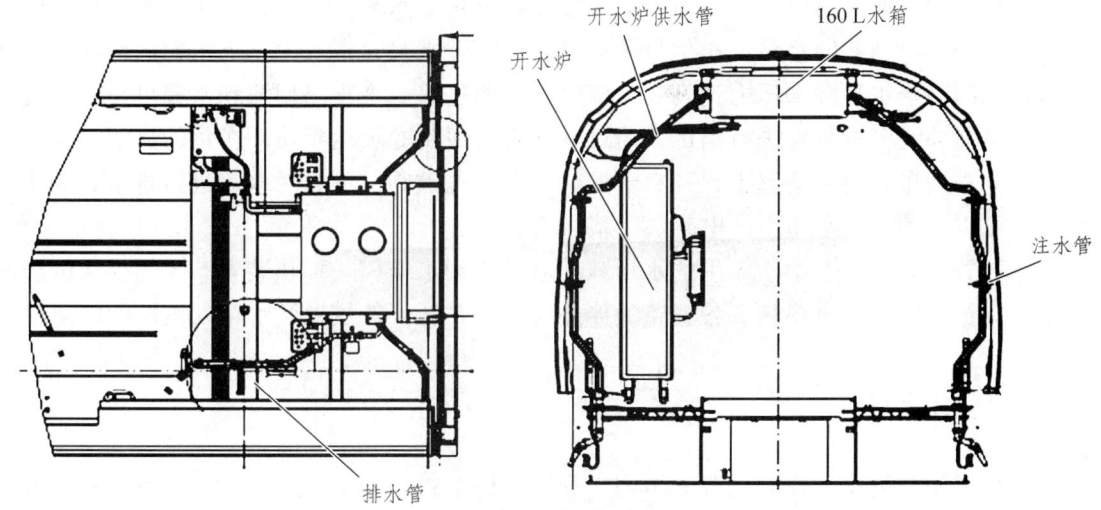

图 10-17 头车 EC01/08 车给水装置组成图

变压器车 TC02/TC07、变流器车 IC03/IC06、头等车 FC05 给水装置包括 300 L 净水箱、注水管路、供水管路和排水管路（见图 10-18）。

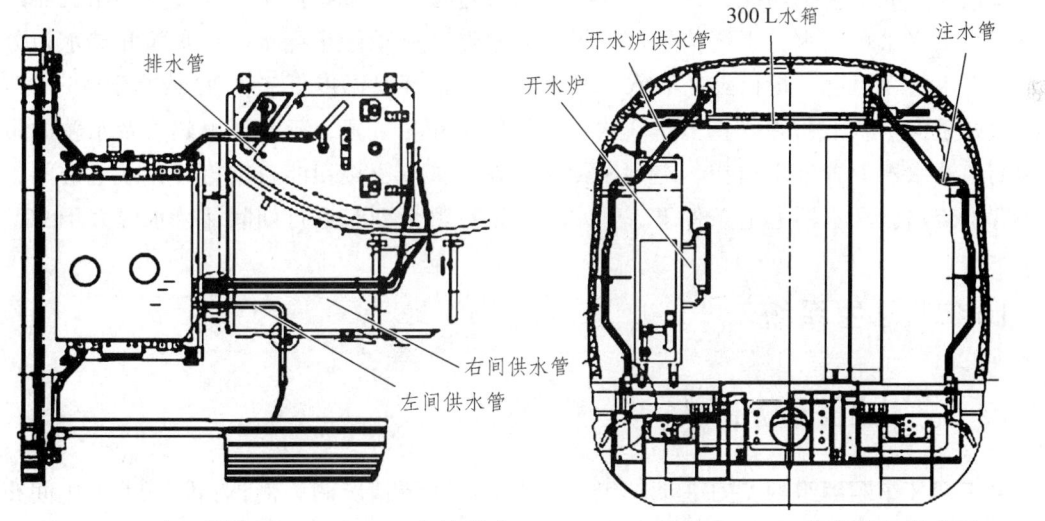

图 10-18 变压器车 TC02/TC07、变流器车 IC03/IC06、头等车 FC05 给水装置组成图

10.4.3 餐车给水系统

10.4.3.1 水箱模块组成

水箱模块由 700 L 净水箱、支撑框架、泵水单元组成。水箱设两个注水管路，水箱底部

装有浮球开关的液位传感器和可拆卸的加热管。支撑框架用于将水箱安装在车下。泵水管路用于吧车的水循环和防冻排空。

10.4.3.2 厨房给水系统应用

水循环过程：通过厨房内的压力开关控制水箱模块上水泵的开关，当车上水阀打开或关闭时，压力开关启动并向水泵传送信号从而启动或打开水泵，实现由车下水箱向厨房用水点供水；在此同时当水箱泵水压力达到一定值时，水通过另一个支路回流到水箱里。泵水过程中水流流经紫外线消毒装置进行消毒，通过分支管路回流的水达到循环净化的目的。

排水：在列车有电的情况下，开启水箱模块上的电磁阀，可以对水箱进行排水；列车无电情况下可以手动打开水箱上的电磁阀手柄进行排水。

防冻装置：为防止冬季水箱里的水结冰，需要启动水箱模块加热装置。水箱模块的防冻装置包括：箱体底部的电热毯、各管路的伴热线、水泵的伴热线以及水箱外表面的防寒材。

10.4.4 开水炉

开水炉根据在列车上安装位置的不同，分为三种型式，即 A 型、B 型、C 型。A 型开水炉安装在 EC01/08、FC05 车，其检修门在炉体右侧（面向开水炉面板）；B 型开水炉安装在 TC02/07、IC03/06 车，其检修门在炉体左侧（面向开水炉面板）；C 型开水炉安装在 BC04 车，其检修门在炉体背后（面向开水炉面板）。

该机具有缺水保护功能，开水器在列车运行过程中，所有控制自动进行，当机器出现故障或列车供水水箱缺水，干烧信号灯闪烁，开水器会自动停止烧水。烧水箱和储水箱分开，生水与开水绝无混合，提供纯正开水。当电热开水器环境温度低于 4 ℃ 或高于 45 ℃，开水器自动处于保护状态，并停止工作。饮水机加装了除垢装置，延长了电热管及水箱的维修保养周期。开水器设置排水按钮，在列车到达终点后，按压按钮能自动打开排水电磁阀，水经底部管子流出。开水器通电条件下，开水器可以在整个列车运行期间保持水温大于 90 ℃。

10.5 卫生系统

10.5.1 卫生设施总体布局

以一列 8 车厢编组的 CRH3 动车组上卫生设施布置情况图为例，标准-标准卫生间布置在 TC02/07、IC03/06 车的 C 位置，通用-标准卫生间布置在 FC05 车的 E 位置，EC01/08 车没有卫生设施。在每辆有卫生设施的车下 D 位置吊装一个 450 L 的污物箱，用于收集来自卫生间便器的污水废物。

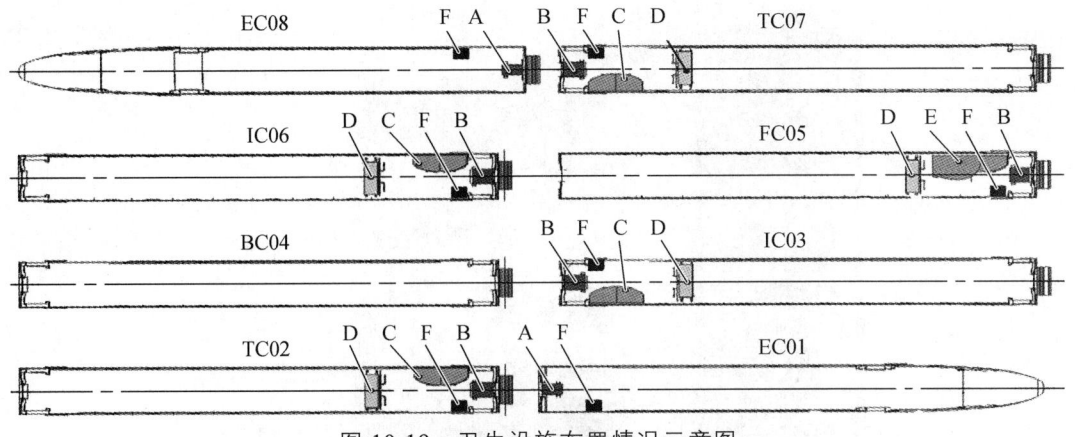

图 10-19 卫生设施布置情况示意图

10.5.2 标准卫生间

TC02/07、IC03/06 采用双标准卫生间，其包括双标准卫生间、洗手系统、坐便器以及卫生间内的设备件。标准卫生间采用模块化设计，卫生间地板、墙板、洗手系统、坐便器等集成为一个模块，减少了卫生间与车上接口，而且接口形式简单，便于安装与调整。标准卫生间分为左右间，右间作为卫生系统的主模块（卫生系统的主控制板安装在此间里），左间作为辅件；左右间外部轮廓和内部设施完全一样，两个模块对称布置在车上。每个标准卫生间由地板、墙板、顶板、门、洗手系统、坐便器以及内部的设备件组成。标准卫生间示意图及实物图如图 10-20 所示。

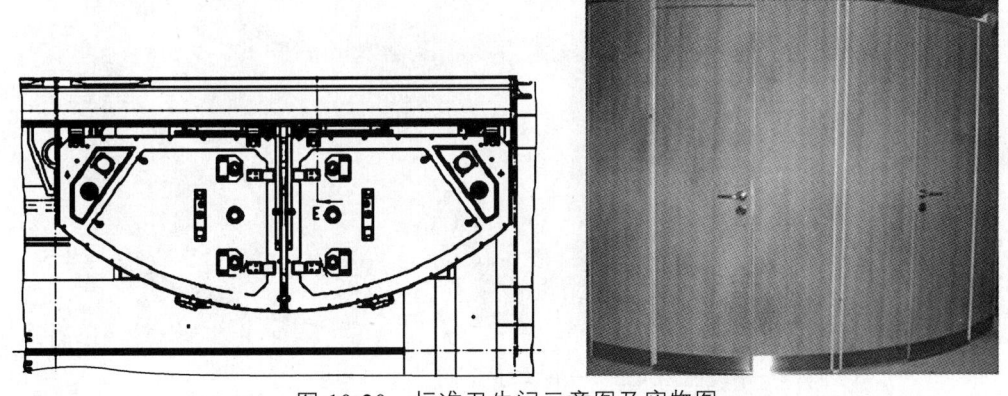

图 10-20 标准卫生间示意图及实物图

10.5.3 标准卫生间设备

标准卫生间的设备主要包括纸巾盒、便纸架、垃圾桶、镜子门、洗手器系统等，如图 10-21 所示。

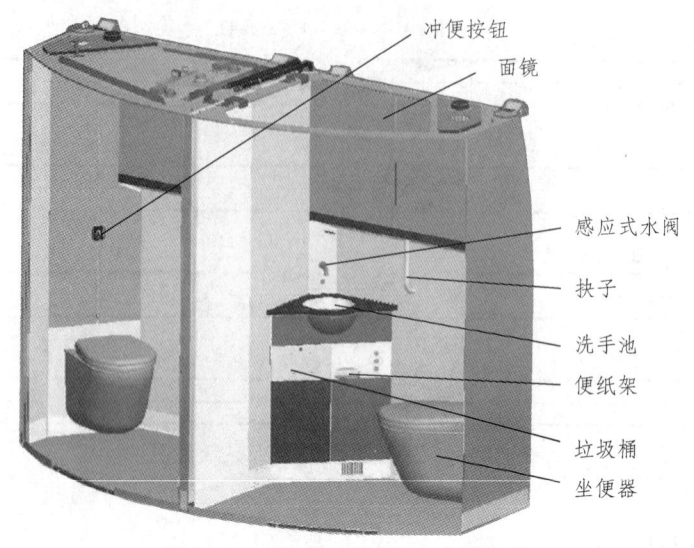

图 10-21 标准卫生间组成模拟图

10.5.4 一等车卫生间

FC05 车卫生间采用通用卫生间和标准卫生间组合形式。通用卫生间其最大的特点是内部空间大，内部设施能够满足残疾人使用的要求。采用按钮控制的电动门，整个模块的设计更具人性化。通用卫生间组成包括地板、墙板、顶板、门、洗手系统、坐便器以及内部的设备件组成。一等车卫生间整体模拟图如图 10-22 所示。

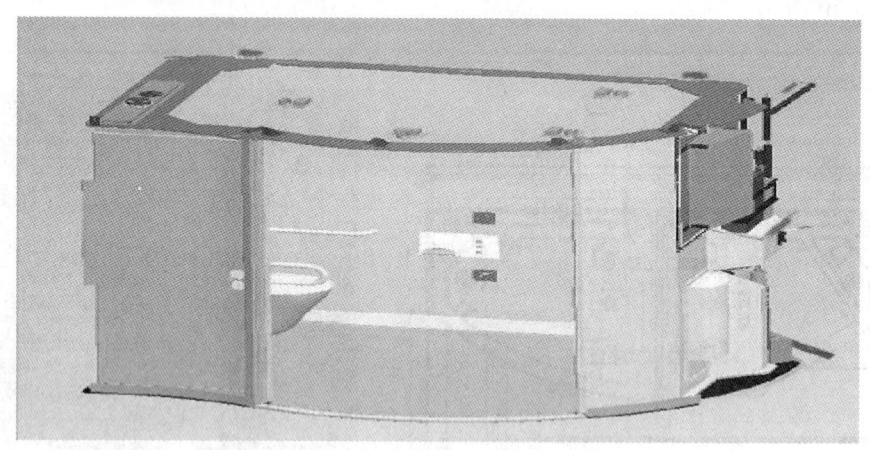

图 10-22 一等车卫生间整体模拟图

10.5.5 集便装置

动车组采用真空推拉式集便装置，其优点是结构设计紧凑，便于安装，用水量较少，系统全部为微机控制，系统故障时，比较容易更换。其缺点是对零部件的可靠性要求比较高，对维护技术的要求较高。

集便装置组成包括两套便器、冲便按钮、车上排污管及伴热、车下排污管及伴热、车下污物箱以及系统控制板（安装在卫生间墙板后）。两套便器工作相对独立，共用一个污物箱。

集便装置正常使用时只需按下冲便按钮，以后的所有冲水循环动作完全由集便装置系统控制器控制进行；对于运行中的有些故障，系统可以通过自我诊断方式和卫生系统的故障常规清除方式自动检测并清除。

整个卫生系统结构紧凑，所有控制集成在主卫生间控制板上。通过主卫生间的控制板可以实现系统的防冻排空，可以检测水箱和污物箱的液位情况和伴热情况，可以控制集便系统的正常运行及故障诊断。

Chapter 1　Outline Introduction

With the rapid development of technology and the acceleration of people's pace of life, high-speed railway came into being to meet people's needs for the modernization of transportation and gradually became the general trend of railway development in the world.

1.1　Development of foreign high-speed railway

Railway, a new means of transportation, has developed rapidly all over the world and played a great role in promoting the development and prosperity of social economy and culture at that time since the British built the world's first railway in 1825.

Japan is the first country in the world to build a practical high-speed railway. On October 1st, 1964, Japan's Tokaido Shinkansen was opened, with the maximum operating speed of 210 km/h. Tokaido Shinkansen has achieved excellent economic and social benefits, and Shinkansen is known as "the backbone of Japan's economic takeoff".

Countries all over the world have planned and constructed high-speed railways since then. There are three climax in the construction and development of high speed railway.

(1) From the 1960s to the late 1980s—the first climax of high-speed railway construction.

From 1964 to 1990, the high-speed railways constructed and put into operation include: the Shinkansen line of Shangyue, Tohoku, Shanyang and Tokaido in Japan; Atlantic TGV line and Southeast TGV line in France; New line of Hannover vilzburg Expressway in Germany; Rome Florence line in Italy.

(2) From the late 1980s to the mid-1990s—the second climax of high-speed railway network construction.

In the late 1980s, great attention were paid to high-speed railway and the related research which brewed the second construction climax of high-speed railway. The second construction peak was formed in Europe in the 1990s. In 1991, the tilting train model X2000 was put into use in Sweden; In 1992, Spain introduced the technology of Germany and France to build the Madrid Seville high-speed railway line; In 1994, Britain and France were connected through the Geely tunnel, which was the first international connection line of high-speed railway; In 1997, the "Eurostar" from Paris connected Germany, the Netherlands, Belgium and France.

(3) Since the mid-1990s till now—the third climax of high-speed railway construction.

In the mid-1990s, the third climax of high-speed railway construction and research came into being. The climax spreads to Oceania, North America, Asia and the whole Europe.

1.2 Development of high-speed railway In China

China's high-speed railway started later than the developed countries, but it has developed rapidly since the 21st century. Its rapid development, large construction scale and huge transportation capacity can be described as the world's first.

In the mid-1990s, China's railways faced a situation of slow speed and insufficient transport capacity, which was difficult to meet people's travel needs.

In the ten years from 1997 to 2007, China's railway has carried out six large-scale speed acceleration, and established a complete technical theoretical system and mature technical measures, which provide strong technical support for the construction and operation management of China's high-speed railway.

In January, 2004, the State Council approved the medium and long term railway development programme, which put forward the idea of leapfrog development, and determined the blueprint for China's railway development.

In 2004, China began to introduce foreign high-speed railway technologies. Through continuous learning, researching, developing and innovating, China has systematically mastered the core key technologies and formed an independent intellectual property technology system and standard system. China's construction and application technology of high-speed railway has reached the international leading level.

In 2021, the State Council issued the "14 th five year plan" for the development of modern comprehensive transport system. The development goal of high-speed railway is to achieve a coverage rate of more than 95% for cities with a population of more than 500,000 by 2025, which mainly adopts the high-speed railway network with a speed of 250 km/h and above, and basically eliminate the bottleneck sections of ordinary high-speed railway. The main lines of the national expressway network composed of 7 capital radiation lines, 11 north-south longitudinal lines, 18 East-West horizontal lines, and regional ring lines, parallel lines, and connecting lines are basically put into operation, and the quality of ordinary highways is further improved.

In terms of major railway indicators for comprehensive transportation development, the railway operating mileage will be increased from 146,000 km in 2020 to 165,000 km in 2025; Among them, the operating mileage of high-speed railway will be increased from 38,000 km in 2020 to 50,000 km in 2025.

1.3 Characteristics of high-speed Railway

It is no accident that high-speed railway has been widely welcomed and developed rapidly all over the world. This is not only because the high-speed railway overcomes the shortcomings of ordinary railway, but also has the following advantages when compared with highway automobile transportation and medium and long-distance air transportation.

1. Safety

Safety is always the primary factor when choosing the mode of transportation. Data shows that in the transportation of various countries, the ratio of railway, highway and civil aviation transportation accident rate (casualties per million person kilometers) is roughly 1 ∶ 24 ∶ 0.8. Because the high-speed railway generally adopts the full closure of the line, the automation of operation controland has a series of perfect safety assurance systems, its safety and reliability are much higher than other means of transportation.

2. Large transportation capacity

High speed railway retains the basic characteristics of ordinary railway. Some experts analyzed and calculated that the minimum running interval of high-speed railway multiple units can reach 4 min, and the train density can reach 20 trains / hour. If the number of passengers per train is calculated as 800, deducting the line maintenance time (4h / D), 400 high-speed trains can be operated every day, transporting 320,000 passengers, and the annual average one-way transportation will reach 117 million people. On the other hand, the 4-lane expressway can pass 1250 vehicles per hour in one direction, and 25,000 vehicles per day in 20 hours. For example, large cars account for 20%, with an average of 40 passengers per vehicle, small cars account for 80%, and two passengers per vehicle. The average one-way transportation capacity is 87 million people per year. At present, the largest aircraft can carry 300 ~ 400 passengers, and the flights between the two places are calculated as 20 sorties per day in one direction, transporting 6000 ~ 8000 passengers per day.

3. High speed

High speed is the core factor of high-speed railway technology and its main technical and economic advantages. Up till now, high-speed railway works as one of the transportation modes with the longest distance and the highest speed on land.

4. Low Energy consumption

According to statistical data, the average energy consumption per kilometer of various means of transportation is: aircraft: 2998.8 J, car: 3309.6 J, highway bus: 583.8 J, high-speed railway: 571.2 J. In addition, cars and aircraft use non renewable primary energy-gasoline or diesel (modern new energy-saving vehicles have not been put into mass use), while high-speed railways use secondary energy-electricity. With the promotion and development of new energy sources such as hydropower, solar energy, wind energy and nuclear power, the advantages of high-speed railway in energy consumption will become more prominent. This is also one of the important reasons why countries all over the world choose to develop high-speed railway in the current situation of energy shortage.

5. Less environment pollution

Environmental protection is a global and urgent issue related to human survival and development. Transportation is closely related to the ecological environment. At present, the pollution of transportation to the environment mainly comes from waste gas and noise. According to statistics, in passenger transportation, the converted emissions of carbon monoxide and other harmful substances from various means of transportation are 0.902 kg/person for roads, 0.109 kg/person for railways, and 635 kg/h for passenger planes per hour. As the high-speed railway has achieved electrification, toilet and other facilities and equipment, the railway has basically eliminated the environmental pollution caused by dust, lampblack and other waste gases (substances). In addition, in terms of noise pollution, Japan once took the noise produced by air transportation per thousand person kilometers as 1, then the noise produced by large cars was 0.2, and the noise produced by high-speed railways was only 0.1.

6. Less land occupation

The double track railway covers an area of 13.7 m, and a four lane Expressway covers an area of 26 m. Although the aircraft channel does not occupy land, a large airport covers an area equivalent to that of 1000 km double track railway.

7. Low cost

To a certain extent, the level of project cost is one of the important factors that restrict the rapid development of modes of transportation. Although the engineering cost of high-speed railway is much higher than that of ordinary railway, it is not higher than that of building a highway or airport. According to French data, the cost of French high-speed railway infrastructure is 17% lower than that of four lane highways. The average cost per seat of TGV high-speed train is only 1 / 10 of that of short haul aircraft.

8. High comfort

With the continuous improvement of people's living standards, travel comfort has become one of the important basis when choosing travel modes. The high-speed railway line is smooth and stable, with large curve radius, stable train operation, small vibration and swing amplitude, and fast speed. Due to the use of new materials, the motor car is spacious and bright, with advanced facilities, complete equipment, comfortable riding, large activity radius, etc. The activity space occupied by passengers on the way is much higher than that of cars and planes.

9. Preferable benefit

The daily traffic jams and accidents of highways have brought huge economic losses to the national economy and also seriously affected the harmony and stability of society. The annual cost of dealing with highway congestion and road traffic accidents in EC accounts for 2.9% and 2.5% of GDP respectively. The economic benefits of building high-speed railway are very obvious. According to statistics, Japan's Tokaido Shinkansen was put into operation in 1964, began to make profits in 1966, and gained all its investment in 1971. The southeast line of TGV in France was opened to traffic in 1983 and became profitable in 1984. The construction of high-speed railway in

China is mainly concentrated in large and medium-sized cities with tight transportation capacity, high population density and rapid economic development. Therefore, its investment recovery cycle is expected to be shorter.

1.4 Definition of high-speed railway

High speed railway is an international and contemporary concept with a wide definition. China's high-speed railway is defined as a newly-built railway designed to operate multiple unit trains of 250 km/h and above, and the initial operation speed is not less than 200 km / h.

The classification of railway speed is generally specified as follows: the speed of 100-120 km/h is called normal speed; 120-160 km/h is called medium speed; The speed of 160-200 km/h is called quasi high speed or fast; The speed of 200-400 km/h is called high speed; The speed above 400 km/h is called super high speed.

1.5 Definition and classification of EMU

1.5.1 Basic concept of EMU

The train set obtained by several power cars and trailers, all of which are permanently connected by power cars for a long time, is called EMU. The basic unit of EMU is called power unit. Each power unit is composed of different numbers of motor cars and trailers. The whole train can be composed of several power units as required. Both ends of the EMU are equipped with cabs, which can run back and forth on the line.Therefore, the EMU has strong flexibility and applicability. It can not only adapt to the operation needs of different speed levels by adjusting the proportion of moving trailers, but also meet the needs of different traffic volumes by adjusting the marshalling (see Figure 1-1).

Figure1-1　China's harmony high speed train

1.5.2 Classification of high-speed EMU

According to different standards and methods, EMU can be classified into many different categories, mainly including the following categories.

1. Classification by speed

(1) Quasi high speed EMU: the running speed is 160-200 km/h;
(2) High speed EMU: the running speed is 200-400 km/h;
(3) Ultra high speed EMU: the running speed is more than 400 km/h.

Quasi high-speed EMUs are generally used in intercity railways in China, and high-speed EMUs are generally used across multiple cities and provinces.

2. Classification by traction power

(1) Electric multiple units: Electric traction has the advantages of high traction power, light axle weight, good economy and environmental protection. Therefore, more than 80% of high-speed EMUs adopt electric traction at present although electric traction has a large initial investment.

(2) Diesel multiple units: diesel traction high-speed multiple units are often used in high-speed railway sections that have not been electrified, or as a transitional traction form for the development of high-speed railway construction, because of their advantages such as less investment, fast efficiency and good flexibility.

(3) Maglev EMU: maglev train is a new means of transportation, which has completely different characteristics from traditional trains. It uses the attraction (or repulsion) generated by the electromagnetic system to lift (or lift) the train, so that the whole train is suspended on the guide rail, and uses the electromagnetic force to guide, and uses the linear motor to directly convert the electric energy into the propulsion force to drive the train forward at high speed. The maglev train is suitable for ultra-high speed operation because the wheel rail does not contact and there is no friction wheel rail resistance, and the speed can reach more than 500 km / h.It's safety, environmental protection, small floor area and stable operation.

Except for the Shanghai Maglev Demonstration operation line from Shanghai Longyang Road station to Shanghai Pudong International Airport Station, China's high-speed EMUs are generally electric EMUs.

3. Classification by power configuration mode

1) Power Centralized High-speed EMU

Power centralized high-speed EMU is a EMU with power cars hung at both ends and trailers in the middle.

2) Power Distributed High-speed EMU

Power decentralized high-speed EMU refers to the EMU formed by the formation of a certain number of power cars and trailers.

4. Classification by bogie connection mode

1) Independent high-speed EMU

Independent high-speed multiple units are the traditional connection mode between vehicles and bogies. The body of each vehicle is placed on two bogies, and the vehicles are connected with sealed couplers. After the train is disassembled, the vehicles can work independently.

2) Articulated high-speed EMU

Articulated high-speed multiple units connect the vehicle bodies with elastic hinges and place them on a common bogie. Therefore, each vehicle cannot be disassembled from the train and walk independently.

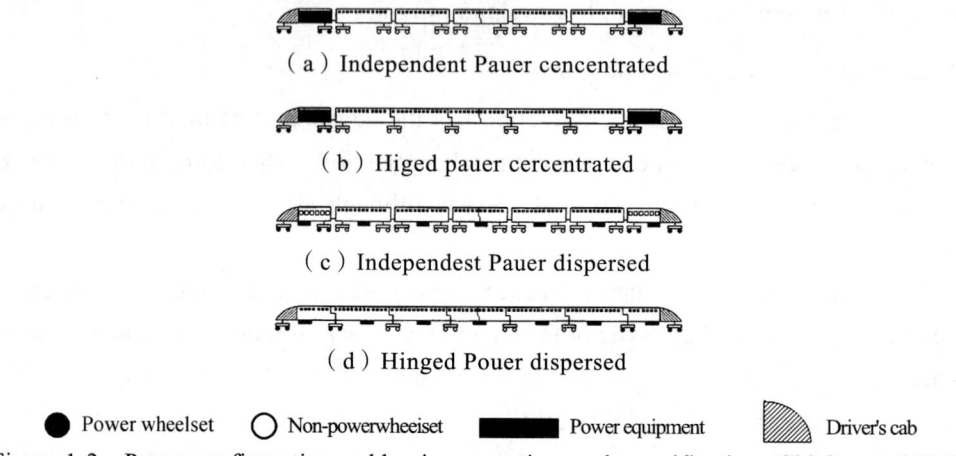

(a) Independent Pauer cencentrated

(b) Higed pauer cercentrated

(c) Independest Pauer dispersed

(d) Hinged Pouer dispersed

● Power wheelset   ○ Non-powerwheeiset   ■ Power equipment   ◩ Driver's cab

Figure 1-2 Power configuration and bogie connection mode cassification of high-speed EMU

According to the combination of power configuration and bogie connection mode, high-speed EMUs can be divided into the above four types, as shown in figure 1-2. China generally adopts independent high-speed EMUs.

1.6 Characteristics and selection of EMU power configuration mode

As mentioned above, there are two ways of power configuration for high-speed EMUs, namely, power centralized type and power decentralized type. The emergence and development of the two forms have their own historical reasons and environmental conditions.

1.6.1 Power centralized type

The power centralized high-speed EMU was first developed in Europe, which is the extension and development of traditional locomotive traction.

The traction force of the power centralized high-speed EMU is provided by the power wheel set concentrated in the power vehicle. Therefore, it brings two noticeable problems: first, the axle load of the power shaft must be large enough to provide the required traction force; Second, the axle load of the power shaft should not be too large, otherwise excessive wheel rail force will be generated during high-speed operation, damaging the rails and lines.

1. Advantages of power centralized high-speed EMU

(1) Because it is similar to the traditional locomotive traction train, the vehicle can be flexibly grouped according to the habit, which is conducive to the flexible use and maintenance management of the vehicle.

(2) Convenient for maintenance. Mechanical equipment and electrical equipment are convenient for monitoring and technical maintenance during operation.

(3) Comfortable. Since the mechanical and electrical equipment are concentrated in the power car and isolated from the passenger trailer, the passenger compartment has small vibration, low noise and good comfort.

(4) Easy to pick and hang. It can facilitate the train to enter the existing line from the high-speed line, and even replace the diesel locomotive to make the train directly enter the non electrified railway section.

2. Disadvantages of power centralized high-speed EMU

(1) Small passenger capacity. Because the power car cannot carry passengers and occupies the marshalling, the passenger capacity is relatively reduced.

(2) The axle load is heavy and difficult to reduce.

(3) Poor braking. The braking capacity of the power car is limited by the adhesion coefficient, which requires the trailer to share part of the braking power.

(4) The large adhesion traction force of the power vehicle is in contradiction with the wheel axle load requirements.

1.6.2 Power decentralized type

The power decentralized high-speed EMU was first developed in Japan. It is developed and extended on the basis of traditional urban rail transit trains.

1. Advantages of power decentralized high-speed EMU

(1) Large passenger capacity. As the power plant and various electrical equipment are distributed in each vehicle, each vehicle can carry passengers, thus the passenger capacity is increased.

(2) Light axle weight. Because the mass and power of power devices, traction motors and other equipment are scattered on each vehicle, it is easier to realize the demand of reducing axle load of high-speed trains.

(3) Good braking.

(4) Because the traction force is scattered on each power wheel, the contradiction between the large traction force and the axle load limit of high-speed trains can be solved.

2. Disadvantages of power decentralized multiple units

(1) Comfort is reduced. Since the power unit is hoisted under each vehicle, the vibration and noise during operation will affect the comfort of passengers in the carriage, and it is still difficult to completely solve the vibration isolation and noise reduction technology at present.

(2) The failure rate of decentralized power equipment is relatively high.

(3) It can only be grouped by units and cannot be driven into non electrified sections for operation, and it is not compatible with the traditional operation and maintenance management system. A new maintenance management system must be established.

Chapter 2 High–Speed Car Body

2.1 The usage of the EMU car body

The part of a vehicle for passengers to ride is called a car body. Its use is mainly manifested in the following aspects:

(1) It is used to install various electrical equipment and mechanical equipment, and protect all kinds of equipment in the vehicle from rain, snow and wind sand.

(2) It is a place for passengers to operate, repair and maintain the locomotive in the place of passengers and crew.

(3) Bearing vertical force: bear the weight of all kinds of equipment in the vehicle, and pass the supporting device to the bogie to the rail.

(4) Transmission longitudinal force: the traction and braking force that is transmitted from the bogey is received, and the traction buffer is passed to the two ends of the car body so that the traction train can operate or brake.

(5)Transversal force: at run time, the vehicle should bear various transverse forces, such as centrifugal force, wind force, etc.

2.2 The primary structure and technical characteristics of the EMU car body

2.2.1 Primary structure

The body structure is the main carrier of EMU. Generally speaking, the main parts of the body structure include: chassis, side wall, roof, end wall and driver compartment structure of the head car.

EMU can be divided into two types: the head car body and the intermediate body. The vehicle body structure is basically the same, the middle body structure is also about the same, it is welded with large hollow aluminum alloy extruded section, The body structure is composed of the bottom frame, side wall, roof, end wall, driver's room, apron structure and so on, which can withstand vertical, vertical, horizontal, twisting and other complex loads. The front end of the driver's cab is equipped with a barrier, the height of the barrier is 150 mm. It is fixed height, not adjustable, in order to facilitate the lifting of the body, four roof spaces are arranged on the chassis.

2.2.2 Technical characteristics of the EMU car body

The design of the EMU has the following obvious characteristics in each type of EMU:

(1) The shape of the vehicle body has a good streamline design to reduce the air resistance and additional resistance generated when the train is running at high speed.

(2) The body has good air tightness to improve and improve passenger comfort.

(3) The body has a good index of lightweight design to reduce the energy consumption of the train during operation.

EMU lightweight car body is mainly manifested in two aspects: one is the body material adopted has low density, high strength, good welding performance, extrusion processing performance is good, good corrosion resistance and other properties of aluminum alloy material; the second is that the body structure adopts the aluminum alloy tube bearing structure. The body bearing structure of EMU adopts the large-size hollow aluminum alloy extruded section of the body, which is welded by the large hollow aluminum alloy extruded section. The structure is also known as the double shell structure. Compared with the single shell structure, the two-shell structure is slightly heavier. However, the hollow profile has the characteristics of high section rigidity, which can improve the overall stiffness of the body structure. At the same time, we can remove the reinforced materials that must be used in the single-shell structure, so that the number of body parts can be reduced. In addition, due to excessive pursuit will light car body for the safety of the car body structure and detrimental passenger riding comfort, therefore, in recent years, as people more and more high to the requirement of ride comfort, car body structure is not only the pursuit of light, but to the reasonable control of the weight of the car body structure. The vehicle body of the EMU adopts the double shell structure, which can improve the vehicle's comfort. The double shell structural profile has a hollow cavity. The body bearing structure of the CRH2 EMU is shown in Figure 2-1.

Figure 2-1　Double shell body structural profile

The CRH2 EMU reflects the overall lightweight design concept of the vehicle. Lightweight considerations in the vehicle is very meticulous, in addition to the main structure, equipment in the car decoration materials, and single line and up and down the floor of the vehicle floor lightweight wires, shielded wire are adopted to facilitate the light weighting of car body.

2.3 The shape and size of the EMU

The CRH2 motor vehicle has a total length of 25,700 mm, a middle length of 25,000 mm, a total length of 201.4 m, a car width of 3380 mm and a car height of 3700 mm.

The body weight of the CRH2 motor vehicle is shown in Table 2-1, and the main technical parameters of the vehicle body are shown in Table 2-2.

Table 2-1   CRH2 vehicle body mass meter

Whole marshalling model	T1c	M2	M1	T2	T1k	M2	M1s	T2c
Body mass/kg	7643	7947	7821	7831	8373	7822	8042	7185

Table 2-2   Main technical parameters of vehicle body of CRH2 EMU

Body length	25,700 mm	Head of the car
	25,000 mm	The middle car
Maximum width of vehicle body	3380 mm	
Maximum height of vehicle (distance rail)	3700 mm	
The floor of the door is at the height of the rail	1300 mm	
Ceiling height	2277 mm	
gauge	1435 mm	
Bogie center distance	17,500 mm	
Fixed wheelbase	2500 mm	
The wheel diameter	860 mm	
Height of coupler distance	1000 mm	
Natural frequency of body bending (in full condition)	$\geqslant 10$ Hz	

2.4 The body structure of the EMU

Type CRH2 EMU car body structure is mainly divided into the first car and car among two kinds, mainly by the underframe, side wall, roof and side wall, car accessories, car tank, front cover equipment under actuator, obstacle and front row), etc (head car include the driver chamber head structure). Two head of car body structure is basically the same, as shown in figure2-2, the middle car body structure is the same, as shown in Figure 2-3, the car body is integral bearing structure type with large-scale hollow aluminum alloy extrusion profile, welded with tube, which can withstand the vertical, longitudinal and transverse and torsion complex load.

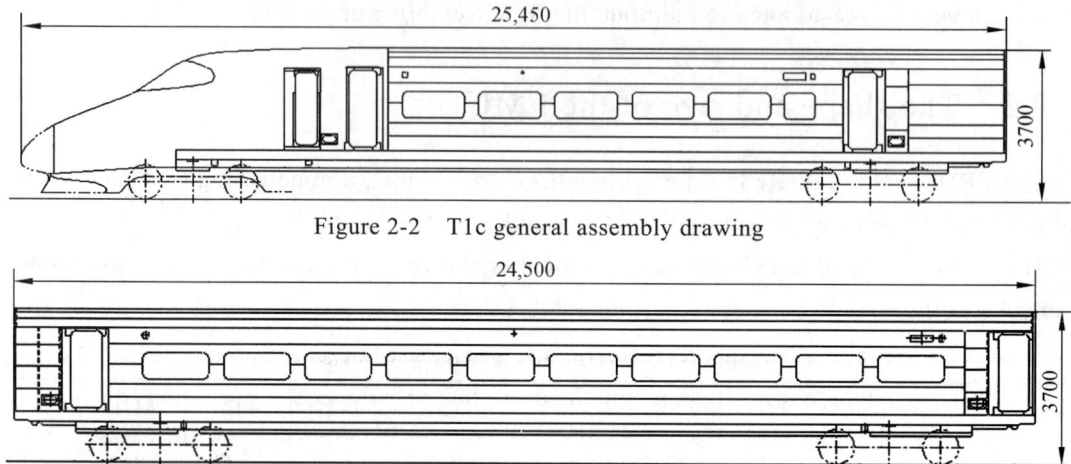

Figure 2-2　T1c general assembly drawing

Figure 2-3　M1 general assembly drawing

2.4.1　Base frame composition

The chassis of the CRH2 EMU is divided into the head car underframe and the middle chassis. The bottom frame of the car is composed of the body chassis and the chassis of the locomotive. The bottom of the T1c is shown in Figure 2-4. As long as the chassis frame is in the middle, the bottom frame consists of a pillow beam supporting the weight of the body and the connecting frame. The side beam, end beam and middle beam of the front and back direction force; Supporting the passenger compartment equipment and passengers and hoisting the equipment under the floor. See Figure 2-5.

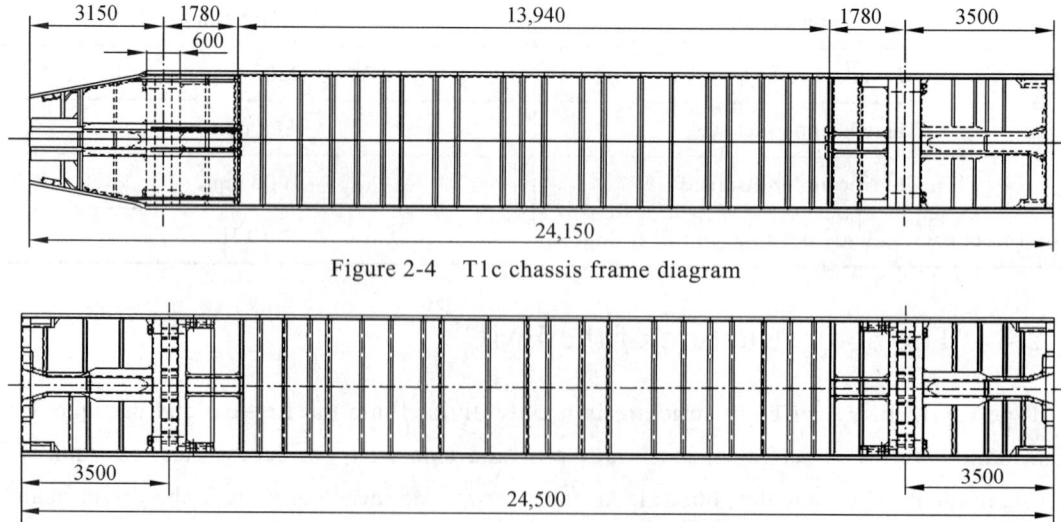

Figure 2-4　T1c chassis frame diagram

Figure 2-5　M1 chassis frame diagram

1. Side beam and end beam

The side girder is the longitudinal girder on the left and right side of the floor under the floor, and it is welded together with the extruded section of the long aluminum alloy, which is the key part connecting the base frame and the side frame to the barrel body, support equipment under vehicle load, floor load, for one-piece structure or packaged. The end beam is the transverse beam at both ends of the base frame, which is welded by aluminum alloy extruded profile and aluminum alloy plate.

2. Sleeper beam

The pillow beam is made of thick wall hollow profile to form a box with a width of 800 mm and a height of 200 mm, which has a high rigidity of torsion and bending. The pillow beam is connected with the side beam in the center of the bogie, and the corresponding structure of the bogie is installed, which can support the load of the vehicle body and avoid the vibration transmitted from the bogie to the floor. The top of the pillow is equipped with a roof seat, which is convenient for rescue and maintenance. The schematic diagram of the pillow beam is shown in Figure 2-6.

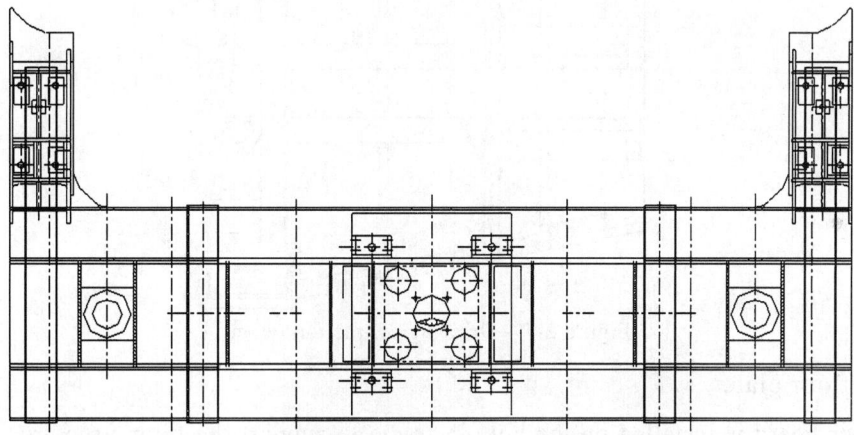

Figure 2-6　Schematic diagram of pillow beam structure

3. Beam

The beam is the transverse beam between the two sides of the beam or the side beam and the middle beam for supporting the installation of the equipment under the floor and supporting the floor. The beam is used as a gas tight floor, and the large sections of aluminum plate with reinforced ribs are used. There is an upward reinforcing rib structure between the front and rear bogie as floor and duct. In the end of the vehicle to ensure that the wind tunnel area is used to strengthen the rib structure, the floor and the wind tunnel are all welded. The lower part of the toilet and washroom is the airtight floor with no reinforcing ribs. The girder shall have the strength required to install the equipment and support the floor. In the large weight equipment installation, there shall be equipment installation seat and reinforcement measures. There is a pipe connecting hole on the beam, and the position corresponding to the installation bolt hole of the equipment under the beam and the floor should be provided with enough dimensional space to ensure that the disassembly work of the floor under the floor is not affected.

4. Towing beam (middle beam)

Traction beam is mainly composed of aluminum alloy extrusion profiles and aluminum alloy plate welding and become, connect body chassis beam and pillow beam, and set corresponding additional structure for coupling buffer device, is to install coupler buffer device. The longitudinal load transmitted by the coupler buffer device is transferred from the plate seat on the traction beam to the traction beam, and then passed through the structure of the pillow beam to the whole body structure to carry out the whole load. Rivet joints are used from the plate seat and the traction beam, and the corresponding parts of the traction beam corresponding to the coupler are strengthened locally. The schematic diagram of traction beam is shown in Figure 2-7.

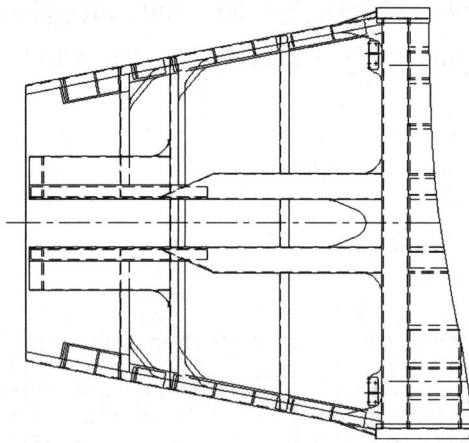

Figure 2-7   Drawing of traction beam

5. The floor plate

The floor board is installed on the bottom frame to support the floor structure, enhance the strength and rigidity of the base frame, and maintain the air tightness structure in the car. Floor board is the section that lengthens in body lengthways, as special floor structure part is plane also can.

6. Head base

It is suitable for the structure of curved side beam, medium beam and reinforcing beam. The front end of the head should be supported by the head end wall, the front row obstacle, the buffer device, the car hook, the buffer and other corresponding structures.

2.4.2 Side walls

The car body of the head car has a side wall with a side wall on both sides. End wall structure is mainly by the end of the column, beam and the roof arch wall force, according to the vehicle end any arrangement consists of separation between the toilet and wash your face and integral type two kinds, the structure of side wall as shown in Figure 2-8.

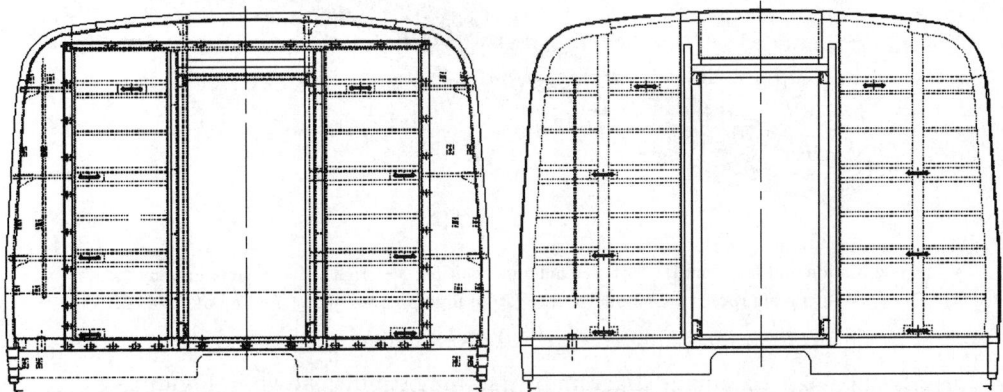

Figure 2-8 Split and integral end wall structure

Train head end wall including the driver chamber side wall, roof, window to install the driver chamber and a former head coupler cover, wireless and its internal structure mainly by car end of end wall column, beam and the roof arch (as shown in Figure 2-9), car connection in the middle part of the side wall is equipped with the breakthrough, folding tent, car shock absorber, High voltage cable wiring, installing ventilation with fresh air to the entry at the same time the corresponding structure of the equipment.

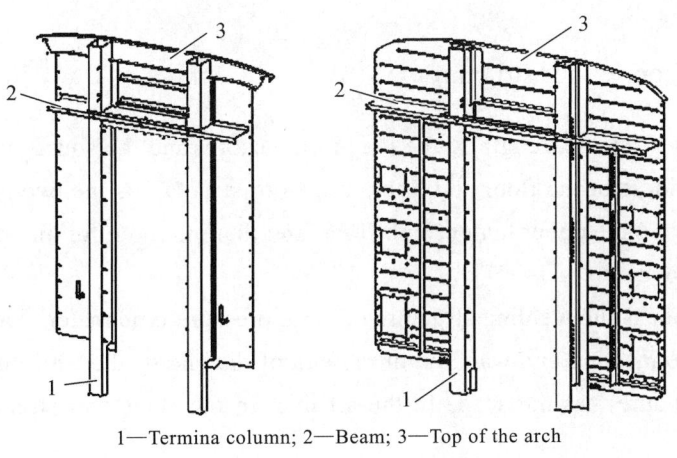

1—Termina column; 2—Beam; 3—Top of the arch
Figure 2-9 End car structure

2.4.3 The roof structure

The roof is made of large hollow extruded sections (as shown in Figure 2-10), and the longitudinal beams are omitted. The welding of the profile is continuous welding along the length of the car body, but the joint position of the side wall and the inside of the car are fixed welding, and the outside of the car is continuously welded.

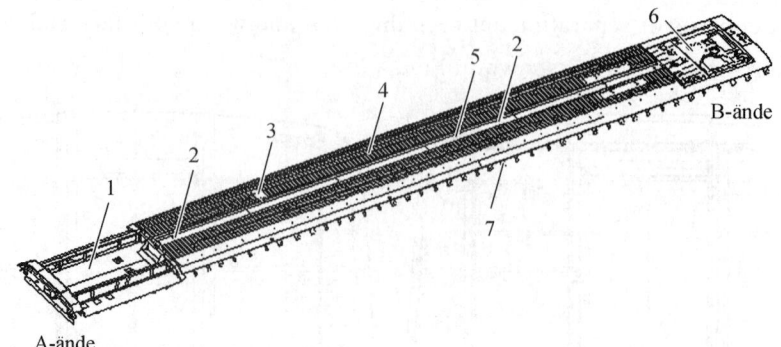

1—Ventilation unit location; 2—Installed antenna position; 3—High voltage cable into my mouth;
4—With a grain roof; 5—Smooth roof; 6—Roof high pressure plate; 7—Top of the arch.
Figure 2-10　Roof structure

There are radio antennas and protective radio antennas on the roof of car Number 1 and Number 0 Setting the TV and FM antenna on the front seat of Number 7.

The roof is the upper part of the vehicle body, which is the base of the installation of the electric bow, the bow cover and the ultra-high voltage cable, and at the end of the car has a high voltage bus connection and installation of the connection structure accordingly.

The roof of the passenger compartment, the ordinary car and the soft seat are all made up of the universal central ceiling, the side ceiling and the rack. Set extra-high voltage cables on the roof.

2.4.4　Guest room floor structure

The floor has sufficient strength to the load in the cabin, and the sound insulation structure is considered in the middle of the floor and floor. The floor structure is the two-layer structure of the lower airtight floor and the upper honeycomb floor, and there is room for air conditioning duct and seat wiring in the floor.

The airtight floor is the welding structure of large pressure type material and floor bracket. At the car and of the connecting end wall But at the end of the end of the wall, the side of the end of the wall is to make sure that the space in the air duct in the floor will strengthen the rib to the downward direction.

The upper floor USES an aluminum honeycomb sandwich board with a total thickness of 21.7 mm, In order to reduce the noise of the solid, the floor liner USES a refractory rubber gasket.

Between the airtight floor and the upper floor, the air duct of fresh air, air conditioning and exhaust loop is arranged in the direction of the rail, and the insulation material with a thickness of 20 mm is pasted on the airtight floor. In addition, the seat is embedded in the floor, and the M12 hexagonal bolt is fixed in the bolt hole.

2.4.5 Headgear and skirt board

1. The structure of the barrier device

In the front end of the driver's cab, the main barrier device is set, as shown in Figure 2-11. The function of the defecation device is to eliminate the obstacles on the middle line, to alleviate the impact of the vehicle on the collision of the obstacle, and to prevent the irregularity of the orbital structure from causing the train to derail. It consists of a delimiter and a buffer. Debugging tools are running structure of snow removal, at the bottom of the flanger is equipped with auxiliary device debugging. The buffer is a multilayer structure composed of five aluminum sheets, which are located in the rear of the snowboard and absorb shock energy through deformation.

Figure 2-11   Main barrier device

The defectors are mainly composed of the baffle and the buffer, and are mounted under the front chassis. Some debugging device installed in a truck frame, the top rail cowcatcher using bolt joint is fixed on the bogie frame, the lower part of the orbital cowcatcher is an adjustable plate, fastening bolt joint to track cowcatcher arm, debugging device structure is shown in Figure 2-12.

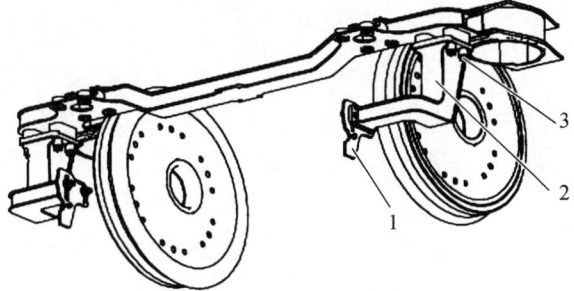

1—Track guard; 2—Rack delimiter arm; 3—Bolt joint M20 (screws, gaskets and pipes) .
Figure 2-12   Structure of baffle

2. Debugging ability

1) The defecation ability of the baffle board

When walking in 200 km/h, you can remove obstacles with a height of 250 mm and weigh less than 100 kg. Static strength can meet the requirements of 137 kN. The height above the orbit is above 150 mm.

2) Cleaning snow ability (including snow plough and stoneware)

When traveling at 240 km/h, it is essential to resist the snow resistance above 18.2 t.

3. Board

1) Bogie skirt board

The bogie is partly constructed to reduce noise. The lower end is 550 mm from the track surface, so as to avoid obstacles to maintenance Consider the loading and unloading problem, the skirt board is divided into two parts. See in Figure 2-13.

Figure 2-13　Bogie skirt board

2) Skirt board

The skirt board are made of large sections in the end of the car. The skirt board is fitted with a variety of floor-to-floor inspection covers and footpads for riding in the tracks.

Chapter 3　Couplers of EMU

At the each end of a railway car, there are couplers (referring to Figure 3-1), which connect the railway car to another one, or connect the EMU train to another train. Normally, the couplers, in term of their usage in EMU trains, can be divided into two main categories: automatic tight-lock couplers and semi-permanent couplers.

An automatic tight-lock coupler is located at each end of a EMU train, It connects the train to the other EMU train (referring to the picture below), or to a locomotive.

Figure 3-1　Automatic couplers

Coupling can be done at low speed without manual assistance, and has the advantage of rigid, slack free and fully-latched connection. An automatic coupler also has pneumatic and electrical connections, which can also make the electrical and the pneumatic connections and disconnections automatically. In addition, with the designed pivot arrangement, it permits both horizontal and vertical track variations.

Semi-permanent coupler connects two adjacent vehicles in an EMU train. The operation of coupler (coupling and uncoupling) can only be done manually. The traction and compression loads are transmitted from one vehicle to the other through two semi-permanent couplers (A and B), which is shwun in Figure 3-2.

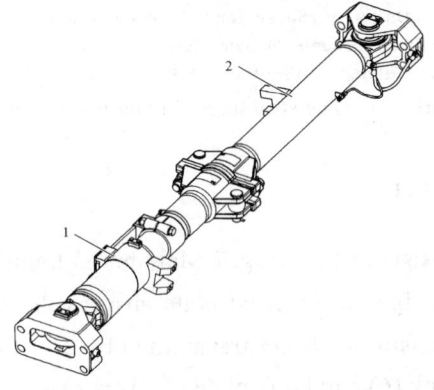

1—Coupler HALF-A; 2—Coupler HALF-B

Figure 3-2　Two Semi-permanent Couplers

3.1 Automatic coupler

An automatic coupler consists of (1) Electric coupler actuator, right, (2). Buffer, (3) Socket joint, (4).Pivot anchor,(5). Support centering, (6). Terminal box, heating, (7). Pneumatic system, (8). Electric coupler actuator, left, (9). Electrical coupler, left, (10). Manual uncoupling, (11). Mechanical coupler, (12). Valve for UC, (13). Valve for MRP, (14) Valve for BP, (15) Electric coupler, right. (Referring to Figure 3-2)

The mechanical coupler front face is in the form of funnel and cone. This enables automatic alignment and centering of the couplers for mating when brought together. The pulling load and the shock is absorbed by the buffer and transmitted to the Pivot Anchor.

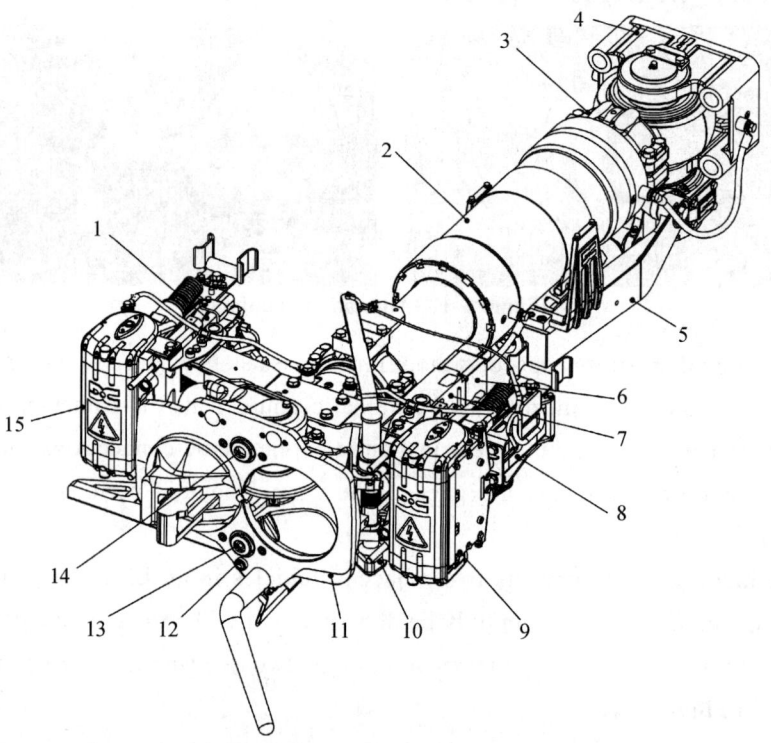

1—Electric coupler actuator, right; 2—Buffer; 3—Socket joint; 4—Pivot anchor; 5—Support centering; 6—Terminal box, heating; 7—Pneumatic system; 8—Electric coupler actuator, left; 9—Electrical coupler, left; 10—Manual uncoupling; 11—Mechanical coupler; 12—Valve, UC; 13—Valve, MRP; 14—Valve, BP; 15—Electric coupler, right.

Figure 3-3　The structure of a automatic couplers

3.1.1　Mechanical coupler

A mechanical coupler consists of 1. Spring, 2 Main pin, 3 Latch rod, 4.Trigger, 5 Hook plate 6. Coupling link. A broad plane edge on the front plate absorbs the compressive and impact loads. During coupled position, the tensile loads get transmitted by coupling link (6) and hook plate (5). A cover protect the coupling link (6) and hook plate (5) from rust and corrosion(referring to Figure 3-4).

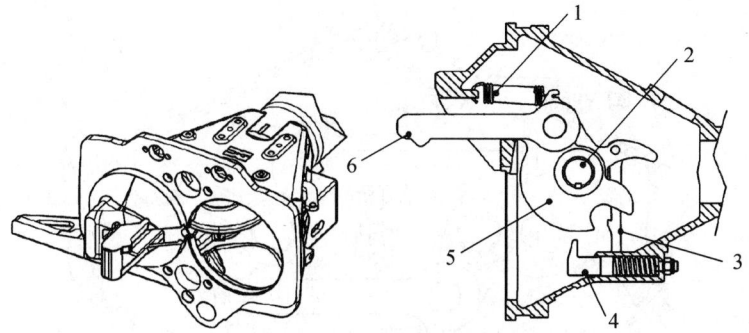

1—Spring; 2—Main pin; 3—Latch rod; 4—Trigger; 5—Hook plate; 6—Coupling link.

Figure 3-4　Mechanical coupler

1. Coupling mechanism

Figure 3-5 shows the two mechanical coupler heads ready to couple. This is the normal condition of an uncoupled coupler.

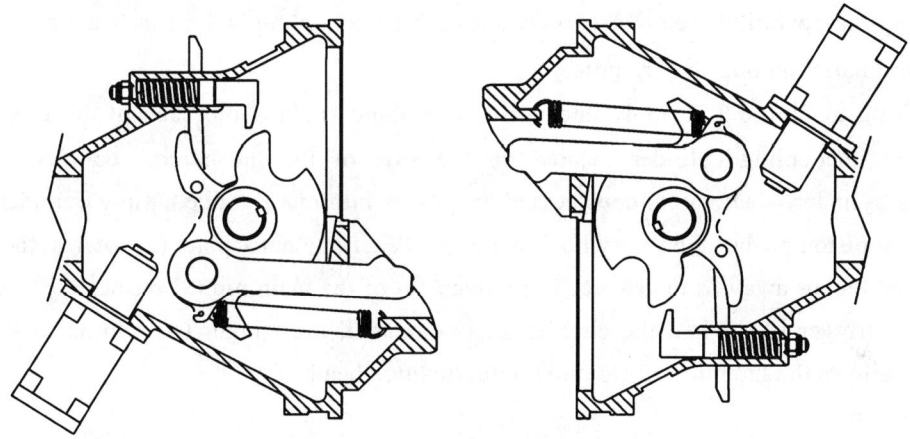

Figure 3-5　Ready for couple

The Figure 3-6 shows the coupled position of couplers. When two couplers are brought close to each other, then the coupling link(6) of the mating coupler seats into the groove of rotary hook plate(5) of the opposite coupler. Similarly, the coupling link (6) of the opposite coupler also seats into the groove of rotary hook plate (5) of the mating coupler.

During this mechanism the coupling link (6) of the mating coupler presses the trigger (4) of the opposite coupler. When the trigger (4) is pressed, the latch rod (3) moves up and causes main pin (2) to release. After release of main pin, the tension spring (1) causes the hook plate (5) to rotate for coupling mechanism.

Once coupling is completed, the coupler links and the hook plates form a parallelogram, which transfers the forces to the main coupler body through the main pin. In the parallelogram position, the two coupler heads form a rigid, slack free and safe connection.

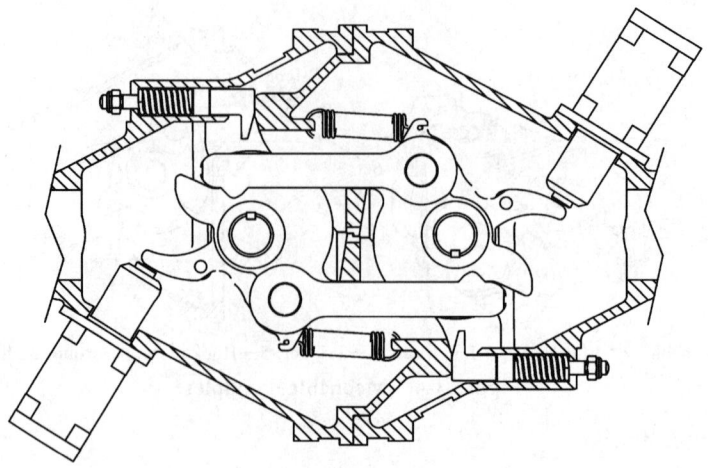

Figure 3-6 Coupled position

2. Uncoupling mechanism

Uncoupling operation separates two vehicles. This uncoupling is done in two ways.

1) Automatic uncoupling (remotely)

Referring to Figure 3-7, apply uncoupling command signal from each of driver's cabins to activate the uncoupling cylinder located on the side of the mechanical coupler. When the uncoupling cylinder is activated, compressed air passes into one the uncoupling cylinders of both couplers, the piston pushes the rotary hook plate (5). When the hook plate (5) rotates, the main pin (2) turns and moves away from groove. The movement of the main pin (2) pushes the latch rod (3) towards the trigger (4). When the coupler gets separated, the trigger (4) returns to its original position. it allows the latch rod (3) to hook onto the latch head.

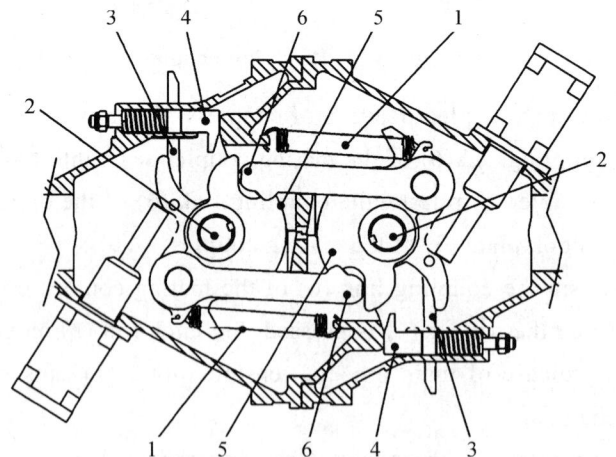

1—Spring; 2—Main pin; 3—Latch rod; 4—Trigger; 5—Hook plate; 6—Coupling link.

Figure 3-7 Uncoupled position

2) Manual uncoupling

The manual uncoupling can be done with uncoupling device named uncoupling handle, which is adjacent to the mechanical coupler. Pulling the uncoupling handle to rotate the hook in the mechanical coupler to get the couplers uncoupled. After the vehicles are separated and uncoupling handle released, the spring along with the springs in the mechanical coupler return to its uncoupled position.

3.1.2 Buffer

Buffer is a shock absorber, which absorbs pulling and compression loads from the mechanical coupler.

3.1.2.1 General description of the buffer

The buffer consists of hydraulic buffer, friction spring, buffer tube, guide rail (referring to Figure 3-8).

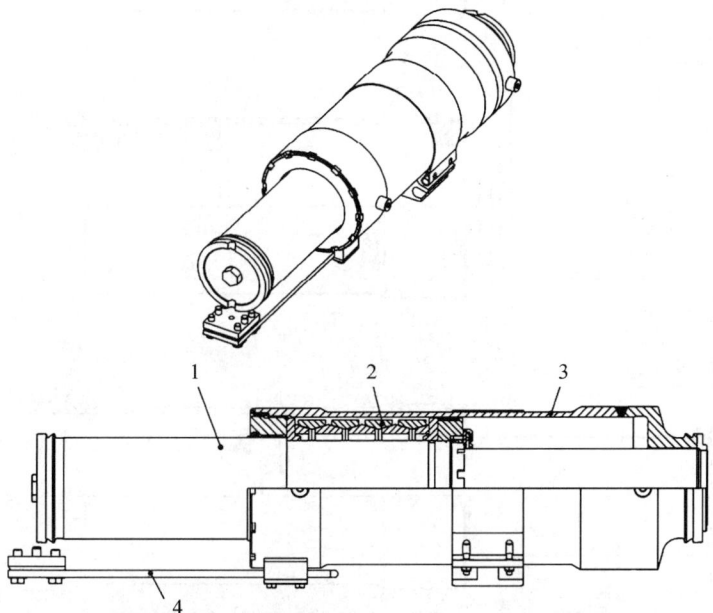

1—Hydraulic buffer; 2—Friction spring; 3—Buffer tube; 4—Guide rail.
Figure 3-8　Buffer

The pulling and compression loads are transmitted to the vehicle from the mechanical coupler through the friction spring (2). The spring (2) absorbs the loads and transmits to the hydraulic buffer (1) and then to the pivot anchor, which is fixed to the vehicle under frame. The guide rail (4), fixed at the bottom of the buffer tube (3), prevents the rotation of the buffer in the buffer tube. This in turn prevents the rotation of automatic coupler.

3.1.2.2 Working principle of the buffer

Referring to Figure 3-9 for the different positions of hydraulic buffer under compression and traction loads.

A. Buffer at normal position (no buff or draft loads).

B. Buffer under compression loads (maximum stroke).

C. Buffer under traction loads (maximum stroke).

The hydraulic buffer is a gas-hydraulic shock absorber that absorbs the main buff forces.

When buffer is subjected to buff loads, the buffer moves over a stroke 200 mm. The indicator, mounted on the front socket joint, shears-off 8 mm before the full stroke, to indicate that the buffer is subjected to maximum force. When buffer is subjected to draft loads, the buffer moves over a stroke of 30 mm. The friction spring absorbs the main draft forces.

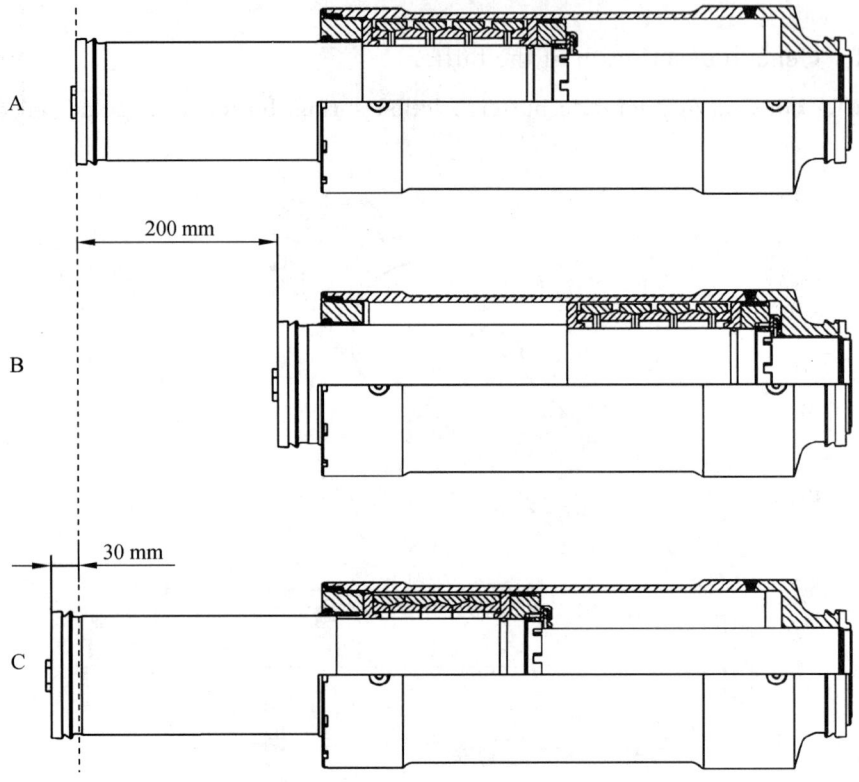

Figure 3-9　Compression and traction of buffer

3.1.3　Coupler hatch

3.1.3.1　Coupler hatch mechanism

The coupler hatch mechanism consists of the following main components: train interface, hatch interface, hatch (Figure 3-10).

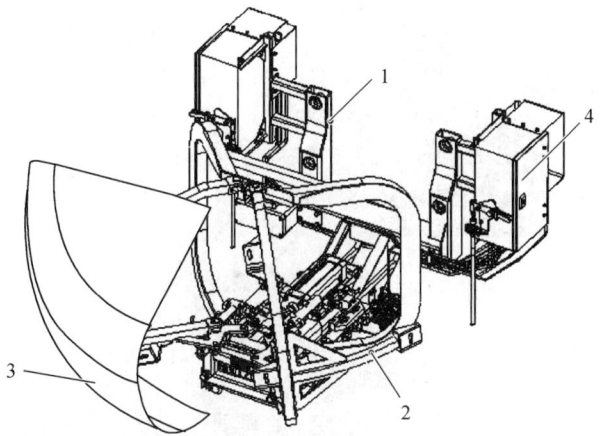

1—Train interface; 2—Hatch interface; 3—Hatch; 4—Hatch control unit.
Figure 3-10 Coupler hatch

Hatch mechanism can be operated automatically by an OPEN/CLOSE command given from driver's desk panel (1) through a rotary switch (2). The hatch mechanism can also be manoeuvred locally with push buttons in the Hatch Control Units (HCU) or by manual operation in case of power supply failure. (referring to Figure 3-11 (A) for hatch mechanism in closed position. referring to Figure 3-11 (B) for hatch mechanism in open position)

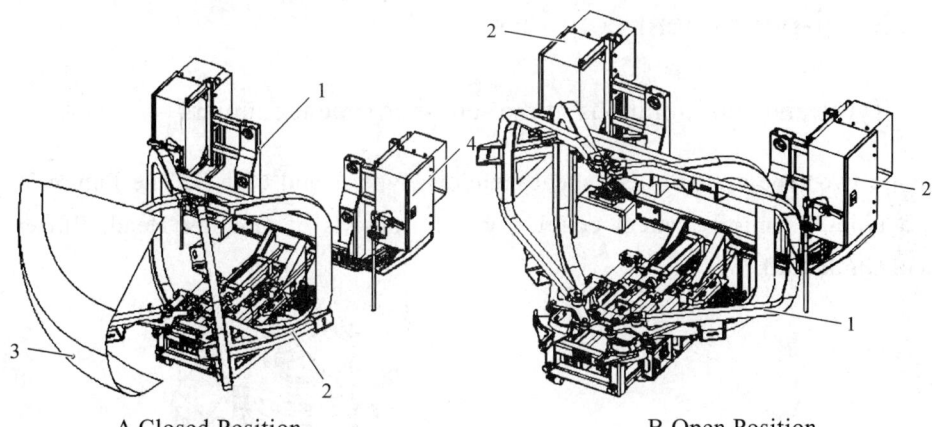

A Closed Position   B Open Position
Figure 3-11 Hatch mechanism in closed and open position

3.1.3.2 Hatch control unit

Refer to Figure 3-12 for hatch control unit. The Hatch Control Units (HCU) are assembled on trainset interface, which contains the electric equipment. The unit have removable covers, which enable access to the push buttons (1) for local control (unlock, open and close) of the hatch echanism. The unit has a connection (4) for external air supply in case of failure of the trainset pressurized air system. A 3-way valve (3) enables switching between internal and external air supply. If no external air supply is connected, the system will drain to make manual operation possible. A removable key (2) can be used to isolate electrical and pneumatic supply to allow safe work on the hatch mechanism.

1—Push buttons (local control); 2—Removable key; 3—3-way valve; 4—Connection, external air.
Figure 3-12　Hatch control unit

3.2　Semi-permanent couplers

3.2.1　Types and configurations of the semi-permanent couplers

There are two type of semi-permanent couplers, type A and type B. The Figure 3-13 below illustrates a type-A semi-permanent coupler, which consists of Coupler Head, Buffer, Bearing Bracket, and Guide Rail.

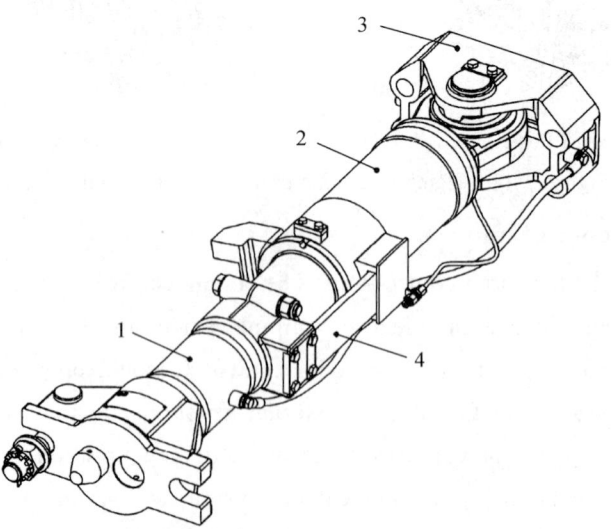

1—Coupler head; 2—Buffer; 3—Bearing bracket; 4—Guide rail.
Figure 3-13　Semi-permanent coupler of type A

The coupler mounted on the vehicle with a bearing bracket. The buffer cushions the draft and buff loads and absorbs the shock. The guide rail prevents the rotation of hydraulic buffer inside the buffer tube and thereby rotates the coupler head. The spherical rubber bearing minimizes the shock of pulling and compression forces and extends the life of the pivot.

The Figure 3-14 illustrates the type-B semi-permanent coupler. The coupler head is same with the one of the type A coupler, but it is welded to the main coupler body to form a stiff coupler tube.

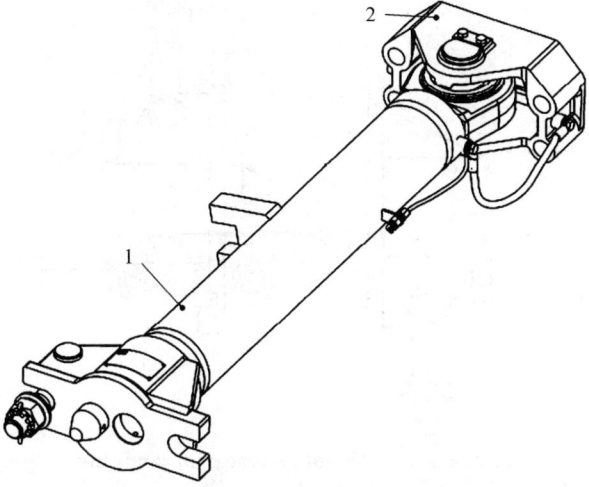

1—Coupler tube; 2—Bearing bracket.
Figure 3-14　Semi-permanent coupler of type B

The coupler head is illustrated in the Figure 3-15. The compression and impact loads are transmitted to the bearing bracket through the specially-designed front face of the coupler head. For type-A semi-permanent coupler, the traction loads are transmitted through the eye screws (1) to the buffer and then to the vehicle under frame, for type-B semi-permanent coupler, the traction loads are transmitted through the tub to the vehicle under frame. The coupling / uncoupling is done manually with eye screws (1) and castellated nuts (2).

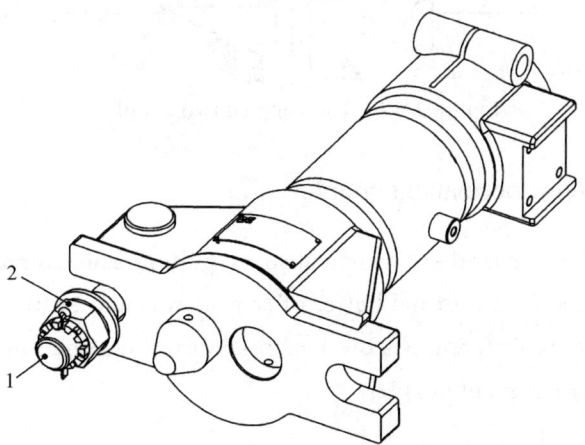

1—Eye screw; 2—Castellated nut.
Figure 3-15　Front face of a coupler

3.2.2 Coupling and uncoupling

The type-A coupler is at one end of a vehicle and the type-B coupler is at the end of the other vehicle. Coupling and uncoupling can only be done manually. Figure 3-16. shows two semi-permanent couplers (type A and type B) which are ready for coupling. At this time the two eye screws of the couplers are turned away from the face of the couplers to prevent damage.

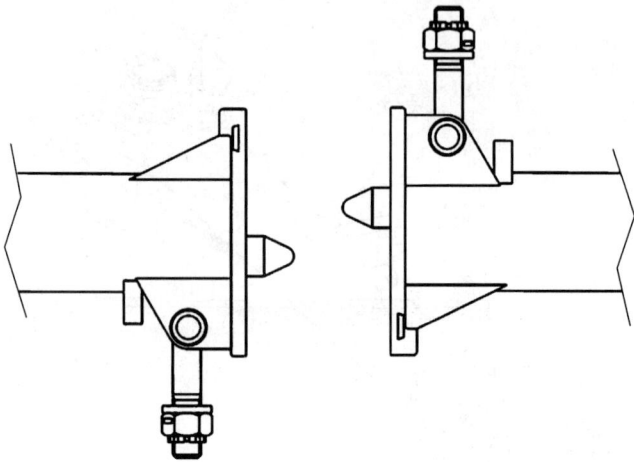

Figure 3-16   Couplers ready for coupling

After the faces of the two couplers are brought together, the eye screws are fitted and tightened behind the flange of the opposite couplers and tighten (referring to the Figure below). They form a permanent connection between two vehicles of a EMU train.

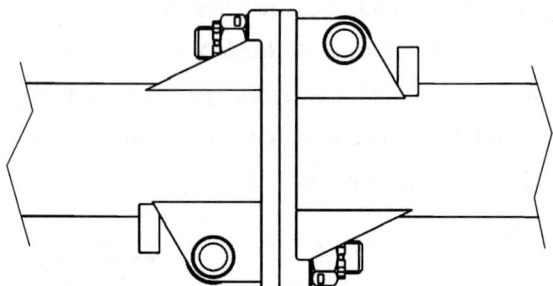

Figure 3-17   The coupled two couplers

3.2.3 Buffer of semi-permanent coupler

The buffer is a shock absorber, which absorbs pulling and compression loads from the mechanical coupler. The structure of the buffer of semi-permanent buffer is same with the one on automatic coupler. The only difference is on the stroke of buffer. The Figure below illustrates the stroke of buffer of semi-permanent coupler.

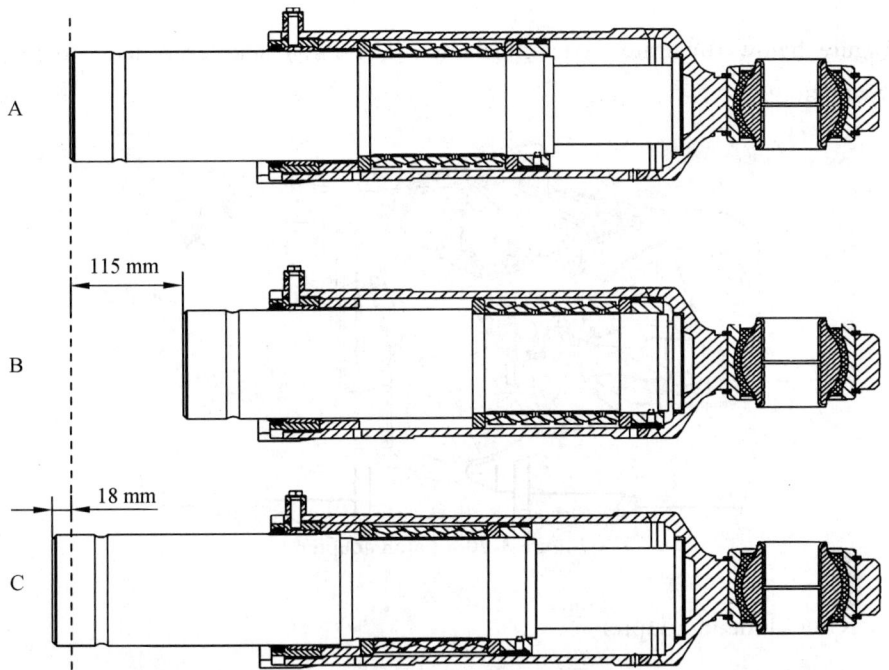

A—Buffer at rest (no buff or draft C loads); B—Buffer under compression load (maximum stroke);
C—Buffer under pulling load (maximum stroke).
Figure 3-18　Buffer of semi-permanent coupler

3.3　Coupler adapter

The coupler adapter is used for a temporary coupling between a knucklehead type coupler and an automatic coupler. The Figure below illustrates a coupler adapter, which consists of a latch adapter and a knucklehead adapter.

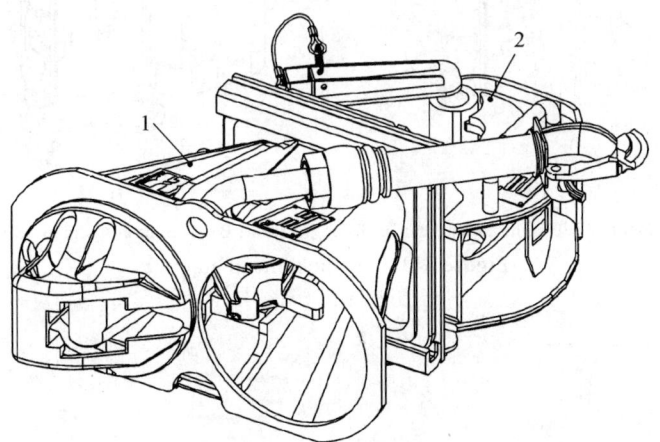

1—Latch adapter; 2—Knucklehead adapter.
Figure 3-19　Coupler adapter

3.3.1 Latch adapter

The Figure below illustrates a latch adapter. The latch adapter is used to mate with the automatic coupler.

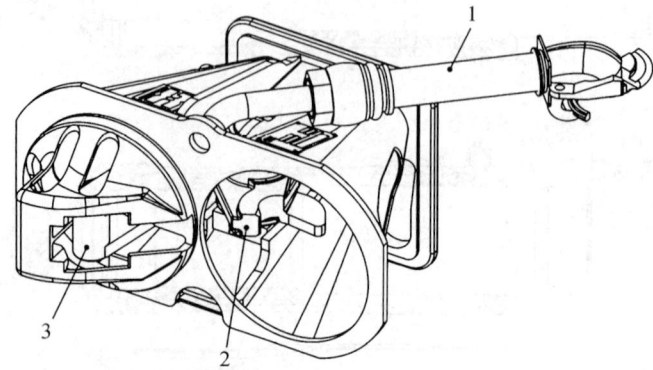

1—Air connection; 2—Hook plate; 3—Coupling link.
Figure 3-20   Latch adapter

3.3.2 Knucklehead adapter

The knucklehead adapter is a special type of design, which allows the coupler adapter to be coupled to train set, mounted on Chinese type 13 and 15 knucklehead couplers.

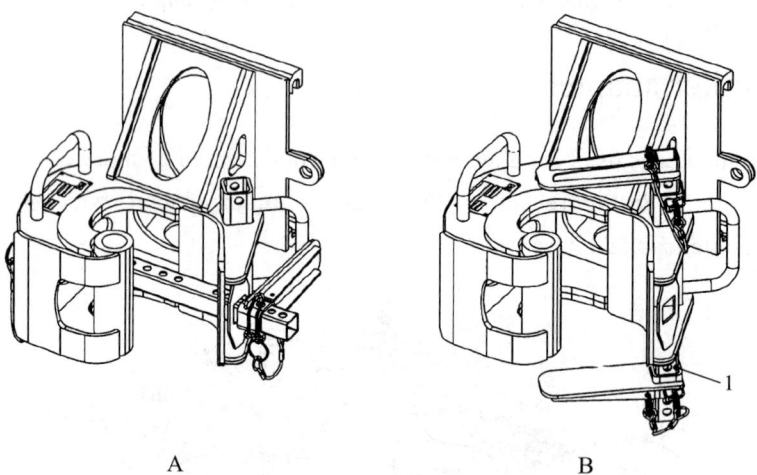

1—Height adjustment; A—Height adjustment in stored position; B—Height adjustment in mounted position.
Figure 3-21   Knucklehead adapter

Chapter 4   Bogies

The EMU trainset normally consists of eight vehicles, 4 motor cars and 4 trailer cars. Each vehicle has two bogies. The bogies can be classified as motor bogie and trailer bogie. The motor bogie is shown as Figure. 4-1, and the trailer bogie is shown as in Figure. 4-2. The bogies are of modular design. The major modules are similar in all bogies.

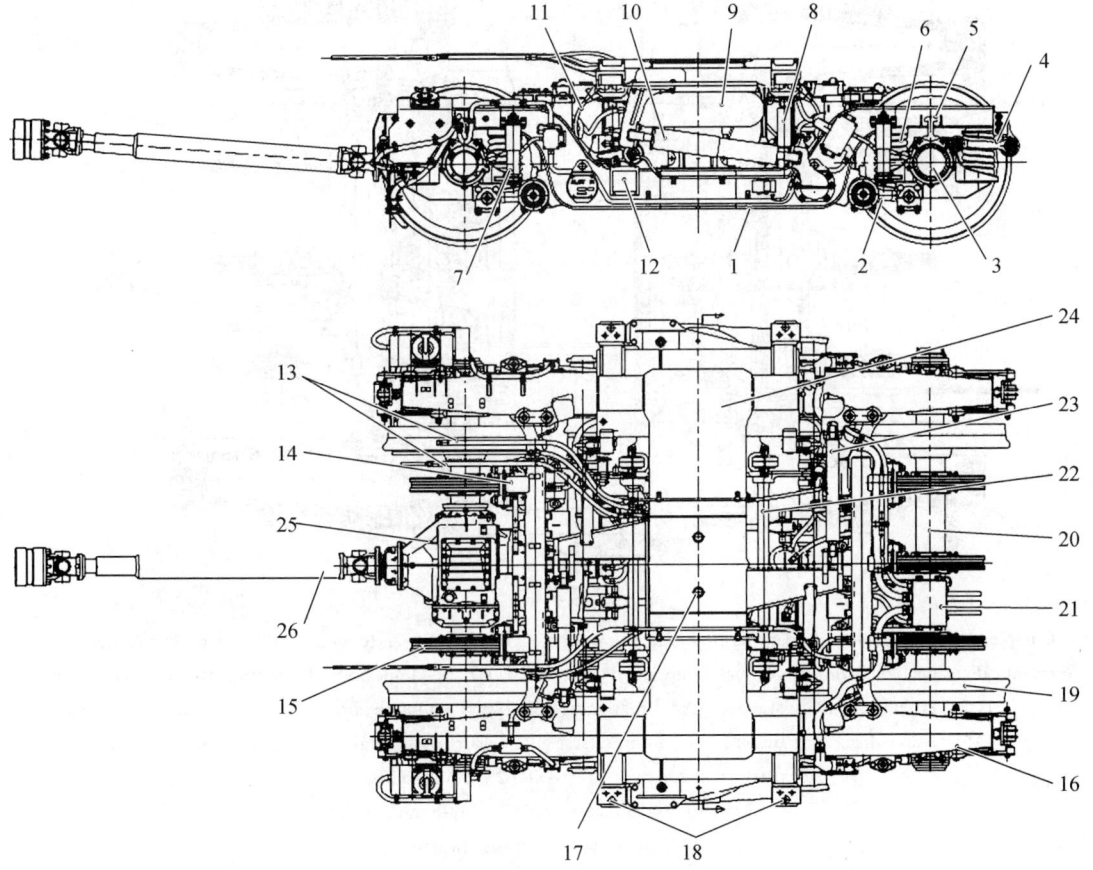

1—Complete; 2—Motor bogie–motor axle with sanding system, left side; 2—Lower rod assembly; 3—Axle box; 4—Push rod; 5—Vertical stop link; 6—Helical springs; 7—Primary vertical damper; 8—Secondary vertical damper; 9—Air spring; 10—Anti yaw damper; 11—Vertical secondary stopper; 12—Brake indicator; 13—Pneumatic connection; 14—Brake calliper; 15—Brake disc; 16—Bogie frame; 17—Bolster guide; 18—Body-bogie support; 19—Solid wheel; 20—Electrical end box; 21—Axle; 22—Anti roll bar assembly; 23—Horizontal damper; 24—Body-bogie bolster; 25—Gearbox; 26—Cardan shaft.

Figure 4-1   Motor bogie

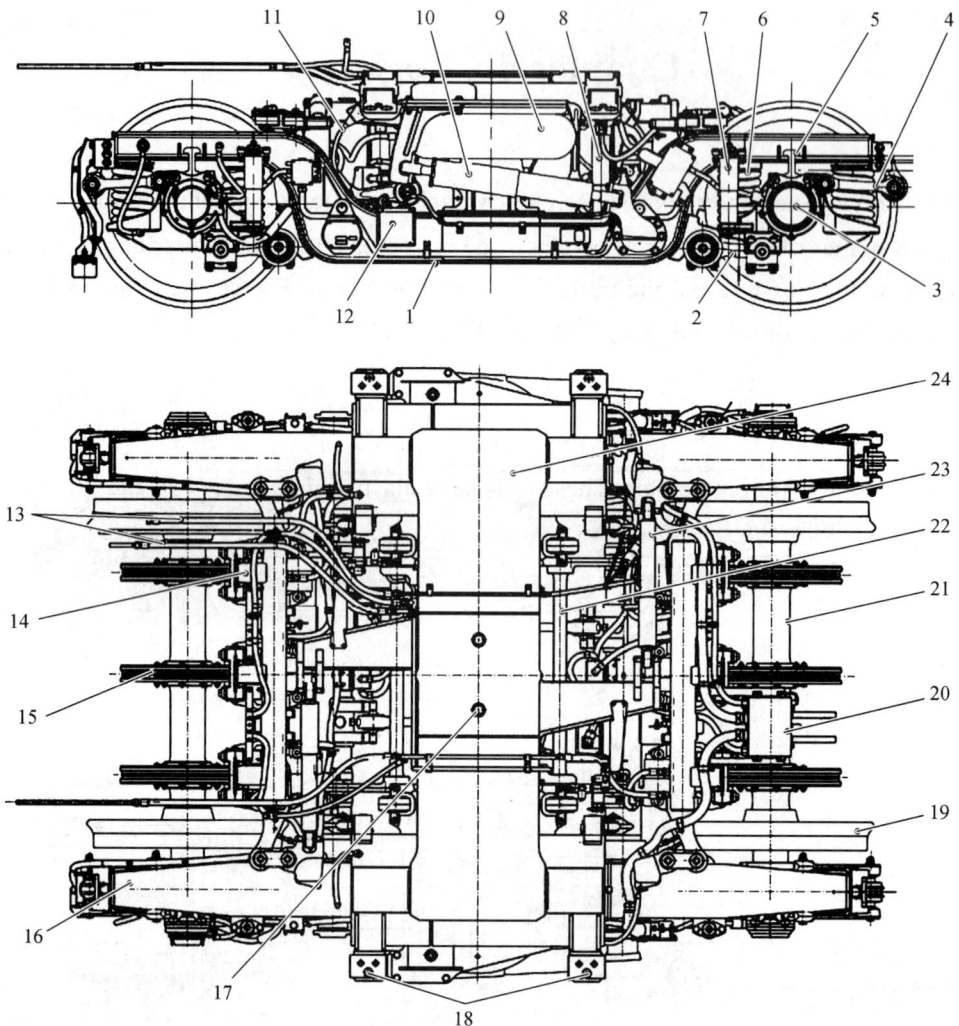

1—Complete 1 trailer bogie with parking brake; 2—Lower rod assembly; 3—Axle box; 4—Push rod; 5—Vertical stop link; 6—Helical springs; 7—Primary vertical damper; 8—Secondary vertical damper; 9—Air spring; 10—Anti-yaw damper; 11—Vertical secondary stopper; 12—Brake indicator; 13—Pneumatic connection; 14—Brake caliper; 15—Brake disc; 16—Bogie frame; 17—Bolster guide; 18—Body bogie support; 19—Solid wheel; 20—Electrical end box; 21—Axle; 22—Antiroll bar assembly; 23—Horizontal damper; 24—Body-bogie bolster.

Figure 4-2 Trailer bogie

The whole body structure rests on the bogies through bolster (24). The bogie and the body structure are fastened through supports (18) provided on the bogies. The bolster (24) has a boxed structure to accommodate the two auxiliary reservoirs. These reservoirs are for the pneumatic system of the secondary suspension air springs.

The 'Z' type traction system transmits tractive and braking forces from the bogie to body. The 'H' shaped bogie frame (16) is fabricated with alloyed steel and is suitable for high speed operations. The bogie frame (16) is connected to the four axle boxes (3) with lower rod assembly

(2) and push rods (4).

The wheel set consists of two solid wheels (19) and an axle (21). The wheels (19) are interference fitted to the axle (21).

The body of the axle box (3) is made of nodular cast iron. The axle box (3) has tapered roller bearings with preassembled cartridges and polyamide cage. Axle box absorbs axial thrust raised due to rail wheel interaction. The axle box consists of integrated sensors to sense the parameters such as bearing temperature, speed, anti skid. An earth / traction return current device is also provided on the axle box for return current path.

The suspension between axles of a bogie is called primary suspension. In bogies, two sets of helical springs (6) are seated firmly on the spring seat, which is an integral part of the axle box (3). A vertical damper (7) is parallel to the helical spring (6) to suppress the bouncing effect of the bogie while on run. The axle box is anchored to the bogie frame (16) by lower rod assembly (2) and push rod (4) set at different heights. These rods have elastic joints at the two ends.

The suspension between bogie frame and body is called secondary suspension. The air spring (9) of secondary suspension enhances the riding comfort. The air spring system in the secondary suspension absorbs the vertical and lateral loads between the vehicle body and bogie. A levelling valve (load sensing device) controls the operation of air spring. If the air spring is deflated, a special rubber pad (auxiliary emergency spring) in series with the air spring, takes the load and permits the vehicle to run without speed limitations.

In addition to air spring (9) assembly in secondary suspension system, several dampers are provided, Two secondary vertical dampers (8) per bogie are provided diagonally parallel to the air spring assembly to suppress bouncing effect while on run. Two horizontal dampers (23) per bogie are arranged diagonally to absorb lateral oscillations to help easy curve negotiation. Two anti-yaw dampers (10) per bogie are fitted between bogie frame and body-bogie bolster (24). These anti-yaw dampers control small amplitude bogie rotational movements while negotiating curves at high speeds. Consequently, undue wear of the wheels through lateral forces on the rail is eliminated. A yaw detection sensor that measures the yaw movement at bogie frame level is provided only for the first trainset.

The motion is transmitted to the wheels from traction motor via cardan shaft (26) connected at one end to a torque limiting joint (safe-set joint), which, in turn, is interference-fitted to the traction motor shaft (arranged lengthwise in the motor bogie underframe). The other end of the cardan shaft is connected to the reduction gearbox (25) mounted on the inner axle of the motor bogie.

The gearbox (25) is mounted on the centre of motor axle. It consists of reduction gear arrangement assembled inside the gearbox casing. It is coupled with cardan shaft through flange coupling. The reduction gear is equipped with an oil gauge and electric sensors to determine the oil level. The relative signal is transferred to the TCMS (Train Control and Monitoring System) during sufficiently long stops at stations. Safe-set is a coupling device, which connects the shaft of the traction motor at one end and to cardan shaft at the other end. This coupling has torque setting system. By adjusting the hydraulic pressure, the release torque can be set to the required level. When the pre-set torque exceeds the specified limit, the shear rings open up and release the oil pressure in the coupling, then the safe-set coupling slips. This occurs in milliseconds. After pressure release, the coupling runs freely on the shaft.

Two antiroll bar assemblies (22) are connected between bogie frame and body-bogie bolster (24). This antiroll bar assembly consists of a roll bar supported by two hangers with elastic articulation. The antiroll bar system prevents the vehicle body from rolling, on the bogie.

4.1 Bogie frame

Bogie frame is an H-type constructed, with non alloy steel frame, referring Figure 4-3. H-type steel frame consists of two solid longitudinal beams connected by tubular cross-members. The longitudinal beams are made up of welded metal plate. Tubular cross-members are made up of pressed steel. Bogie frame consists of fabricated and machined brackets to accommodate the components of bogie. Bogie frame with fabricated brackets is stress-relieved to relieve the stress developed during the welding process. The frame is machined to accurate dimensions after the welding and stress-relieve processes. Bogie frame rests on primary suspension coil.

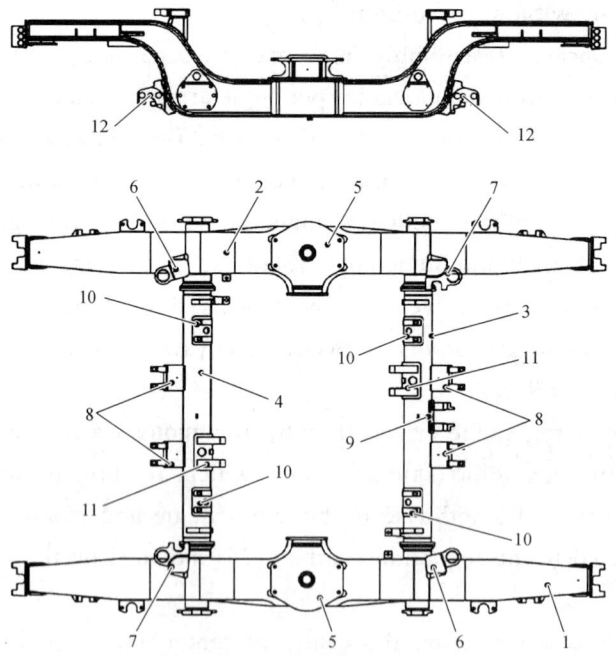

1—Complete longitudinal beam-left; 2—Complete longitudinal beam-right; 3—Rear tubular beam assembly;
4—Front tubular beam assembly; 5—Secondary suspension support; 6—Brake tubular girder support;
7—Lateral damper support; 8—Brake transom support; 9—Gear box reaction support;
10—Anti-roll bar support; 11—Traction rod support;
12—Support fastening for axle box.

Figure 4-3 Bogie frame

4.2 Wheelset with axle box

Each bogie consists of two wheelsets with axle boxes. Each wheelset is a rotating component with the power of traction motor which drives the trainset through the cardan shaft. The whole bogie rests on the wheelset with axle box through the primary suspension coil springs. It takes the weight of trainset through the primary suspension. Each wheelset carries a maximum axle load of 17 tons.

4.2.1 Wheel

Refer to Figure 4-4, wheel is a mono block structure made up of R8T steel. It is a one-piece circular component of 890 mm diameter alloy steel. Wheel sample test pieces are subjected to tensile test, chemical analysis, impact test, hardness test on the cross section of the rim, checks for direction of the residual stresses, micro structure, grain size, and ultrasonic examination before the machining operation. Wheel is a machined component. In the centre there is a machined bore of 192 mm diameter which accommodates the axle with interference fit. The wheel is designed to withstand fatigue load, vertical load, lateral load and high speed.

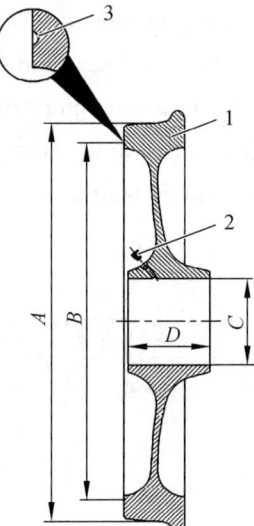

1—Wheel; 2—Screw; 3—Machined groove (serviceable limit indication).
Figure 4-4 Wheel

The wheel tyre consists of tapered rolling profile with a radius which acts as a differential to negotiate the track curves. Wheel flange prevents the wheels from derailment. Rim portion of the wheel is hardened and tempered to reduce wear and tear due to friction. Wheel is an ultrasonically tested component and free from the internal defects. The wheel bore is concentric with the tread diameter of the wheel. There is a through hole of 5 mm diameter, which is provided on the outer diameter of the hub to the wheel bore. It is used for oil injection while removing the wheels from axle. The hole is protected by a screw (2) in the normal working condition. The permitted dimensions of wheel are given below.

Dimensional details:

Wheel diameter:　　　new 890 mm (Fully worn limit is 810 mm);
Tyre width:　　　135 mm Hub fitting diameter 192 mm;
Minimum outer diameter of hub:　　240 mm;
Hub width:　　　　　　　180 mm.

On the wheel face with a diameter of 794 mm indicates the serviceable limit of the wheel. The wheels are painted to prevent corrosion.

4.2.2　Axle

Axle is made of an alloy steel forged material. It is a machined component. The seating positions of the axle are finished by grinding operation. The axle is ultrasonically tested to avoid internal defects. Forged axle sample pieces are subjected to chemical analysis, tensile test, resilience test, rotary bending fatigue test, microscopic examination and the ultrasonic examination to ensure the quality of the axle.

The axle is accurately machined by grinding to accommodate the wheelset with axle box components. It consists of brake disc seat wheel seat and the axle box bearing seats of grinding. Tapped holes at the two end faces of the axle accommodate the end plate that locks the axle box bearing complete. At the centre of the trailer axle there is a through bore with a diameter of 65 mm, which is used for periodical ultrasonic testing with bore probe.

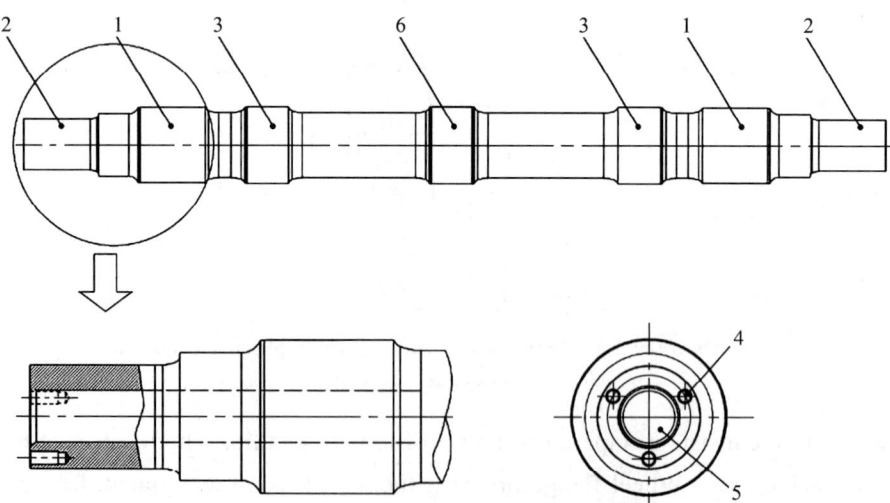

1—Wheel seat; 2—Axle box bearing seat; 3—Brake disc seat; 4—Tapped holes end cap locking;
5—65 mm diameter bore; 6—Brake disc seat (centre).

Figure 4-5　Axle

4.3 Axle box

Referring to Figure 4-6, axle box body is made up of nodular cast iron and is a machined component. It consists of a machined bore at the centre, which accommodates the tapered bearings. Axle box body consists of circular shape rings at the two ends to accommodate the coil spring.

Axle box end faces consist of tapped holes to fix the intermediate front cover. Intermediate front cover consists of speed and temperature sensor provisions.

Axle box with bearing assembly is fitted at the two ends of the axle. Primary suspension coil springs rest on axle box which takes the bogie load. These bearings are assembled to the axle by press fit. Tapered bearing unit which has one end locked by end cap is fitted on axle. Bearings are lubricated by grease. A return current device is fitted on the axle box. Intermediate front cover and front cover consist of O-rings to prevent grease leakage. All end cover fasteners are torque tightened. The axle boxes are equipped with the following devices:

- Bearing temperature sensors (BTS);
- Speed sensors for antiskid device (BCU);
- Speed sensors (LKJ) • Speed sensors (ATP);
- Earth current return devices (ECR) or Traction current devices (TCR).

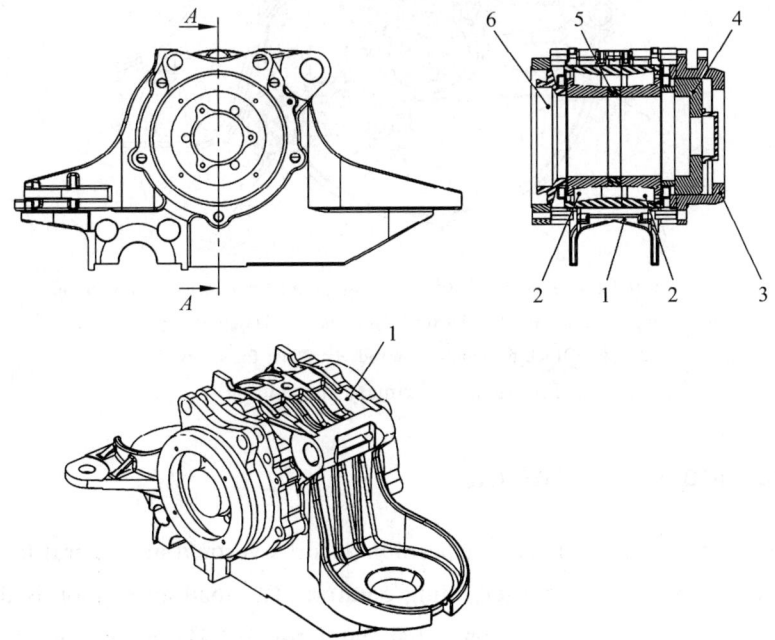

1—Axle box; 2—Tapered bearing; 3—Intermediate front cover (left); 4—End cap; 5—Spacer; 6—Axle.
Figure 4-6 Axle box

4.4 Primary suspension

Referring to Figure 4-7, primary suspension transmits the vertical forces. It consists of external spring group, internal spring group and vertical damper. External and internal spring groups consist of external and internal coil springs. These springs are made of spring steel round wire and are subjected to fatigue test. Wire diameter of the outer spring is 29.5 mm and the inner spring diameter is 20 mm. These springs are laid between the bogie frame and axle box. Primary suspension consists of two sets of spring group and one vertical damper on each axle box.

A lower rod assembly is connected between the axle box and the bogie frame. The lower rod is connected to axle box though block for connection by screws. Complete push rod (4) assembly is connected to the axle box top and the bogie frame by the bolted fastenings. The elastic joints in these rods guide the axle box for uniform suspension.

A vertical stop link is fitted on the axle box. This is used to control the bogie frame height at 'no load' condition. In addition to the coil springs, dampers are fitted to the bogie frame for primary suspension which reduce the vehicle vibration and absorb the spring damping during the vehicle movement.

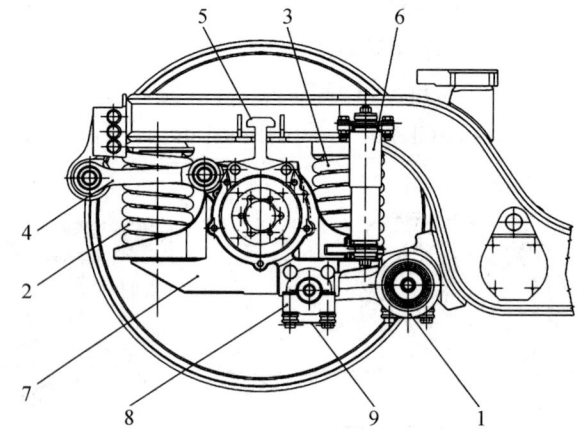

1—Lower rod assembly; 2—External spring group; 3—Internal spring group;
4—Complete push rod; 5—Vertical stop link; 6—Damper; 7—Axle box;
8—Block for connection rod; 9—Plate for screw.

Figure 4-7 Primary suspension

4.5 Secondary suspension

Referring to Figure 4-8, secondary suspension absorbs vertical and lateral loads between the bogie and body which ensures passenger riding comfort. The load absorption is done by two air spring assemblies (1), vertical (6), horizontal (7) and anti-yaw (4) dampers on each bogie. These are fitted between body bogie bolster and bogie. It ensures constant trainset height through the levelling valves on each bogie. Secondary suspension consists of air spring assembly, vertical damper, horizontal damper. In case of a problem with the air spring or with air supply to air spring, the vehicle body will be lowered onto the emergency spring. Then, emergency spring works alone. In this conditions, the trainset must run on reduced speed to ensure safety and comfort of the passengers.

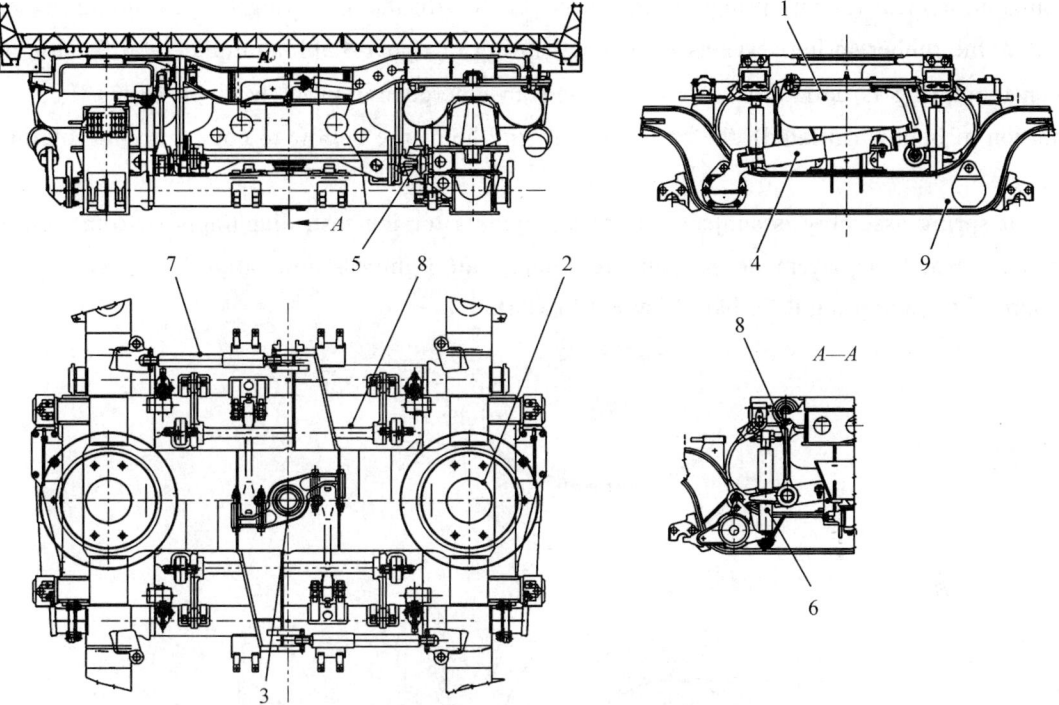

1—Air spring; 2—Bogie-car body link; 3—Traction system; 4—Anti-yaw damper; 5—Lateral rubber stop; 6—Vertical damper; 7—Horizontal damper; 8—Anti roll bar; 9—Bogie frame.

Figure 4-8　Secondary suspension

4.5.1　Air spring assembly

There are two air spring assemblies on each bogie. Referring to Figure 4-9, two air springs are connected with a double balancing valve. Main air comes to the air spring through the levelling valve. They are two auxiliary reservoirs in series which support the air spring system.

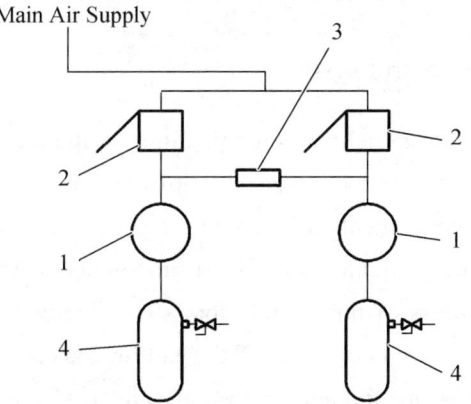

1—Air spring; 2—Levelling valve; 3—Double balancing Valve; 4—Auxiliary reservoir.

Figure 4-9　Air supply line diagram

Referring to Figure 4-10, air spring assembly consists of the following components: air spring diaphragm, conical rubber spring, arranged in series with the air spring (when the air spring is deflated, the rubber spring serve as emergency spring), upper diaphragm plate and friction plate (when the spring is deflated). Air spring and an emergency spring work in series. In normal condition of bellow (inflated), the emergency spring helps the bellow to cope with the rotation of the bogie.

Air spring assembly is subjected to tests, such as torsion test, diaphragm deformation with maximum radial displacement, pressure resistance, air tightness and fatigue test. The bursting pressure of the air spring is 20 bar (1 bar = 100 kPa).

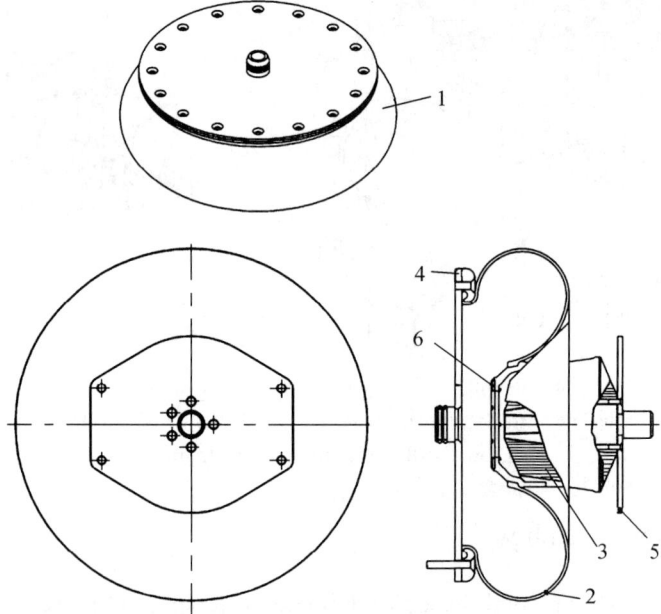

1—Air spring assembly; 2—Air spring diaphragm; 3—Conical rubber spring (Emergency spring);
4—Upper diaphragm plate; 5—Lower plate; 6—Friction plate.
Figure 4-10 Air spring assembly

4.5.2 Air suspension control system

Air suspension control system helps to charge and vent the air spring bellows of the vehicle. It also regulates the level of vehicle body regardless of the vehicle load. Air suspension permits a restricted amount of spring movement on account of platform boarding levels. Air suspension control is designed accordingly to hold the air spring bellows beneath the vehicle body at a constant spring height regardless of the vehicle load. The device that controls this function is a levelling valve which charges, vents or cuts off the bellows according to the difference between the preset length of the actuating linkage (set-point) and the momentary spring height (actual value).

4.6 Bolster

Bolster (Figure 4-11) is an intermediate component between the vehicle body and bogie. Each bogie has one bogie bolster. It rests on the secondary suspension springs. The vehicle body is connected to the body bogie bolster at four corners of body support brackets with bolted fasteners. The body bogie bolster has a boxed structure to accommodate the two auxiliary reservoirs required for the pneumatic system of secondary suspension air springs. It transmits the vehicle loads to bogie through secondary suspension. The secondary suspension dampers and the anti roll bar hangers are also connected to the bolster. It consists of a pivot pin to assemble the traction equalizer. Both sides of the body-bogie bolster consist of plates for lateral stop. Body bogie bolster consists of support brackets for body connection.

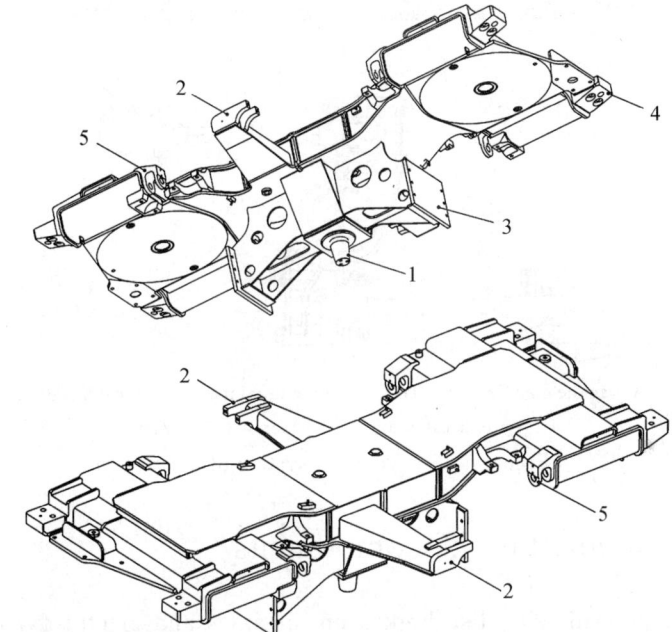

1—Pivot pin; 2—External support; 3—Plate for lateral stop; 4—Body support bracket;
5—Support vertical secondary stop.
Figure 4-11 Bogie bolster

4.7 Traction system of the bogie

Referring to Figure 4-12, traction system connects the bolster to bogie frame by linkage system. This system is assembled at the centre of the bogie. Each bogie consists of one traction system. Traction system consists of Traction Rod , Complete Equalizer , Joint for Traction Rod , It transmits the longitudinal forces of a bogie to the vehicle body. The bolster consists of a pivot at the centre. Traction system equalizer (1) is assembled to the pivot pin through the spacer and conical bushes (3) with three screws. Both ends of the equalizer are connected with traction rod joints with screws and nuts. Traction rods with joints are bolted to bogie frame brackets.

Traction rod joint consists of a pin, cylinder and a joint. It provides spherical movement in the traction system. These joints are assembled at the traction rod which has a bore of 103 mm. Pin consists of two holes of 25 mm diameter. The traction rod is used to assemble the complete equalizer to bogie. The elastic joints are tested for reinforcement, geometric, mechanical loads and static stiffness test.

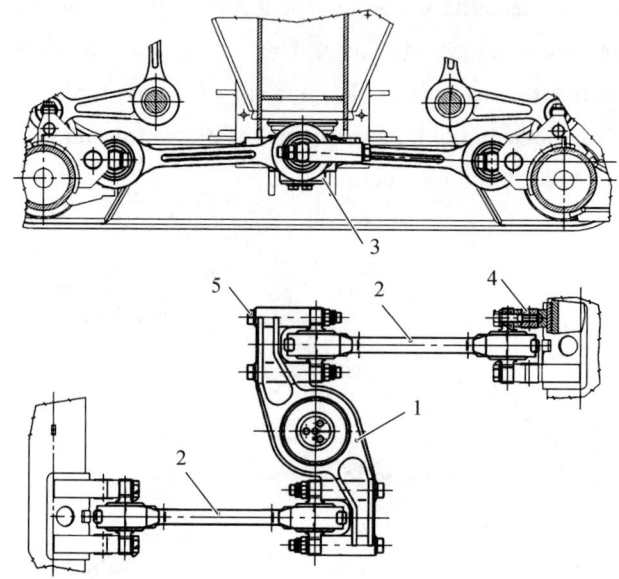

1—Complete equalizer; 2—Traction rod with joints; 3—Conical bushing;
4—Cylindrical Nut M24; 5—Screw M24×220.
Figure 4-12　Traction system of bogie

4.8　Bogie mounted brake components

The trainset is equipped with disc brakes on all axles and electro-dynamic brakes on the driven axles. All axles are equipped with 640 mm diameter axle-mounted disc brakes, made of steel, with reduced ventilation. There are 3 brake discs on the trailer axle and 2 on the motor axle.

Referring to Figure 4-13. the brake cylinder and the calliper for each brake disc are of conventional type, with built in automatic slack adjuster. The brake cylinder and calliper for parking brake are of integrated spring types. The brake pads are sintered type; designed for a maximum permitted temperature of 600 °C and a maximum wear of 30 mm.

The brake equipment is mounted on two brake transoms. These transoms are mounted on the bogie frame with brake transom supports. The brake cylinders are connected commonly through a pneumatic pipeline to activate braking system. The pneumatic air supply to the brake cylinder is supplied by brake control units which are located in under frame of all vehicle.

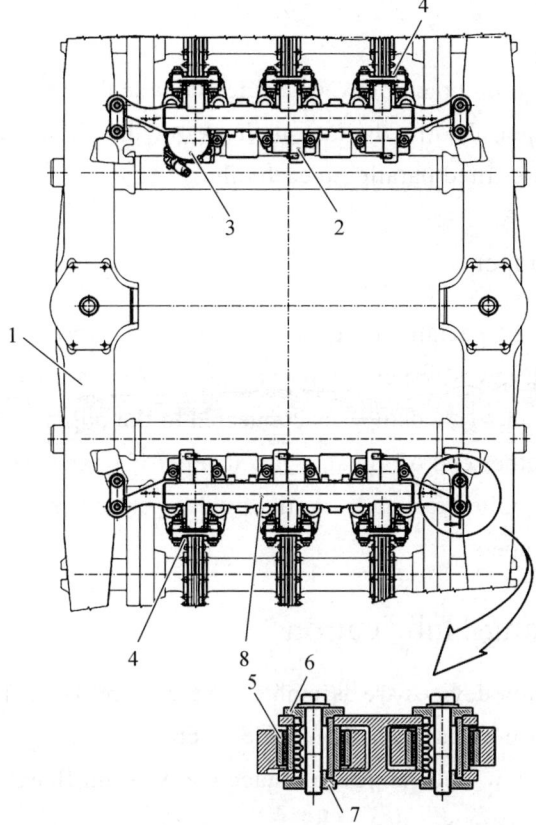

1—Bogie; 2—Brake calliper Unit (conventional); 3—Brake calliper Unit (Parking); 4—Sintered brake pad;
5—Upper elastic bush for brake transom; 6—Brake transom fastening bush;
7—Brake transom fastening bush 8—Brake transom.

Figure 4-13   Brake assembly for bogie

4.9   Damper

4.9.1   Vertical damper

Damper for primary suspension is assembled between the bogie frame and axle box. It absorbs shocks and vibrations of the vehicle. One end of the damper is fixed on a plate with two elastic joints. This plate is fixed to the bogie frame on the support. The other end of the damper is fixed to the axle box with two elastic joints. Joints are tightened by nuts. Each primary suspension of one bogie consists of four dampers.

Vertical dampers for secondary suspension are mounted on support brackets on bogie frame and brackets of body-bogie bolster. Secondary suspension consists of two vertical dampers on each bogie, and absorbs the vehicle vibrations and shocks. It consists of mounting joints at both ends which are perpendicular to each other.

4.9.2 Horizontal damper

Horizontal dampers are mounted between bogie frame and body-bogie bolster with brackets and bolted fasteners. Damper absorbs the lateral shocks of the vehicle body. Damper consists of joints at both ends which are fitted parallel to each other.

4.9.3 Anti-yaw damper

Anti-yaw Dampers are specially designed dampers to control small amplitude sinusoidal rotation movements. Anti-yaw dampers improve the bogie stability by reducing the vehicle vibrations. One end of the anti-yaw damper is connected to the bogie frame with a support bracket and bolted fasteners. The other end of the anti-yaw damper is connected to the body bogie bolster with a support bracket and bolted fasteners. Anti-yaw damper consists of joints at both ends. Each bogie has two anti-yaw dampers.

4.10 Wheel flange lubrication

Wheel flange lubrication devices are assembled to the trainsets. A flange-lubricating device is located on trailer wheel axle of each leading bogie of end vehicles (MC1 and MC2). The flange lubrication device lubricates wheel flanges to reduce the wear on flanges. The lubricant moves to the rails through the wheel flanges.

A wheel flange lubrication device consists of a pump unit, filter, spray nozzles, flexible air hoses and the lubrication hoses. Pump unit and other components are located on vehicle body and only the pipes and the nozzles are on the bogie.

There are two pump units in one trainset, one pump unit is mounted on MC1 and the second pump unit on MC2. When the trainset is in motion, the electronic control device emits electrical pulses which actuate the solenoid valve corresponding to the running direction. When the trainset moves in the direction of MC1 vehicle, pump feeds the spray nozzles placed before the right and left wheel of trailer axle of MC1, at that time, second pump unit on MC2 does not work. When the trainset moves in the direction of MC2, pump feeds the spray nozzles placed before the right and left wheel of trailer axle of MC2, at that time, pump unit on MC1 does not work.

The system is activated as per the trainset running direction at predetermined intervals of time or space, according to the trainset speed. Usually, one lubrication cycle is carried out every 300 meters. The lubricating oil is of bio-degradable type made of vegetal oils.

4.11 Sanding system

Referring to Figure 4-14, sanding operation increases the friction between wheel tread and rails during the vehicle starting sequence and in gradients. During sanding operation dry sand is injected to the rails through nozzle. Sand boxes contain dry sand. Each motor axle is provided with a sander on each wheel. Each sand box has two pneumatic input connections. One connection maintains a continuous flow of air to keep the sand dry, the other connection for sanding. The sand will be sprayed to rails with compressed air when the driver operates the sanding lever manually. Sanders are electrically heated. Sanding system consists of sand box, sand box lid, sand tube heater, nozzle, coupling and support brackets.

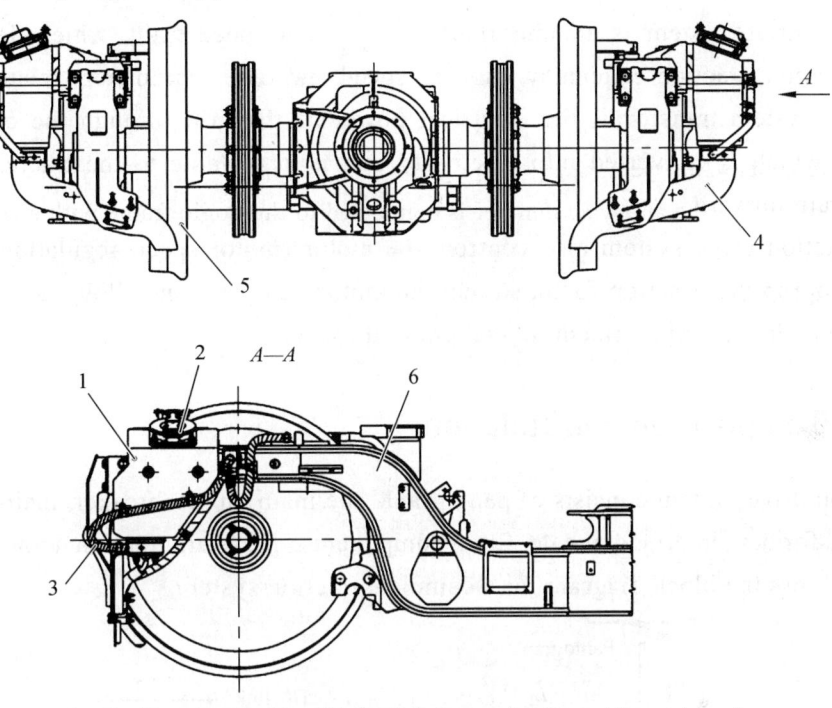

1—Sand box; 2—Sand box lid; 3—Spiral wrap; 4—Support for sand nozzle;
5—Motor wheelset; 6—Bogie frame.

Figure 4-14　Sanding box layout

Chapter 5　The Traction System of EMU

Traction drive system is an important part of high speed train, which determines the running direction, traction efficiency, running speed and other parameters related to motion. The traction system transforms the electrical power of the grid through the electric power conversion, which is converted into electricity that is acceptable to the traction motor and drives the train forward.

The traction drive system also controls the motor (motor speed regulation) in order to output the appropriate traction force, so that the motor vehicles can follow the instructions of the driver's cab in any environment, at the required speed.

5.1　Composition and function

Traction drive system consists of pantograph, the main circuit breaker, main transformer, current transformer, intermediate dc filter components, inverter, traction motor and so on. Figure 5-1 shows the block diagram for a complete traction system.

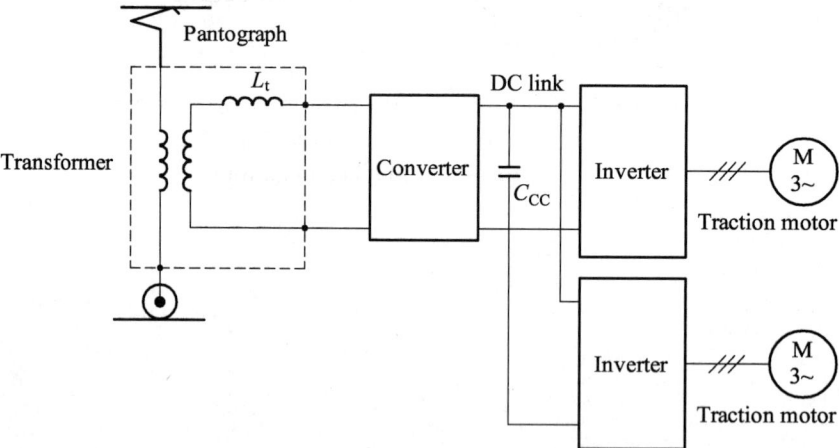

Figure 5-1　Basic components of the traction system

The effect of the electric bow is to transfer the electrical energy of the power grid to the moving car when it needs energy. When a moving car does not need to be electrified, the pantograph lowered, which separates the moving car from the high voltage. The electric bow is usually installed on a pedestal with an insulated column, which can be installed on the body of the vehicle, and the separation between the high voltage and the vehicle body. It is important to note that when used, the insulating column must be kept clean, otherwise the impurities attached to it are likely to reduce the insulation level, resulting in the risk of being overwhelmed by high voltage breakdown.

The role of the main circuit breaker is to cut or connect the main circuit and the grid when the electric bow is raised.

The function of the transformer is to convert the high voltage obtained by the pantograph to the electric energy with the appropriate voltage level, so as to facilitate the converter to control the electric energy. Transformers are large in size and weight, so they are usually mounted on trailers.

The converter is used to transform the electrical energy from the transformer which after stabilized to the traction motor. Usually a pre-class pulse rectifier rectifies the AC current from the transformer to a stable DC current, and then the converter inverts the DC current to deliver the power to the traction motor.

Normally, the motor is controlled by a special TCU, combined with the driver's room command information and the car's own condition, such as the car weight, slope and other information, Output the appropriate traction force, so as to achieve constant speed or variable speed traction of the EMU. At present, the converter in the motor vehicle has regenerative braking function, that is in the case of braking (electric braking), it can also run in reverse, the braking energy feed back to the grid. The traction motor runs as a generator and convert mechanical energy into electrical energy.

Converter as energy conversion device, its energy consumption is relatively large, and will produce a larger quantity of heat inevitably, Therefore, the converter also requires a special cooling device. For the moment, the cooling method is generally divided into water cooling and air cooling combined cooling, and it also needs to be cooled by a special cooling unit.

5.2 Pantograph

The pantograph acts as an electrical contact between the catenary and the electrically operated vehicle, it is a high-voltage device that receives power from 25 KV, 50 Hz ac catenary, the rails on the line can be used as a backflow conductor. There are two types of pantographs, single-armed and double-armed, and all of the current ones used in China are single-armed pantographs.

The design of the pantograph should have the highest operational reliability and meet the required contact pressure, even in high-speed operating conditions.

5.2.1 Structure and composition

Pantograph generally includes chassis, damper, the Lifting device, emergency drop device (ADD), upper arm, lower arm, carbon skateboarding, arch, guide bar, etc, the overall structure of the pantograph is shown in Figure 5-2.

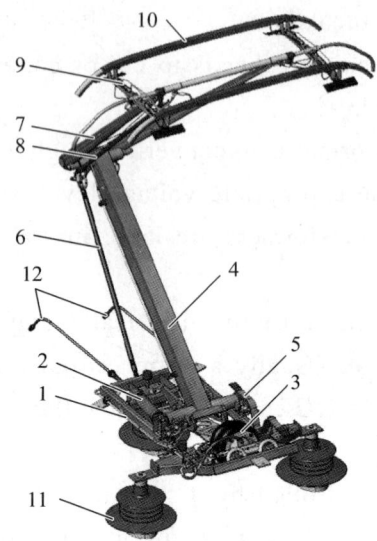

1—Pedestal; 2—Amortisseur; 3—Rise bow device; 4—Lower arm; 5—Bow assembly; 6—Lower guide rod; 7—Upper arm; 8. Upper guide rod; 9—Pantograph bow; 10—Carbon skateboard; 11—Insulator; 12—Insulated hose.

Figure 5-2　The general structure of the bow

The pantograph chassis is made of steel, and the upper and lower arms are made of lighter aluminum alloy material and fixed to the base frame. As shown in Figure 5-3.The entire pantograph was mounted on three insulators and rigidly secured with appropriate fasteners. Because insulators are susceptible to contamination and are relatively fragile, such as being easily damaged when hit by other objects, insulators are designed to be individually disassembled for easy replacement.

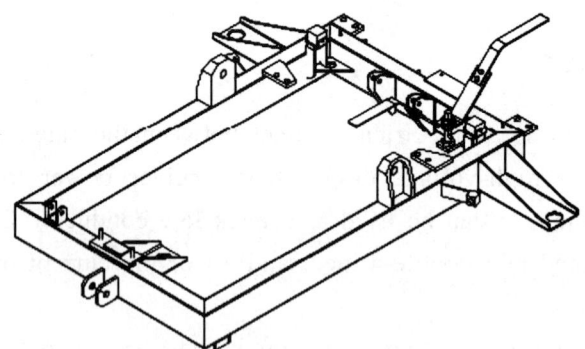

Figure 5-3　Pantograph base frame

The insulator is made of ceramic material. In the ascending position, the entire structure of pantograph can transmit electrical power, is a charged conductor, and the lower part of the insulator is the body of the vehicle. The body of the vehicle and the pantograph are insulated from the insulator. Therefore, the insulator is one of the safety components on the pantograph.

The raising device includes a pneumatically operated airbag driving device and an air lifting device. As shown in Figure 5-4.Whenever the compressed air passes into the airbag drive, the raising device will move and turn the lower arm upwards. Thus, the upper arm moves upward until the head bow touches the catenary.

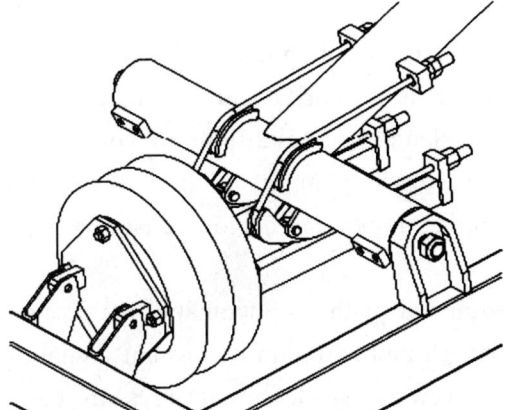

Figure 5-4　The schematic of lifting bow device

One end of the damper is fixed on the bottom frame, while the other end is fixed in the lifting device (lower arm) of the raised bow mechanism. The damper can reduce the impact of the pantograph on the roof when lifting the and lowering the bow, and can also absorb the pantograph vibrations caused by the interaction between the vehicle movement and the contact network.

In descending position, the pantograph is placed on three rubber shock absorbers, the head bow is placed on the bow assembly. Three rubber shock absorbers carry the entire structure of the electric bow. The head bow is put in place by bow assembly.

The bow assembly shape is designed to ensure that no damage occurs when the head bow is lowered. As long as the bow is fixed properly, it can prevent the tilt and bending of the bow.

The lower guide rod is supported by the rising bow and dropping bow operation. This will help guide the lower arm in place to prevent slanting and bending. One end of the lower guide rod is connected to the chassis and the other end is connected to the top end portion of the lower arm.

The upper arm is made of aluminum alloy, designed to keep the head bow in place.

The upper guide rod can keep the head bow in level position. Put the head bow accurately at an average height. This helps to achieve the equal or even wear of two carbon boards. The upper guide rod is made of aluminum alloy.

The head bow includes: bracket frame, transverse spring, bow Angle, carbon skateboard, pneumatic hose connection (ADD). It is designed to withstand horizontal and vertical shocks. In addition, the constant contact pressure of catenary can also be maintained.

The head bow is made up of rigid frames with two brackets, which are fitted with a carbon skateboard. The frame hangs from four springs and is mounted vertically in the bracket.

In addition, two transverse springs are placed between the head bow and upper arms to ensure horizontal bounce. This suspension structure allows the Carbon skateboard frame to move flexibly in the longitudinal direction, this will be able to cushion the impact of the vertical, to protect the carbon skateboard.

The main material of the carbon skateboard is the synthetic high-strength carbon, which has to be smooth to make sure that no spark occurs when collecting electricity. The automatic dropping device monitors the skateboard conditions by compressed air. In the pantograph of EMU, carbon skateboard is filled with compressed air, when the Carbon skateboard broken or damaged, the automatic dropping device can detect the pantograph damage to emergency drop bow.

The pantograph is equipped with a pneumatic lift system to ensure the dynamic characteristics of the pantograph and maintain a constant contact pressure with the catenary. The pneumatic lifting system can adjust the contact pressure between the carbon skateboard and the catenary.

The pneumatic lifting system and the automatic dropping device can get compressed air from the air circuit. The airbag cylinder operated by the compressed air system allows the pantograph against the catenary. When the compressed air is discharged from the airbag drive, the pantograph will be moved down by its own weight.

5.3 traction transformer

The principle of the transformer is to use the mutual inductance principle of alternating current, and the primary voltage is induced to the secondary by the conjugate coil. The required output voltage can be obtained through the design of different original, secondary coil turns ratio. Due to the high voltage of the contact network, the voltage level of 25 kV is obviously not able to be carried directly into the vehicle. As a result, the voltage transfer device is required to reduce the voltage from the grid to power the converter. The main working principle of the transformer is basically the same, which uses the primary and secondary side windings to transfer energy through the coupling of the iron core.

Figure 5-5   Actual drawing of the traction transformer

Because the traction transformer capacity is very large, and installed in the high-speed movement of the motor car, therefore, it is necessary to reduce the weight as much as possible. For example, the total weight of the CRH2 is less than 3 tons. Figure 5-5 shows the actual drawing of the traction transformer.

5.3.1 Structural features

The transformer that used in the CRH2 type EMU, The windings contains an primary winding and three secondary windings (two traction winding and a auxiliary winding) The windings are shown in Figure 5-6:

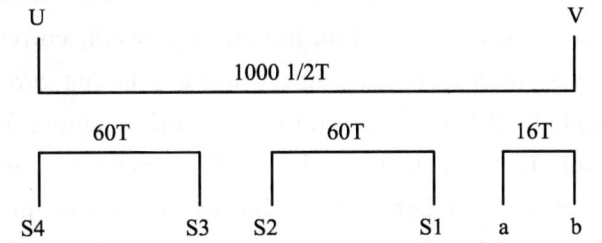

Figure 5-6　Winding of traction transformer of CRH2 EMU

Its structural features are:

(1) The secondary winding is two independent windings, each winding is connected with a traction converter device, make the secondary winding has high reactance and weak coupling, ensure that the traction conversion device has the characteristics of stable operation. In addition, in order to accommodate the capacity of each secondary winding, the primary winding is conFigured with two parallel wires.

(2) To reduce weight, the primary coil was made of aluminum coils.

(3) Side of a winding grounding, secondary winding side and three winding side of heat resistant epoxy resin insulating casing adopted at the center of the 11 root copper wire injection forming integrated terminal board, relative to the terminal side of a three winding is used and raises two center conductor.

5.4　Traction converter

5.4.1　Overview

The traction converter is the critical equipment of the moving vehicle, and is also one of the key technologies of the vehicle. Its working principle: using the new type of power semiconductor devices (such as IGBT or IPM, etc.), Uses the advanced PWM pulse modulation technology, intelligent control of power, in order to realize the output power for precise control of the traction motor.

The external and internal structure of the traction transformer is shown in Figure 5-7.

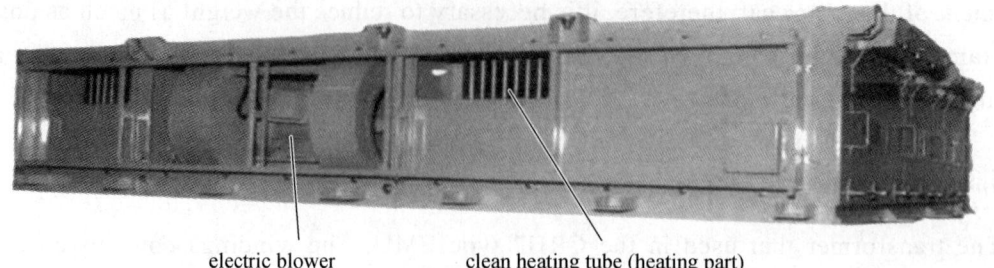

electric blower   clean heating tube (heating part)

Figure 5-7　Appearance of traction converters for CRH2 EMU

Due to train from the ac power input power for single-phase alternating current (ac), and general for the three-phase ac motor traction motor, as a result, current transformer usually adopt a level before pay - direct link, the single phase alternating current (ac) for middle dc rectifier, and then through the PWM inverter for three-phase ac output for ac motor, in order to realize the basic control. In the design of the traction converter, advanced four-quadrant technology is adopted, namely: When the moving car is in traction, the transformer can transfer electrical energy from the grid to the traction motor. When the moving car is in brake condition, the traction motor becomes the generator state, and the transformer sends the electrical energy generated by the traction motor to the ac power grid. At present, all mobile vehicle converters running in our country have regenerative braking function.

Since the traction transformer is also an energy conversion device, it also needs to be specially cooled by its additional cooling equipment. Usually the traction transformer is cooled by the combination of water cooling and forced air cooling.

5.4.2　Construction

As described in the previous section, the traction converter contains a pre-level cross-section and a PWM inverter. Since the energy needs to flow in both directions, the first of these is usually a four-quadrant rectifier. The four-quadrant converter also has a different structure for different moving cars. Traditional four quadrant converter structure as shown in Figure 5-8, is made up of four power switch bridge type circuit, namely each bridge arm has a power device (IGBT or IPM), against each power device and a diode to be used for two-way transmission of energy and necessary fly-wheel circuit. Due to train traction converter used in the power is relatively large, the voltage level is relatively high, therefore there are different schemes for the treatment of this pulse rectifier. Among these schemes, as shown in Figure 5-9, there are three level-converter schemes with diode clamp for CRH2, two rectifiers parallel scheme for CRH5, and single bridge arm double-tube parallel scheme for CRH3. Look from the design thought, CRH2 model of three-level converter can reduce the pressure drop of single pipe, which can improve system capacity, in the middle of the same dc voltage, reduce the single pipe pressure drop. And take three level output, second harmonic content is low, so you can save the volume and weight are relatively large second harmonic filter, reduce the volume and weight of the converter. In parallel with double rectifier, it can be used to output smaller grain wave, which is beneficial to the stabilization of the middle dc. Using double pipe parallel scheme, the capacity of the system can be improved, and the dc loss can be reduced by using a more pressure-resistant switch tube. At present, the choice of several kinds of schemes for moving cars in our country has to do with the selection of main circuit.

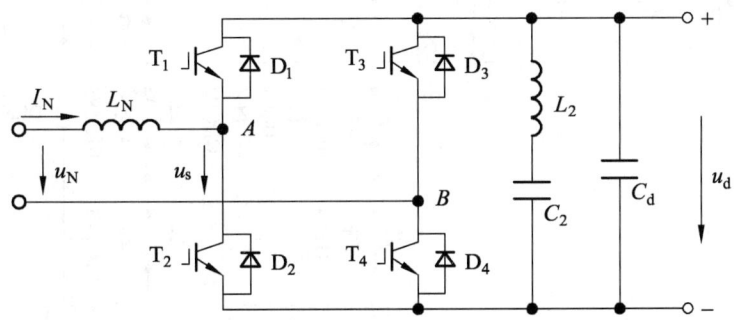

Figure 5-8 Traditional four-quadrant converter schematic

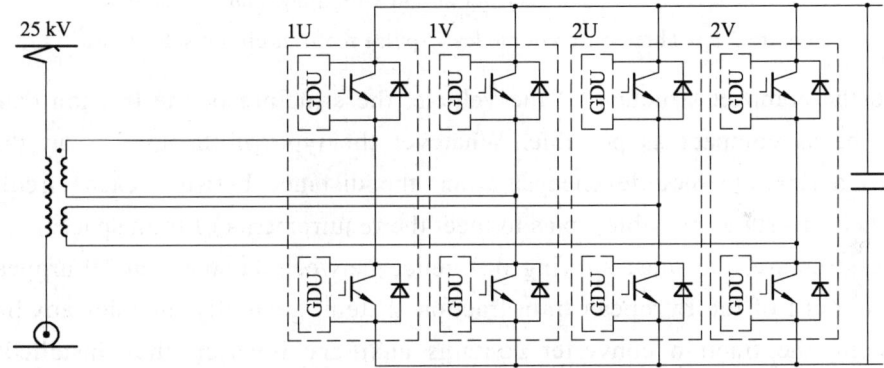

(a) The pulse transformer for parallel scheme of double converter

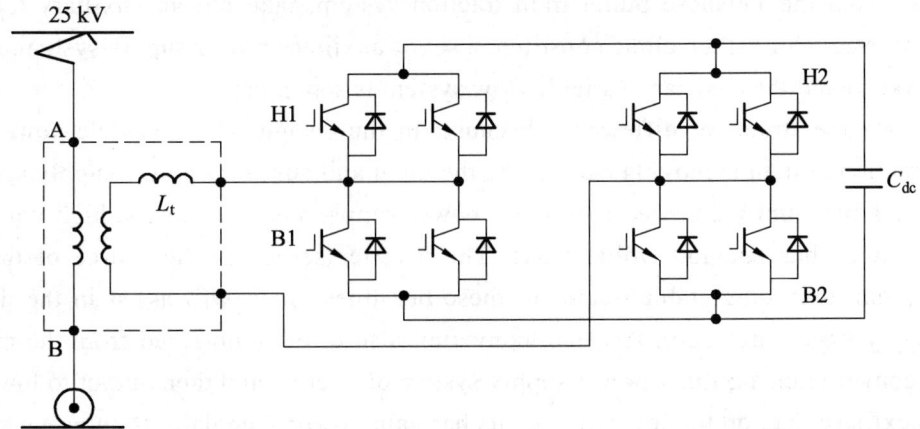

(b) The pulse convertor for a single bridge two-tube parallel scheme is adopted

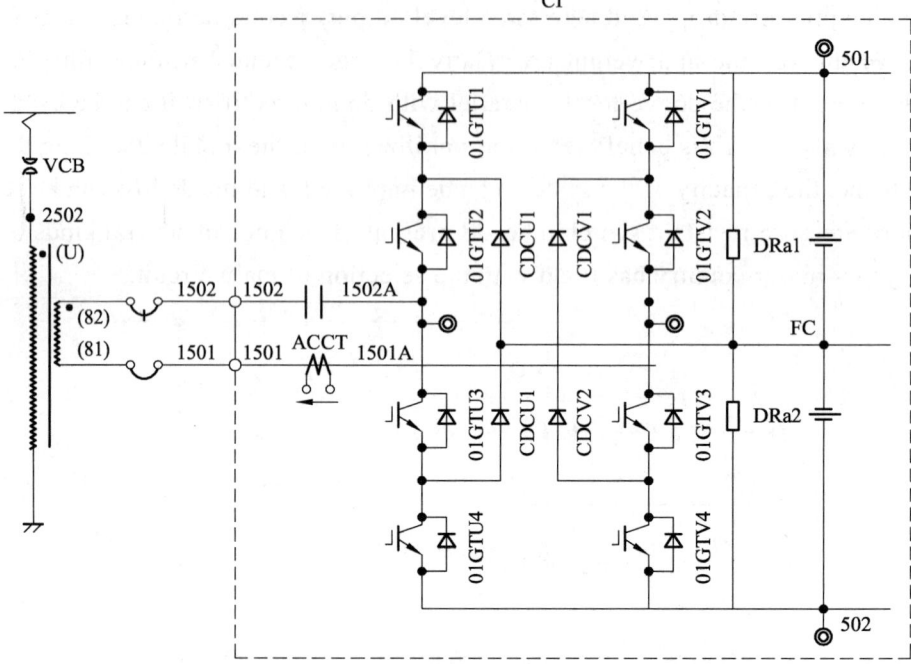

(c) The three-level pulse rectifier circuit with diode clamp is adopted

Figure 5-9　Three different modes of pulse rectifier circuit schematics

  Due to the compact structure of the vehicle, the structure of the traction converters is required to be as compact as possible. Whatever the type of the motor car, the traction converter as a separate module encapsulation, the distance between each circuit element requirements as nearly as possible, so as to meet the requirements of train space.

  On the structure, the most striking difference between Japanese and European mobile workshops is Lord of the European train traction system, generally includes auxiliary power supply system, the traction converter contains auxiliary inverter, they installed together, wrapped in a converter box, adopt the method of centralized inverter and concentrated heat dissipation; And the Japanese bullet train traction system, take out an auxiliary tap on the main transformer alone, then alone constitute a set of auxiliary power supply system, the main traction system and the auxiliary variable flow system is separated.

  Generate the structural differences because, in the design of the vehicle power supply system, traction system is moving car will be the main and auxiliary power supply system are designed to have a unified power supply bus power supply system, namely, high voltage bus, medium voltage bus and low voltage bus. The inverter serves as the source of the power supply system, providing stable output to these bus lines. So it will assist in the design of power supply system design in the main converter, also directly obtained from the middle of the main converter dc auxiliary power supply system of energy, and then output to low voltage bus bar, auxiliary load on the low voltage bus bar gain power. The daily train group separates the auxiliary power supply system from the main traction system as a special part. A secondary winding is specially designed to provide electricity to the auxiliary system. An auxiliary converter is specially designed for the auxiliary system. According to different loads in the car, the auxiliary converter outputs multiple voltages of different systems to supply power to different loads.

The difference between these two structures leads to a significant difference in the principle and performance of the work.

Since the auxiliary power supply system of the Japanese system is supplied directly from the auxiliary winding of the traction transformer, the auxiliary power supply system is in a state of power loss when the main circuit breaker is disconnected (over phase) or the overhead contact line is temporarily without power. If the train is over phase frequently, the auxiliary power supply system will start and stop frequently.

The situation of European EMU is different, because the auxiliary power supply system and the main converter are integrated. The auxiliary power supply system obtains electric energy from the intermediate DC of the main converter, while the main converter has regenerative braking function. Therefore, when the high-speed train is in operation, the auxiliary power supply system can still obtain electric energy from the intermediate DC of the intermediate main converter even when the main circuit breaker is disconnected or the contact line is without power for a short time. So the auxiliary power system will work smoothly all the time.

5.4.3 Operating principle

The working principle of the converter is shown in Figure 5-10. As already known, when the converter works, after the main transformer sends high voltage, the four-quadrant converter changes it into stable intermediate direct current. Then, the PWM inverter obtains electric energy from the intermediate DC link, and inverts the three-phase alternating current to drive the traction motor to run. The following is respectively introduced the two main parts, four quadrant converter and PWM inverter working principle. The single bridge arm double-tube parallel scheme of CRH3 is taken as an example to illustrate.

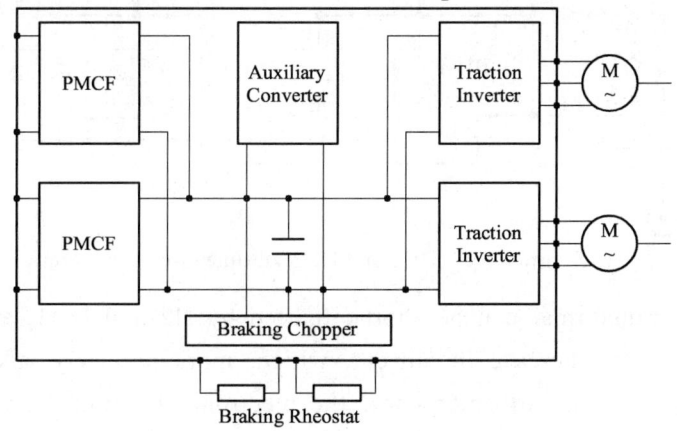

Figure 5-10   converter works schematically

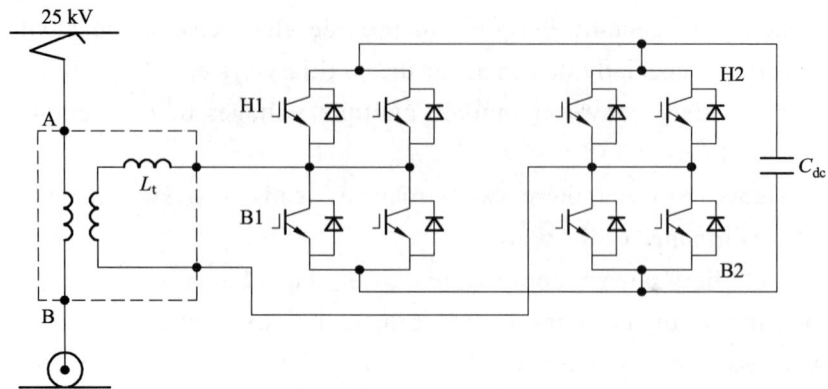

Figure 5-11 quadrant converter works schematic

As shown in Figure 5-11, each bridge arm is fitted with two parallel IGBT to increase the capacity of the load current of the same bridge arm. Each IGBT has a built-in anti-parallel diode. In the description below, DH1, DH2, DB1, DB2 will be used to refer to the diodes associated with IGBT H1, H2, B1, B2, etc.

The four quadrant converters can work in traction and braking, and present the principle of the two different working conditions respectively.

(1) traction condition

When the work is in traction, the four-quadrant converter is the equivalent of performing a "rectifier" function. Fixed in the carrier frequency of 250 Hz and duty ratio variable (PWM) cases, using a logic (below will carry out specific analysis) control of four quadrant converter. Therefore, if there is a positive and half wave of line voltage on the transformer terminal A and B, A certain element (such as H2) can be controlled within a certain period (T_{ON}). Figure 5-12 shows the circuit diagram of the DH1 and H2.

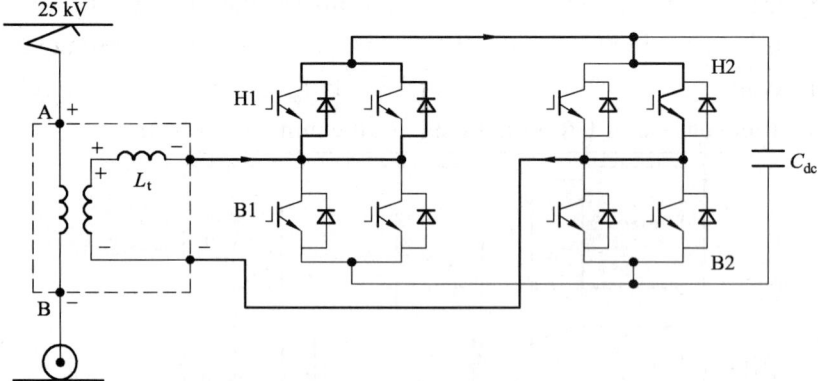

Figure 5-12 DH1 and H2 lead time circuit diagram

In fact, the transformer can be short-circuited by H2 and DH1, and the inductor "Lt" operates with a linear increase in current, which, more precisely, accumulates a specific amount of energy. In case of emergency, the electronic traction regulator can control the shutdown of H2 (T_{OFF}). The energy accumulated by "Lt" is transferred to the output filter (represented by the capacitor "Cdc") through the diode DH1-DB2, as shown in Figure 5-13:

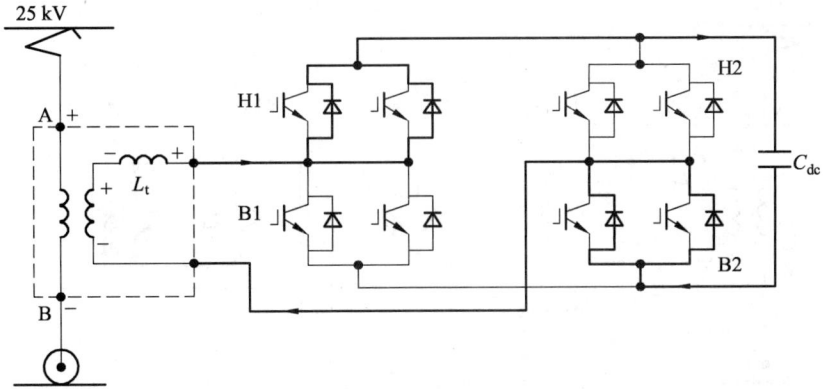

Figure 5-13 DH1 and DB2 lead time diagram

The voltage present at the output terminal of the main transformer (which in turn flows through the filter capacitor) consists of the sum of the vectors of the transformer secondary voltage and the automatic induced voltage of the inductor "Lt". As a result, the T_{ON} in the IGBT is adjusted appropriately to significantly change, specifically, the energy accumulated by the "Lt" and the value of the rectifier voltage present on the output filter. The loop T_{ON}-T_{OFF} is completed after conducting B1 and diode DB2. Figure 5-14 shows the circuit diagram for B1 to be connected to DB2.

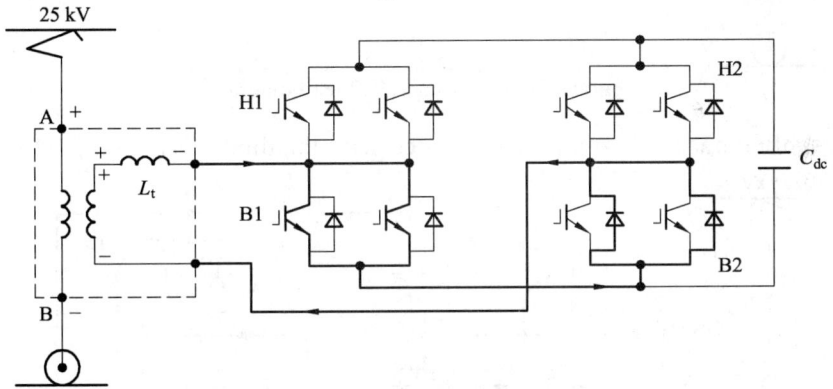

Figure 5-14 B1 and DB2 lead time diagram

The effect obtained on the main transformer is the same as that analyzed in Figure 5-22 (short circuit on the output terminal), but obtained through a different IGBT-DIODI connector. This facilitates the dissipation of heat generated during the IGBT switching process because the two related IGBTs are located in two separate power modules. In the case of DB1 off (T_{OFF}), the energy accumulated by the "Lt" is transmitted to the output filter in the same pattern. The principle of operation remains unchanged during the negative polarity half wave of the line voltage, except in relation to the conduction of current by other power supply components.

For example, B2-DB1 and DH2-H1 are switched on alternately, as shown in Figure 5-15 and 5-16.

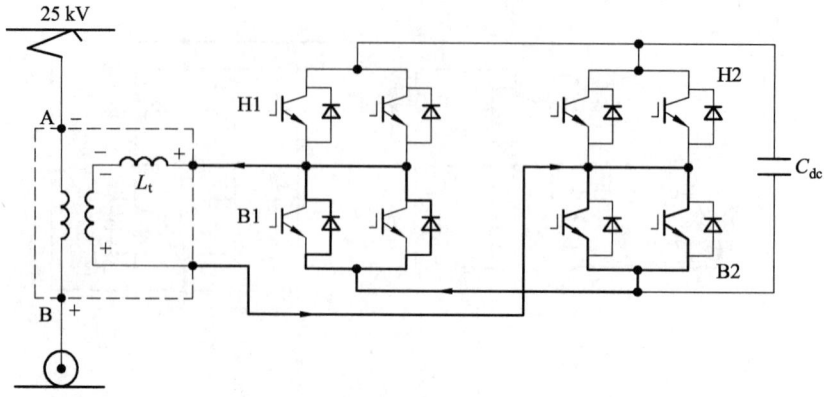

Figure 5-15　B2 and DB1 guide circuit diagram

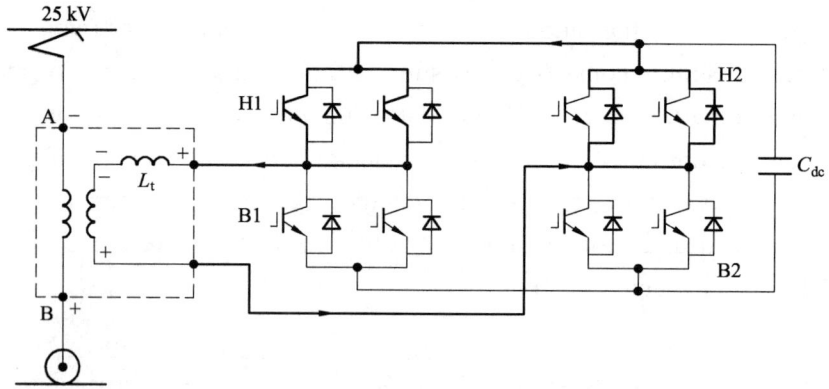

Figure 5-16　H1 and DH2 lead diagram

In the disabling phase (T_{OFF}), it is associated with the diode DH2 and DB1 connectors.

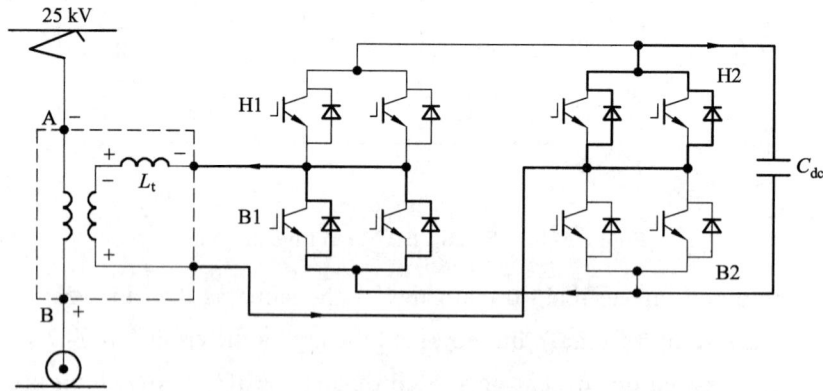

Figure 5-17　DH2 and DB1 guide circuit diagram

The way to generate PWM is: The logical way constitutes a triangle wave (carrier), with fixed frequency and amplitude (f=1350Hz), Divided by a sine wave (modulation), the sine wave frequency is 50Hz (the same as the line voltage), the amplitude and the phase are variable. The intersections of the carrier and the modulated wave generate PWM, as shown in Figure 5-18.

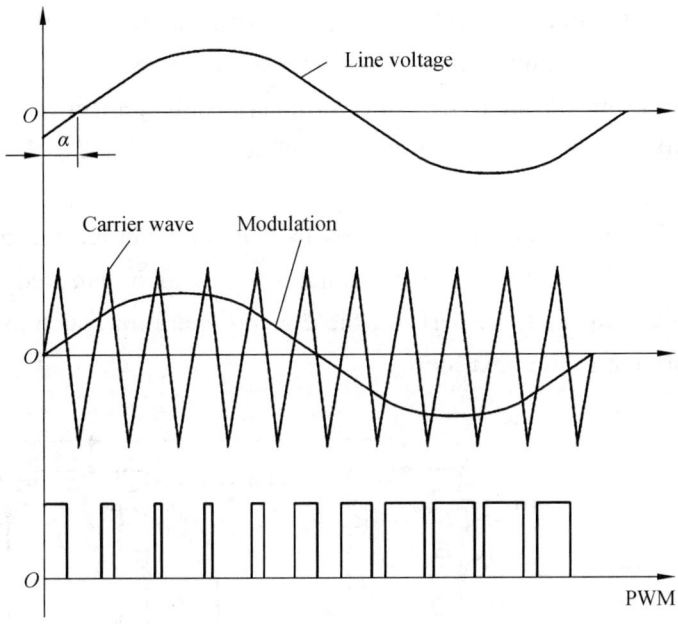

Figure 5-18 PWM modulation principle diagram

(2) Braking condition

When four quadrant converter working in braking condition, in the implementation phase of electric braking, energy recovery can be draw energy from the four quadrant (Cdc) in the output filter capacitor to the main traction transformer secondary to achieve. All of these are closely related to the voltage in the 25 kV circuit and the phase of the voltage across the secondary winding. In addition, the important results of the dispersed inductance of power transformer should be realized at high value. Assume that 25 kV line pressure on normal polarity half wave, and then to the transmission of energy from the condenser to "Cdc" filter (see Figure 5-19) to the main transformer secondary, need connector H1 and B2 into conduction:

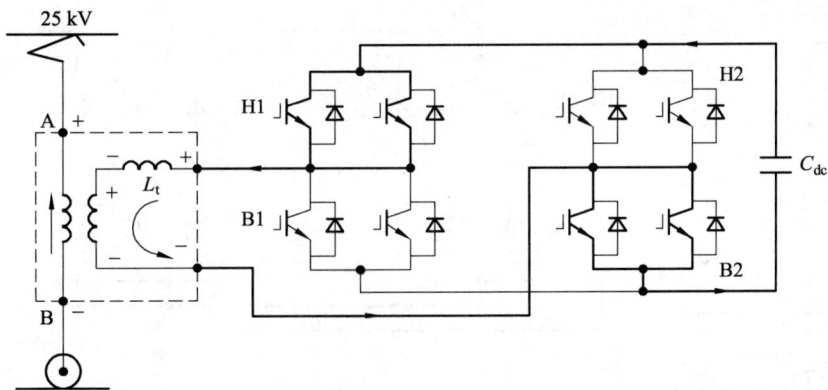

Figure 5-19 H1 and B2 conduction circuit diagram in the braking phase

There are two important things to note in this stage:

1. The current of the inductor "Lt" is increasing (rising), and it is clear that the current of the secondary winding of the power transformer is also the same.

2. Induced current on power transformer primary winding form phase and line voltage, even allow transformer used as generator (related to the line), and then send the default intensity of electric current.

By the IGBT T_{ON} of connector, and then to a certain phase, the phase of secondary transmission terminal short-circuit power transformer, which can reduce the circulating current of the same transformer. To perform the closing operation, such as closing IGBT B2, the current flows through to the next loop.

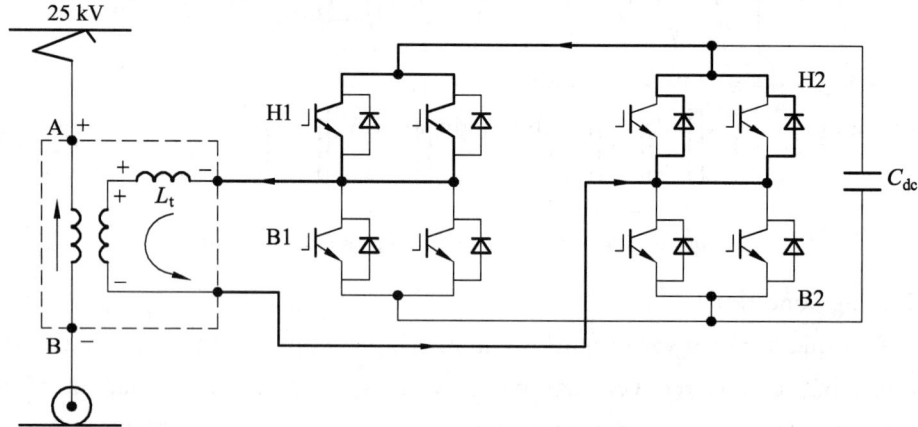

Figure 5-20　H1 and DH2 conduction circuit diagram in the braking phase

At this stage, as shown in Figure "Lt" inductance is used as a generator, and such as the transformer current to keep the same direction, will produce a negative growth. After this stage, another T_{ON} will be generated, as shown in the Figure 5-20. The next one (short circuit for transformer secondary winding) will easily close the H1.

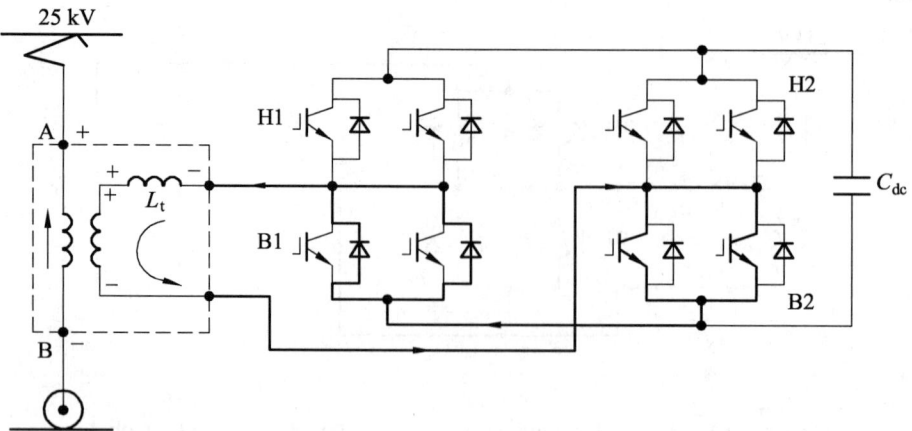

Figure 5-21　DB1 and B2 conduction circuit diagram in the braking phase

As shown in Figure 5-21, the current increases negatively. However, H1 and B2 are switched on alternately to dissipate heat. By modulating T_{ON} and T_{OFF} properly, a preset amplitude of current can be delivered to the high voltage line. When the high voltage circuit has negative half-wave, the operation of the chopper in four quadrants remains the same, except the order in which IGBT is directed. In fact, during T_{ON}, the connector h2-b1 will be controlled; During the T_{OFF}, h2-dh1 and H1 - the DB2 connector will alternate. Two trains drive failure cases, IGBT of the reversing frequency will be decreased from 250 Hz to 250 Hz, so the line "pick up" frequency should be 332 Hz, to optimize the harmonic interference and drive launch.

The above is the working principle of the pulse rectifier.

For several existing models, in addition to type CRH2 for three-level inverter structure, several other models in the same inverter main circuit, three-phase bridge type full bridge inverter, its structure as shown in Figure 5-22.

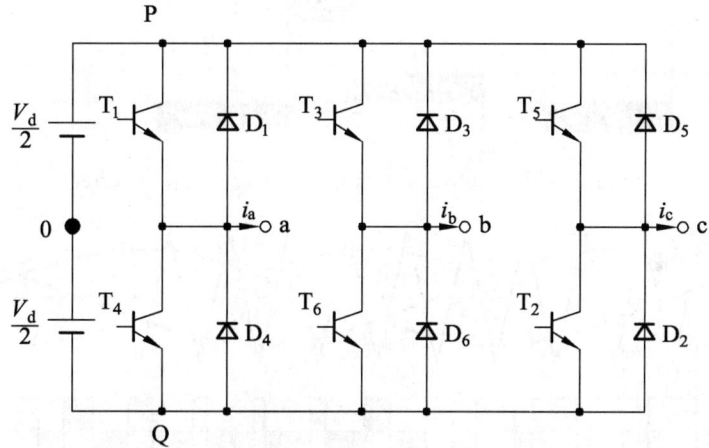

Figure 5-22 Main circuit schematic of the inverter

Figure 5-23 is used as an example to illustrate the working principle of an inverter.

As shown in Figure 5-23, in the inverter shown in Figure 5-22, only the switching signals of each IGBT need to be given in sequence as shown in the following Figure, that is, T1 to T6 are switched on at a distance of 120 degrees, and each time a 180 degree Angle is switched on, line voltages Vab, Vbc and Vca as shown in the Figure can be obtained. So you have an alternating square wave output.

But when the load is ac motor, the output pulse of the square wave voltage is very large and cannot be controlled by the torque of the motor. So it cannot adapt to the demand of the train, adopted PWM modulation method, which USES a high frequency carrier (usually a triangle wave) and we need the sine wave modulation wave superposition, to produce a series of pulse width, thus to get the switch signal of each switch tube. The details are shown in5-24.

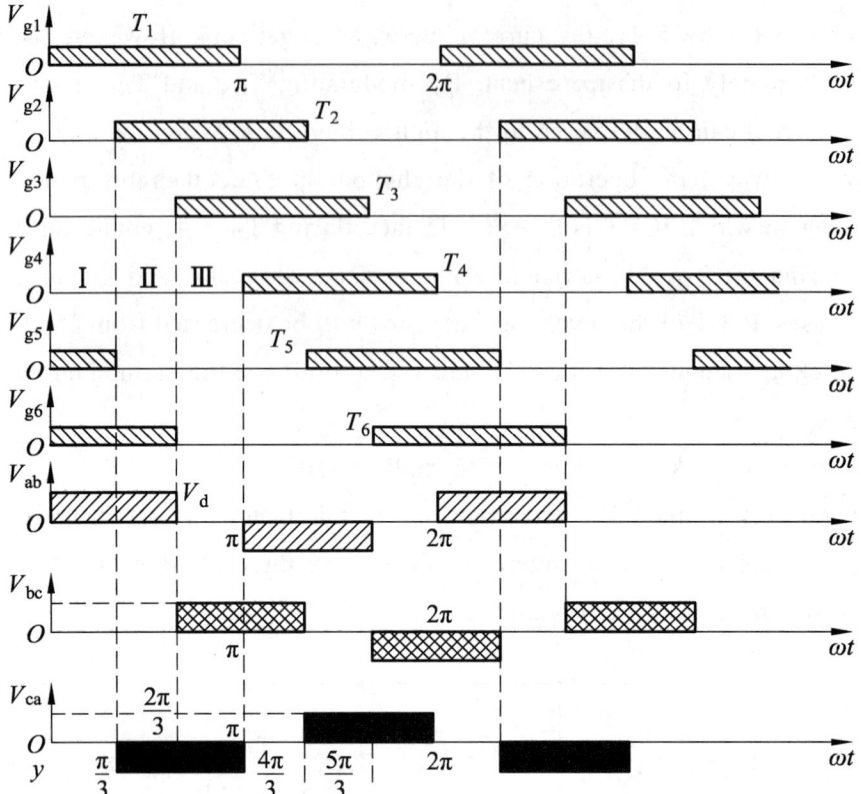

Figure 5-23 Output voltage of a square wave inverter

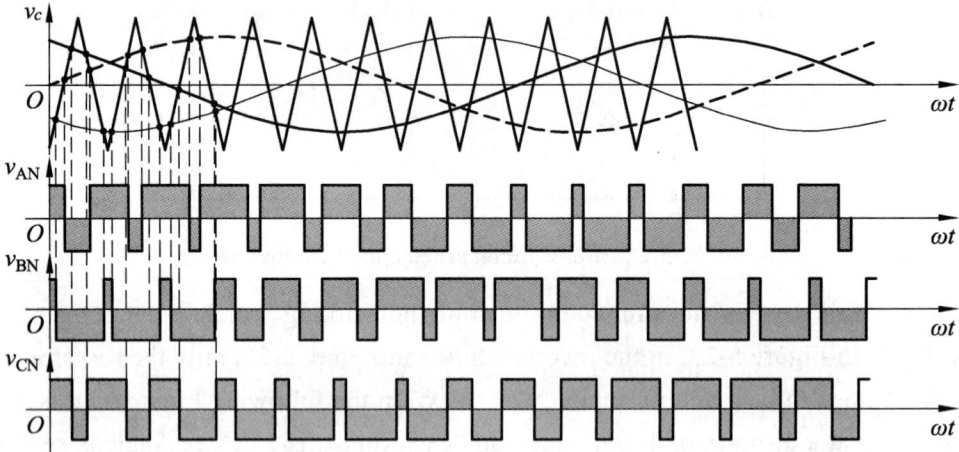

Figure 5-24 Sinusoidal modulation of PWM pulse width modulation method

The resulting output voltage is very close to the sine wave. If the modulation wave generated through the proper control, coupled with the appropriate algorithm, combined with the output value and the change of the given value, will be able to precisely control the output frequency and amplitude of sinusoidal wave, thus greatly improve the quality of the output power and more accurately to control the motor.

The control methods of the inverters are different, there are advantages and disadvantages to this algorithm, but it is usually based on the spatial vector control algorithm, which is controlled by the characteristics. The space vector control is also called the direct torque control in the motor control algorithm, The idea of this control method is, We either current or voltage control motor, at the end of the day is to control the output torque, and output torque and rotor flux of the single value function, only variation and flux linkage. In this case, the rotor magnetic chain is directly observed and controlled by the rotor, which is the precise control of the output torque of the motor.

5.5 Traction motor

An electric motor is a mechanical device that converts electrical energy and mechanical energy into one another. There are many kinds of electric motors, such as ac asynchronous motor, ac synchronous motor, dc motor, stepping motor, linear motor, etc. The traction motor used in EMU in China is AC asynchronous motor.

Ac asynchronous motor has the characteristics of simple structure, easy maintenance and long service life. But as a result of ac motor speed, motor structure and power supply frequency, only the power supply frequency is certain, so the speed regulation for ac motor is particularly difficult, therefore, in the field of locomotive traction with the situation of the dc motor is more. But over the years, the development of power electronic technology, especially the emergence of frequency conversion technology, the application of pulse width modulation technology, makes the ac motor speed control is more and more convenient, therefore, the application of ac asynchronous motors has been widely used in the fields of locomotive traction and large scale hydropower station.

The structure of the traction motor is simple, which consists of the rotor, stator, rotor bearing, outer cover and lead.

5.6 Vacuum breaker

A vacuum breaker (VCB) is a high-voltage electrical switching device. The purpose of installing the vacuum circuit breaker is to cut off the overcurrent quickly, safely and accurately when the circuit after the secondary side of the main transformer fails. At the same time, it is usually open and close the main circuit of a switch, it both circuit breaker and switch two functions. Figure 5-25 shows the appearance of a VCB.

The vacuum circuit breaker is equipped with static and dynamic contacts in a closed vacuum container. Through the static and dynamic contacts, the current is cut off by taking advantage of the high insulation resistance and arc diffusion in the vacuum. It is typically installed on the top of the car.

Figure 5-25　The appearance of a VCB

5.6.1　Structure and performance parameters of VCB

The VCB consists of the following basic components

(1) Bracket: the frame for installing all functional components.

(2) Vacuum arc extinguishing chamber: arc extinguishing element to realize circuit closing and breaking function.

(3) Conductive circuit: it is connected with the moving end and the static end of the arc extinguishing chamber to form a current channel.

(4) Transmission mechanism: the motion of the operating mechanism is transmitted to the arc extinguishing chamber to realize the closing and opening operation of the arc extinguishing chamber.

(5) Insulation support: insulation support parts will be each functional component, frame together to meet the insulation requirements of the circuit breaker.

(6) Operating mechanism: power driving device of circuit breaker closing and dividing

The performance parameters

For VCB, we typically have the following requirements for performance:

(1) The high insulation level

(2) Low sensitivity to climate conditions

(3) Small dimension

(4) Disconnect the ability

(5) The service life is long

(7) Less maintenance work

5.6.2　Working principle

When the total wind pressure is sufficient, the solenoid valve connected to the "VCB together" after the instructions, the solenoid valve action, allowing the total duct of compressed air into the high-pressure cylinder. Using the pressure of compressed air to top the connection mechanism, the main contact point of the high voltage circuit is connected by the force of mechanical lever. At the same time, when the metal piston of the high-pressure cylinder is lifted, a holding coil is provided at the top of the high-pressure cylinder, and the piston is tightly sucked by the holding coil to produce a contact pressure so that the main contact is kept in close contact with each other. When the main contact in close contact, the electromagnetic valve absorbs, release the action VCB compressed air.

VCB disconnect process is relatively simple, when it received a "VCB disconnect" command, the high voltage cylinder to maintain the coil loss of power, under the action of the spring through mechanical levers high-pressure main contact will disconnect.

Chapter 6 Brake System

6.1 Main types of brake system

Stopping the train set or decreasing its speed purposefully means brake. A Brake system is the device that used for brake purpose. A moving vehicle has kinetic energy, which must somehow be removed to make stop. For a vehicle of mass travelling at a certain speed, its kinetic energy is half mass times square of speed. For a high-speed EMU, several different ways of dissipating energy have been exploited by the engineers to make it to stop safely. They are friction brake and electro-dynamic brake. The friction brake can be categorized to two subclasses: automatic air brake, and electro-pneumatic brake.

6.1.1 Automatic air brake

The schematic diagram below illustrates the main components of a simplest automatic air brake.

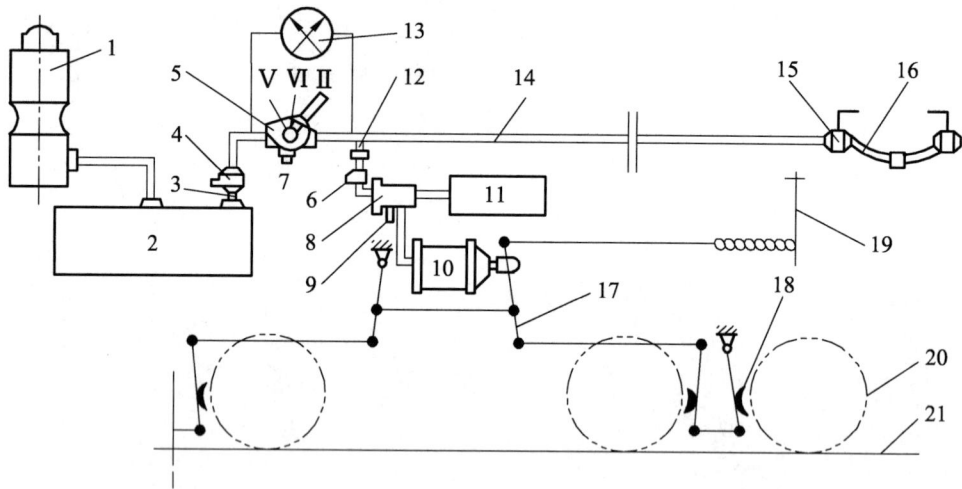

1—Compressor; 2—Main reservoir; 4—Compressed air feeder; 5—Driver's brake valve; 8—Brake control vale(on vehicle);
10—Brake cylinder; 11—Auxiliary reservoir; 14—Brake pipe; 15—Cock; 16—Hose;
17—Rigging; 18—Brake block; 20—Tread of wheel.

Figure 6-1 Main components of the automatic air brake

First, the compressor driven by electric motor charges the main reservoir with compressed air, until the main reservoir reach it maximum pressure (900 kPa). When the driver place the brake valve in the "release" position, the compressed air in the main reservoir will fills into the brake pipe. Thus the pressure in the brake pipe is rising and the vehicle's brake control valve will react to connect the auxiliary reservoir to brake pipe to fill it with compressed air until it reach the its working pressure (700 kPa). At the same time the brake control vale connects brake cylinder to its air exit port and the compressed air in the brake cylinder will exhaust. As the air escape, the piston will be pushed back by its spring and with help of brake rigging to make the brake block to be removed from contact with the wheels. The train brake will be released. And the auxiliary reservoir will be recharged ready for another brake application.

When the driver place the brake valve in the "application" position, the compressed air in the brake pipe will escape. Thus the pressure in the brake pipe is decreasing, to which the vehicle's brake control valve will react to connect the auxiliary reservoir to brake cylinder to fill it with compressed air. The piston will be pushed out by the pressure against the spring and with help of brake rigging to make the brake block to contact with the tread of wheels and apply pressure on it.

The brake pipes run the length of the trains, which are connected between vehicles by flexible hoses which can be uncoupled to allow the vehicle to be separated. The brake pipes transmit the variation in pressure to control the brake on each vehicle. With a continuous brake pipe connecting all the coaches or wagons in the train, the driver can change the air pressure in the pipe with the driver's brake vale easily and thus control the brakes of the whole train.

6.1.2 Electro-pneumatic brake

But purely air brake rely on the transmission of an air pressure signal along the brake pipe, which is initiated from the front of the train and has to be sent to every vehicle along the train to the rear. There is always a appreciable time lapse between the reaction of the leading vehicle and the reaction of the one at the rear. It is not suitable for the high-speed EMU train, can only be used as a back-up brake system.

In fact the brakes used as the service brakes are electro-pneumatic brakes. E-P brakes use a number of train wires connected to a driver's brake "valve" or controller. A main reservoir pipe is provided along the length of the train and the auxiliary reservoirs of each vehicle is always fully charged so that a constant supply of air is available on all cars. The brakes are controlled by a BCU(brake control unit) which receive the brake signal sent by the driver's brake valve through the train wires. First the BCU produce a pre-control air pressure, which will work on its relay valve which will connect the auxiliary reservoir to brake cylinder. The auxiliary reservoir fill in the brake cylinder with the compressed air whose pressure is same with the pre-control air pressure.

6.1.3 Dynamic brake

Dynamic brake is a train brake system where the traction motors are used to provide a braking force by reconnecting them in such a way that they become generators. When braking, the traction motors are acting as generators, which means the traction motors are hard to turn. The motor car's wheels are what are turning the traction motors and they are geared to the traction motors when it generating power. Thus the braking force is caused.

The train's kinetic energy can be converted into electric power and be transmitted back to overhead line to be used by other trains nearby. This is regenerative brake. But the power developed by a braking train may not be accepted by the line if no other trains are drawing power so trains equipped with regenerative braking will usually have resistor grids as well to exhaust the excess energy. This is rheostatic brake.

6.2 Introduction to brake system of EMU train

The brake system of the EMU train is normally achieved by the use of 2 different brake system: electro-pneumatic brake and electro-dynamic brake, with automatic air brake as a back-up. An electro-pneumatic brake system and electro-dynamic brake are microprocessor)controlled with extensive brake management that controls, manages and diagnoses all the equipment involved in braking process excluding parking brake equipment. The automatic air brake with distributor helps in rescue during service brakes fail. This system is purely air type, fully independent from the main service brake system which is controlled by the brake management via microprocessor based electronic control units.

6.2.1 Service brake

The brake handle in the driver's cab sends a brake signal to the train line. This train line carries the signal to each brake control unit of different vehicles, which generates the brake signal for electro-dynamic brake and to electro-pneumatic brake system for friction brake. In service brake application, electro-dynamic braking is applied first and followed by electro-pneumatic braking. On the motor axles, electro-pneumatic braking is withdrawn through the excitation of the interlock solenoid valve by the traction regulator. In the position of maximum service brake application, the system is applied to the maximum electro-dynamic force on the motor axles and a pneumatic force on the trailer axles to ensure the performance capabilities required. At low speeds (less than 10 km/h) and in the event of electro-dynamic brake failure on the motor axles, the pneumatic brake is activated through the deactivation of the interlock valve. Electro-pneumatic effort is applied on trailer axles only when electro-dynamic braking has reached its maximum value. During service braking, traction is isolated.

6.2.2 Emergency brake

In emergency braking condition, the traction and electro-dynamic brakes are isolated.The pneumatic brake applies its maximum braking force by exhausting brake pipe pressure into atmosphere.The emergency braking can be controlled by the following apparatus:

• Brake hand-lever on emergency braking position-in this position, safety loop is open and all the vehicles apply the maximum pneumatic brake force.

• Push button in the driver's cabin.

• Safety devices (signalling system).

• Safety loop cut under abnormal conditions.

• Passenger alarm.

When the push button in the driver's cabin is pressed, the safety loop along the trainset is opened and the brake pipe is vented by the emergency valves on each end vehicle, and the distributor valve applies maximum braking effort.

The automatic brake (not the electro-pneumatic brake) guarantees the safety of the emergency application. During emergency application, opening of the safety loop isolates the electrodynamic brake and also de-energises the valve on back-up brake, in order to isolate the recharge of the brake pipe.

6.2.3 Passenger alarm brake system

All vehicles are equipped with a passenger alarm brake system. This brake system comprises of two brake handles in each passenger compartment. The operation of the brake handles by passenger exhausts the brake pipe air into the atmosphere. This action can be neutralized by the driver. When passenger alarm handle is activated, the following actions take place:

• A visual and buzzer signal is given to the driver in the driver's cabin.

• The solenoid valve of an emergency brake panel in the leading car is de-energized, causing an emergency brake.

• Valve on back-up brake unit is de-energized in order to inhibit recharge of the brake pipe. Passenger alarm operation can be stopped, when passenger alarm handle is reset by the driver.

6.2.4 Back-up brake

In the event of a failure in the electronic control unit or in rescue mode, the trainset can proceed using the indirect back-up brake pipe. Then the brake is controlled by the pressure in the brake pipe (600 kPa air pressure) which is regulated by time depending brake valve installed on driver's desk, which is activated by a manual lever of the back-up brake. The back up brake system has emergency brake function with the emergency brake distance.

On each vehicle, a spring actuated distributor generates the signal due to reduction in brake pipe and signal is sent to relay valves. During back-up brake operation, electro-dynamic brake is isolated. A pressure switch on the brake pipe and a micro switch on back-up brake handle isolate traction effort.

6.2.5 Parking brake

The trainset is equipped with spring-operated parking brake device, fed from the main brake reservoir. It has manual release device, which can meet the requirement of safe parking without rolling on a 30% slope.

Pushing buttons located in the driver's cab result in application / release of parking brake to the trainset and to the coupled trainsets (in case of multiple composition). The status of the parking brake is indicated on the driver's desk as applied or released, by the driver push button, and detected by pressure switches. Parking brake application is isolated during running of the trainset.

Handle of mechanical release device is provided near the parking brake cylinder. The parking brake application and release status of spring brake is indicated through the colours. Red colour with a black centre spot indicates application of parking brake and green colour indicates release of parking brake.

6.3 Working principles of brake system for EMU

Figure 6-2 illustrates the configurations and working principles of brake system.

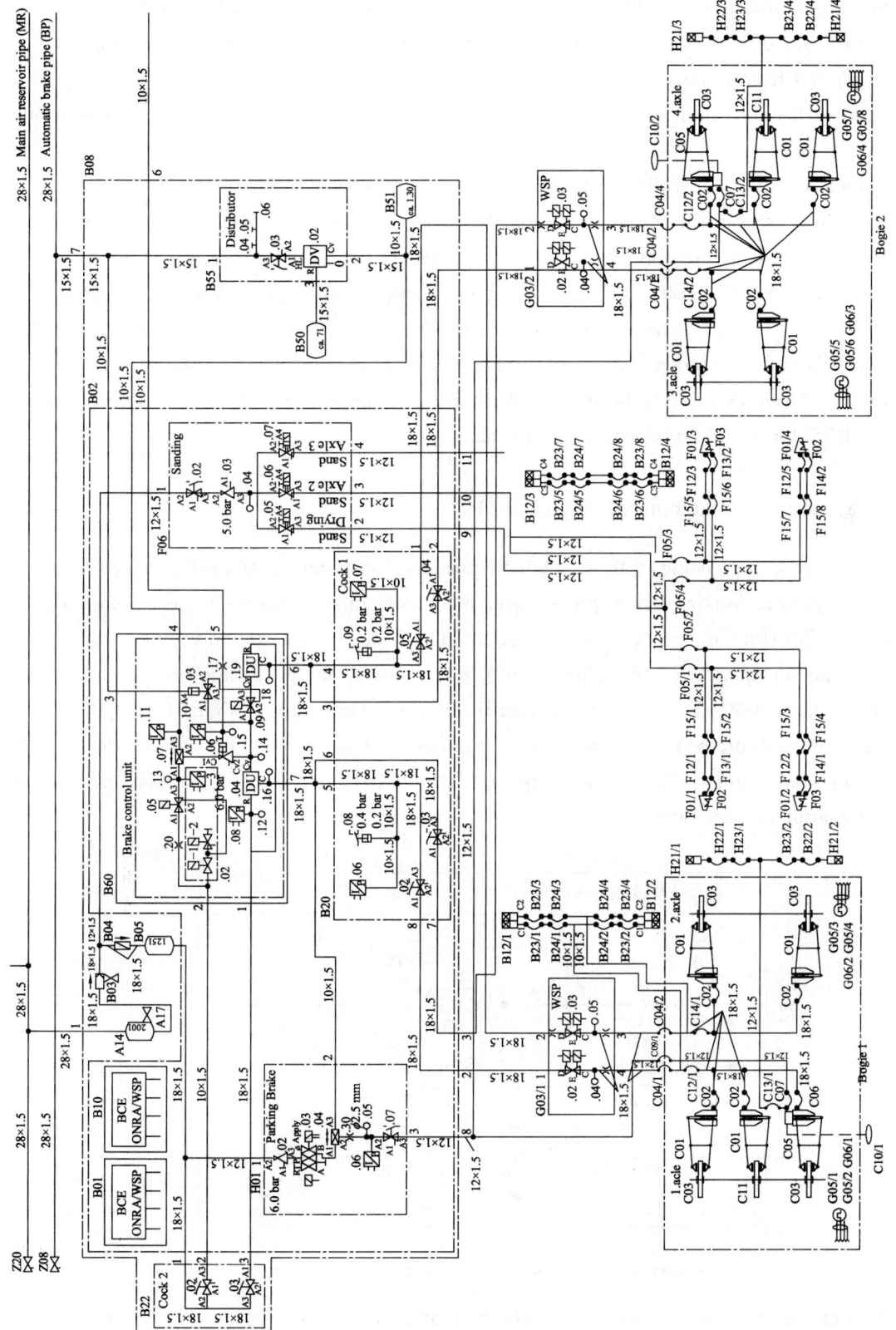

Figure 6-2 Schematic pipe diagram of EMU brake system

- 207 -

The microprocessor-based Electronic Brake Control Unit (EBCU) (B01) performs the local brake control functions. BCU is used to receive and interpret the brake demand signals as well as the other signals from trainset to control the electro-pneumatic brake system. The microprocessor functions also includes fault diagnosis as well as fault indication to facilitate maintenance and operation.

Compressed air for operation of friction brake system is tapped from the Main Air Reservoir Pipe (MR). The pressure in MR is monitored by a pressure switch, which is connected to the propulsion interlock circuit. This pressure switch prevents the vehicle from being moved, if the pressure level in the main reservoir pipe is not sufficient. The compressed air passes through a check valve (B04) to the auxiliary brake reservoir (B05) of the brake equipment with a capacity of 125 litres. This brake equipment (B04 and B05) is located in the brake frame (B08). In case of MR pressure loss, the check valve (B04) ensures that the air pressure is reserved in the auxiliary brake reservoir (B05) for operation of the friction brakes.

6.3.1 Service brake control (Figure 6-3)

The service brake system of trainset adopts pneumatic-dynamic-combined braking mode and the electro-dynamic braking takes precedence. If the dynamitic braking force, whose control depends on TCU(Traction Control Unit), is not enough, electro-pneumatic brake will be followed. The electro-pneumatic brake control unit (B60) is responsible for pneumatic brake control. The pressure regulator (B60.02) modulates the electric friction brake demand signal from BCU (B01) into a proportional pre-control pressure. The signals to the pressure regulator (B60.02) are application/release signals. The pressure regulator (B60.02) is equipped with a charging magnet valve and venting magnet valve.

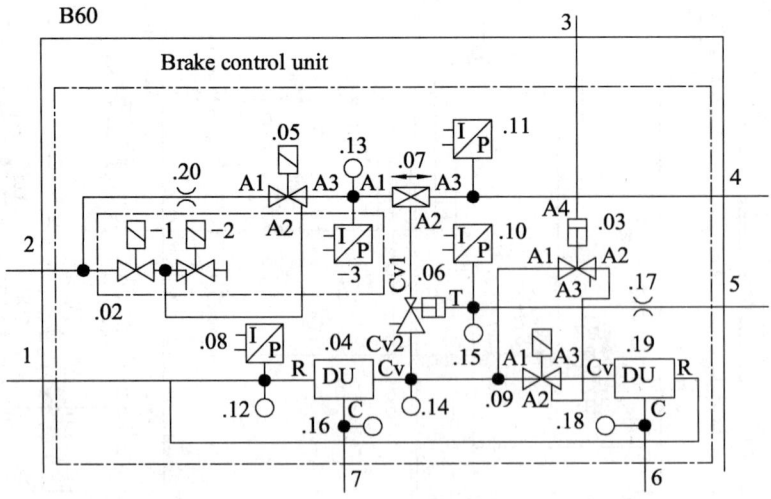

Figure 6-3 Schematic pipe diagram of B60 module

The signal of pressure transducer (B60.02-3) indicates the actual pressure level in the brake control unit (B60). If the signal from pressure transducer (B60.02-3) does not match with the commanded pressure, the charging magnet valve or venting magnet valve are controlled by BCU (B01) to obtain the correct pressure level in the control volume. This technique provides a high accuracy, linearity and repeatability.

The BCU Control can also control compressed air flowing to the emergency magnet valve (B60.05). The emergency magnet valve (B60.05) is energized under normal service brake condition which allows the control volume air pressure from pressure regulator (B60.02) to pass via the load dependent pressure limiting valve (B60.06) to relay valves (B60.04 and B60.19). The pressure limiting valve (B60.06) is provided for protection of bogie equipment in case of failure of electronic indication generation of brake cylinder pressure. For service brake, the load correction is performed electrically via brake demand signal from BCU (B01) to the pressure regulator valves (B60.02).

The air supply to brake control unit (B60) can be isolated by vented stopcocks (B22.02 and B22.03).Stopcock (B22.02) is used for isolation of direct electro-pneumatic brake and stopcock (B22.03) is used for isolation of friction brake (direct electro-pneumatic brake and indirect brake). For good accessibility these stopcocks (B22.02 and B22.03) are mounted outside the brake container (B02) but in the brake frame (B08).The stopcocks (B22.02 and B22.03) electrical signals are read by EBCUs which can also be read by the Train Control and Monitoring System (TCMS).

6.3.2 Back-up brake (Figure 6-4)

In case of failure of electro-pneumatic direct brake system or in rescue mode, the trainset proceeds using back-up brake system, which is automatic air brake system. The brakes in back-up brake system are controlled by the pressure in automatic brake pipe, which is regulated by the driver's brake valve type-FB11 (D02) installed on driver's desk. Automatic brake pipe can also be controlled from a rescue locomotive or from a recovery trainset.

Back-up brake control system is a brake operating mechanism, which is used as auxiliary control for vehicles with electro-pneumatic brake. During rescue operation, this brake system can also be operated as automatic air brake if electro-pneumatic brake is not available. With driver's brake system, the pressure in automatic brake pipe is regulated after activation, and thus the indirect brake of trainset can also be operated as a another service brake for rescue operation.

The direct release distributor valve (B55.02) is set to 6 bar nominal BP (brake pipe) release pressure. Operation of the brakes of the trainset is done through a Traction/Brake Controller (TBC) (D01). TBC (D01) supplies electrical signals, which are transmitted electrically in the trainset via discrete wire and/or bus system. Brake demand signals are transmitted to each vehicle for operation of direct electro-pneumatic brakes. Pressure in automatic brake pipe is thus kept above nominal release pressure for service braking and is lowered in case of automatic trainset stopping or emergency braking. For this reason, deadman's valve (N02) is also connected to automatic brake pipe.

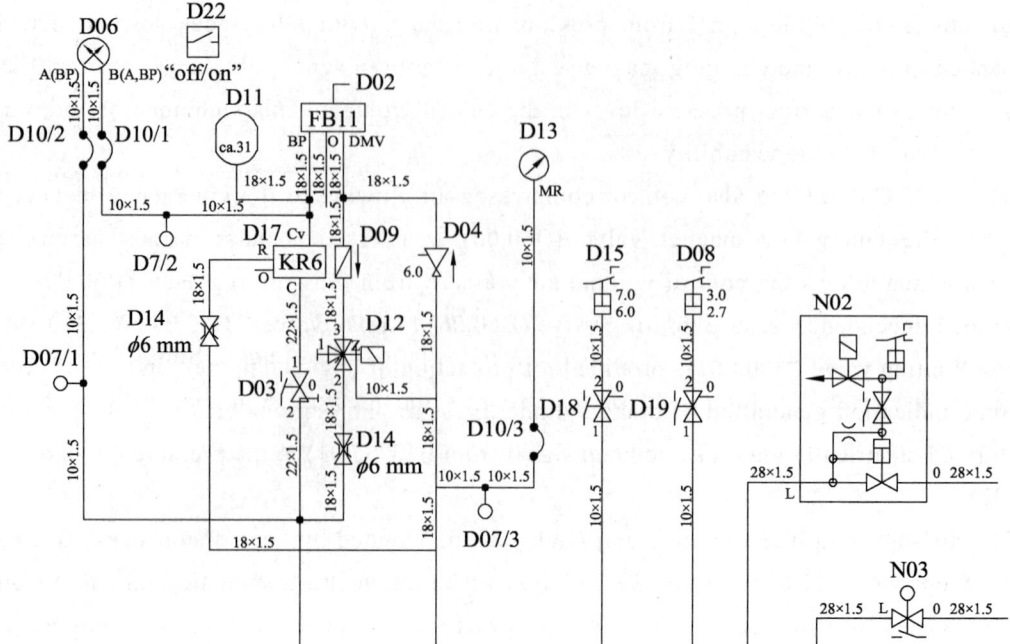

Figure 6-4　Schematic pipe diagram of back-up brake control system

In normal operation, the Back-up brake system achieves the following basic functions:

(1) Isolation is achieved by a "shut-off" switch (D22) arranged in driver's control desk. In normal operation mode via TBC (D01), as long as there is no request for automatic trainset stopping or emergency braking, the isolation magnetic valve (D12) and the emergency brake valve (N02) are energized. Due to this, the compressed air passes from the pressure-reducing valve (D04), check valve (D09) and flow throttle (D16) into the automatic brake pipe.

(2) The pressure-reducing valve (D04) regulates the nominal pressure to back-up brake system equipment. The flow throttle (D16) limits the feeding capacity in such a way that the automatic action of the indirect brake is still guaranteed.

When emergency braking is initiated by the TBC (D01) or other emergency and automatic trainset stopping equipment, all the emergency brake valves (N02) present in the trainset are de-energized and thus the automatic brake pipe is exhausted through a large port. In addition, pressure maintenance is prevented by interrupting supply voltage of isolation magnetic valve (D12).

6.3.3　Emergency brake

During an emergency brake application, the electrical emergency brake control loop is opened and Automatic Brake Pipe (BP) pressure is vented via deadman's valve (N02). Subsequently emergency brake cylinder pressure is applied via BP controlled distributor valve (B55.02).

Simultaneously after opening the electrical emergency brake control loop the emergency magnet valve (B60.05) is de-energized (fail-safe principle), so that air pressure from auxiliary brake reservoir (B05) flows via double check valve (B60.07) to the load dependent pressure limiting valve (B60.06) and relay valves (B60.04 and B60.19) initiating a load weighed emergency brake application. In case of emergency brake and when interlock valve (B60.09) is out of order, the bypass piston valve (B60.03) ensures that the air pressure is applied to brake cylinders on the motor axles. Load dependent pressure limiting valve (B60.06) limits the pre-control pressure to relay valves (B60.04 and B60.19) as per the pneumatic load weight. Simultaneously, during emergency brake application, BCU (B01) also sets the pressure regulator valves (B60.02) to emergency brake pressure.

In case of non availability of electro-dynamic brake, the pneumatic friction brake compensates the electro-dynamic brake force of the relevant vehicle (example: by opening the relevant interlock valve (B60.09) and by applying the brake cylinder pressure).

Individual axles in the vehicles can be manually isolated by means of stopcocks with electrical switches (B20.02, B20.03, B20.04 and B20.05) in brake cylinder supply pipe to isolate the brake control unit (B60) and release the air-applied brake cylinders (example: in case of failure of pressure regulator B60.02 or emergency magnet valve B60.05).

6.3.4　Brake indication

TCMS reads the information about the condition of brakes (released/applied) from pressure switches (B20.08 and B20.09). This brake equipment is installed in the brake container (B02). A duplex pressure gauge (D06) is provided in the driver's cabin to indicate pre-control and the automatic brake pipe pressure level. The duplex pressure gauge (B11) shows the brake cylinder pressure of motor and trailer axles in driver's cabin. Pressure gauge (D13) is provided to indicate main air reservoir pipe pressure. All the above gauges (D06, B11 and D13) are provided with lighting (supply voltage of 24 VDC).

For a visual brake test, brake indicators (B12) are installed outside the bogie, on both the sides, to show green sign for released brakes and red sign for applied brakes. Parking brake indicators (H21) are also provided to indicate the parking brake pressure.

6.4　Brake calliper unit

6.4.1　Introduction

The trainset is equipped with disc brakes on all axles and all of them are equipped with 640 mm diameter axle-mounted disc brakes, made of steel, with reduced ventilation. Normally, there are 3 brake discs on the trailer axle and 2 on the motor axle.

The brake caliper unit is a combination of a brake caliper and brake cylinder, providing automatic slack adjustment for pad and disc wear. The brake caliper unit used as a service brake, has a brake cylinder. The brake cylinder and the calliper for each brake disc are of conventional type, with built in automatic slack adjuster. Consequently, the clearance between the disc and pads for smooth running remains virtually constant at the "brake release" position. The brake pads are sintered type; designed for a maximum permitted temperature of 600°C and a maximum wear of 30 mm.

The brake equipment is mounted on two brake transoms. These transoms are mounted on the bogie frame with brake transom supports. The brake cylinders are connected commonly through a pneumatic pipeline to activate braking system.

The pneumatic air supply to the brake cylinder is controlled by brake control units which are located in under frame of all vehicles.

6.4.2 Structure of brake calliper unit

The brake caliper units serve either as service brakes or as service and parking brakes. The brake caliper unit used as a service has no spring actuator. The brake caliper unit used as a service and parking brake, has a brake cylinder with a spring actuator. The spring actuator serves in application of brake and secures a parked vehicle in the absence of compressed air.

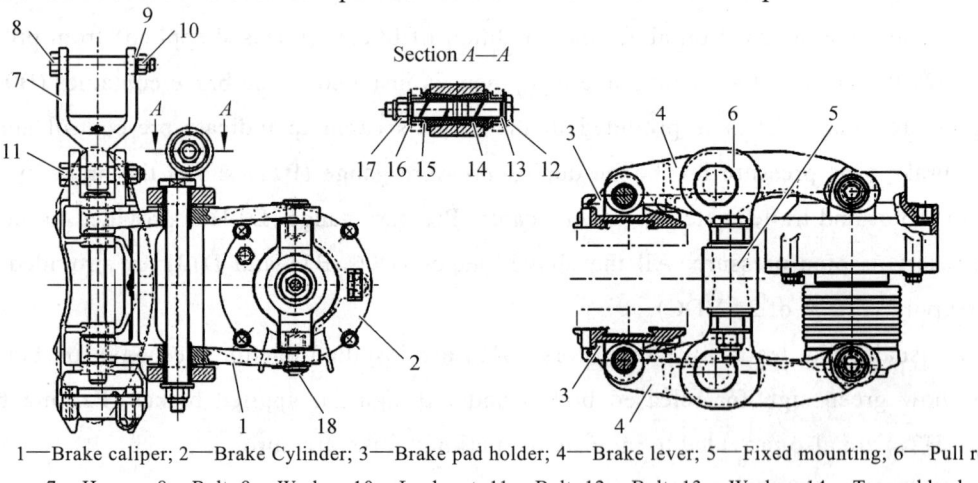

1—Brake caliper; 2—Brake Cylinder; 3—Brake pad holder; 4—Brake lever; 5—Fixed mounting; 6—Pull rod; 7—Hanger; 8—Bolt; 9—Washer; 10—Lock nut; 11—Bolt; 12—Bolt; 13—Washer; 14—Tapered bush; 15—Flanged bush; 16—Washer; 17—Lock nut; 18—Pivot screw

Figure 6-5 Brake calliper unit

The brake caliper unit consists essentially of the brake cylinder without the spring actuator, the brake caliper and the brake pad holders with snap lock gates.

The brake caliper units are held in the bogie by a three-point fastening arrangement. The three-point fastening arrangement comprises of fixed mounting as part of the pull rod, and two hangers which are hinged to the brake pad holders with bolts. The pull rod is suspended from the bogie by the fixed mounting with its bolt in the tapered bushes. The bolt is supported in the bogie by two flanged bushes, two washers and lock nut. The hangers are attached to the bogie with bolts. Pin joints and resilient tapered bushes allow the brake caliper units to adjust to the axial movements of the wheelsets.

The brake caliper is a preassembled member. It consists of two torsionally rigid brake levers that articulate on the pull rod. The brake pad holders are mounted on one end of the brake levers. The opposite ends of the brake levers have tapping holes for the pivot screws that carry the brake cylinder.

The parking brake is operated centrally from the driver's cabin. The spring actuator has manual release gear to release the parking brake mechanically in case of emergency.

Service braking charges the brake cylinder and causes the brake pad to clutch the brake disc. Brake force is built up as the brake pads are applied to the brake disc.

Venting the brake cylinder releases the service brake. The return spring in the brake cylinder moves the brake levers to the release position. Charging the spring actuator releases the parking brake. When the actuator springs are tensioned, the brake levers go to the release position. In the absence of release pressure, the parking brake can be released mannually with the mechanical emergency release gear.

6.4.3 Brake cylinder

Brake cylinders with automatic slack adjustment are used to operate the friction brakes. Being small and compact, the brake cylinders are most suitable for installation in brake callipers for disc brake actuators. Brake cylinders are essentially distinguished by their integral, force controlled slack adjustment mechanism which is designed as a single acting clearance adjuster. During brake application, the slack adjuster quickly and automatically corrects the increasing brake pad clearance due to wear. This clearance is hence maintained across the entire range of slack adjustment. An approximately constant piston stroke with low air consumption is obtained, there is no need to adjust the brake rigging manually.

The cylinder body is an aluminium die casting with a smooth piston running surface, a high proportion of contact and resistance to wear. The piston is sealed by a low temperature resistant rubber packing with grease pockets. This guarantees a long service life as well as minimum leakage and maximum dependability. The slack adjuster is locked reliably by a positively acting geared coupling, even when the brakes are released. The brake cylinder is protected from water ingress. The unloaded cylinder chamber communicates with atmosphere through a breather plug located at the lowest point.

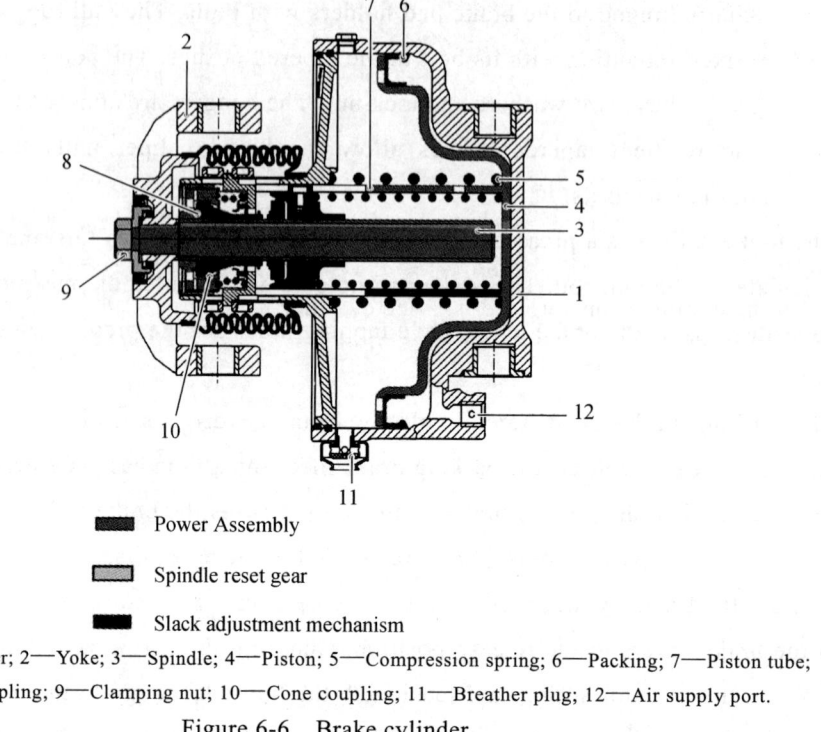

Power Assembly

Spindle reset gear

Slack adjustment mechanism

1—Brake cylinder; 2—Yoke; 3—Spindle; 4—Piston; 5—Compression spring; 6—Packing; 7—Piston tube; 8—Gear coupling; 9—Clamping nut; 10—Cone coupling; 11—Breather plug; 12—Air supply port.

Figure 6-6 Brake cylinder

6.4.3.1 Working process of brake cylinder

The compressed air delivered to the brake cylinder after braking is initiated, is converted into piston force. This force is transmitted to the spindle by the piston tube and the cone coupling, which are moved back to the release position by the compression spring when the cylinder is vented.

6.4.3.2 Slack adjustment mechanism

The single acting slack adjustment mechanism is automatic. The slack adjustment mechanism corrects excessive brake pad clearance that is caused by wear due to braking.

6.4.4 Brake cylinder with spring actuator

The brake cylinders are a combination of an air powered service brake cylinder having a built in single acting slack adjuster and a spring actuated cylinder. The spring actuated cylinder is positioned at right angles to the service brake cylinder.

The main components of the spring actuated cylinder (2) are piston (14) and compression spring (13). The force of the compression spring (13) acts on the wedge (16) through piston (14), spindle (12) and tube (11), and is relayed through the service brake cylinder (1) to the brake caliper linkage.

During normal operation, the spring actuated cylinder is released with compressed air, but it can also be released quickly by hand if necessary. If minimum release pressure is available, a manually released spring actuator will be reactivated automatically.

The manual release gear (3) is located on the spring actuated cylinder (2) and is operated manually. It serves to release the parking brake when no release pressure (7) is available for the spring actuated cylinder (2). The manual release gear expands the compression spring (13) until the piston (14) is supported on the cylinder bottom and the spring force can no longer act on the wedge (16) through the spindle (12). The spindle (1) is moved simultaneously to the release position by the compression spring of service cylinder.

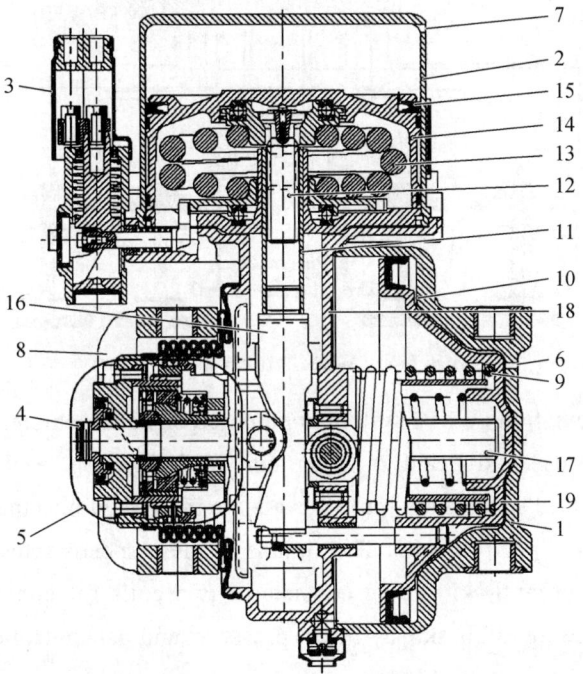

1—Service brake cylinder; 2—Spring actuated cylinder; 3—manual release; 4—Spindle reset mechanism; 5—Slack adjustment mechanism; 6—Air supply port, C; 7—Air supply port, F; 8—Yoke; 9—Compression spring; 10—Packing ring; 11—Tube; 12—Spindle; 13—Compression spring; 14—Piston; 15—Sealing ring; 16—Wedge; 17—Spindle; 18—Housing; 19. Piston.

Figure 6-7　Brake cylinder with spring actuator

A service brake cylinder with a spring actuated cylinder has the following advantages:

① No need for complicated, space wasting handbrake linkage.

② Since the spring actuated cylinders are actuated pneumatically, trainset entire parking brake can be operated centrally from the driver's cabin.

③ Constant force can be caused by the spring actuated cylinder, because the latter acts on the brake rigging through the service brake cylinder.

④ Added security in the event of a service brake failure. In an emergency, brake can be applied safely using a centrally controlled spring actuated cylinder.

6.5 The wheel slip protection (WSP)

The microprocessor based wheel slide control system consists of speed sensors, rotating pole wheel, control units, anti-slip valves, as shown in the Figure below

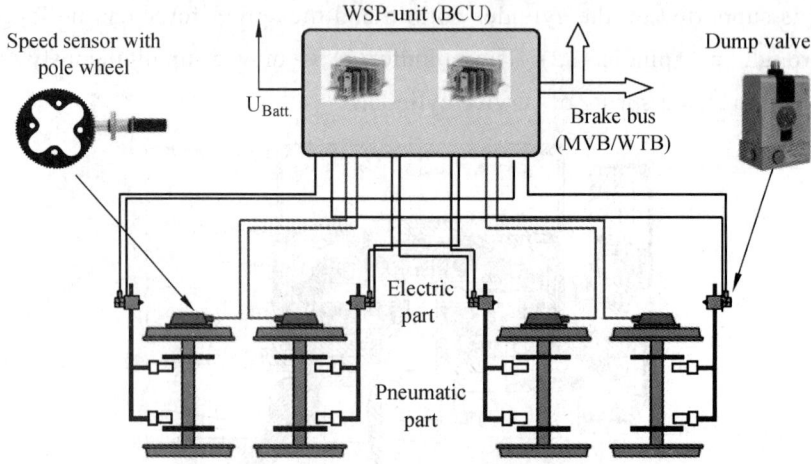

Figure 6-8 Wheel slip control system

The Wheel Slip Protection (WSP) system is mounted on each vehicle, there are two electronic control units EBCU1 (B01) and EBCU2 (B10)) for WSP function, each one includes anti-skid valves, single channel speed sensors and pole wheels are integrated into the axle bearing unit. Each axle is equipped with two speed sensors. The signals of these speeds sensors are feed back to two independent EBCUs. Each anti-skid valve consists of two coils for control of charging and two coils for control of venting of brake cylinder pressure and is controlled by two independent EBCUs.

WSP function includes the Detection of Non Rotating Axle (DNRA) functionality also. DNRA functionality detects locked axles and indicates them as a failure message for each locked axle., if the speed signal of an axle drops below a certain speed threshold, the locked axle is detected This speed threshold depends on the current reference speed for DNRA function. For example, for a reference speed of about 200 km/h, the speed threshold is about 100 km/h. In case of a single speed sensor failure at one axle, the DNRA function still works on this axle. It is continuously monitored by the electronic control units if there is an open or short circuit in the control of anti-slip valves.

The microprocessor based wheel slide control system forms a close loop. First the speed sensor detects the speed of wheel without physical contact and sends a proportional frequency signal to control unit, which indicates the speed of the vehicle. The control unit evaluates the frequencies of all speed sensors from all vehicles. If the deceleration exceed the limit, it will generates signals enabling the anti-slip valves (G03.02 and G03) to discharge the brake cylinder. The control loop adjusts the brake cylinder pressure to the instantaneous wheel-to-rail adhesion and keeps the wheels within their optimum range of slip. The control unit ensures maximum possible brake force transmission.

6.6 Air supply system

The air supply system of a EMU train consists of main air supply unit and auxiliary air supply unit.

6.6.1 Main air supply unit

An EMU train are normally equipped with two air supply units (A01) mounted on the underfloor of the cars. Each air supply unit contains a main compressor of screw type SL22 (A01.01) and a Duel-chamber Air Drier (A01.04). The compressor motors are supplied by the 440 V, 60 Hz, 3 AC busbar of the on-board power supply. The main compressor is connected to a duel-chamber air dryer and to a condensate collecting tank (A15) with anti-freezing-provisions. Air from the air supply unit is fed to the train line main reservoir (MRP) pipe which is coupled to the adjacent cars via hose pipes. The MRP pipe is used to supply the compressed air for all cars.

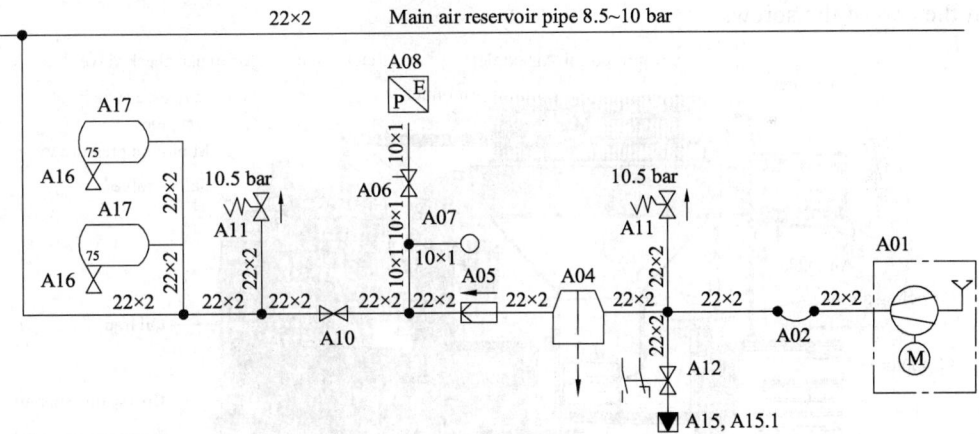

A01—Air compressor; A08—The pressure sensor; A03—Safety valve; A04—Air dryer; A17—Main reservoir; A11—Safety valve; A15—External air supply; A05—Oil filter; A07—Testing fitting.

Figure 6-9　Air supply unit- pneumatic diagram

6.6.1.1 Main compressor

The main compressor is normallly of screw type. Figure 6-10 illustrates the structure of a main compressor.

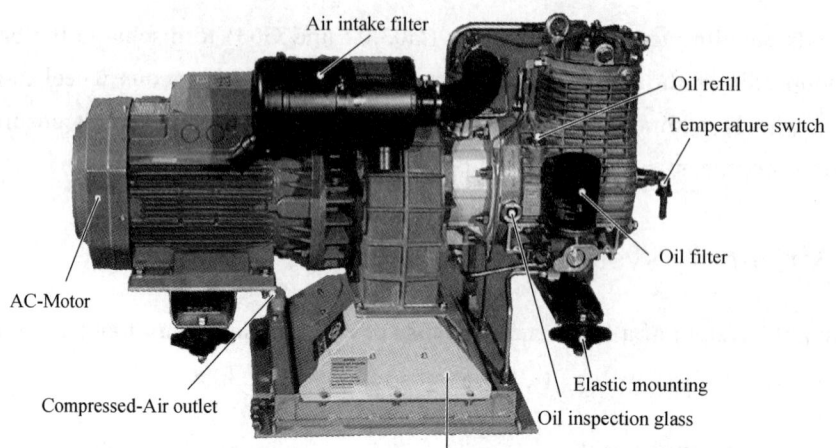

Figure 6-10 A screw compressor

6.6.1.1.1 Working principles of main compressor

Rotary-screw compressors use two meshing helical screws, known as rotors, to compress the gas (Referring to the Figure 6-11). In an oil-flooded rotary-screw compressor, lubricating oil bridges the space between the rotors, both providing a hydraulic seal and transferring mechanical energy between the driving and driven rotor. Gas enters at the suction side and moves through the threads as the screws rotate. The meshing rotors force the gas through the compressor, and the gas exits at the end of the screws.

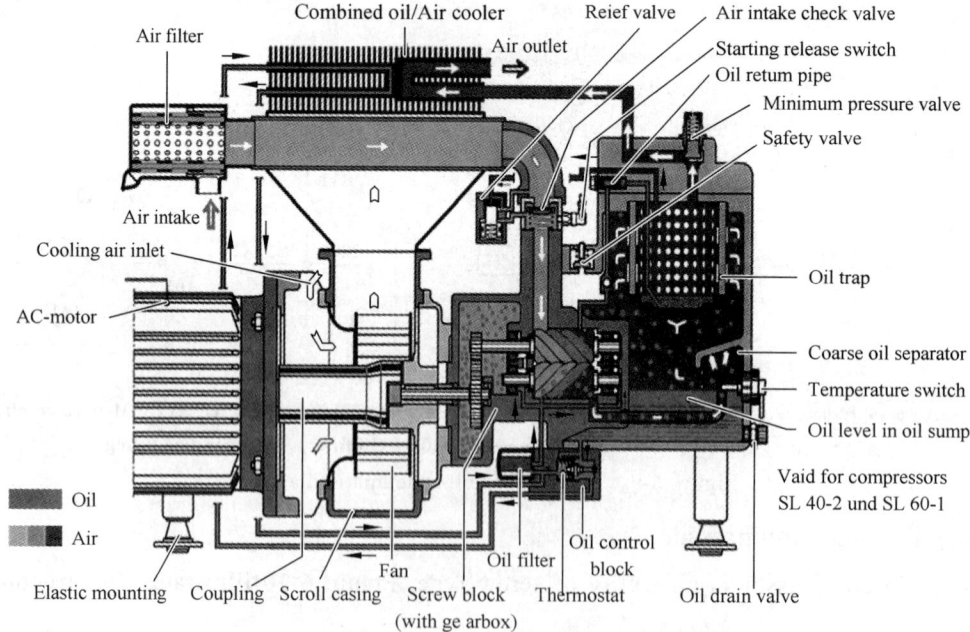

Figure 6-11 Schematic diagram of a screw compressor

The effectiveness of this mechanism is dependent on precisely fitting clearances between the helical rotors and between the rotors and the chamber for sealing of the compression cavities.

However, some leakage is inevitable, and high rotational speeds must be used to minimize the ratio of leakage flow rate over effective flow rate.

6.6.1.1.2 Control of main compressors

The compressor management determines one preferred main compressor of the two main compressors. The preferred compressor is replaced by the other available compressor if the preferred compressor is not available anymore. The preferred compressor is also replaced by the other available compressor if the run time of the preferred compressor is more than 50% within 1 hour. The compressor is activated if the average MRP value is less than 850 kPa, the second compressor is activated if the average MRP value is less than 830 kPa.

Within one 8-car trainset the two compressors are switched on one after the other to avoid a break down of the electrical power supply. If the availability of electrical power of a 8-car trainset is reduced at maximum one compressor in the affected 8-car train set is activated. When the train is set into service and the MRP level is less than 700 kPa then all available compressors in train run. This decreases the necessary time to build up 1,000 kPa in the MRP.

6.6.1.2 Air dryer

The compressed air is passed through a pressure vessel with two "towers" filled with a media such as activated alumina, silica gel, molecular sieve or other desiccant material. After it has been disposed of, the relative humidity is less 35% and this can meet the use requirement at the temperature of − 40 °C

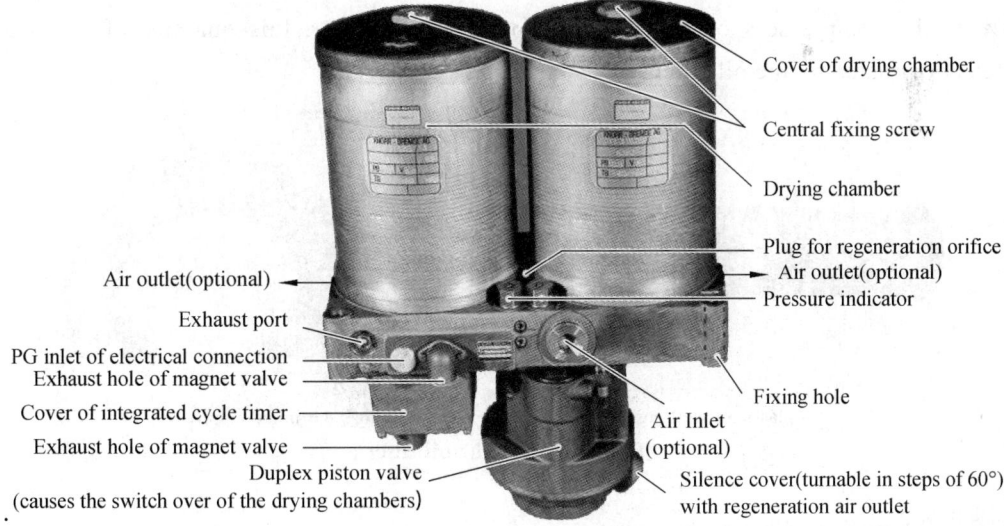

Figure 6-12   Air dryer

This desiccant material attracts the water from the compressed air via adsorbtion. As the water clings to the desiccant, the desiccant "bed" becomes saturated. The dryer is timed to switch towers based on a standard NEMA cycle, once this cycle completes some compressed air from the system is used to "purge" the saturated desiccant bed by simply blowing the water that has adhered to the desiccant off.

The duty of the desiccant in the chamber is to bring the pressure dew point of the compressed air to a level in which the water vapour will no longer condense, or to remove as much water from the compressed air as possible.

The methods used for the regeneration of the desiccant vessel Heatless "pressure-swing" drying, which uses part of the dry compressed air coming from the other vessel to dry the desiccant in the vessel being regenerated at lower pressure. 17% ~ 20% purge rate. Normally one chamber of the dual-chamber dryer is in the absorbing-water condition and the other in the regeneration condition. The alternate conversion of the function is controlled by a electronic conversion calculagraph, the cycle period is about 120 s.There is also a electric heater at the drain valve in case of icing; a muffler is located at the drain jaws.

6.6.1.3 Safety valve

Two same safety valves are installed in the main air supply unit, one is set to 1.05 MPa, the other is set to 12 bar to protect the air system and the compressor.

6.6.1.4 The oil filter

After the compressed air has been dealt by oil filter, the oil content is less than 0.1 mg/ m3, the oil filter should be drained of the oil every period of time.

The compressors oil consumption highly depends on the compressor type, oil properties and its operation conditions, and hence is not constant. Particularly at high operation temperatures, up to 50% of the compressors oil consumption pass the air dryer, this quantity of oil is almost completely extracted by the oil filter.

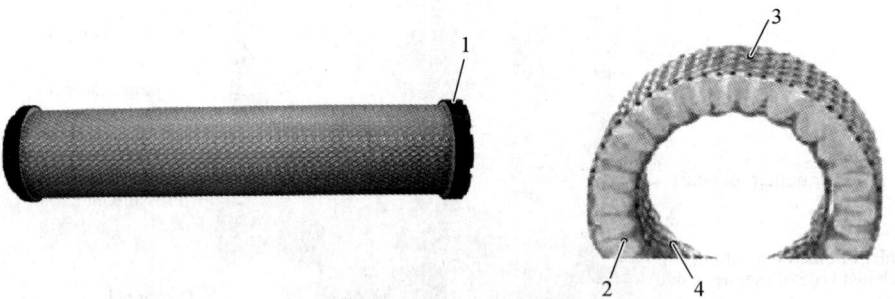

1—plastic caps; 2—glass-fibre layer; 3—outer support; 4—inner supplrt.
Figure 6-13　The oil filter

6.6.2　Auxiliary air supply unit

In case of MRP is lower, the auxiliary air supply unit will supply compressed air to the pantograph reservoir, components of the auxiliary air supply unit are shown in Figure 6-14.

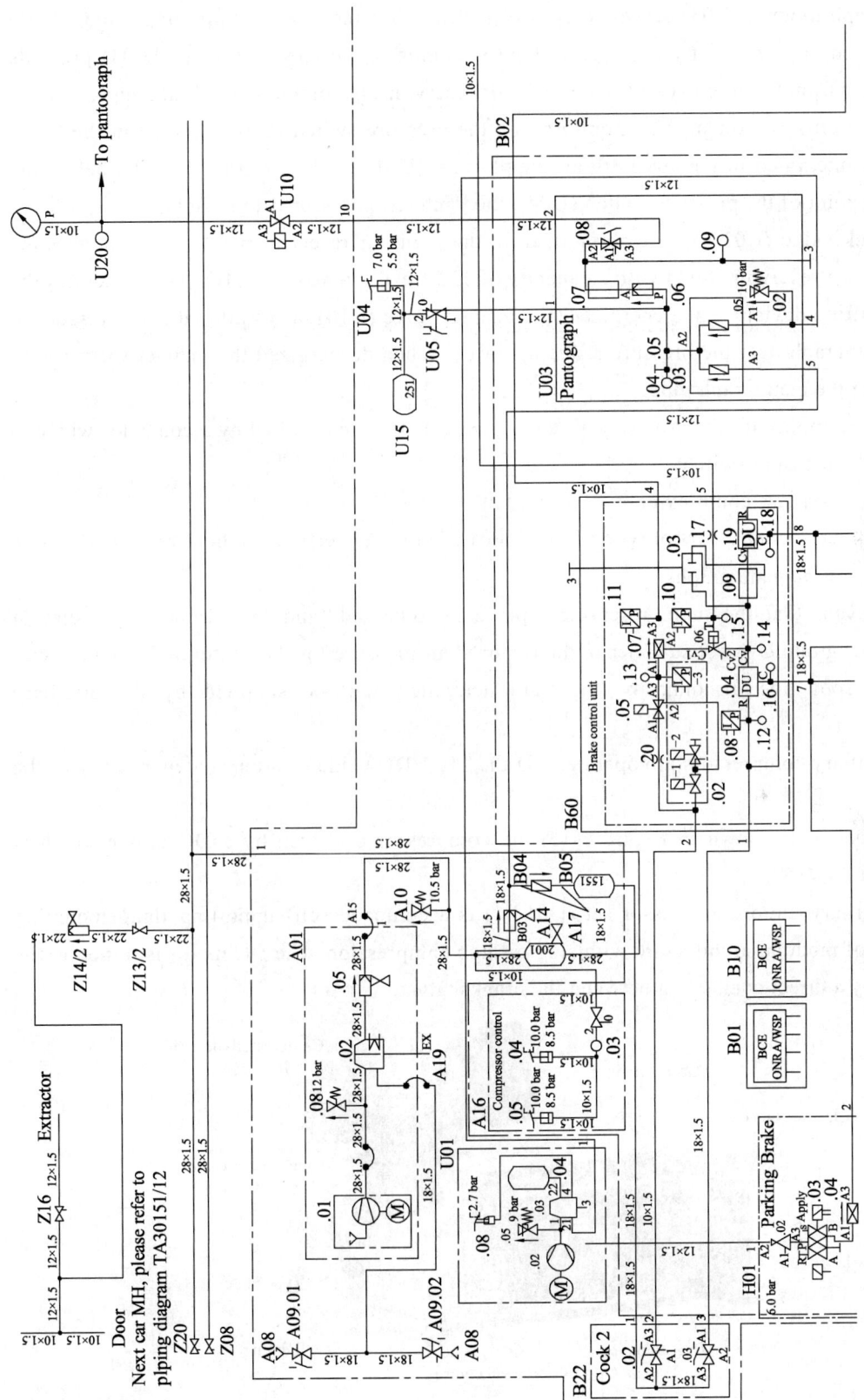

Figure 6-14　Schematic diagram of brake system (part)

Pantograph module (U03) serves to control and monitor the auxiliary air supply unit (U01) and compressed air supply of current collector (pantograph).The check valve (U03.03) prevents compressed air from flowing back into the main air reservoir pipe or automatic brake pipe.

The main air reservoir pipe is monitored by the pressure switch (U04), located in the brake frame (B08), integrated in the auxiliary air supply unit (U01). If the air pressure falls below the lower switch point of the pressure switch (U04), the panto-compressor is to switch ON.

Via check valve (U03.03), air pressure from the main air reservoir pipe or automatic brake pipe is fed to the reservoir (U15) with a capacity of 25 litres. The magnet valve (U10) operates the pantograph lifting device. When energized, the magnet valve (U10) opens allowing air pressure to raise the pantograph over the pressure reducing valve. When deenergized the magnet valve (U10) closes venting the pantograph pipe.

The power supply for the auxiliary air supply unit (U01) is controlled by a contactor which is operated by the pressure switch.

6.6.2.1 Auxiliary compressor

Two auxiliary compressors of type LP115, located at the underfloor of the cars, are available in the vicinity of the pantographs.

In the event that the main reservoir pipe is not charged (and the available pressure at compressed air group U is not sufficient), the required air pressure for the pantograph, main circuit breaker and roof line disconnector for train activation will be supplied by the auxiliary compressors.

The auxiliary compressors are operated via the 110 VDC vehicle battery independently of the catenary.

A compressor is shown in Figure 6-15, the compressor is driven by a DC motor which is powered with 24 VDC.

The auxiliary motor-compressor set (U01.02) is a compact, self-supporting flangemounting construction of modular architecture with single-stage compression. The DC motor is joined to the compressor by a direct connection between the crankshafts.

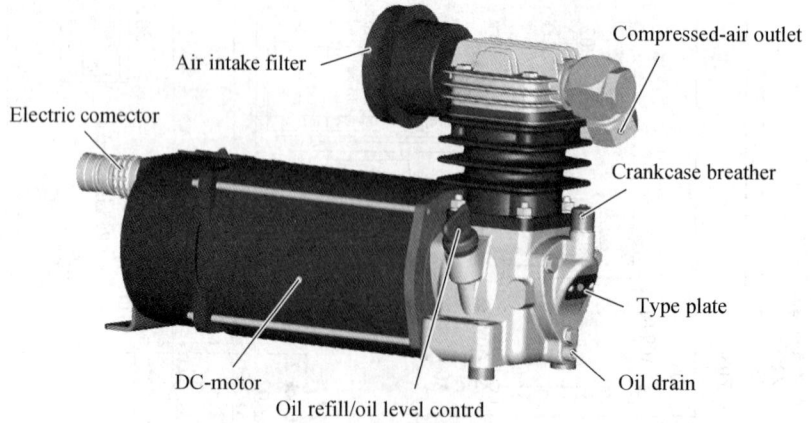

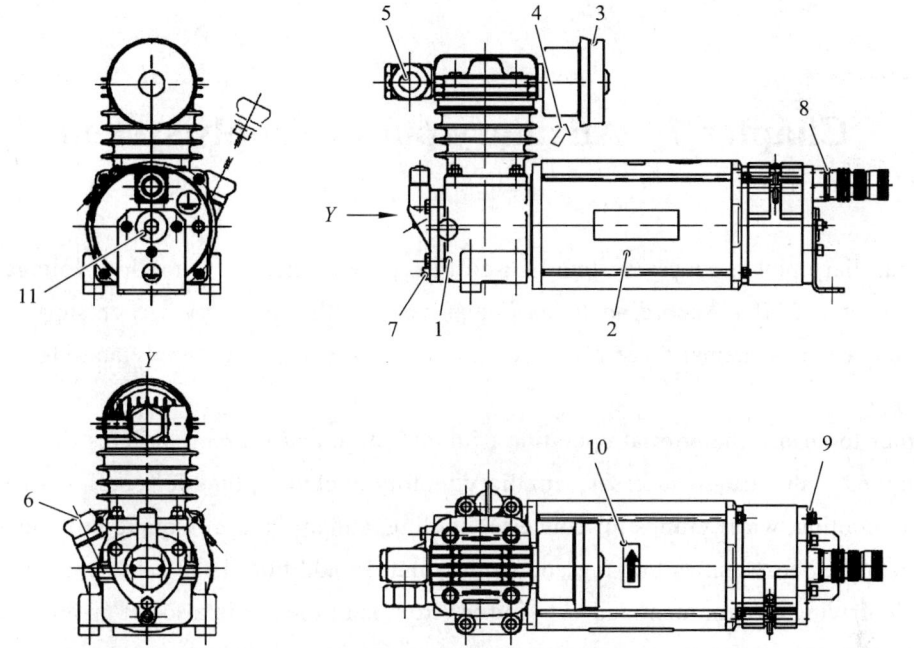

1—Compressor; 2—DC motor; 3—Dry type air filter; 4—Air inlet; 5—Air outlet; 6—Oil filter hole; 7—Oil drain; 8—Connector; 9—Ground; 10—Rotation clockwise; 11—Hole to view direction of rotation.

Figure 6-15   Auxiliary motor-compressor set

6.6.2.2   Control of auxiliary compressors

After the auxiliary compressor is enabled by the CCU it is controlled locally by the brake control module (B02) in the TC02 / TC07 cars. The auxiliary compressor is activated during train activation when the auxiliary air pressure is below the starting threshold of 550 kPa. There will be a message displayed at the driver's MMI to inform about the necessary activation of the auxiliary compressor. The train activation procedure itself is not changed but needs some more time if the auxiliary compressor is needed to provide the required air pressure. The auxiliary compressor is switched off when the level rises above the stopping threshold of 800 kPa, and be off for 90 min if the maximum allowed running time of 10 min is exceeded.

Chapter 7 Auxiliary power supply system

The auxiliary power supply system is used to supply electricity to the low voltage electrical equipment of the EMU. According to particular voltage the auxiliary power supply system is divided into two subsystems: three-phase AC medium voltage power supply and DC low voltage power supply.

In order to ensure the normal operation of the traction and braking systems of the EMU, the car is equipped with various necessary auxiliary motors, including fans for cooling, oil pumps for transformer cooling, water pumps for converter cooling, and air compressors to provide air sources for pneumatic devices such as braking and pantograph. In addition, in order to ensure a good and comfortable driving environment and working environment, the car is also set up air conditioning, electric heater, fan, refrigerator, electric boiler and other electrical appliances, which need three-phase AC medium voltage power supply. At the same time, DC low-voltage power supply is required to provide uninterrupted power to the network control management system of EMU, lighting and so on .

Between the AC and DC auxiliary power supply and the necessary auxiliary electrical equipment mentioned above, the auxiliary power supply distribution line running through the whole train and the distribution cabinet distributed in each carriage are connected into a closed loop to complete the electricity distribution. These wire and distribution cabinets are the distribution section of the auxiliary power supply system.

7.1 Composition and operation principle of auxiliary power supply system

The EMU is normally composed of 2 power units with symmetrical layout as (M+T+M+T)+(T+M+T+M) type. The input of the auxiliary power supply system comes from the traction power supply system, but the auxiliary converters of CRH3 EMU are independent from the traction converters. Each power unit has one single auxiliary converter and one double auxiliary converter, which are installed on two trailers separately. The operation principle is shown in Figure 7-1.

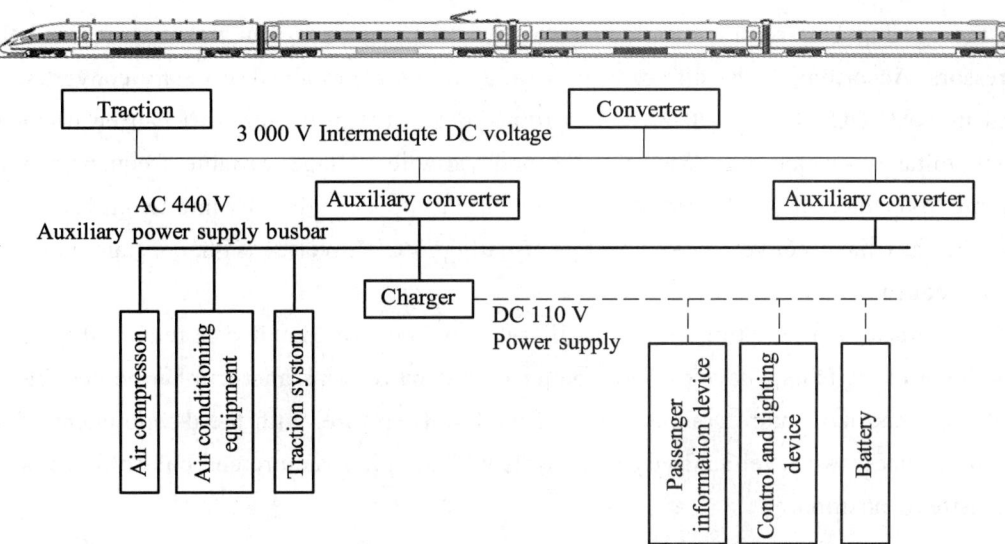

Figure 7-1　Schematic diagram of EMU auxiliary power supply system

The auxiliary converters located in two trailers transform DC 3000 V from the middle link of traction converters into 3φAC440 V and supply power to the AC 440 V bus grid to ensure the cooling use of air compressors, air conditioners and traction systems of each vehicle. Then the 3φ AC 440 V is transform to DC 110 V through the charger for passenger information system, controlling and lighting, and charging the battery at the same time. Main technical parameters are revealed in Table 7-1.

Table 7-1　Main technical parameters of auxiliary power supply system

Auxiliary converter	quantity	Each train has two single converter 2 dual converters.
	capacity	160 kV·A
	circuit structure	DC-AC
		filter capacitor +PWM+ transformer、EMC filter
	input	DC 3000 V (The intermediate voltage of the traction converter)
	output	AC 440(1±5%)V 60(1±1%) Hz
Battery charger	quantity	2 per train
	capacity	60 kW
	input	The three-phase alternating current output of the auxiliary converter
	output	DC 110 V(+25%, -30%)

7.2　Auxiliary converter

The three-phase AC medium voltage supply subsystem uses auxiliary converters to generate a voltage of 3φAC 380 V, 50 Hz which supplies power to the cooling fans of traction motors on the

EMU, the cooling fans of traction converters, the oil pumps of main transformers and the air compressors. According to the different input side, the main circuit of auxiliary converter can be divided into AC-DC-AC and DC-AC. According to the different output, it can be divided into constant voltage constant frequency(CVCF) and variable voltage variable frequency(VVVF); According to the electric level series of the main circuit, it can be divided into two levels and three levels. The auxiliary converter of EMU is usually CVCF inverter with constant voltage and constant frequency.

The characteristics of three-level auxiliary converter are that it can reduce the withstand voltage level of switching devices, have better output waveforms and less harmonics, but adopt more devices and have more complex control modes. Therefore, with the development of power electronic devices, two-level auxiliary converters with simple structure and control have occupied the mainstream position.

7.2.1 Auxiliary converter device composition

The input of the auxiliary converter comes from the traction converter intermediate circuit DC 3000 V, and the output is 3ϕAC 440 V, 60 Hz after processing by the auxiliary converter. CRH3 and all auxiliary converters of CRH380B EMU simultaneously supply power to a 3ϕAC 440 V, 60 Hz bus connecting the whole train (8 vehicles), and each auxiliary converter is synchronized through the bus.

Buses are coupled during train operation. In case of failure, the coupling contactors of the double auxiliary converters can be turned on to isolate the units.

Auxiliary converters include switches, protection components, various monitoring equipment and power modules.

Figure 7-2 shows the main components and positions of the single auxiliary converters of EMU, and Figure 7-3 shows the composition of the mounting plate of the single auxiliary converters.

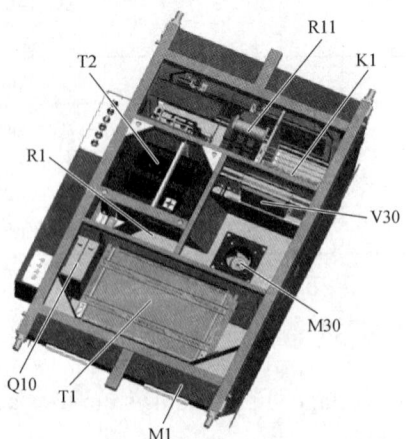

Figure 7-2 The main components of the single auxiliary converters of EMU

In Figure 7-2, K1 SIBCOS-M2500 is the main controller, M1 is the built-in fan, M30 is the main fan, Q10 is the coupling circuit breaker, R1 is the filtering choke, R11 is the precharge resistor, T1 is the pulse width modulation inverter, T2 is the transformer, and V30 is the capacitor.

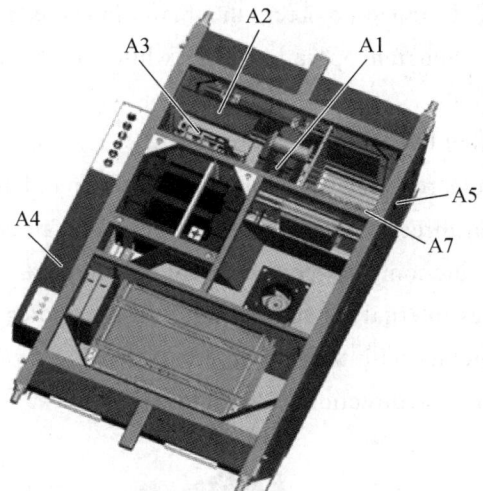

Figure 7-3   The composition of the mounting plate of the single auxiliary converters of EMU

In Figure 7-3 A1 is the mounting plate for contactor and precharged contactor, A2 is the mounting plate for 3AC voltage detection, A3 is the mounting plate for external power supply contactor and output fuse, A4 is the mounting plate for filter capacitor, A5 is the mounting plate for transformer, and A7 is the mounting plate for contactor.

The single auxiliary converters of CRH3 and CRH380B EMU are forced air cooled. As shown in Figure 7-4.

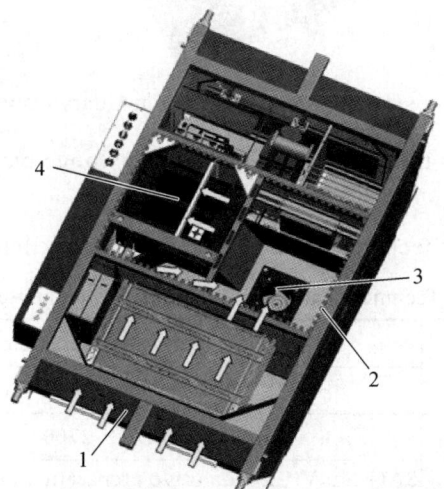

Figure 7-4   Forced air-cooled main air flow by single auxiliary converters of EMU

In Figure 7-4 the No.1 is the air filter, No.2 is the partition board, No.3 is the main fan M30, No.4 is the exhaust outlet on the bottom cover.

Air is introduced by two dual-nozzle grilles mounted on the front of the housing, and is then directed through the heat sink of the power module [T1], which extends into the duct. The main fan [M30] blows cold air into the middle compartment, the cold air then passes through the transformer [T2], and finally discharged through the two vent grilles located at the bottom.

The cooling system is designed to keep the main fan speed as low as possible, which minimizes dirt, noise levels, and fan operation time while maintaining optimal ventilation and cooling.

The main fan is controlled by the main controller SIBCOS-M2500 [2K1] [3K1] according to the temperature. Each module reports the temperature of the radiator to the controller, which monitors the temperature and directly turns on or off the main fan according to the temperature. Fan control can achieve full autonomy, without external interference.

Built-in fan [M1] ensures internal air circulation. These modules work continuously, and they turn themselves on or off together with the system controller. Figure 7-5 shows the position of the built-in fan on the housing and the direction of the internal air flow.

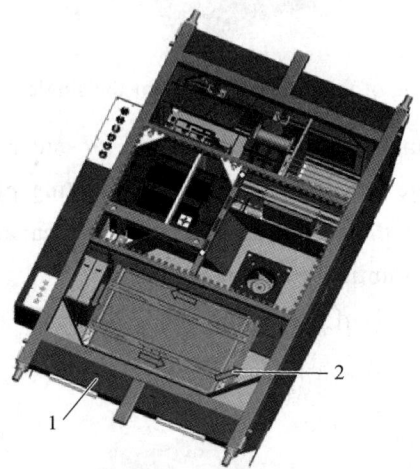

Figure 7-5　Forced air cooling system of auxiliary converters of EMU

In Figure 7-5, the No.1 is the built-in fan [M1] on the hinge plate, and No.2 is the internal air flow.

Table 7-2 shows the main technical parameters of single auxiliary converters for EMU.

Table 7-2　Technical parameters of auxiliary converters for EMU

content	parameters
capacity	2×160 kV·A （$\cos\phi=0.9$）
input voltage	DC （2700～3600） V
output voltage	3AC 440 V （Locomotive preparation under parking conditions： 345 V） （60±1） Hz （Locomotive preparation under parking conditions： 47 Hz）
Heat dissipation mode	Forced air cooling
Overall dimensions	1886 mm×2978 mm×699.5 mm
weight	About 1450 kg

7.2.2　Circuit of auxiliary converter

The main circuits of auxiliary converter is DC-AC type. The DC-AC auxiliary converter takes power from the DC grid or directly from the intermediate DC link of the traction converter, and converts DC to three-phase AC by the inverter. DC-AC auxiliary converters have been widely used in locomotive, EMU, urban rail and other applications.

Due to the high input voltage, it is generally necessary to add a step-down device to ensure the voltage level required by the output auxiliary electrical equipment. There are two manners, one is to invert first, and then reduce the higher AC voltage to the required voltage level through the three-phase step-down transformer; The other is to reduce the DC input voltage to a suitable value through a step-down circuit, and then invert it.

Figure 7-6 and Figure 7-7 respectively show the circuit structure of the two auxiliary converters.

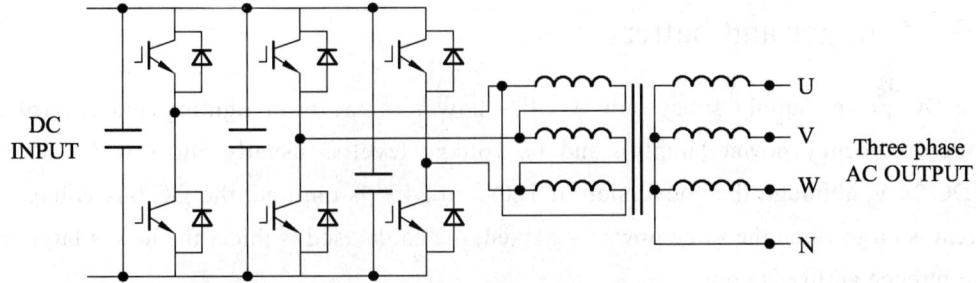

Figure 7-6　Schematic diagram of the direct-AC auxiliary converter circuit (mode 1)

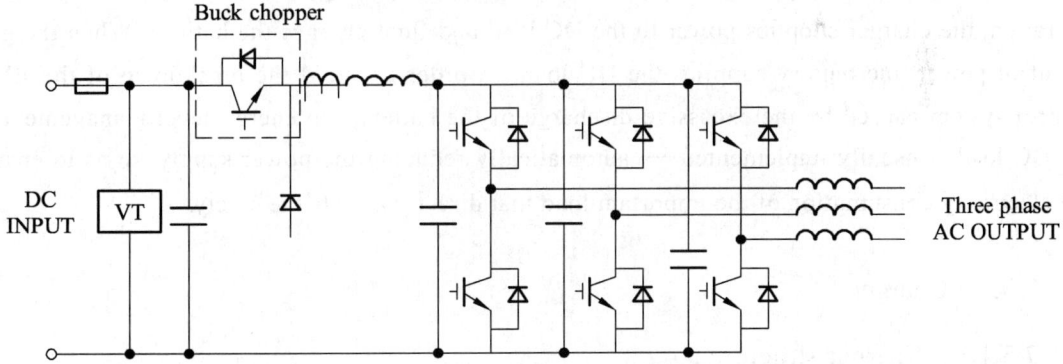

Figure 7-7　Schematic diagram of the direct-AC auxiliary converter circuit (mode 2)

In order to obtain good quality three-phase AC power supply, it is usually necessary to add filtering link. In Mode 1, the three-phase inductor/capacitor filter or three-phase LC filter may be placed between the inverter and the step-down transformer or may be placed behind the transformer. In mode 2, the filter is placed after the output of the inverter.

In the first mode, the Δ-Y transformer not only realizes the function of step-down, but also realizes the mutual isolation between the high-voltage input power supply loop and the load loop. This circuit is characterized by a small number of switching components and simple control. The disadvantage is that the output three-phase voltage is easily affected by the DC input voltage, and when the DC input voltage is high, the inverter switching components required high withstanding voltage and high cost. Therefore, the mode is more suitable for the traction converter with middle DC link power supply.

In the second way, different circuits can be adopted to achieve voltage reduction. The simplest is a single tube buck chopper, as shown in Figure 7-7. It has the following characteristics: (1) the inverter input voltage is kept constant through the closed-loop control of step-down chopper, so as to eliminate the influence of input voltage fluctuation on the output of three-phase inverter. (2) There is only one high-power and high-voltage IGBT element in the whole circuit, and the inverter can choose the IGBT element of lower voltage level to reduce the equipment cost. But this way does not realize the isolation between the input and output, and also should set load protection circuit after the buck chopper lost control.

7.3 Charger and battery

The DC power supply subsystem supplies power to the train lighting and control system (including emergency power supply), and its voltage level is usually DC 110 V. CRH5 EMU adopts DC 24 V, although the conversion of 110 V to 24 V is omitted, the DC bus voltage is low, the current is large when the same power is played, the cable used is thick, the loss is large, and the anti-interference ability is poor.

The DC power supply adopts the combination mode of charger and battery. During normal operation, the charger supplies power to the DC load and float charges the battery; When the grid is out of power, the battery supplies the DC load. In order to avoid the breakdown of the EMU control system caused by the excessive discharge of the battery, the energy level management of the DC load is usually implemented——automatically reducing the power supply, so as to ensure the electricity consumption of the important load that directly affects the safety.

7.3.1 Charger

7.3.1.1 Charger structure

Each EMU traction unit equipped with 1 charger, suspended under No.4 cars and No.5 cars. The BC is powered by a 3ϕAC 440 V, 60 Hz bus, which is transformed into DC 110 V to supply power to batteries and other DC loads. The DC 110 V bus is connected through the whole line.

The charger includes switch and protection parts, as well as many monitoring devices and power modules. The structure of the a charger is as show in Figure 7-8, Figure 7-9 and Figure 7-10.

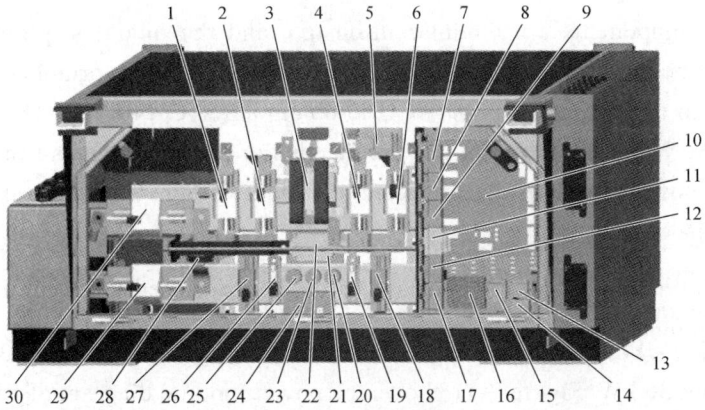

1—FuseF4; 2—FuseF10; 3—Contactor Q1; 4—Fuse F3; 5—Fixed frame A2; 6—BK fuse F9; 7—Voltage sensor T6; 8—Output voltage sensor T20; 9—Output voltage sensor T23; 10—Master controller K1; 11—DC 110 V ground fault check T22; 12—Input voltage sensor T4; 13—fan A1-Q15; 14—Motor protection switch fan A1-F15; 15—contactor A1-Q12; 16—Fuse A1-F1 to A1-F8; 17—Input voltage sensor T3; 18—BN2 Fuse F11; 19—BD fuse F7; 20—EMC Electromagnetic compatibility V25; 21—NTC resistor; 22—Decoupling diode R20; 23—EMC Filter capacitor V26; 24—BN2/BS2 Contactor Q2; 25—EMC Filter capacitor V27; 26—BD Fuse F8; 27—BN2 Fuse F12; 28—Battery current sensor T24; 29—Fuse F1; 30-Fuse F2.

Figure 7-8　The layout of switching equipment and control devices for EMU charger

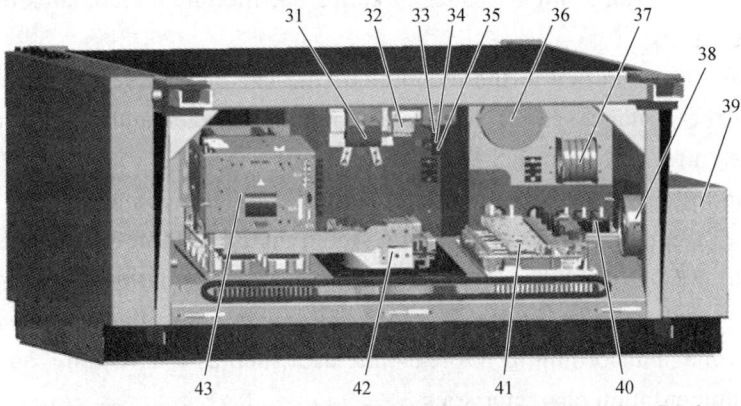

31—Input contactor Q3; 32—Discharge contactor Q4; 33—Precharge resistor R11; 34—Precharge resistor R12; 35—Precharge resistor R13; 36—Internal fan M2; 37—Iron ring V4; 38—Internal fan M3; 39—Capacitor base A4; 40—terminal A5; 41—Charger module T2; 42—Mounting plate A3; 43—Charger module T1.

Figure 7-9　Module layout of EMU chargers

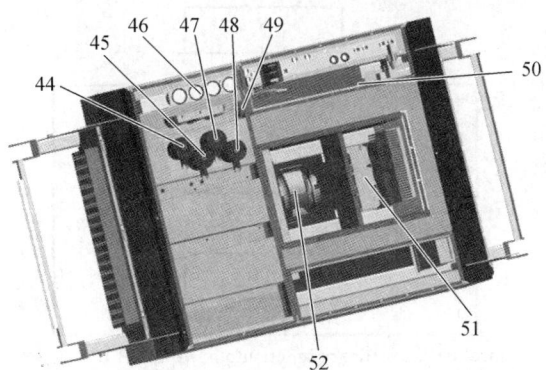

44—Filter R4; 45—Filter R2; 46—Mounting plate A4; 47—Filter R3; 48—Filter R1; 49—Current sensor T21; 50—iron core V11; 51—Input filter R5; 52—Main fan.

Figure 7-10　Layout of the middle cabinet without bottom cover of EMU charger

The box and components are modular in design, and the modules, protection devices and power modules can be quickly separated without special tools.Under normal conditions, the BC is directly connected to the output of the D-ACU to obtain a 3φAC 440 V, 60 Hz power supply with an output of 60 kW. When the train control unit sends the startup command through MVB, if the DC 110 V external power supply is disconnected, the input voltage is normal, and BC is not faulty, then BC starts normally.

In case of external power supply, BC is provided by external power socket 3φAC 380 V, 50 Hz power supply, output 36 kw.

In the case of "parking and servicing", the BC is provided by ACU with3φ AC 345V, 47Hz power supply, output 36 kW. Figure 7-11 shows the power module diagram of EMU chargers.

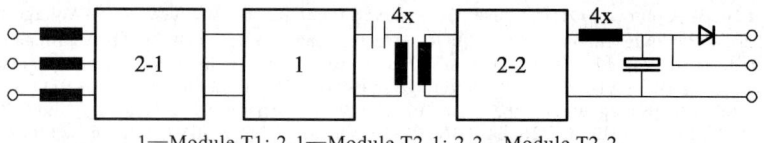

1—Module T1; 2-1—Module T2-1; 2-2—Module T2-2.
Figure 7-11 The power module diagram of EMU charger

Module T1 is controllable high-frequency converter. Module T2 contains one input rectifier and four output rectifiers.

Several sensors are installed in the module circuit. The current sensor detects current of the device and load, the voltage sensor detects the output voltage, and the voltage, current and temperature of the battery are recorded.

The main controller K1 loads the powerful control program, commands the charging module T1, T2 and high-frequency transformer 4X to transform three-phase AC input voltage (440 V/60 Hz) into the DC 110 V output voltage with electrical isolation , to charge the battery, at the same time, it supplies power to the DC load. The main controller K1 can also regulate the battery charging voltage according to the real-time data such as temperature, so as to conform to the temperature compensation characteristics.

7.3.1.2 Control system of the charger

Figure 7-12 shows the control system diagram of EMU chargers.

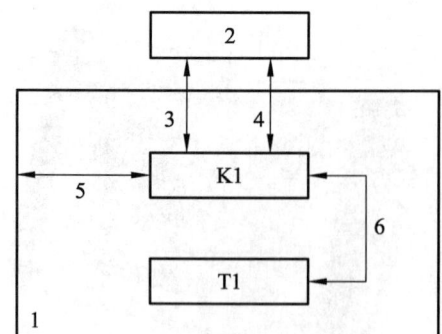

1—BC; 2—Central control unit; 3—Binary input output; 4—MVB Bus; 5—RS232 serial interface; 6—CAN bus; K1—Main control unit; T1—Power module.
Figure 7-12 the schematic diagram of charger control system

The BC control system consists of a main controller K1 and a power module T1. K1 is used to monitor the BC and has a more advanced function, it provides signal to CCU through the MVB. The internal communication of BC control system uses CAN bus.

7.3.2 Battery

EMU battery pack and charger are paired, each traction unit is equipped with one group, which is suspended under 4 cars and 5 cars. The battery pack consists of two battery seats. Each battery seat is equipped with 84 FNC 1502 HR* cells in series, as shown in Figure 7-13.

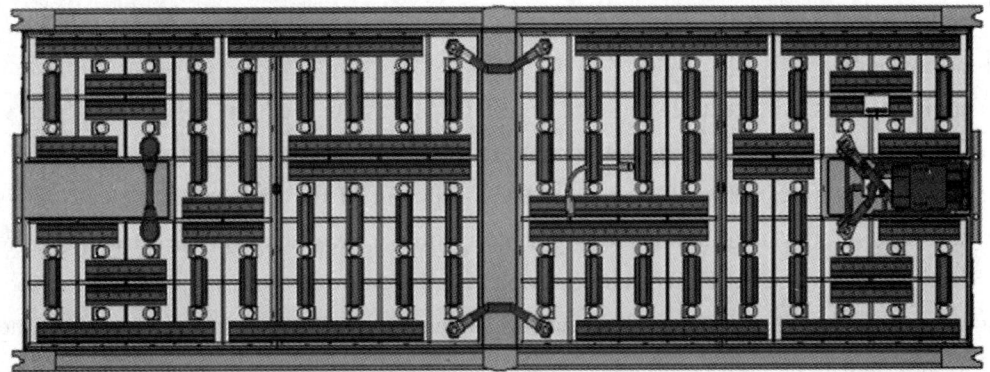

Figure 7-13   Profile of EMU batteries

The interconnection of single batteries enables the nominal voltage of the battery pack to reach 100.8 V, the capacity to reach $2\times160A\cdot h$, the maximum discharge current to reach 545A, and the battery type is NiCd.

When the train is under no network voltage, the DC 100.8 V battery system can keep the auxiliary equipment such as internal lighting, external lighting, emergency ventilation, on-board safety equipment, broadcasting and communication system running within the time specified in the parking plan.

The assembly method of the single battery can ensure that the creepage gap specification of the 100.8 V battery pack meets the requirements of DIN EN 50272-2 and iec50124 standards.

7.4   The power distribution system

Distribution system plays the role of electrical bridge between power supply and load in auxiliary power supply system, connecting power supply device, electrical equipment and control and protection equipment into a closed loop, so as to complete the transmission, distribution and conversion of electricity.

When the auxiliary power is started, power is first transmitted to the bus, and the power supply bus runs through the whole train through the power connector at the end of the car between the car and the car. The power is transmitted to the power distribution cabinet of the car by the dividing device of each car, and then distributed to various loads by the power distribution cabinet.

The power distribution system mainly includes two equipment: distribution cable and distribution cabinet. According to the purpose division, the car body wiring has three types power, broadcast and network control, we mainly discuss the power wiring here; According to the location of the car body wiring in the vehicle, it can be divided into two parts: inside the car and under the car wiring. The power distribution cabinet is used in conjunction with the wiring and is mostly installed in the car, which is convenient for the operation and maintenance of the EMU mechanic. Due to the design habits and manufacturing process of each manufacturer, there are great differences in the layout of wiring and the structural function of the distribution cabinet. The number is huge and complex, and the voltage level is various, and they are almost all over every part of the car body.

In addition, since the electrical control logic of EMU is the medium voltage and high voltage electrical systems is controlled by the low voltage electrical system, and the medium voltage electrical system supplies power to the auxiliary equipment of the high voltage electrical system, in fact, the low voltage, medium voltage and high voltage electrical systems are highly related. Taking the starting process of EMU as an example, it goes through three stages in sequence:

Stage one: Low voltage DC system startup. It mainly includes lighting equipment, network control system and two-stage equipment, as well as traditional control circuit of pantograph and main circuit breaker, which occurs before the lifting bow is closed and is powered by vehicle-mounted battery.

Stage two: the medium voltage AC system startup . It mainly includes traction and braking auxiliary devices such as traction ventilator, brake air compressor and air conditioning unit in passenger compartment, and prepare for the train operation, this happens after the pantograph raising is off, and the main traction circuit is put into operation except for the motor converter and traction motor. The auxiliary converter that takes power from the DC link in the middle of the traction converter is started and connected to the grid to the medium voltage AC bus to supply power for the above mentioned equipment. At the same time, the charger is started continuously, the DC bus is powered by the charger, and the battery is also changed from the discharge status to the charging status.

Stage three: High voltage traction system startup. The driver starts the traction motor under the given conditions of driving signal, then the train runs.

Chapter 8 EMU Network Control Technology

8.1 Overview

8.1.1 The purpose of the EMU network control system

The EMU network control system (hereinafter referred to as TCMS) realizes information transmission through the bus running through the train, centrally manages the relevant information of vehicle operation and on-board equipment action, provides effective guidance for the operation of drivers and attendants, and provides support for the maintenance of equipment and passenger services. TCMS system has five major functions of information transmission, logic control, screen display, fault diagnosis and user support. CRH3 type EMU is a typical representative of China's high-speed EMU, and this paper introduces the EMU network control technology by taking CRH3 EMU as an example.

8.1.2 Abbreviated terms of EMU network control technology (Table 8-1)

Table 8-1 Abbreviated terms of EMU network control technology

Abbreviated Terms	Description
TCMS	Train control and management systems
ACU	Auxiliary converter unit
BCU	Brake control unit
CC	Vehicle control
CCU	Central control unit
CI/O	Input/output devices
DC	Driver's cab
DS	door
DMI	ATP monitor
MMI	Driver monitor
ET	Ethernet
FAS/SD	Fire alarm system/smoke detector
GW	gateway
RP	Repeater
KLIP	SIBAS KLIP device
HVAC	Heating, ventilation and air conditioning controls

Table

Abbreviated Terms	Description
MVB	Multifunctional vehicle bus
OL	Joystick
TCU	Traction control unit
TR	Train radio
WC	lavatory
WTB	Stranded train bus

8.2 EMU network control system composition

Taking the CRH3 type EMU as an example, the network of each EMU includes gateway GW, central control unit CCU, traction control unit TCU, brake control unit BCU, auxiliary control unit ACU, as well as charger unit BC, air conditioning control unit HVAC, door control unit, passenger information central controller PIS-STC, man-machine display interface MMI, distributed input and output station SIBAS KLI and other equipment. These smart devices are connected to the EMU network via the train bus WTB or the vehicle bus MVB.

The EMU network diagram structure is shown in Figures 8-1, 8-2, 8-3, 8-4, 8-5 and 8-6.

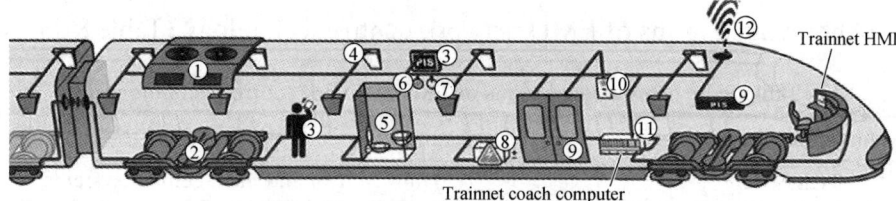

Figure 8-1　EMU network wiring diagram

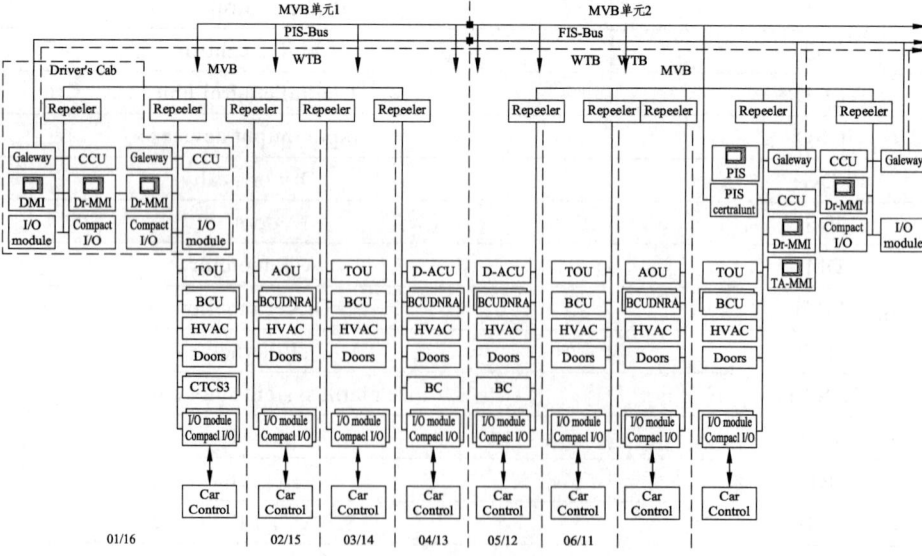

Figure 8-2　EMU network topology

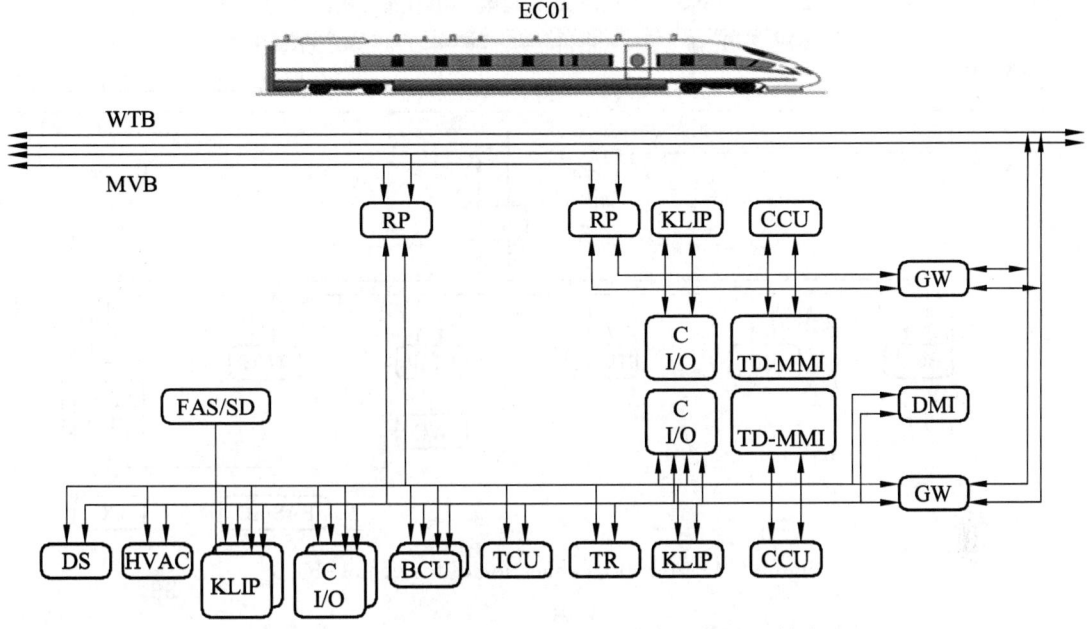

Figure 8-3　Network connection of the EC01 vehicle

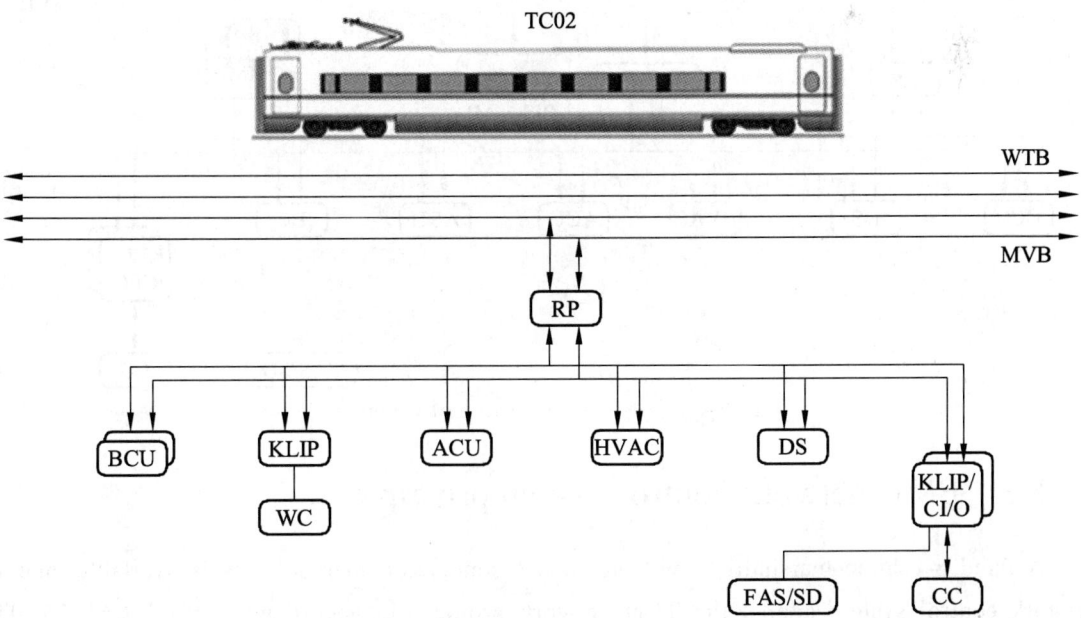

Figure 8-4　Network connection of vehicle TC02

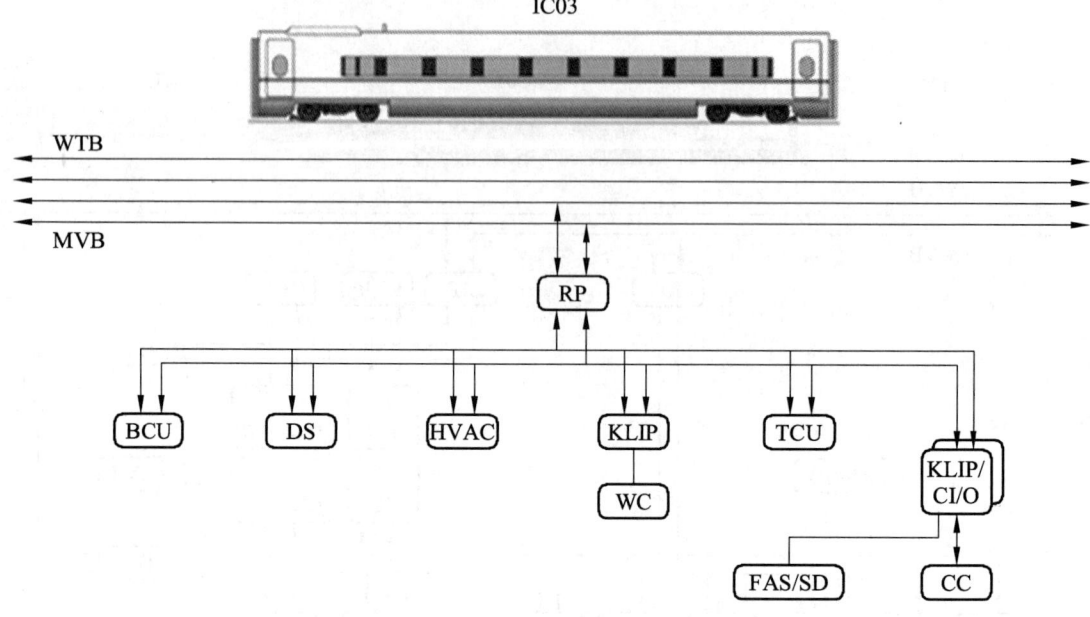

Figure 8-5   Network connection of the vehicle IC03

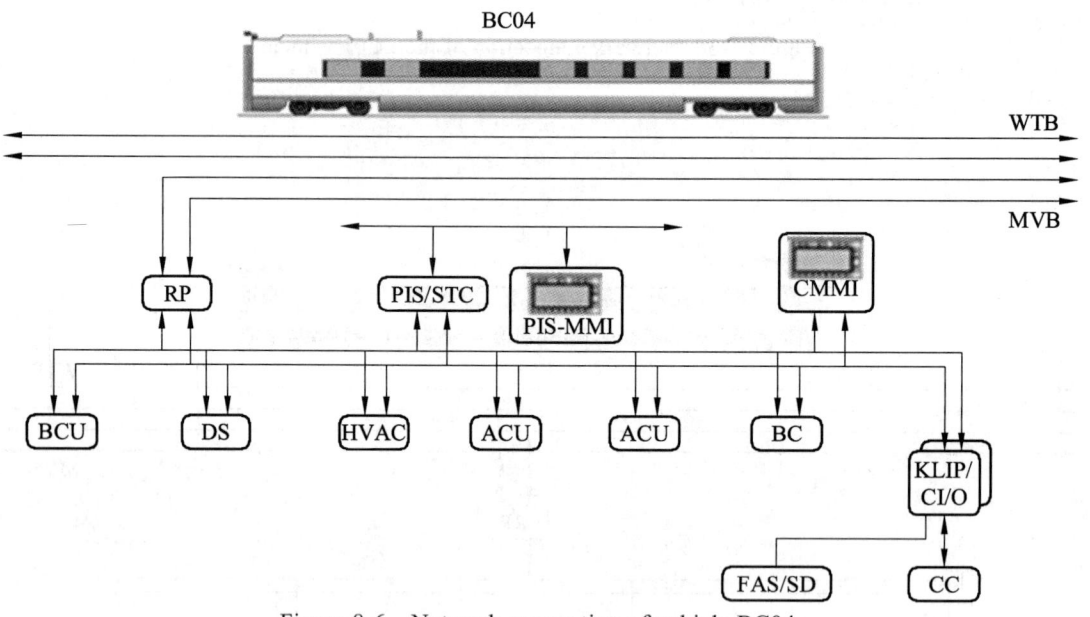

Figure 8-6   Network connection of vehicle BC04

8.3   EMU network control system principle

A fixed 8-vehicle marshalling with up to 2 reconnection marshallings is available, and its network control system adopts the TCN network protocol in accordance with IEC61375. The communication network of the EMU is divided into two levels: the train-class network and the vehicle-class network. TCN Gateway connects train-level networks and vehicle-level networks.

The train-level network uses the WTB bus to run through the whole train, and undertakes the function of network interconnection when reconnecting. The whole train is divided into two power units, each of which is a power unit. The two units are connected by WTB to complete the transfer of train-level information. The network within each power unit is a vehicle-level network. MVB-EMD bus connection is adopted between different vehicles in each power unit, except for the head car and the rear car each set up 2 repeaters, the rest of the car is provided with a repeater; Each vehicle device is also connected by MVB-EMD bus, and different smart devices inside the same vehicle are connected to the MVB-EMD bus. These smart devices typically include central control units, displays, TCUs, and ACUs.

Whether it is a train-level bus or a vehicle-level bus, the communication line dual-channel redundancy design is adopted, which is the redundancy of the communication line. When one communication line fails, the system can automatically switch to another communication line. In addition, there is equipment redundancy, which is generally equipped with two key control signal devices for the acquisition of EMUs, which are redundant with each other. For example, the gateway and the central control unit, because of their vehicle control and bus management functions, the gateway and the central control unit are hot-standby redundant configuration in each power unit. For the WTB bus, the central control unit automatically selects one of the main devices through the competition mechanism of the underlying protocol chip, and the other central control units are the backup masters, and monitors the working status of the current master in real time. When the main central control unit fails, the standby central control unit will take over the responsibilities of the main central control unit, exercising WTB bus management and control functions. The sovereign switchover is an automatic switching mode, which does not require human intervention, and the sovereign switching does not cause the interruption and failure of the train control function. For the MVB bus, each power unit is a separate MVB network, and the bus management, redundancy, and switching mechanisms within each MVB network are consistent with the WTB.

Whether it is a train-level bus or a vehicle-level bus, the communication line dual-channel redundancy design is adopted, which is the redundancy of the communication line. When one communication line fails, the system can automatically switch to another communication line. In addition, there is equipment redundancy, which is generally equipped with two key control signal devices for the acquisition of EMUs, which are redundant with each other. For example, the gateway and the central control unit, because of their vehicle control and bus management functions, the gateway and the central control unit are hot-standby redundant configuration in each power unit. For the WTB bus, the central control unit automatically selects one of the main devices through the competition mechanism of the underlying protocol chip, and the other central control units are the backup masters, and monitors the working status of the current master in real time. When the main central control unit fails, the standby central control unit will take over the responsibilities of the main central control unit, exercising WTB bus management and control functions. The sovereign switchover is an automatic switching mode, which does not require human intervention, and the sovereign switching does not cause the interruption and failure of the train control function. For the MVB bus, each power unit is a separate MVB network, and the bus management, redundancy, and switching mechanisms within each MVB network are consistent with the WTB.

A train of 8 cars is composed of two power units, each power unit is an MVB (multi-function vehicle bus) network segment, each MVB adopts the main chain-branch structure, each vehicle is equipped with a repeater, and the MVB in a basic unit is divided into multiple branches. In this way, even if there is a network communication failure of a subsystem device, at most, it will only affect the communication between the network and the subsystem in the car, and will not affect the network communication of the entire basic unit.

The network control system adopts distributed control technology, that is, distributed acquisition and execution, and centralized control and management. It is composed of traction control unit TCU, brake control unit BCU, charger control unit BC, auxiliary converter control unit ACU, door control unit DCU, fire detection and smoke alarm control unit FAS/SD, intelligent display unit, etc., and communicates through MVB bus or WTB bus and central control unit CCU.

8.3.1 Multi-function vehicle bus MVB

MVB is designed for railway train (vehicle) equipment interconnection and development of highly reliable and strong real-time fieldbus, its connection mode, MVB according to the transmission medium different ESD, EMD, OGF, a MVB network structure should include one or more bus segments, their respective characteristics:

(1) Electrical short-distance dielectric ESD. ESDs are differential transmission wire pairs according to RS485 that can support up to 32 devices over a transmission distance of 20 m without the need for galvanic isolation. If galvanically isolated is used, the transmission distance can be longer.

(2) Electrical medium distance medium EMD. The electrical medium-distance medium composed of shielded twisted pair can support up to 32 devices within a transmission distance of 200 m, allowing the use of transformers for galvanic isolation, as shown in Figure 8-7.

(3) Optical fiber medium OGF. Through the star coupler outlet, the transmission distance can reach 2.0 km, mainly used in more demanding environments.

(4) 8-bit cyclic redundancy check method is adopted.

(5) The physical layer supports three kinds of transmission media, redundant through the two channels itself, important I/O use double parts, and the redundancy switching process will be carried out in the shortest possible time.

(6) By setting the bus repeater, the network topology can be bus-type, star type or hybrid type.

(7) The data link layer supports three basic data transmission modes: process data, message

data, and supervision data.

(8) The transmission baud rate is 1.5 Mb/s, and the signal adopts bidirectional L-type differential Manchester encoding;

Different network (EMD) endpoints require a dedicated terminal to be conFigured, as shown in Figure 8-8.

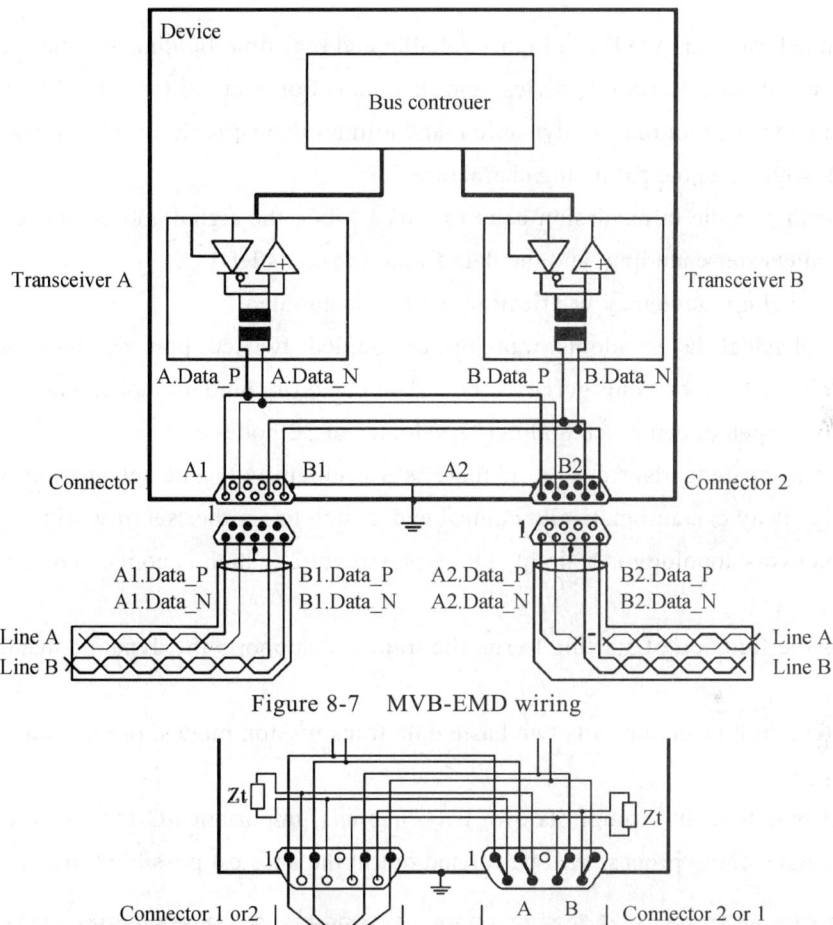

Figure 8-7 MVB-EMD wiring

Figure 8-8 MVB-EMD network terminal

The carriage-level communication network of the EMU adopts MVB vehicle bus, its topology is fixed, can not be dynamically changed, a traction unit 4 vehicles together constitute an MVB network segment. The communication adopts medium-distance transmission medium, that is, shielded twisted pair, which is divided into two redundant wiring in the carriage.

An MVB network segment adopts a structured network structure, that is, each vehicle forms an MVB branch network through the repeater and a traction unit MVB backbone network connection, the advantage of this structure is that the fault of an MVB branch network does not affect the MVB branch network of other vehicles, in the end car due to redundancy reasons there are two MVB segments, respectively, through two repeaters access to the entire MVB network segment, in each segment at both ends are connected to the termination resistance (120 Ω).

8.3.2 Stranded train bus WTB

The stranded train bus WTB is a highly reliable and real-time fieldbus specially developed for the reconnection of railway train vehicles, and its connection method (see fig. 8-9) is particularly suitable for open trains that require dynamic marshalling (also suitable for closed trains with fixed marshallings), which has the following characteristics:

(1) According to the transmission baud rate of 1 Mb/s, the signal adopts bidirectional L-type differential Manchester encoding, and the data frame format is HDLC;

(2) 16-bit cyclic redundancy verification method is adopted;

(3) The physical layer adopts transformer-coupled twisted pair shielded wire, and the transmission channel can be conFigured as redundant or non-redundant mode, and the transmission distance without repeater can reach 860 m (22 vehicles or 32 nodes);

(4) When using redundant design, if there is a problem with one set of train buses that are working, the gateway can automatically control and switch to another set of work;

(5) The network topology is a simple bus-type structure, which is convenient for inter-vehicle wiring;

(6) It has the function of starting to run the train and supports the dynamic marshalling of the train;

(7) The data link layer supports two basic data transmission modes: process data and message data;

(8) WTB is redundant through its own two channels, important I/O is used in two parts, and the redundancy switching process will be carried out in the shortest possible time.

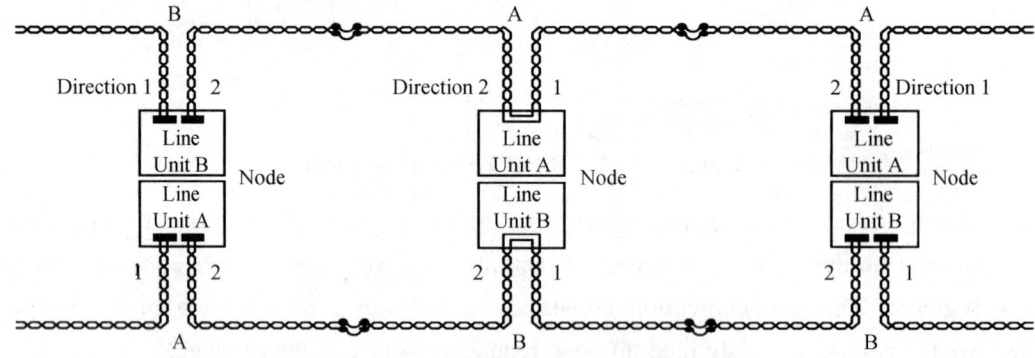

Figure 8-9　Twisted pair train bus WTB connection

The role of the WTB is to connect the two power units so that the necessary train-grade data exchange can be carried out between the two power units. The basis for completing the data exchange between the train network WTB and the vehicle network MVB is the TCN gateway, which is responsible for the data conversion and routing tasks between the two buses of WTB and MVB. Each power unit has two gateways, located in the right cabinet of the driver's cab of the end car (i.e., 1 car and 8 car), which are integrated in two central control units (CCUs) and are redundant with each other, but only the gateway in the central control unit as the main participates in WTB and MVB communication. The gateway is powered on from the central control unit but is not activated.

During the connection and deassembly of EMUs, WTB can dynamically identify the characteristics of network terminals and network topologies, realize the dynamic address allocation of WTB nodes, and automatically complete the relevant configuration of the train level. When the configuration is complete, all train bus devices are given a clear TCN address (i.e. the gateway address activated in each power unit).

8.3.3 Central control unit CCU

There are two central control units (CCUs) in the driver's room of each end car, that is, there are two central control units (CCUs) in the driver's room of each end car, that is, there are two CCUs per basic unit. One of the CCUs works in the master mode and the other works in the slave mode. The CCU at the occupied end of the driver's cab is called the train master CCU, and in addition to the work of the main CCU, it is also responsible for the network control of the entire train. The master CCU of the other base units is called the booted master CCU.

The master CCU of each base unit is responsible for vehicle control within the unit. It reads commands and information from the vehicle bus MVB and the train bus WTB (through its attached gateway) and sends control signals and feedback information to the train bus WTB and the vehicle bus MVB.

The tasks of the central control unit CCU are:

(1) Control of the main circuit breaker and pantograph;

(2) Generation of traction setting points of the traction control unit (TCU);

(3) Transformer protection;

(4) Vehicle power control;

(5) Front-end automatic hook and opening and closing mechanism control;

(6) Generation of higher-level command and control preset values for various devices, such as doors, HVAC, lighting, etc.;

(7) Safety ring, fire alarm system and bogie diagnosis and monitoring;

(8) Digital and analog signal input and output control through distributed input/output stations (SIBAS-KLIP®, MVB-Compact I/O);

(9) Maintenance operation control;

(10) CCU equipment diagnosis, train bus and vehicle bus communication diagnosis;

(11) Connect to the train bus (WTB) through the auxiliary gateway to determine and test the configuration of the EMU and the connecting train.

(12) Run the same program as the master CCU from the CCU, however there is no active process control. Monitor the status of the main CCU from the CCU and be prepared to take over the work of the main CCU in the event of a failure of the main CCU. When a master-slave conversion occurs in a CCU, not only the MVB interface configuration of the CCU is transformed, but their secondary gateways are also converted. The reason is that only the gateway inside the main CCU can be activated, so due to the conversion of the gateway, the initial operation of the train bus (WTB) is triggered at the same time.

8.3.4 Distributed input/output stations

There are two types of input and output stations in the EMU, one is a compact I/O station with a fixed number of input and output points and a very compact structure, and the other is an intelligent peripheral terminal SIBAS-KLIP® whose input and output modules can change with the increase or decrease of the number of input and output channels. Among them, there are two types of compact input and output stations, one is MVB-Compact I/O for collecting special signals in the driver's room, for example, signals from buttons, switches, indicators, circuit breakers, coded plugs and master controllers; The other is used to acquire the PT100 temperature sensor signal.

SIBAS-KLIP® is mainly composed of AS318 module, bus module, input/output module, and power module. AS318 is the interface module between SIBAS-KLIP® and MVB, and the bus module is the bridge for its internal communication; The input and output module can provide 16-bit digital input, 8-bit digital output or 16-bit digital output, 8-bit relay output, 4-channel analog input ($\pm$ 10 V, $\pm$ 20 mA, Pt100), 2-channel analog output ($\pm$ 10 V / $\pm$ 20 mA), and the power supply module is used to convert 110 V voltage on the car to 24 V.

8.3.5 Repeater MVB-Repeater

MVB-Repeater itself does not have the ability to interact with other devices of the MVB bus, it only extends the communication distance of the MVB bus. There are 10 repeaters in the CRH3 EMU, of which there are 2 in each of the two terminals and 1 in the other cars. MVB repeaters not only have signal forwarding, amplification, and shaping effects, but also have fault isolation effects. Once the MVB branch network or equipment communication of a car fails, it can be easily isolated without affecting the normal communication of the MVB bus of other vehicles.

8.3.6 HMI of human interface devices

The HMI of the driver and train attendant is the device that mainly interacts with people in the EMU car network equipment. On the one hand, it accepts the information from the MVB, and after processing, the necessary information is displayed to the relevant personnel through the display interface, and the operator can operate the HMI, input his own intention and information into the HMI, and after processing, store the relevant information in its own storage system or transfer to the MVB network.

8.3.7　Traction control unit TCU

There are 2 traction units in the CRH3 EMU, and two power units in each traction unit. 4 traction converters, located under two end cars and No.3 and No.6 cars, each with a traction control unit. Four traction motors are connected in parallel to provide traction. Each traction converter consists mainly of two four-quadrant choppers (4QC), an intermediate voltage circuit with series resonant circuitry, a brake chopper (BC) and a pulse width modulated frequency converter (PWMI). The intermediate power supply circuit provides power to the train power supply module, the train power supply module is located outside the traction inverter box, which supplies power to the train auxiliary power supply system and on-board equipment including auxiliary equipment such as pumps and fans. The TCU is responsible for the generation and distribution of traction control commands in normal traction mode, automatic speed control mode, emergency traction mode, and protection of traction system components.

8.3.8　Brake control unit BCU

In the CRH3 EMU, each car has a brake control unit, and for redundancy, if one module of the end car BCU fails, another module can replace some of its functions. The BCUs in the trailer also have a redundancy function, which can be replaced by another module in case of the failure of one module.

The brake control unit in each car performs control and diagnostics within its own subsystem, i.e. the braking system of its own vehicle, which includes anti-slip functions. In addition to managing the control and diagnosis of the braking system of the vehicle, the BCU in the end car is also responsible for the braking management task in the traction unit. When the BCU, which is responsible for the braking management in this traction unit, is used as the main control unit of the train, it also undertakes the braking management task of the train.

8.3.9　Battery charger control unit BC

There are two battery chargers on the CRH3 EMU, which are located in the dining car and the first-class car, and the battery charger control system is located in the charger. The input power supply of the battery charger is 3-phase AC440 V, 60 Hz, and the output is DC 110 V, which is the power supply for the 110 V load of the EMU. It has two main control modules, one is the core control module of the charger, which is also responsible for communicating with the vehicle bus MVB, and the other is the power module mainly used for charging.

8.3.10 Auxiliary converter control unit ACU

Each train has an auxiliary converter. Its power input is connected to the middle circuit of the traction converter. The input voltage is labeled DC 3000 V. There are two kinds of auxiliary converters, one is a single auxiliary converter, located under two transformer cars of No.2 and No.7; One is a double auxiliary converter, which is located under the No.4 and No.5 vehicles respectively. The input to the auxiliary converter comes from the intermediate DC link output of the traction converter.

All auxiliary converters simultaneously power a 3AC 440 V, 60 Hz bus that runs through the entire train. The bus is coupled during train operation. In the unlikely event of a bus failure, the coupling contactors of the dual auxiliary converters can be turned on, thus isolating the individual parts. The bus supplies power all large loads in each carriage. Each auxiliary converter is individually synchronized via the 3 AC 440 V, 60 Hz bus.

The output is provided with anti-no-load, short-circuit, and overload and is electrically isolated from the input. The output is not grounded, and a permanent ground fault detection device (for diagnostic purposes) is installed on the secondary side of the output transformer. The auxiliary converter is controlled and diagnosed by its central control system, and in the double auxiliary converter there are two central control systems of the auxiliary converter, which work separately in their respective inverter units, and the two control systems are connected by MVB and finally connected to the vehicle bus MVB.

8.3.11 Door control unit DCU

In CRH3, in addition to the dining car (the dining car does not have an outer door), several external doors of each vehicle have a main door control unit connected to the vehicle bus MVB, and the door control unit of the other outer doors is connected to it through the CAN bus, and then communicates with the vehicle bus MVB by the main door control unit. Read and diagnose sensor and actuator information, monitor the door interlock, receive the corresponding speed signal to perform safety locking.

8.3.12 HVAC control unit for air conditioning units

CRH3 has an HVAC control unit on each car and is connected to train communication and control via the bus MVB. The basic functions of the air conditioning system can be operated by the driver MMI of the cab and the train attendant MMI of the dining car.

8.3.13 Toilet control system WC

The toilet control system in the CRH3 EMU, in addition to controlling the electrical components inside the subsystem to complete the corresponding functions of the toilet, also communicates with the train network control system through the defined input and output signals to provide support for fault inspection, diagnosis and maintenance of train crew and maintenance personnel.

In a vehicle with two toilets, one toilet acts as the main one, responsible for exchanging information with the train network control system. The toilet itself, which is the main, does not have the ability to communicate directly with the MVB, it is connected to the train communication network via SIBAS-KLIP®, mainly some binary status information is fed back to the train network control system, and this information can then be displayed on the conductor's HMI. These information mainly include: error information in the bathroom, empty fault information in the water purification tank, 95% fault information in the sewage tank, high heating system temperature of the sanitation facility, and emergency call information.

8.3.14 Controller of passenger information system (PIS-STC)

Passenger Information Systems (PIS) are used for passenger audiovisual information, train personnel communication and passenger entertainment. Its system controller PIS-STC is the control core of the entire information system PIS and the bridge between the PIS and the train control network. It is responsible for processing information from the MVB bus, the equipment in the PIS, and the GSM antenna, GPS antenna, FM antenna and other devices belonging to the system, and issues the corresponding control instructions or related information to the corresponding target after processing. At the same time, there is a power-down hold function memory in the STC, which can store important operating data, and also make the PIS automatically recover to a previous state after a power failure. PIS-STC manages the passenger information subsystem while also communicating with the train control system.

8.3.15 FAS/SD fire alarm and smoke detection systems

The fire alarm and smoke detection system mainly includes a smoke detection controller, a photoelectric smoke detector and a linear heat detector and other equipment, as well as the corresponding cables. The smoke detection controller and the photoelectric smoke detector are connected by a CAN bus and form a loop.

The advantage of this structure is that when there is an interruption in the loop, the CAN bus can still communicate normally, improving the reliability and safety of the system. In each car's fire alarm and smoke alarm system there is a linear heat detector, it is located in the auxiliary converter or traction converter, and through a special wire and one of the photoelectric smoke detector is connected, when the temperature at the position measured at the linear heat detector exceeds the set value, the two wires connected to it will be short-circuited, so that the photoelectric smoke detector connected to the linear heat detector will be detected, and then through the CAN bus to transmit the corresponding information to the smoke detection controller. Each photoelectric smoke detector generates alarm signals, fault signals, and readiness signals, in addition to providing maintenance and diagnostic information, and their power supply is provided by the smoke detection controller. Photoelectric smoke detectors are distributed in the power supply and are provided by the smoke detection controller. Photoelectric smoke detectors are distributed in cabs, control cabinets, PIS cabinets, and toilets.

8.4 System functions of EMU network

EMU network control system mainly adopts train distributed network communication and control system (DTECS platform), DTECS platform is a set of on-board computer system designed for the control and communication of rail vehicles, mainly to complete the communication management, function control, fault diagnosis, information display and event recording of rail vehicles. A network control system built from several modules of the DTECS platform, called the TCMS system.

The TCMS system has the following characteristics:

(1) Bus transmission, reduce hard wiring, reduce vehicle weight;

(2) Centralized management of vehicle operation status information and on-board equipment status information, improve the degree of train informatization, and support the work of drivers;

(3) Realize the automation of on-board inspection and reduce maintenance work;

(4) Integrate passenger information system functions to support passenger services.

The modular design of the DTECS network control system is particularly suitable for the on-board network control system of rail transit vehicles, and makes the composition of the system very flexible, which not only reduces the system wiring distance, but also is very easy to expand. The EMU network control system mainly refers to the following standards:

EN 50121-3-2:2000 Electromagnetic compatibility test and limit value of electrical equipment for rolling stock;

IEC 60571:1998 Electronic devices for rolling stock in railways;

IEC 61375:2007 Train communication networks;

UIC 556:1999 Information transmission on train buses.

8.4.1 Communication functions

Implement the network communication protocols specified by IEC 61375 and UIC 556 to provide information exchange channels for in-vehicle devices on the network.

8.4.2　Control functions

Based on the network communication function, it completes the logic control, status monitoring, fault diagnosis and other functions of the vehicle system, including the traction system, auxiliary power supply system, braking system, door control system, air conditioning system, lighting system, passenger information system, etc. The control functions mainly include the following:

(1) The network control system has the management function of the vehicle network of the power unit, has the diagnostic function of the train-level bus and the vehicle-level bus and the communication status of the equipment, and the alarm information will be generated when the bus or network equipment communication failure is detected, and the central control unit (including the gateway) is redundant hot standby, and when the central control unit fails or the network segment where the central control unit is located, the central control unit automatically switches to the main control, so that the EMU management function is not affected.

(2) The network control system has the function of train-level and unit-level control and monitoring, that is, to realize the control and monitoring of the EMU or the traction unit. Within the traction unit, it is possible to control and monitor various functional subsystems such as traction, brakes, auxiliary converters, doors, air conditioners, etc. When the traction unit is the main control traction unit, the input operation of the whole train is evaluated, the train control instructions are issued, and the feedback status of the subsystem is monitored to realize the control and diagnosis of the entire EMU.

(3) The network control system has the control function and interface of the traction system. From the train-level control, the generation and distribution of traction control instructions in normal traction mode, automatic speed control mode, and emergency traction mode are considered, and at the same time, according to the monitoring of the operation of the whole vehicle, the control strategies such as traction blockade and power limitation are adopted to protect the traction system components in the above mode.

(4) The network control system monitors and diagnoses the emergency braking loop, parking brake loop, brake mitigation loop, bogie monitoring loop, passenger emergency braking loop, and driver vigilance device, generates traction blockade, maximum commonly used braking or emergency braking command, parking brake instruction and publishes it in full column.

(5) The network control system has a communication interface with the auxiliary converter, according to the working mode and working status of the auxiliary system, automatically complete the failover and redundancy management of the auxiliary system equipment, realize dynamic load distribution and energy management, and realize the input and removal control of all AC loads of the whole train (including air compressors, traction system cooling pumps and fans, traction transformer cooling pumps and fans, air conditioners and other equipment) and DC loads. And the train AC power supply, DC power supply, AC load operation, DC load operation status monitoring

and diagnosis.

(6) The network control system has a communication interface with the door controller to realize the control and status monitoring of the release, opening, closing and locking of the whole train door, and realize the interlock of the door and traction.

(7) The network control system has a communication interface with the air conditioning controller to realize the release of air conditioning control instructions and status monitoring of the whole train, and cooperate with the air conditioning controller to complete energy management. It has an emergency shutdown function for air conditioning in case of fire.

(8) The network control system has a fire alarm monitoring function, which can centrally display the fire alarm loop status and fire alarm parts, and has the function of automatic test of fire alarm loop.

(9) The network control system has the function of controlling and monitoring the internal and external lighting of the whole train. The interior lighting has full lighting and emergency lighting working modes.

(10) The network control system has the control and monitoring of the driver's cab auxiliary equipment (sanding, wheel flange lubrication, front windshield heating, etc.).

(11) The network control system has an information transmission interface between the on-board equipment of the train operation control system, and when the train exceeds the specified speed, it will automatically slow down through the braking system.

(12) The network control system has a constant speed operation control function and a manual set point function for speed adjustment, the required speed is defined by the set point control device, the driver can activate the constant speed operation mode through the man-machine interface or constant speed handle, etc., and the network control system can automatically adjust the traction force or braking force to meet the given speed requirements. The constant speed function should provide speed control modes for reconnect, shunting and car washing.

(13) The network control system has a standby operation mode, and after the train is suspended, the EMU automatically completes the system detection and temperature regulation in the vehicle according to the return to operation time. In the maintenance mode, it can perform automatic tests of high voltage, traction, braking, air conditioning, fire alarm system and report detection faults, and achieve energy saving by controlling the air conditioning lighting load in the maintenance operation mode, and can exit the mode at any time to return to operation.

(14) In addition to the maintenance operation mode, the network control system also has a variety of operating modes such as emergency traction mode, terminal change operation mode, and drag mode to meet the various needs of actual operation.

(15) The network control system provides the control function of reconnection and decoupling, and cooperates with the mechanical and electrical reconnection interface to complete the reconfiguration function of the train in the reconnection and decoupling mode, and meets the reconnection control function of different driver control terminals of the different driver control

terminals of the two 8-car marshalling EMUs. The WTB bus is used to achieve reconnection, and 2 columns of reconnection marshalling are realized, and the group can be connected to the form of head-tail, tail-tail, and tail-head. Each marshalling node acts on the WTB bus at the same time, and in order to realize the reconnection control function, the identification of the number of marshallings, the identification of the reconnection location, the identification of the non-reconnection terminal, the identification of the main control group, the identification of the active grouping, the recognition of the driving direction are realized in turn, and finally the reconnection marshalling topology is constructed. The control and diagnostic functions of the network control system after reconnection are not affected by train marshalling changes.

(16) The network control system monitors and diagnoses important subsystems and equipment, and transmits them through process data or message data. With fast and reliable fault troubleshooting and fault isolation capabilities, EMU diagnostic system failure does not affect the normal operation of EMUs.

(17) The network control system monitors, troubleshoots and protects the safety-related status of the bogie, including: bogie lateral stability monitoring, non-rotating shaft monitoring, wheel-to-wheel shaft temperature, traction motor bearing temperature, gearbox bearing temperature monitoring. Features early warning, alarm and automatic speed limiting.

(18) The important equipment of the network control system such as the central control unit and the human machine interface display are equipped with redundancy and automatic switching functions.

8.4.3 Monitoring display function

The system can monitor and alarm the performance of the EMU and various important components in real time to ensure the safety of the operation of the EMU. The monitoring information of the system generally includes the working status of the braking system, the braking action, the status of the electrical system on the car, the status of the door, etc. Through the system monitoring, the hidden dangers of the accident can be found in time for timely maintenance. Monitoring and diagnostic data are displayed in real time via the driver display to support the driver in driving safely.

8.4.4 Troubleshooting and storage functions

The network system completes the collection, analysis, dumping and display of the fault data of each component of the vehicle. Fault information is displayed on the driver's desk via a display screen, and diagnostic information can be uploaded to ground maintenance and service systems for long-term storage and in-depth ground analysis.

Diagnostic systems provide effective support for the maintenance and overhaul of train personnel (drivers, crews) and maintenance personnel during EMU operation, maintenance and repair. An EMU is a complex system consisting of multiple distributed control units. The diagnostic system is able to identify, evaluate, report on most failures that may occur in all modes of operation, including impact on other systems, and provide operational guidance. The functions of the diagnostic system are integrated in the HMI. EMU diagnostics are composed of two parts: a central diagnostic system and a diagnostic subsystem. The diagnostic subsystem diagnostics traction, braking, etc., and reports possible faults and individual functional limitations to the central diagnostic system, which stores, classifies and displays them.

The fault storage area is used to permanently store the event data (fault data, environmental data, protocol data) of the entire vehicle, and the data acquisition of all systems is based on the system time as a synchronization mode. The stored data is easy to refer to when overhauling personnel are working. A fault store is an event-driven, failed data store. Reserve a fixed storage area in the fault store for each failure code. For each code, record at least the first failure and the last 3 failures. Fault storage distinguishes between historical failures and current failures. The network control system has an easily accessible portable device transmission interface and a wireless information transmission interface, which can collect data and analyze portable equipment, and can also wirelessly transmit the data recorded by diagnostic equipment to the ground maintenance base as needed.

Through the human-computer interaction function of driver and crew display, driver and crew can observe the operating status of the vehicle online in real time, or control the operating status of related systems through the display.

Chapter 9 HVAC System

9.1 Overview

Heating, Ventilation and Air Conditioning system (HVAC) provides air conditioning to driver's cabin and passenger saloons of vehicles in the trainset, which consists of 2 packed driver-cabin HVAC Unit (one in each driver cabin of MC1 and MC2 vehicles) and 8 packed passenger-saloon HVAC Unit (one in each vehicle). According to their usage, HVAC unit could be divided into 2 categories, one is cabin HAVC, the other is saloon HAVC. The two categories are seminar, so we take the later as the example to illustrate HAVC's principles and structures. The saloon HAVC is shown as the Figure 9-1.

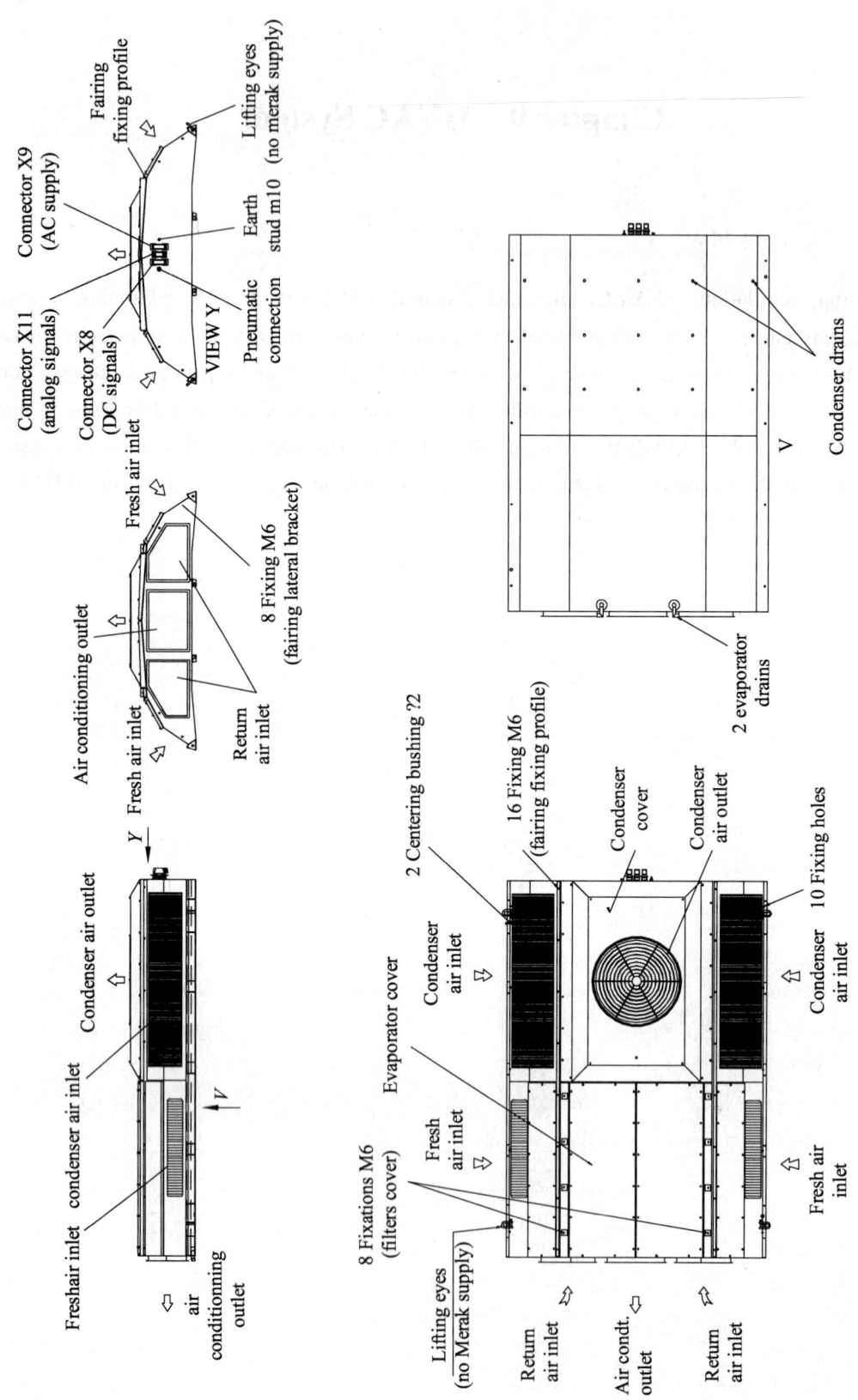

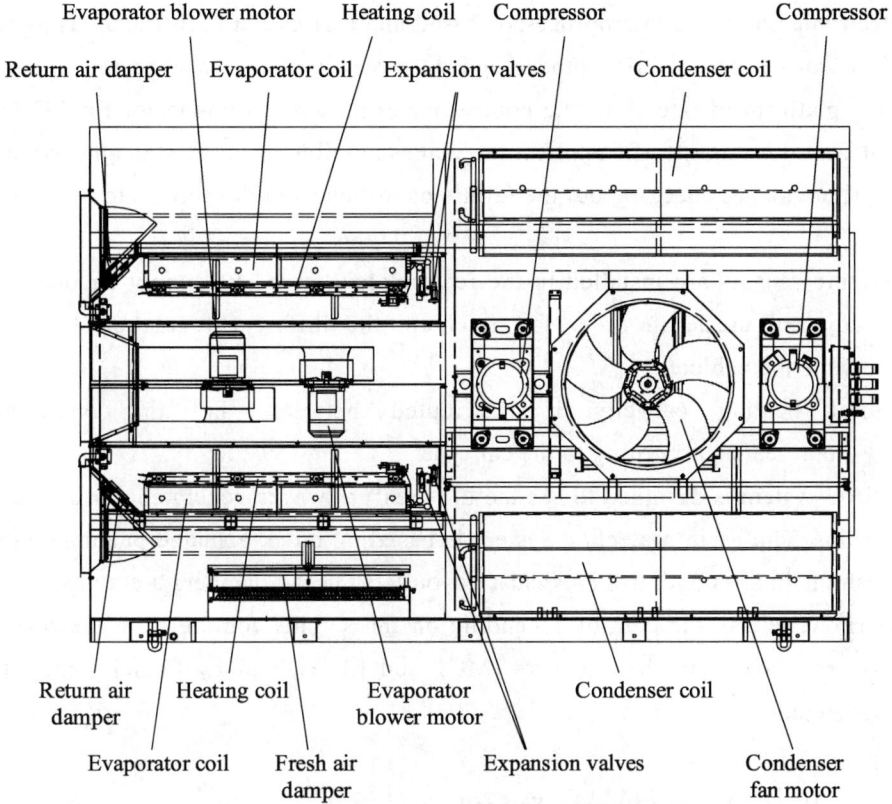

Figure 9-1 HVAC Unit Main Components Layout

9.1.1 Air handling process

Fresh air enters HVAC unit through two side grids (fresh air inlet) in the evaporator section of the unit. It is mixed with return air, which returns from passenger area and enters the unit through two return air inlets, located at the evaporator end of the unit. This air mixture is treated, in cooling mode, the refrigerant evaporation causes that the heat in the air is absorbed when passing through the fins; in heating mode, the treated air (return air + fresh air) goes through the heating coils arranged in parallel with the evaporator coils, thereby the air is heated. Afterword, this air mixture is impelled to passenger saloon by means of the air distributions ducts coupled to the HVAC unit. The exhaust air is exhausted to the exterior through the exhaust unit connected to saloon with an exhaust ducting system.

9.1.2 Characteristics of the HVAC system

The electrical connection of the HVAC system components with the train systems is made by means of connectors, to ease the mounting and dismounting tasks of the components themselves, and of any element. Therefore, in future major revisions, the HVAC system can be dismounted and extracted from the car, to perform such tasks in a suitable environment.

The electronic control is microprocessor based and carries out such functions as temperature regulation, control of the operating modes and diagnosis, which is packed in the control panel, located in the platform of one end, The control panel provides a connector for PC, that, with a dedicated software for this specific application, makes possible to find and diagnose the failures of the HVAC system, makes checking out the failure conditions and the actions to be taken whenever feasible.

Temperature sensors are installed in the recirculated, fresh and supply air ducts, and in the saloon and adjacent areas, in order to effectuate the different regulation functions of the temperature inside the vehicle.

The total heating capacity is distributed between the air conditioning units and auxiliary floor heaters according to the car type.

The HVAC system is designed to subdue the pressure waves generated during the running of high-speed trains. The basic protection system is based on quick actuated pneumatic dampers set up at the fresh air intakes and at the exhaust air outlets. These dampers are actuated at the same time by the HVAC electronic control depending on the signals coming form the pressure waves protection system located in the end cars (MC1 and MC2), and by tunnel signal through car information system.

9.2 Principles of HVAC system

9.2.1 Refrigeration system principles

9.2.1.1 Latent heat

State is the physical condition, or form, of a substance at any given time. Matter can exist in solid, liquid or gaseous state. All substances exist in one of these three states.

Change of state is the change of a substance from one state to another. When ice melts, it is just water changing its state from solid to liquid. Boiling water changes from liquid state to gaseous state. The change of state that we are concerned with is the change of refrigerant from liquid to gas. Adding heat causes the liquid refrigerant to vaporize. Removing heat causes the refrigerant to change from a vapour to a liquid.

Pressure variations can modify the temperatures at which a change of state occurs. If the pressure is lowered, the temperature at which the refrigerant changes from a liquid to a vapour drops. If the pressure is increased, the temperature at which the refrigerant changes from a vapour to a liquid is raised. Changing the refrigerant pressure allows the system to use air at the same temperature to both vaporize and condense the refrigerant.

A change of state is always accompanied by a release or absorption of heat. When a substance changes from a solid to a liquid or from a liquid to a gas, heat is absorbed. When a substance changes from a gas to a liquid, or from a liquid to a solid, heat is released.

Latent heat is the energy absorbed or released by a substance during a change in its physical state (phase) that occurs without changing its temperature. The latent heat associated with vaporizing a liquid or condensing a vapour is called the heat of vaporization.

The most efficient way to transfer heat from one area to another (in the specific case of refrigeration, to remove heat from an area) is to make use of latent heat. Vaporizing a liquid inside of the car body causes it to absorb heat, which then becomes latent heat in the refrigerant gas. This vapour can then be pumped to the outside of the car, and condensed. When it is condensed, it gives up its latent heat to the outside air. The refrigerant can then be returned to the car interior and vaporized again to absorb more heat. This is what an air conditioner does, as explained in the next section.

9.2.1.2　Refrigeration cycle

Figure 9-2 is a flow diagram of the air conditioner portion of the HVAC system. The Figure shows how the refrigerant moves through the mayor components of the system. Notice that the system is divided into high and low pressure areas by the compressor and expansion valve, and into gas and liquid by the evaporator and compressor. The refrigerant flows in a continuous circle:

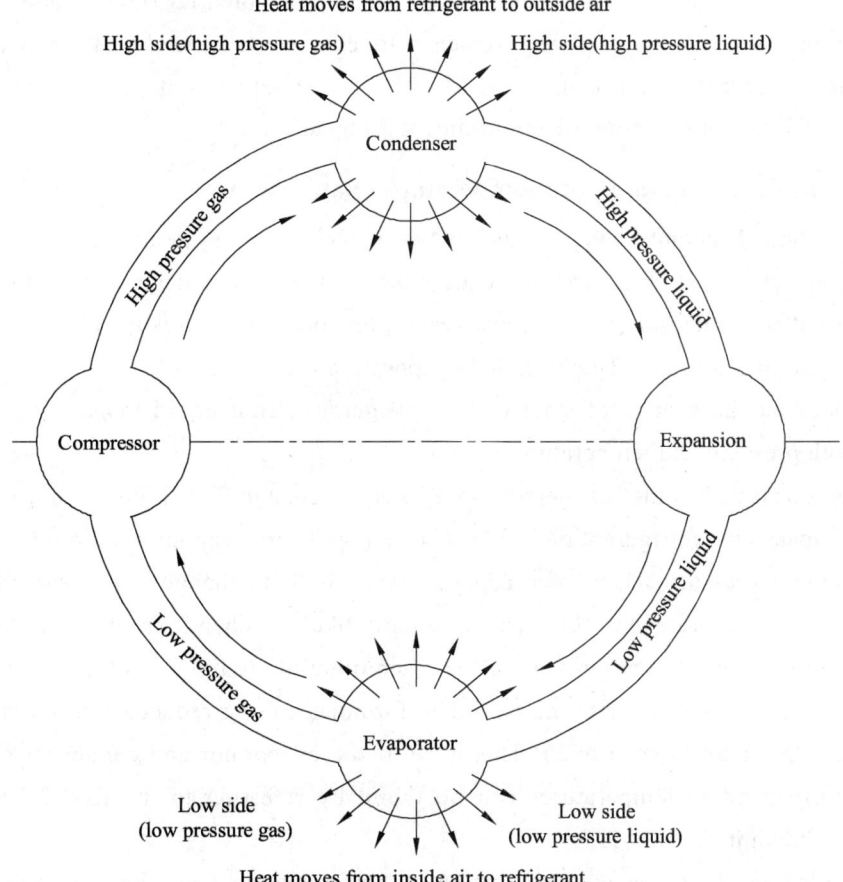

Figure 9-2　Refrigeration cycle

(1) Changing from a liquid to a gas to absorb heat in the evaporator;

(2) Being pressurized by the compressor;

(3) Giving up heat in the condenser and changing back into a liquid;

(4) Being metered by the expansion valve to reduce its pressure before it enters the evaporator.

9.2.1.3 Refrigerant

The refrigeration cycle is based on the principle that a volatile liquid absorbs heat in evaporating or changing from a liquid to a vapour, absorbs heat. There are many liquids that can be used to produce cooling by causing them to change from a liquid to a vapour, but some are better suited for use in a refrigerating system than others because of their physical and chemical properties. A refrigerant suitable for use in an HVAC system should:

- Be non-flammable, non-explosive, and non-toxic.
- Be stable. Must not combine with material used in the equipment.
- Require low or moderate operating pressures.
- Be readily available.

This system uses the alternative refrigerant R-407C ($CH_2F_2/CHF_2CF_3/CH_2FCF_3$), a chlorine-free hydrofluorocarbon, with zero Ozone Depletion Potential (ODP) index and it fully complies with the Montreal Protocol requirements. Its characteristics and performance are similar to those of the refrigerants traditionally used for this type of applications (chlorofluorocarbonated refrigerants—CFC's), but reducing the environmental impact.

9.2.1.4 Refrigerant's pressure-temperature relationship

Note that the refrigerant changes state in two places in the system: the condenser and the evaporator. In the condenser, high pressure causes the refrigerant to change from a hot gas to a hot liquid. This is called condensation. In the evaporator, low pressure causes the refrigerant to change from a cold liquid to a cold gas. This is called evaporation.

Remember that the change of state of the refrigerant (from liquid to gas or gas to liquid) varies with both pressure and temperature:

(1) Adding heat makes the refrigerant more likely to change from a liquid to a vapour, while removing heat makes the refrigerant more likely to change from a vapour to a liquid.

(2) Raising the pressure makes the refrigerant more likely to change from a vapour to a liquid, while lowering the pressure makes the refrigerant more likely to change from a liquid to a vapour.

Refrigerant temperature and pressure affect each other along tightly defined lines, which can be predicted by formulas that relate the two. The formulas can be reduced to a chart that relates temperature and pressure to each other. Therefore, if the evaporator and condenser pressures are known, the corresponding temperatures can be found by referring to the R-407C temperature-pressure chart shown in Table 9-1.

Using the same chart, the pressure inside of any component can be determined from the temperature. For instance, this chart allows the technician to determine the temperature of the refrigerant in the evaporator by reading its pressure. Allowing two or three degrees for heat transfer through the evaporator metal allows the technician to determine the approximate temperature of air leaving the evaporator by finding evaporator pressure.

Table 9-1　Temperature-pressure chart for R-407C (liquid and saturated vapour)

Temperature		Vapor pressure (PSI)	Temperature		Vapor pressure (PSI)
/°C	/°F		/°C	/°F	
−31.7	−25	3.6	18.3	65	104.8
−28.9	−20	6.1	21.1	70	115.2
−26.1	−15	8.8	23.9	75	126.2
−23.3	−10	11.9	26.7	80	137.8
−20.5	−5	15.2	29.4	85	150.2
−17.8	0	18.9	32.2	90	163.4
−15	5	22.9	35	95	177.4
−12.2	10	27.3	37.8	100	192.1
−9.4	15	32.0	40.6	105	207.8
−6.7	20	37.2	43.3	110	224.4
−3.9	25	42.7	46.1	115	241.9
−1.1	30	48.7	48.9	120	260.5
1.7	35	55.2	51.7	125	280.1
4.4	40	62.1	54.4	130	300.9
7.2	45	69.5	57.2	135	322.9
10	50	77.5	60	140	346.2
12.8	55	86.0	62.8	145	370.8
15.6	60	95.1	65.5	150	396.9

9.2.2　Electric heater principles

The electric heater operates on the principle of electrical resistance. Electrical resistance, measured in Ohms , is one of the three main properties of electricity, along with electrical pressure (voltage) and the number of electrons moving past a particular point in the circuit (electrical current or amperage). These electrical properties work to produce heat in the electric heater coil.

9.2.2.1　Current and resistance

Current is thought to consist of electrons travelling between atoms. It is measured in amperes, or amps (A). The electrical pressure that causes the electrons to move is called voltage. A substance that allows electrons to flow is called a conductor. As current flows through any type of conductor, the natural resistance of the conductor material opposes it. This resistance is caused by the reluctance of the atoms to give up or receive electrons.

One side effect of using voltage to push electrons against resistance is the production of heat. This heat can be thought of as being caused by the friction of the electrons trying to move past the reluctant atoms. Therefore, using high voltage to push many electrons through a high resistance conductor can produce a large amount of heat. In many electrical circuits the heat is unwanted, and can severely damage the equipment if not removed. However, the electric heater assembly is designed to produce as much heat as possible from the available electric current.

9.2.2.2 Heater basic construction

The heater assembly is a complete electrical circuit fed by the VAC car power. The element of the heater coil is composed of a metal alloy made of atoms that are very reluctant to give up electrons. This metal is said to have high resistance.

As electrical current is pushed through the heater coil by the voltage electrical supply, the friction between the electrons and atoms creates heat, called resistance heat. The resistance heat causes the coil to become very hot. The blower directs air over the coil. The coil heat is transferred to the air as it passes over the heater coils. The warmed air then enters the passenger compartment. To ensure that the coil does not overheat, the coil electric circuit is interlocked to the blower system. Therefore, the coil cannot heat up unless the blower motor is running. The coil also contains thermal protection devices: an over temperature thermostat and two over temperature fusible links.

9.3 The HVAC unit

The schematic diagram of the refrigeration cycle is shown in Figure 9-3.

The low-pressure vapour that leaves the evaporator is sucked through suction line into the compressor. During compression, the vapour undergoes an increase in pressure and temperature that is a function of both the car interior and outside ambient temperatures. The temperature of resulting compressed vapour is higher than a condensing temperature. A solenoid bypass valve, located between the high and low pressure areas of the system, adapts the compressor capacity to the evaporator real charge. The compressor has a suction vibration absorber at the input line and a discharge vibration absorber and a check valve at the output line. The check valve has a floating piston with positive closing action to insure that refrigerant entrained in the condenser coil is not permitted to return to the compressor during periods of shut down. The high-pressure high-temperature vapour is discharged by the compressor and flows through the check valves to the condenser coils.

The refrigerant vapour flows from compressor to the condenser coil, and then towards the charging valve, the dehydrator filter and the sight glass / moisture indicator.The condenser coils with cooling fins, remove heat from the refrigerant vapour. As the high-pressure high-temperature vapour passes through the coil of each condenser, outside ambient air is drawn through the coil fins by the condenser fan motor and heat is removed from the refrigerant by air flowing over the condenser coils. This removes the heat that the refrigerant absorbed from the car interior by the evaporator. As the heat is removed from the vapour, the cooling vapour condenses to as low a temperature as can be obtained by the condenser fans.

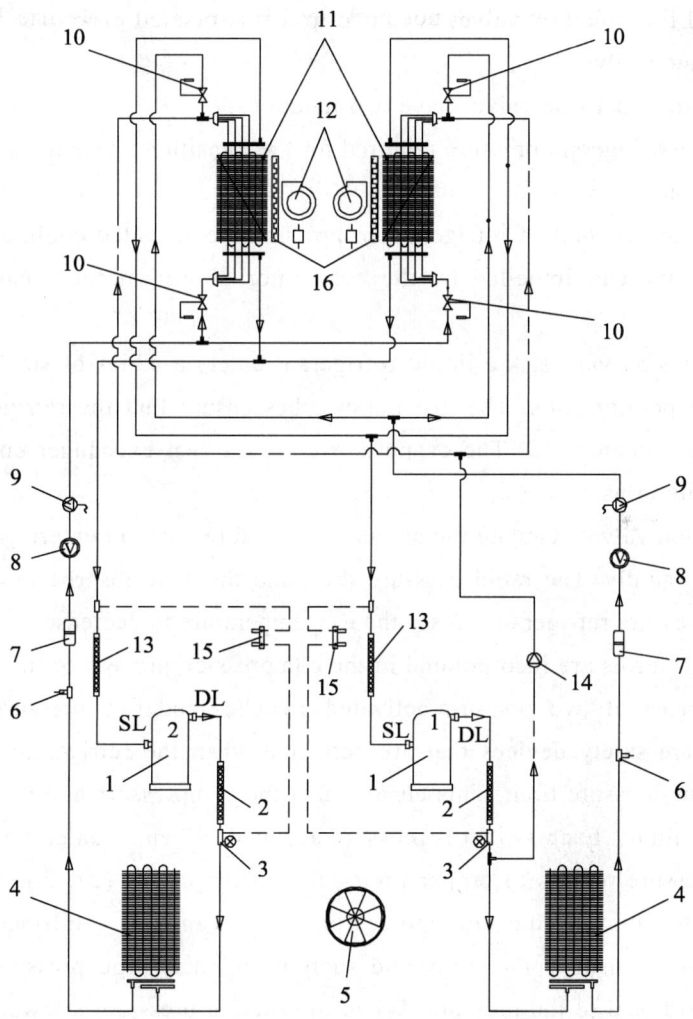

1—Compressor; 2—Discharge vibration absorber; 3—Check valve; 4—Condenser coil; 5—Condenser fan motor;
6—Charging valve; 7—Dehydrator filter; 8—Moisture sight glass; 9—Liquid line solenoid valve;
10—Thermostatic expansion valve; 11—Evaporator coil; 12—Evaporator blower motor;
13—Suction vibration absorber; 14—Bypass solenoid valve; 15—Refrigeration controls;
16—Electrical air heater assembly.

Figure 9-3 The schematic diagram of the HVAC unit

The charging valve is useful to carry out maintenance operations such as vacuuming and charging the refrigerant in the circuit.

The moisture sight glasses enable checking the relative dryness (moisture content) of the liquid refrigerant in the system. The sight glasses also enable detecting a shortage of refrigerant or a restriction in the liquid line. This condition is indicated by a noticeable bubble flow in the refrigerant, which can be seen through the sight glass.

The liquid refrigerant output of the sight glass is then rerouted to the liquid line solenoid valves. These valves are microprocessor activated to control the flow of refrigerant through both evaporator coil circuits. This enables the control of full cooling or partial cooling. The liquid output of the liquid line solenoid valves is routed to the associated evaporator coil circuit via the thermostatic expansion valves.

The thermostatic expansion valves have two functions:

a. To reduce the refrigerant pressure required for the transition phase (evaporation) to occur in the evaporator coil, and

b. To regulate the amount of refrigerant to produce the expected cooling on the air coming from the inside of the car, impelled by the evaporator blower motors, that goes through the evaporator coils.

From the expansion valves, the liquid refrigerant enters a series of small distributor tubes, which lead into evaporator coils. The distributor tubes ensure that the refrigerant is distributed evenly inside the evaporator coil. The evaporator coil is a heat exchanger built of copper pipes joined with aluminium fins.

As the expansion valves regulate the amount of liquid refrigerant entering the evaporator, the pressure decreases rapidly. The rapid pressure drop and the heat absorbed from the car interior vaporize the low-pressure refrigerant causes the car temperature to decrease.

Refrigeration controls are incorporated in the compression process of the refrigeration cycle. These controls consist of two pressure-activated switches and two pressure transducers. The pressure switches are safety devices that are activated when the refrigerant pressure reaches a high-pressure or low-pressure limit. This ensures that the compressors and the system as a whole operate within safe limits. Each switch is pressure actuated. When actuated, the switch opens (cut out). When the pressure returns to proper limits, the switch closes (cut in). The open or closed status of each switch informs the microprocessor, which can then implement the programmed action. The pressure transducers monitor the suction and discharge pressures and develop an analog signal proportional to the pressure. When the suction pressure is lower than the reference value or the high pressure exceeds the reference value, the temperature control implements modulated cooling before the cut-out limit is reached.

The section of the refrigerant circuit that goes from the output of the thermostatic expansion valve to the compressor input is known as the low-pressure side, while the section between the exit valve of the compressor and the entrance of the expansion valve is called the high-pressure side.

HVAC unit technical data is shown in Table 9-2.

Table 9-2   HVAC unit technical data

Cooling capacity (text = 40°)	44 kW
Heating capacity	29 kW
Total air flow	4,300 m³/h (±10%)
Fresh air flow (cooling)	1,400 m³/h (±10%)
Return air flow (cooling)	2,900 m³/h (±10)
Refrigerant	R-407C
AC Power supply	400 V, 50 Hz, 3 phases
Voltage admissible Variation	±10%
Frequency admissible variation	±5%
DC Power supply	24 VDC

9.3.1 Compressors

The compressor aspirates the cold gases coming from the evaporator coil at low pressure and compresses them, turning them into overheated, high-pressure gas.

The compressors used for this unit are scroll type, namely ZR125-KCE-TFD-522 by COPELAND (Figure 9-4). This type of compressors has few moving parts and no dynamic suction or discharge valves. In addition, they cause very low vibration and sound levels and are resistant to the stresses caused by liquid sludge, flooded starts, and debris commonly found in refrigeration systems.

Both compressors are mounted on one compressor bench attached to the unit by means of four shock absorbers that eliminate any vibration and reduce any noise.

The compressors suction and discharge pipes have been provided with hose vibration absorbers to provide greater resistance against wearing and reduce vibration and noise. The suction line vibration absorber has a 35 mm, whereas the one for the discharge line is ϕ22 mm.

The refrigeration controls are installed close to each compressor. These controls include, for each compressor two safety pressure cut-out switches for high and low pressure and two pressure transducers for high and low pressure too.

The pressure-switches are safety devices that operate when the refrigerant pressure drops to values lower than the minimum (low pressure) or when it exceeds the maximum (high pressure). This way of operating ensures that both the compressor and the system will work within safety margins. When actuated, the switch opens (cut-out). When the pressure returns to within proper limits, the switch closes (cut-in). The open or closed status of each switch notifies the microprocessor, which can then implement the programmed action.

The pressure transducers monitors the suction and discharge pressures and develop an analog signal proportional to the corresponding pressure. When the suction pressure is less than the reference value or the high pressure exceeds the reference value, the temperature control implements modulated cooling before the cut-out limit is reached.

In addition, the pressure control assembly includes high and low pressure valve access ports for quick pressure gauges connection and easy maintenance operations.

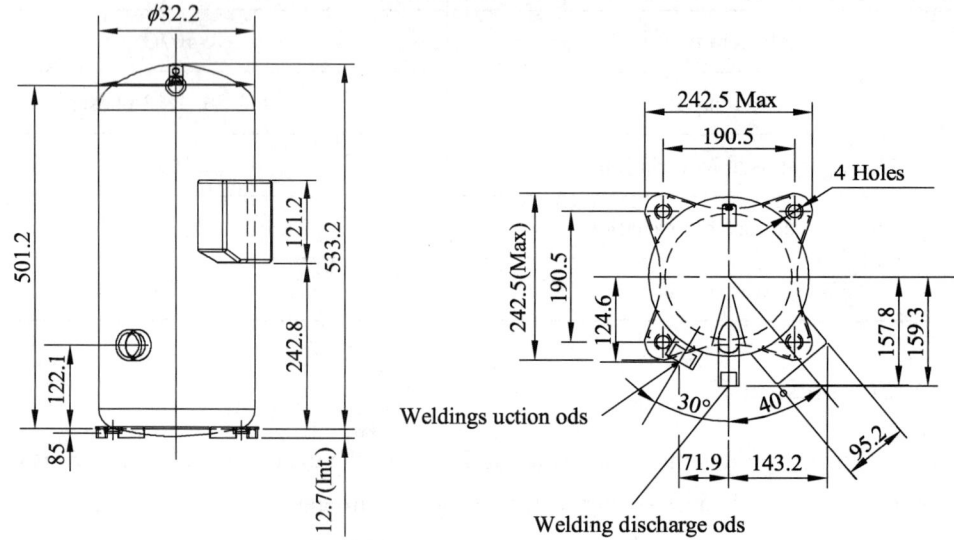

Figure 9-4   Refrigeration compressor

Compressor technical data is shown as Table 9-3.

Table 9-3   Compressor technical data

Model	Copeland ZR125-KCE-TFD-522
Type	Scroll
Refrigerant	R-407C
Type of power regulation	by hot gas bypass
Voltage	400 V, 3 phase (±10%)
Frequency	50 Hz (±5%)
Oil capacity	3.25 litres
Oil type	Polyolester Copeland 3 MA (32 cSt)
Quantity	2

9.3.2 Condenser

9.3.2.1 Condenser coils

The gas comes out of the compressor at a high temperature and pressure and reaches the condenser coil. Since the gas temperature is much higher than the ambient air temperature, the heat dissipates into the air passing through the coils. The gas temperature drops so much that it condenses.

Each condenser coil is made of a set of 3/8" diameter copper pipes ranged in parallel, equidistant spacing and laid across the airflow, expanded to be one with the 0.18 mm alum fins, with a 2.5 mm between spacing, arranged perpendicularly to the pipes.

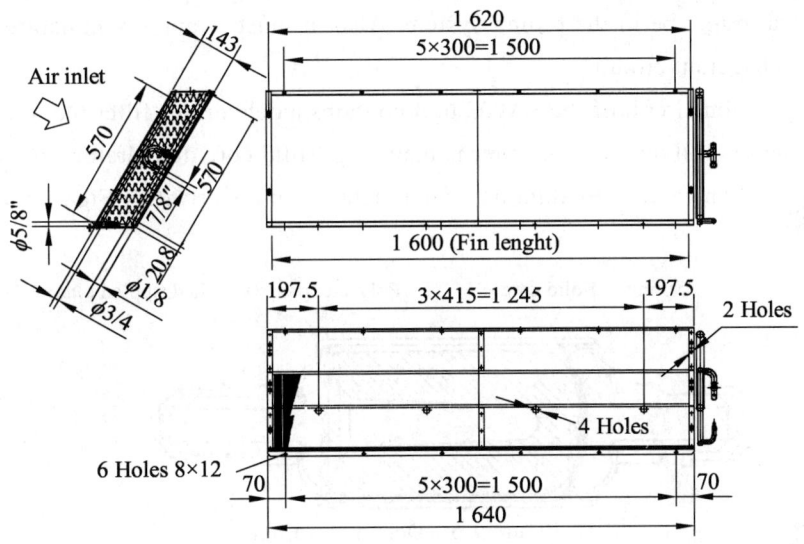

Figure 9-5　Condenser coil

Condenser coil technical data is shown as Table 9-4.

Table 9-4　Condenser coil technical data

Type	24T-6F-1600 L
Tubes, elbows, junctions, collectors	Copper
ϕ tube	3/8"
Fins	Aluminium, 0.18 mm thickness
Spacing between fins	2.5 mm
Frame	Galvanized steel sheet, 1 mm thick
Fasteners and rivets	Stainless steel
Test pressure	30 bar in water, at 30 °C
Quantity	2

9.3.2.2 Condenser fan motor assembly

To obtain a better distribution on the coil heat exchanging surface, the air from the outside is introduced through the condenser coils by two fans. This assembly consists of an axial fan whose outer diameter is 750 mm, made up of 5 blades with a 37° inclination angle. The fan is actuated by an asynchronous motor (1.8 / 1.3 kW at 400 VAC, 3-phase, 50 Hz) revolving at 1,000 / 750 r.p.m., with IP-56 protection and Class F insulation.

9.3.3 Dehydrator filter

The purpose of the dehydrator filter is to arrest any solid particle (dirt, rust or welding particles, etc) that might be in the piping system. Also, it must retain any moisture and acids that might hold the refrigerant circuit.

Each refrigeration circuit of the HVAC unit contains a dehydrator filter mounted on the liquid line, at the condenser coil outlet. This filter is made of a solid core dehydrator cartridge, made of a mixture of silica gel and activated alumina; and a metal filter (referring to Figure 9-6).

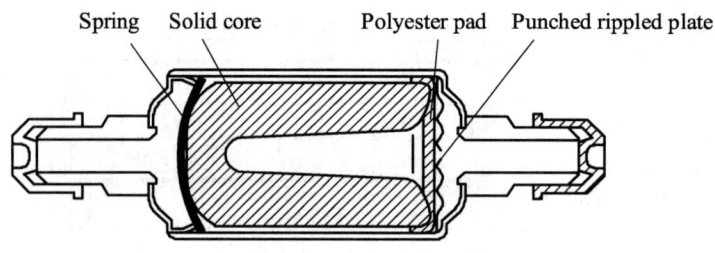

Figure 9-6   Dehydrator filter

9.3.4 Evaporator

9.3.4.1 Evaporator coil

The evaporator coil is formed by a set of 1/2" diameter copper pipes. It has 0.1 mm aluminium fins with a 2.5 mm space between them. The refrigerant liquid circulates inside the pipes and the fins and pipes are cooled when this liquid evaporates, and air circulating in there is also cooled before being blown into the cabin.

The coils are fed by one thermostatic expansion valve that distributes the refrigerant through the small distributor orifices inside the serpentine pipes of the evaporator coil. As a consequence, there is a pressure drop and the refrigerant temperature goes down too.

Table 9-5 Evaporator coil technical data

Type	10T-4F-1175 L
Tubes, elbows, junctions, collectors	Copper
Ø tube	1/2"
Fins	Aluminium, 0.18 mm thickness
Space between fins	2,5 mm
Frame	Galvanized steel sheet, 1 mm thick
Fasteners and rivets	Stainless steel
Test pressure	30 bar in water, at 30 °C
Quantity	2

9.3.4.2 Evaporator blower

Treated air is forced into the car by two evaporator fan motor assemblies consisting of a centrifugal fan with galvanised plate blades and forged steel hub mounted on a three-phase single shaft motor with 0.75 kW at 400 V, 50 Hz, running at 1,500 r/min.

9.3.5 Thermostatic expansion valves

The expansion valves are meant to allow the passing of liquid into the coil in the appropriate amount in order to obtain a correct evaporation of the refrigerant at the outlet. At the same time, it ensures an adequate differential pressure between the high and low pressure sides in the refrigeration system.

For these purposes, the valve consists of a valve body connected to a bulb by means of a capillary tube (Figure 9-7). The body is mounted on the liquid line and the bulb is fixed to evaporator outlet, on the suction line.

The bulb holds a small amount of refrigerant. The free space in the bulb, the capillary tube and the free space above the valve are full of saturated vapour at the pressure corresponding to the bulb temperature. The space below the diaphragm is in contact with the evaporator; therefore, the pressure here is the evaporation pressure.

The opening degree of the valve is determined by the pressure caused by the bulb charge temperature which is exerted on the upper side of the diaphragm and by the pressure below the diaphragm, which is the addition of the evaporation pressure plus the pressure of the spring acting on the lower side of the diaphragm.

Therefore, the thermostatic expansion valve works because of the pressure differential between the vapour pressure in the evaporator and the charge pressure in the bulb. Since the thermal bulb is in touch with the suction line, the pressure on this bulb depends on the temperature of such line, which makes it possible to control it.

The thermostatic expansion valve is provided with a pressure equalizing line connected to the evaporator outlet, by the thermal bulb, to compensate the pressure drops caused by the distributor and the evaporator surface. The role of the liquid distributor is to achieve a uniform feeding of the coil.

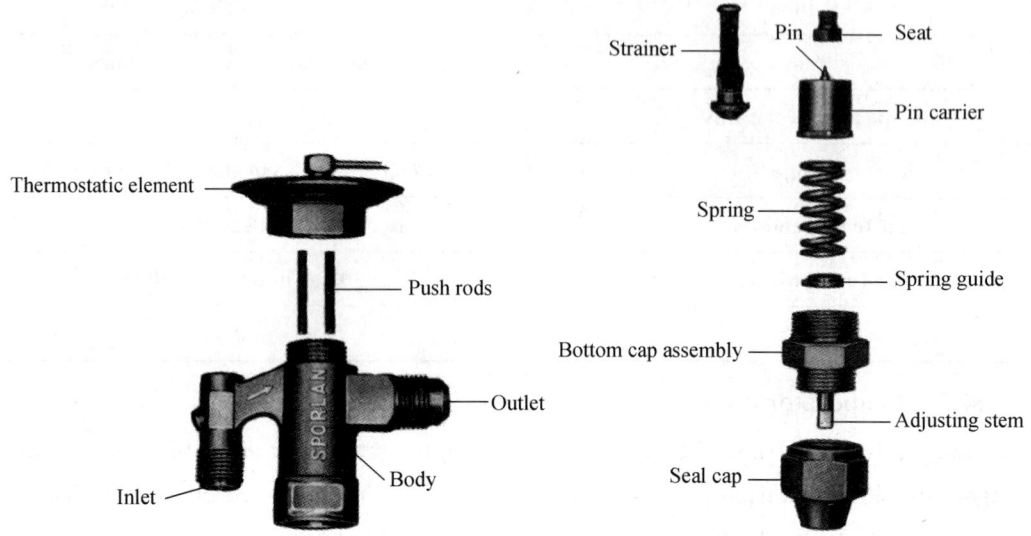

Figure 9-7 Typical thermostatic expansion valve

Expansion valve's technical data is shown as in table 9-6.

Table 9-6 Expansion valve technical data

Connections	1/2" ~ 5/8" weld
Evaporation temperature	−50 °C ~ +10 °C
Gas injection	Controlled by refrigerant reheating
Bulb max. temperature	100 °C
Max. Test Pressure	28 bar
Quantity	4

9.3.6 Air heater assemblies

The package HVAC unit includes two electric air heater assemblies installed in parallel with each evaporator coil that supply the passenger saloon with a 29 kW overhead heating power.

Each air heater assembly stage is protected against over temperature by two safety thermostats. The first one disconnects the heating contactors when the temperature reaches around 90 °C, and then connects them again when the temperature drops to safe operating limits (69 °C).

The second safety thermostat trips the air heating circuit breakers if the temperature reaches around 125 °C. The HVAC control will send the fault via MVB.

9.3.7 Electrical and electronic control panel

The control system is based on a microprocessor, which controls all the normal functions: preconditioning, ventilation, cooling and heating, as well as provides information to the train communication network via the MVB interface.

The control panel contains all the necessary elements (contactors, relays, circuit breakers, etc), to manage each working mode of the passenger saloon. The control panel for MC1 and MC2 coaches also includes pressure waves and cabin HVAC control systems.

Taking the temperature signals sent by different sensors, the control sends the necessary commands to set off the necessary elements involved in each specific situation, in order to get the temperature set point for the cabin in a given time.

Furthermore, this electronic control carries out some other operations such as storing in a memory the compressors motors working times, and keeping record of the main temperatures for future maintenance purposes and also in order to verify the performance of the unit.

The data stored in memory can be read and processed by means of a laptop computer provided with a software application, which has been especially developed with the purpose of obtaining a suitable preventive maintenance.

9.3.8 Pressure waves protection system

The pressure waves protection system is designed to avoid a strong variation of pressure inside the cars uncomfortable for the passengers. The system is composed by:

a. 4 pressure wave transducers located in the front part of the end cars (MC1 and MC2), one in each side. This means two sensors per end car with a total of four sensors per train.

b. 2 Electronic control cards located inside the control panel of the cars MC1 and MC2 (two control cards per train).

c. Quick reaction dampers for fresh air inlet and exhaust outlet in the car installed in all the cars, as well as drain dampers installed in the HVAC unit.

The pressure waves transducers are electrically connected to the corresponding control card. Therefore, any high variation of exterior pressure is registered by the pressure waves control card which processes the information and sends an electric signal to the mechanical actuators of the exhaust and fresh air dampers in order to speedily close the dampers.

The pressure waves control card produces an output signal. This signal is passed over the electrical train wire interconnected to the actuators of the exhaust and fresh air dampers of all cars in the trainset to optimize the response time.

Chapter 10 High-Speed EMU Service System

The service system includes the EMU passenger information system, lighting system, kitchen facilities and equipment, water supply and sanitation system from the aspects of passenger information exchange and catering equipment. The main function of the passenger information system is to facilitate and guide the passengers to reach the destination smoothly, and provide high-quality entertainment services to the passengers during the journey. The lighting system is to ensure that passengers have sufficient light source during the ride, can carry out reading, entertainment and other activities; due to the characteristics of the use of EMU, kitchen equipment on the one hand emphasizes the safety and health of food on the train, on the other hand, due to the short travel time of the bullet train itself, speed has also become an important technical requirement. Water supply device is based on the kitchen water, sanitary water and drinking water three aspects of its composition structure is introduced; the health system highlights its unique and user-friendly facilities, making the advantages of the EMU health system clear.

10.1 Passenger information system

Passenger Information System (PIS) is a general term for in-car facilities and equipment that provide passengers with timely and accurate Information about the journey through sound and visual information, guide them to their destinations smoothly, and make their life on the road safer, more comfortable and convenient. PIS can be divided into: announcement and communication subsystem, information display subsystem, video and audio entertainment subsystem.

10.1.1 Notification and communication subsystem

The announcement and communication subsystem is composed of the following main components: PIS System controller (STC), PIS Man-Machine-Interface (PIS-MMI), PIS control centered tracking (CCT), internal communication station, fire box, loudspeaker, GPS antenna, GSM antenna, UIC bus, PIS data bus, etc.

The functions of the notification and communication subsystem are divided into the basic functions of notification and internal communication and the extended functions of notification. The basic functions of notification and internal communication are available in every single EMU. In the reconnected EMU, the basic functions of each EMU and the whole train are also available. The basic functions of the notification include full-column notification, optional notification, and notification when a CCT fails.

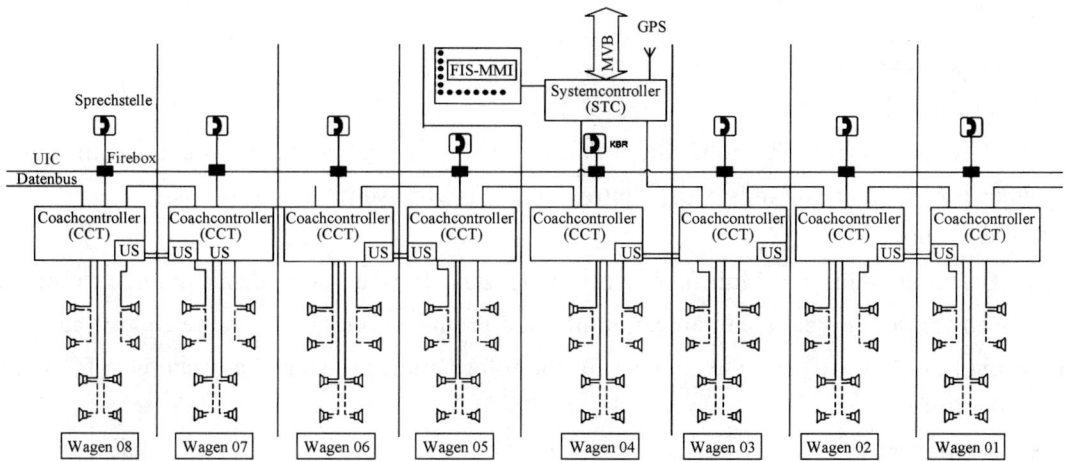

Figure 10-1　PIS Notification and communication subsystem composition diagram

1. System controller（STC）

STC is the control core of the whole information system PIS, and also the bridge connecting PIS and train control network.It is responsible for processing the information from the MVB bus, PIS, as well as the GSM antenna, GPS antenna, FM antenna and other devices belonging to the system, After processing, the corresponding control instruction or relevant information is sent to the corresponding target.At the same time, the STC has a power-off hold function memory, which can store important operational data, but also enables the PIS to automatically restore to the previous state in case of power failure.

2. PIS man-machine interaction interface（PIS-MMI）

PIS-MMI is the main interface for real-time communication between PIS and human beings. It is responsible for feedbacks of information from PIS or control network to operators, and also sends operators' requirements to PIS system.

3. PIS coachcontroller（CCT）

Each coach is equipped with a CCT and can communicate with the STC via the PIS data bus through a unique address.

4. Communication station, fire box, loudspeaker

The internal communication subsystem of each coach contains an internal communication station, a fire box and a CCT connected to the speaker. The CCT and the fire box are installed in the PIS cabinet. The fire box of each car is connected to the UIC bus.

5. GPS antenna, GSM antenna

The GPS antenna and GSM antenna receive the necessary signals and transmit them to STC for further processing. The information transmitted by GPS guarantees to trigger the announcement and possible content display when it reaches or passes the specified driving position.

GSM can receive digital voice notification (DVA) and advertising text information to STC for processing.

6. Bus system

1）UIC bus

The UIC bus is used for notification and internal communication. LF signals from internal communication stations and individual control signals are transmitted on this bus.

2）MVB bus

MVB Bus is short for Multifunction Vehicle Bus. It is a serial data communication bus, mainly used for the internal communication of fixed grouping vehicles. It is the control bus of the vehicle level of the EMU, and the channel for the information exchange between the STC and the CCU in the PIS.

3）PIS data bus

PIS data bus realizes the communication between STC and CCT. Transfer configuration, display, and control data from the CCT to the STC, and the diagnostic data from the CCT to the STC. On a reconnected EMU, the STCS of the two EMUs exchange information via the PIS data bus.

The basic communication function is to realize the dialing of each communication station through the dialing key on the internal communication station, which can be realized in the single bullet train or the heavy linkage train. However, this function is only available when the CCT is connected. Once the CCT fails due to a fault, this function will be unavailable.

The notification extension function can only be initiated by the internal communication station in the train cabin area. There are three types of options: The first is to all the EMU or adjacent EMU speakers; the second, to the operator in the EMU or with the EMU announcement car selection; the third is to the operator in the EMU or with the EMU announcement level of choice.

10.1.2 Information display subsystem

The main function of information display subsystem is to transmit display contents and display instructions to passenger information display and side destination display. The contents displayed on the passenger information display (station guide, news, advertisements, etc.) are edited by the computer on the ground and stored in the IC memory card. Read through the IC card reading and writing device in the driver's cab, input to the train information control device, and issue the display information and instructions of the train number information display. Its main components are: monochrome LED information display, related communication bus, GSM antenna, GPS antenna, CCT.

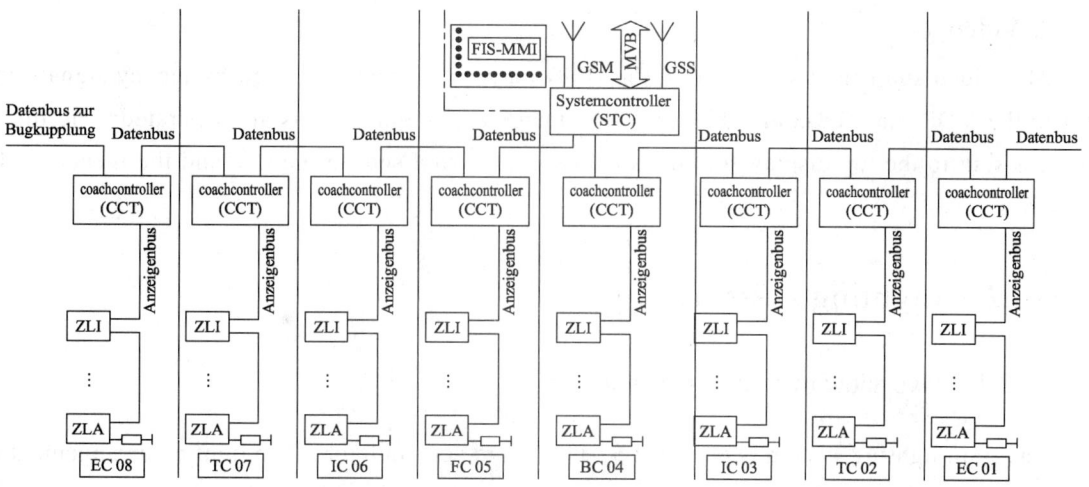

Figure 10-2 PIS information display subsystem diagram

The display system of each carriage includes external information display, internal information display and display bus. The display control can be divided into two different modes: automatic display control (normal mode) and manual display control (only used for internal display of the train).

10.1.3 Audio-visual entertainment subsystem

The system is designed to make passengers in the first class car (FC05) more comfortable, allowing for music or video entertainment during the journey. It is divided into two subsystems: audio system and video system.

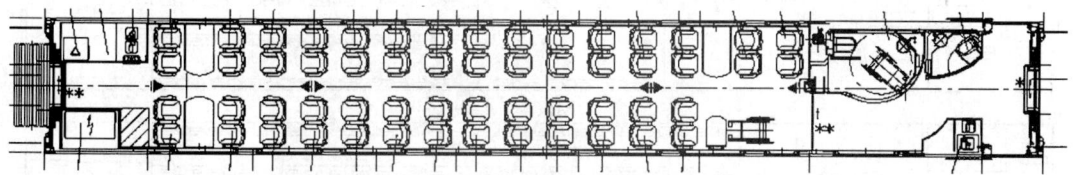

Figure 10-3 Video display in FC05 car layout diagram

The course of work:

1. Audio

The SCT transmits the LF signal from the UKW radio receiver or MP3 player to the CCT in the form of digital signal through the audio bus, where it is selected by the PIS MMI together with the sound signal from the video and transmitted to the AEU in the seat of the FC05 and to the top speaker (background music).

The LF signal is transmitted from each AEU headset as an analog signal. Each passenger can change the channel and volume of the voice individually through the keyboard. The volume of background music can only be changed by the PIS-MMI of each EMU.

2. Video

The Video and sound signals from the DVD player are tuned into high frequency signals and sent to the VDR via a coaxial cable. In VDR, image and sound signals are separated; The Image signal is sent to the top display, and the sound signal is first sent to the CCTand the thence to the audio bus.

10.2 Lighting system

10.2.1 Overview of lighting system

The train lighting system is powered by 110 V and accumulators. The lighting arrangement of the whole train is shown in attached Figure 10-2.It can be seen from the Figure that ordinary lighting is arranged in the middle of the roof and the junction between the side wall and the roof. These lights are usually fluorescent lamps, which are converted from DC 110 V to AC 220 V. There are reading lights above the seats in the car and halide lights in the dining car. These lights are converted from DC 110 V to DC 24 V.

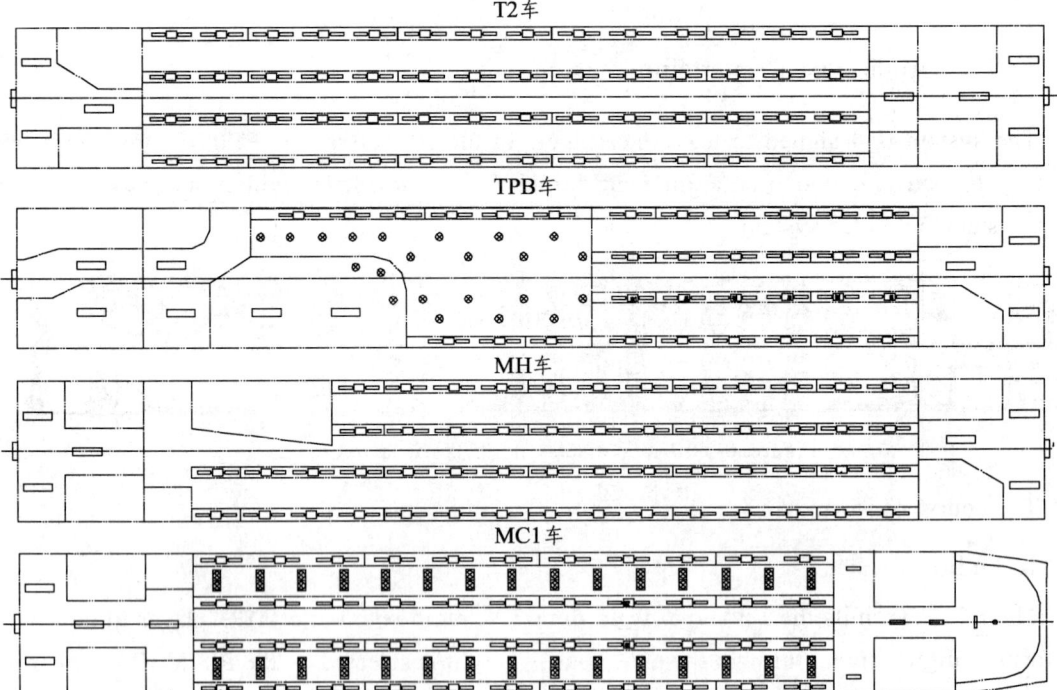

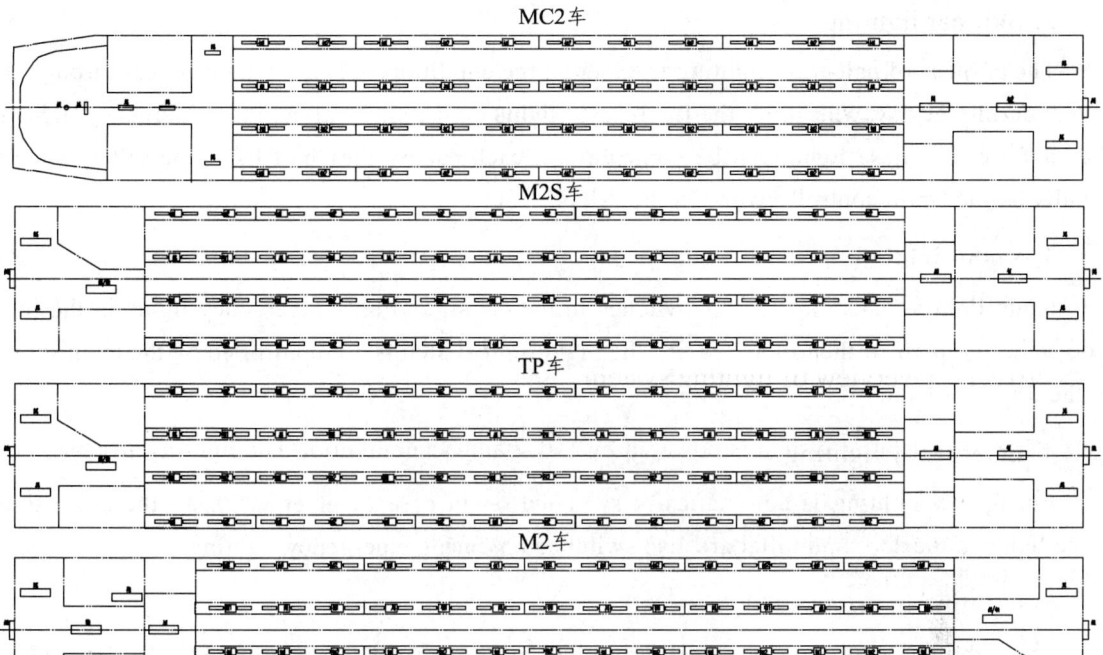

Figure 10-4　Lighting layout of the whole train

The lighting control switch in the car is divided into whole car lighting, half car lighting, night lighting, emergency lighting and fault display, etc. Lighting can be controlled either in the compartments or from the driver's cab.

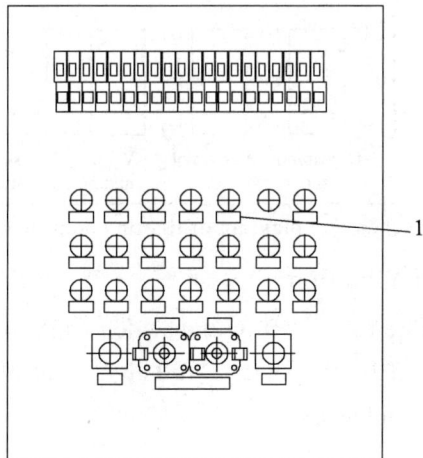

Figure 10-5　Schematic diagram of the lighting control switch in the driver's cab

1. All car lighting

The whole car lighting means that all the lighting in the car is working. If the video display is turned on, the 2 lights above it are off.

These lights can be controlled in each car by the "all-light controller" switch, usually by the "train control" switch in the driver's cab.

2. Half car lighting

The purpose of half-train lighting is to set up the conditions when the train passes through the tunnel during the day, when only the fluorescent lights on the side wall and the emergency lights in the roof are lit. These lights can be controlled in each car by the "half-light controller" switch, usually by the "train control" switch in the driver's cab.

3. Night lighting

Night lighting is controlled by switches in the cabin, and only emergency lights in the roof, side walls and parts of the toilets are lit. The night light switch is not controlled by the main switch in the driver's room.

4. Emergency lighting

Emergency lighting is automatically switched on in case of emergency. At the same time, some lights in the door and toilet are also switched on during emergency lighting.

5. Lighting in driver's cab

The lighting in the driver's cab is controlled by the "driver's cab light controller" switch on the driver's control platform. The position is shown in the following Figure 10-6 three-band switch, which can make the light on the left side of the driver shine alone or make both lights in the driver's room shine.

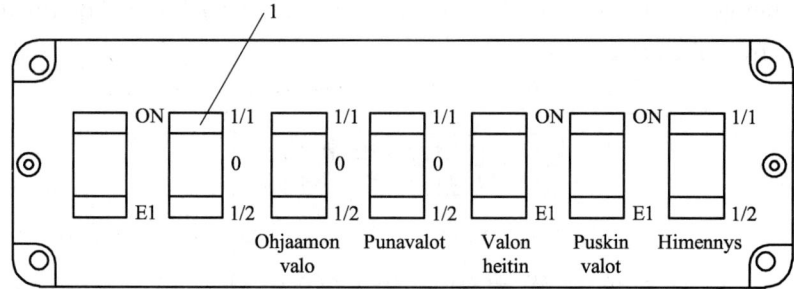

Figure 10-6 Schematic diagram of lighting control in driver's cab

6. Turn off the lights and operation

The lighting in the car can be turned off by the switch "light off Control", and the lighting in the whole train can be turned off by the switch "full light controller" in the driver's room. The lighting in the dining car and cabin has its own control switch.

7. Reading lamp

The reading light is mounted in the luggage rack above the seats, and the switch is mounted with the light and controlled by the passengers themselves.

8. The dining car lighting

In addition to fluorescent lights, there are halide lights in the dining car. The lighting of these lights is controlled by the dining car switchboard alone.

10.2.2 Maintenance of lighting

When illume appears problem commonly, it is lamp tube appeared problem normally, accordingly, need to replace lamp tube above all. When replacing the lamp does not work, the power converter may be faulty. For the reading light in the room and the spot light in the dining car, 24 V voltage halogenated lamp is used; When replacing the lamp doesn't work, the switch may be faulty.

10.3 Kitchen facilities and equipment

1. Instructions for kitchen Facilities and equipment (Figure 10-7)

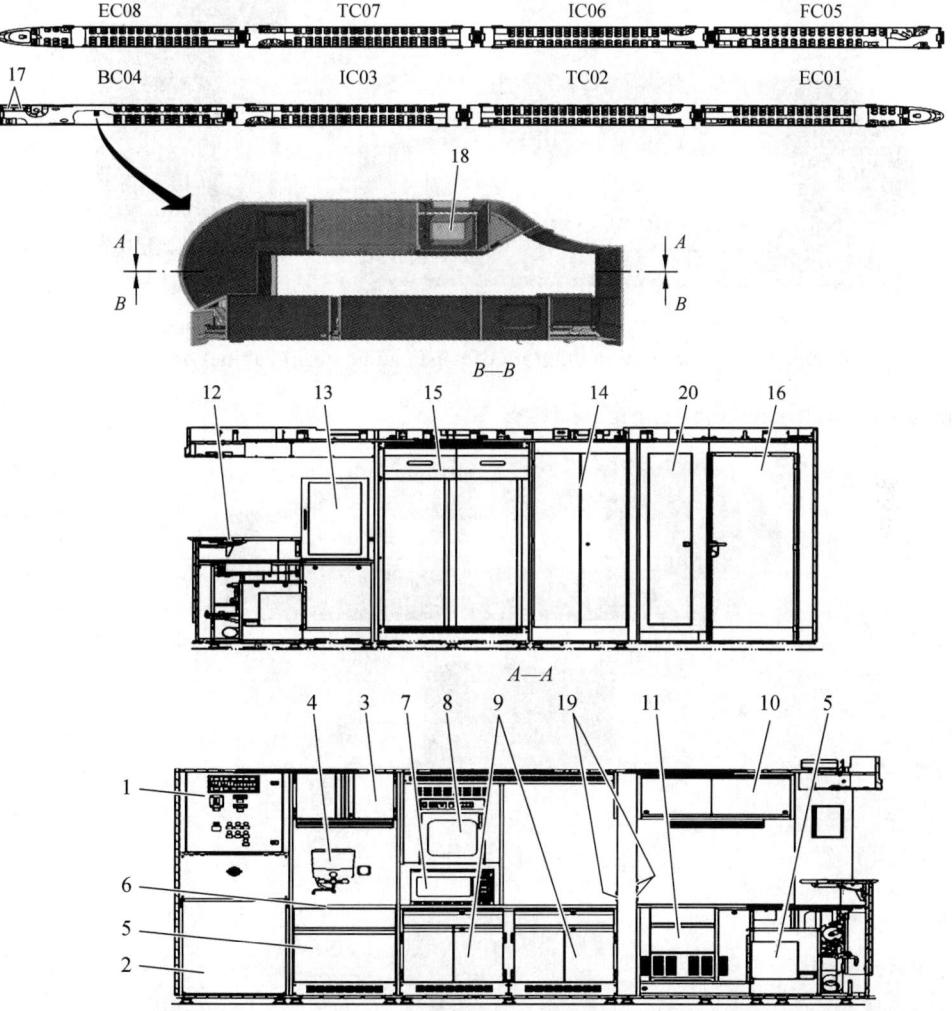

1—Control panel; 2—Waste trolley; 3—Cupboard; 4—Hot water boiler; 5—Waste drawer; 6—Sink; 7—Microwave oven; 8—Steamer; 9—Storage compartment; 10—Cupboard; 11—Icemaker; 12—Bar workdesk; 13—Show case; 14—Hot water dispenser module; 15—Refrigerator module; 16—Entrance door; 17—Galley storage; 18—Hot water dispenser; 19—Socket; 20—Wardrobe.

Figure 10-7 Structure of kitchen facilities and equipment

1) The door

Enter the kitchen work area through the door in the passenger/bar area. This door has a lock on the passenger/bar side, so access to the work area is only possible with a key. There's no door lock on the work area side.

2) Kitchen unit

(1) Waste and control cabinet unit is shown as in Figure 10-8.

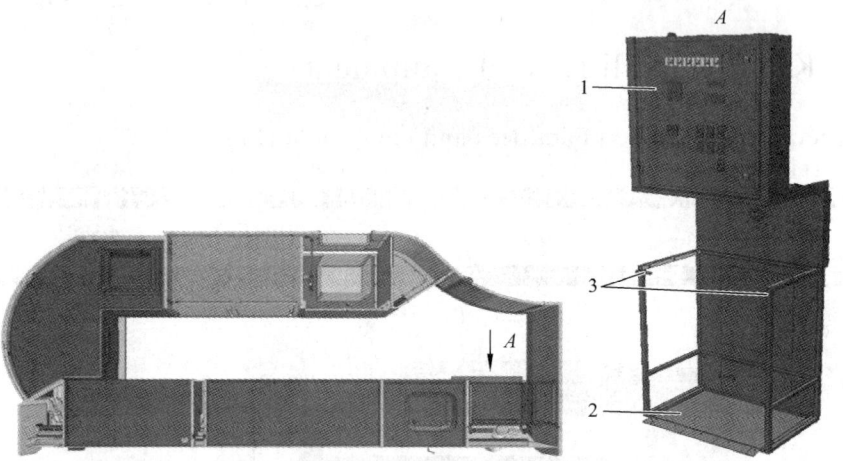

1—Control cabinet; 2—Two garbage truck storage areas; 3—locked car tank.
Figure 10-8 Simulation diagram of waste and control cabinet unit

(2) The tank unit is shown as in Figure 10-9.

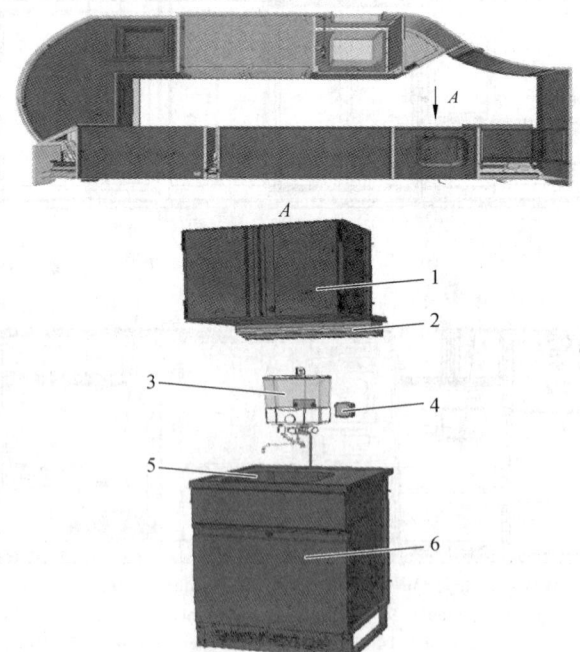

1—Wall cupboard; 2—Workplace lighting; 3—Hot water boiler; 4—Socket; 5—Sink; 6—Waste drawer.
Figure 10-9 Simulation diagram of flume unit

(3) The heating unit is shoun as in Figare 10-10.

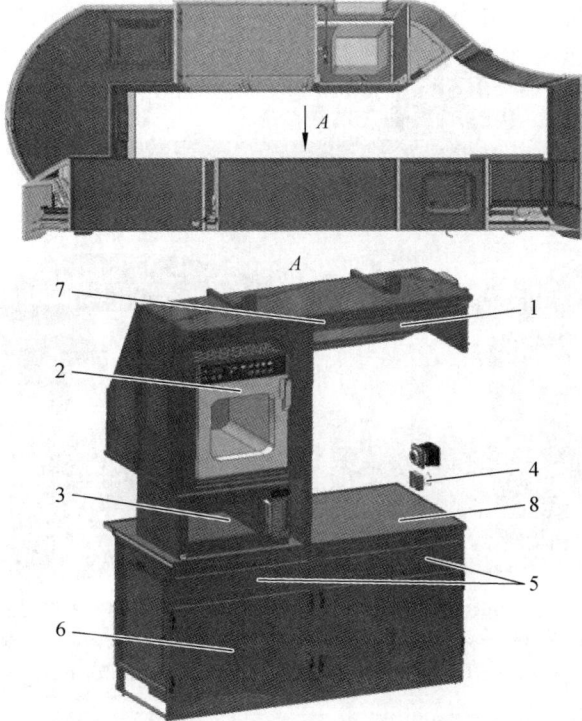

1—Workplace lighting; 2—Steamer; 3—Microwave oven; 4—Socket; 5—Drawe;
6—Storage compartment; 7—Cooker hood /; 8—Workdesk.

Figure 10-10 Simulation diagram of heating unit

(4) Cold and hot beverage units is shown as in Figure 10-11.

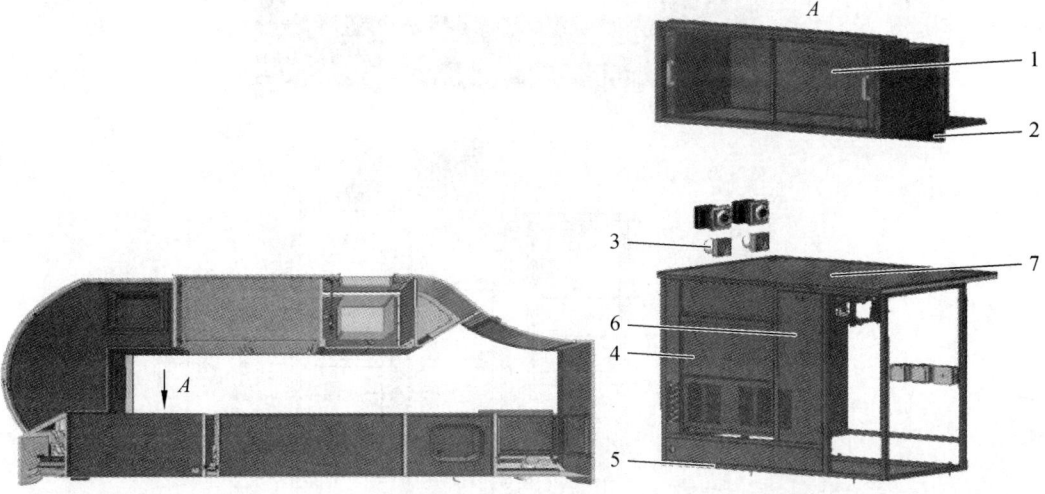

1—Wall cupboard; 2—Workplace spotlight; 3—Socket; 4—Icemaker; 5—Revision opening;
6—Revision opening; 7—Workdesk.

Figure 10-11 Simulation diagram of cold and hot beverage unit

(5) The counter unit is shown as in Figure 10-12.

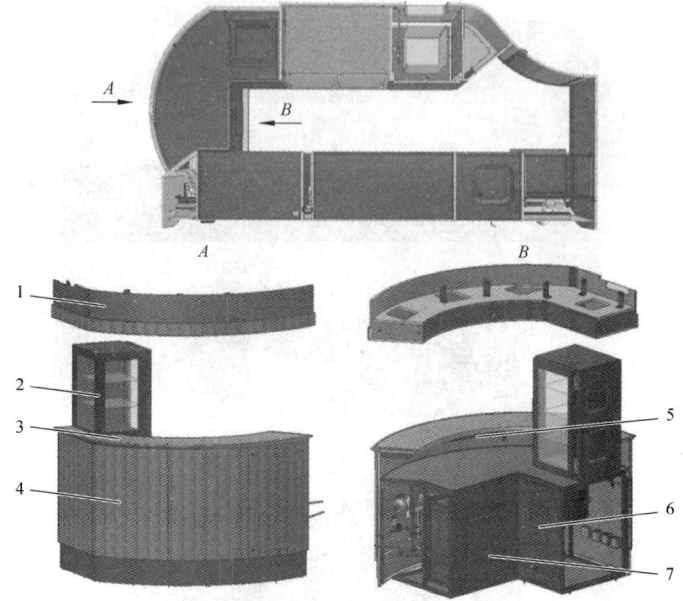

1—Counter superstructure; 2—Showcase; 3—Bar workdesk /; 4—Revision opening;
5—Workplace spotlight; 6—Revision opening; 7—Waste drawer /.

Figure 10-12　Simulation diagram of counter unit

(6) Cooling unit is shown as in Figure 10-13.

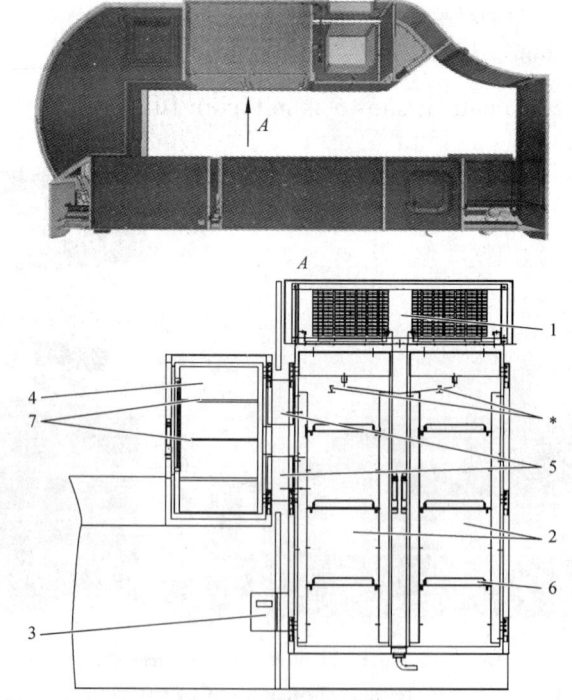

1—Refrigerating unit; 2—Refrigerator; 3—Refrigerator control; 4—Showcase;
5—Air duct; 6—Support; 7—Glass insert.

Figure 10-13　Cooling unit structure

(7) The boiler unit is shown as in Figure 10-14.

The boiler unit is equipped with a hot water panel. The unit is closed using two sliding doors, lock with a latch lock (square lock).

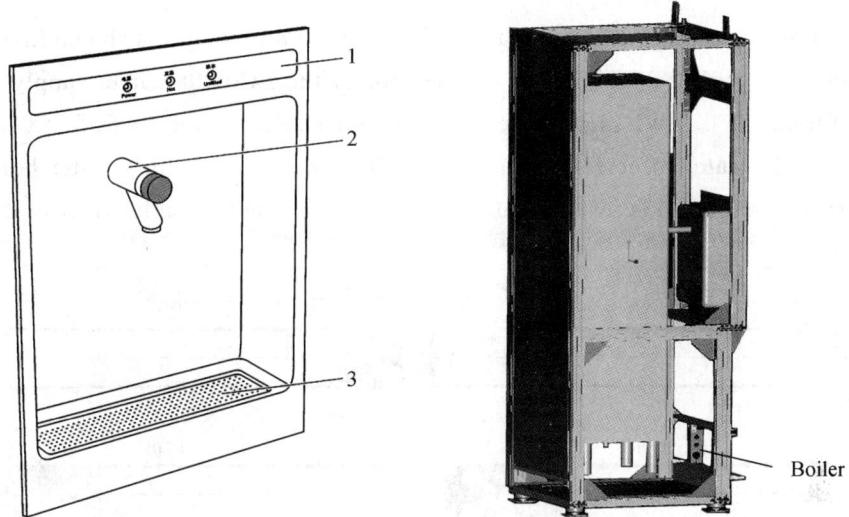

1—Indicator panel; 2—Water tap; 3—Water drain.

Figure 10-14　Boiler unit schematic diagram and simulation diagram

(8) Kitchen storage unit is shown as in Figure 10-15.

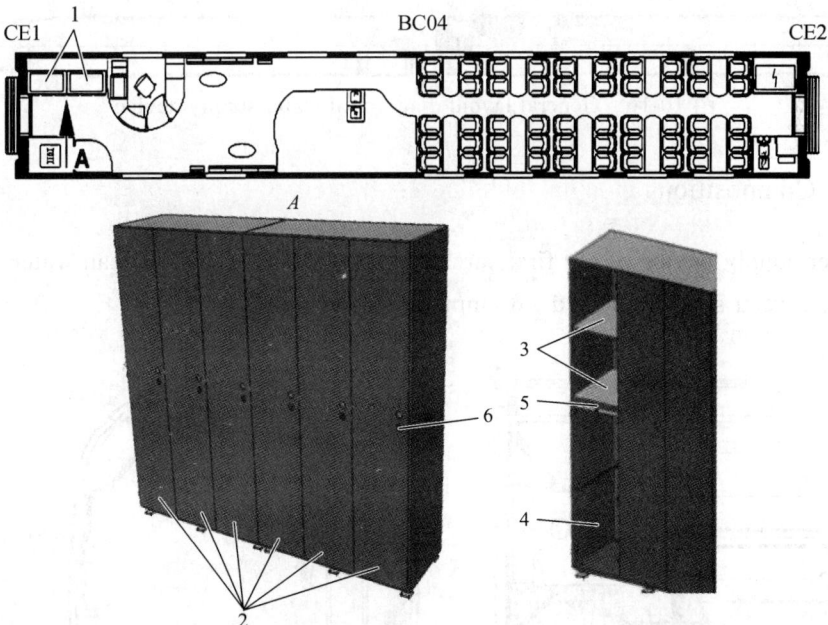

1—Galley storage module; 2—Storage cabinet; 3—Container insert; 4—Trolley run-in cabinet; 5—Trolley locker; 6—Door lock.

Figure 10-15　Simulation of kitchen storage unit

10.4 Water supply device

10.4.1 The overall layout

The layout of sanitation facilities on a CRH3 train with 8 carriages is shown in Figure 10-16. A 160 L clean water tank (A) is installed on the roof of the EC01/08 car to supply water to the boiled water furnace (F); 300 L clean water tank (B) is installed on the roof of TC02/07, IC03/06 and FC05 to supply water to corresponding toilets (C and E) and boiling water boilers (F); the 700 L water tank module (G) is installed under the BC04 vehicle to supply water to the kitchen of the dining car.

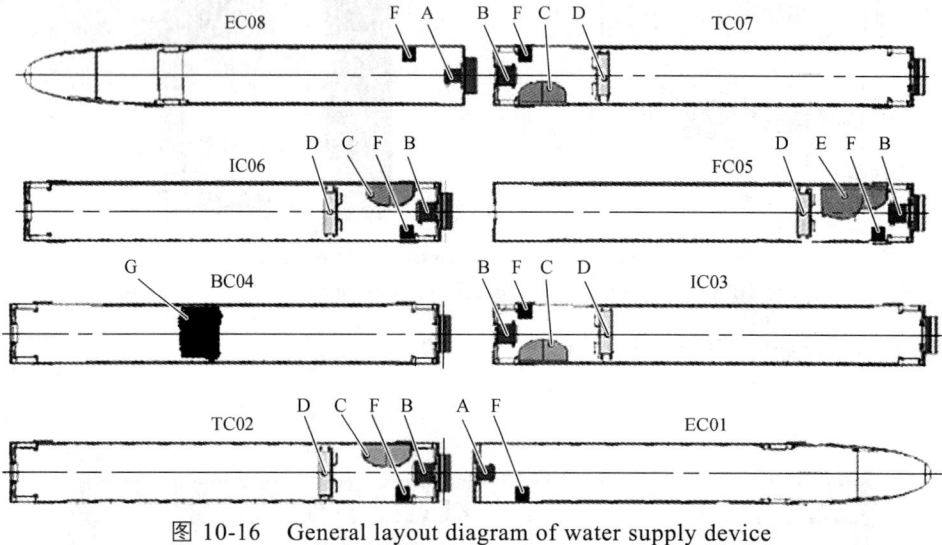

图 10-16 General layout diagram of water supply device

10.4.2 Composition

The water supply device of the first car EC01/08 includes a 160 L clean water tank, a water injection line, a water supply line and a drainpipe (see Figure 10-17).

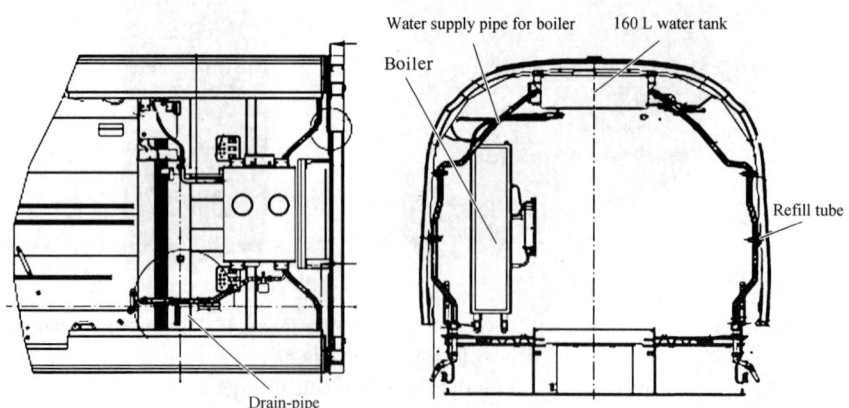

Figure 10-17   Composition diagram of water supply device for head car EC01/08

Transformer car TC02/TC07、converter car IC03/IC06、first class FC05 water supply device includes 300 L clean water tank, water injection line, water supply line and drain line (as shown in Figure 10-18).

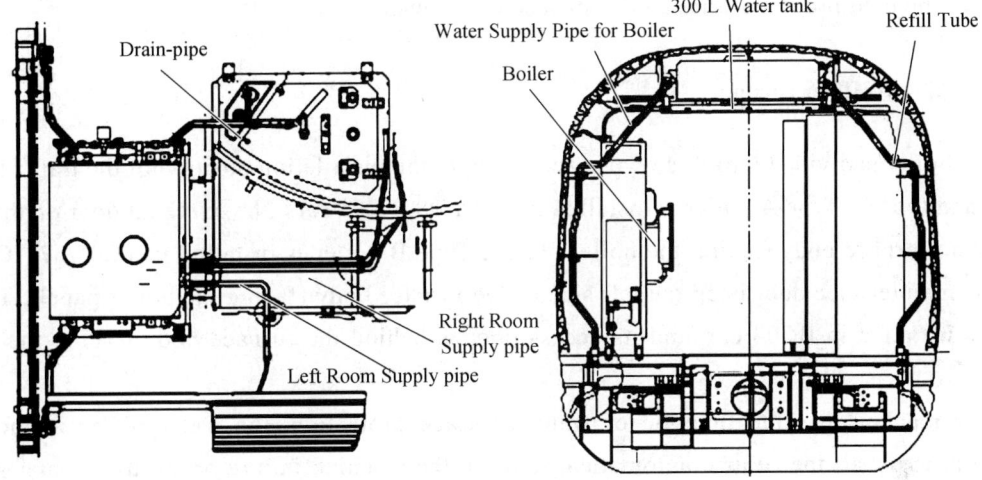

Figure 10-18　Transformer car TC02/TC07、converter car IC03/IC06、first class FC05 water supply unitconstitutional diagram

10.4.3　Dining car water supply system

10.4.3.1　Tank module composition

The water tank module is composed of 700 L clean water tank, supporting frame and pumping unit. The water tank is provided with two water injection lines, the bottom of the tank is equipped with a floating ball switch level sensor and a detachable heating pipe. The support frame is used to mount the tank under the car. The pump pipe is used for water circulation and antifreeze emptying of the bar car.

10.4.3.2　Kitchen water supply system application

Water circulation process: The switch of the water pump on the water tank module is controlled by the pressure switch in the kitchen. When the water valve on the vehicle is opened or closed, the pressure switch starts and transmits a signal to the water pump to start or open the water pump, so as to realize the water supply from the water tank under the vehicle to the kitchen water point; At the same time, when the pump pressure of the tank reaches a certain value, the water returns to the tank through another branch. In the process of pumping water, the water flows through the ultraviolet disinfection device for disinfection, and the water returns through the branch pipe to achieve the purpose of circulation purification.

drainage: When the train has power, open the solenoid valve on the tank module to drain the water tank; When the train has no power, the solenoid valve handle on the water tank can be manually opened for drainage.

Anti-freezing device: To prevent the water in the tank from freezing in winter, it is necessary to start the tank module heating device. The anti-freezing device of the water tank module includes: the electric blanket at the bottom of the box, the hot wire of each pipeline, the hot wire of the water pump and the cold proof material on the surface of the water tank.

10.4.4　Boiling furnace

The boiler is divided into three types according to the installation position of the train: Type A, type B and type C. Type A boiler is installed in EC01/08, FC05 cars, the overhaul door on the right side of the furnace body (facing the boiler panel); Type B boiler is installed in TC02/07, IC03/06 cars, the maintenance door is on the left side of the furnace body (facing the boiler panel); Type C boiler is installed in BC04 car, and its access door is behind the furnace body (facing the boiler panel).

This machine has the function of water shortage protection, the water boiler in the train running process, all the control automatically, when the machine failure or the train water supply tank water shortage, dry burning signal lights flashing, the water boiler will automatically stop boiling water. The boiling tank is separated from the storage tank, and the raw water and boiled water are not mixed, providing pure boiled water. When the ambient temperature of the electric water heater is < 4 °C or > 45 °C, the water heater is automatically under protection and stops working. The water dispenser is equipped with descaling device to prolong the maintenance cycle of electric heat pipe and water tank. The water boiler is equipped with a drainage button. After the train reaches the destination, press the button to automatically open the drainage solenoid valve, and the water flows out through the bottom pipe. When the water heater is powered on, the water heater can keep the water temperature > 90 °C during the whole train operation.

10.5　Health tsystem

10.5.1　General layout of health facilities

Take for example the layout of sanitation facilities on an 8-car CRH3 bullet train, Standard - standard toilets are arranged in position C of TC02/07 and IC03/06, The general-standard toilet is located in position E of the FC05, Ec01/08 has no sanitary facilities.A 450 L sewage tank will be hoisted under each vehicle with sanitation facilities at position D for the collection of sewage waste from toilet toilets.

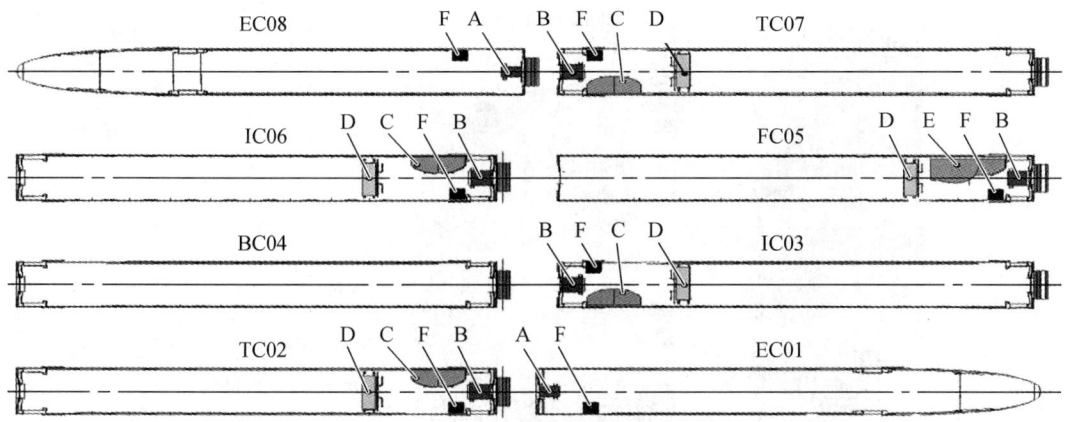

Figure10-19 Schematic diagram of the layout of health facilities

10.5.2 Standard toilet

Tc02/07 and IC03/06 adopt double standard toilet, including double standard toilet, hand-washing system, toilet seat and toilet equipment. Standard toilet adopts modular design, bathroom floor, wall panel, hand-washing system, toilet seat and other integrated into a module, reduce the bathroom and car interface, and interface form is simple, easy to install and adjust. The standard toilet is divided into left and right parts, the right as the main module of the health system (the main control board of the health system is installed in this room), the left interacted as auxiliary parts; the exterior contours between left and right are exactly the same as the interior facilities, and the two modules are arranged symmetrically on the car. Each standard bathroom consists of a floor, wall panels, a top plate, a door, a hand-washing system, a toilet seat, and internal equipment.

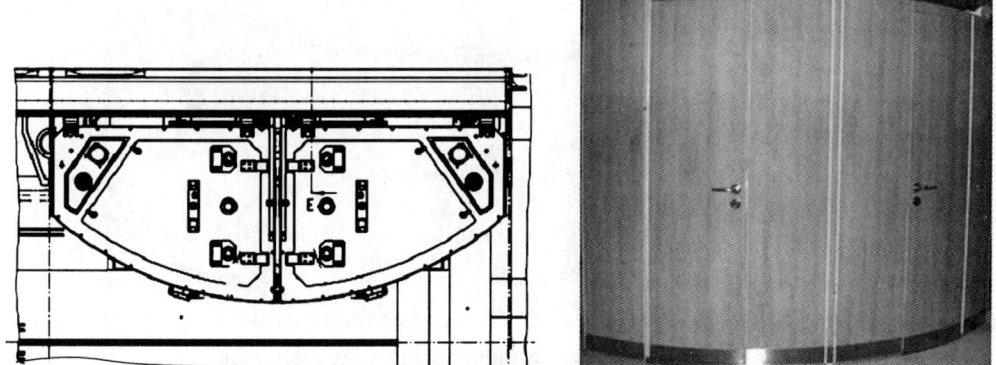

Figure10-20 Standard toilet drawing and physical drawing

10.5.3 Standard toilet equipment

Standard toilet equipment mainly includes tissue box, toilet paper holder, trash can, mirror door, hand washing system, etc.

- 285 -

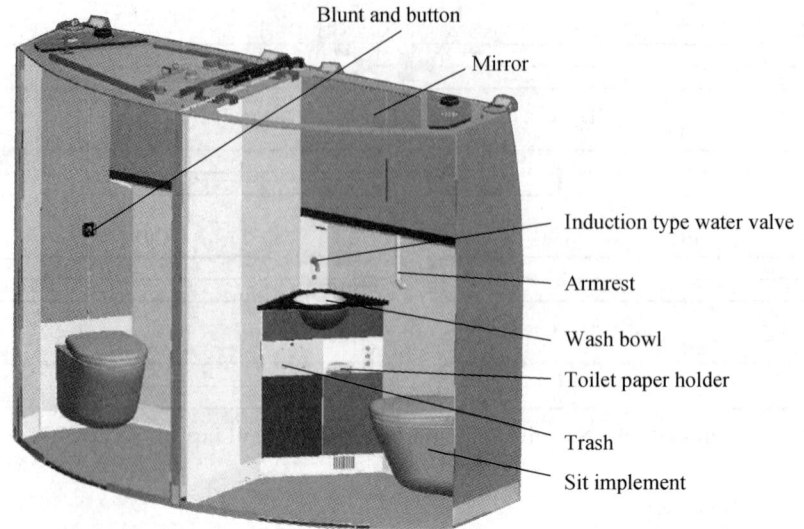

Figure 10-21　Standard toilet composition simulation diagram

10.5.4　First-class car toilet

FC05 vehicle toilet adopts the combination of general toilet and standard toilet. The biggest feature of the universal toilet is its large internal space, and the internal facilities can meet the requirements of the disabled. The electric door controlled by the button makes the design of the whole module more humanized. The general toilet consists of floor, wall panel, top plate, door, hand-washing system, toilet seat and internal equipment components.

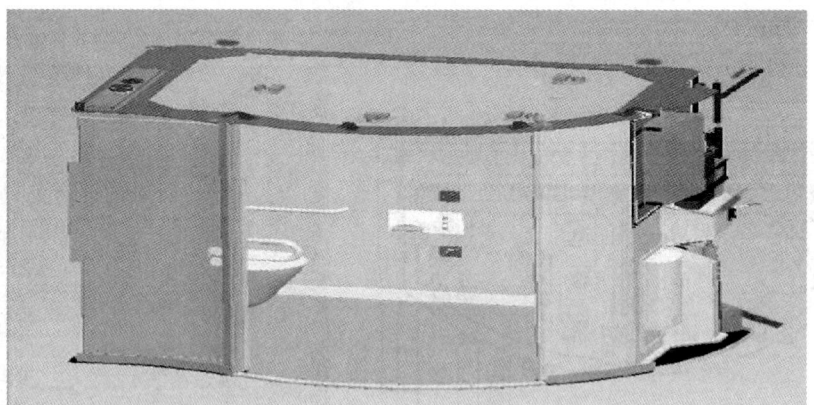

Figure 10-22　First class car toilet overall simulation diagram

10.5.5　The toilet collecting device

CRH3 EMU adopts vacuum push-pull collecting device, which has the advantages of compact structure design, easy installation, less water consumption, the system is all microcomputer control, it is easy to replace the system failure. Its disadvantage is that the reliability of components is relatively high, high maintenance technology requirements.

The toilet collecting device comprises two sets of toilet, toilet flushing button, on-board sewage pipe and heat tracing, under-car sewage pipe and heat tracing, under-car sewage tank and system control panel (installed behind the toilet wall panel). The two sets of toilets work relatively independently and share a trash bin.

When the collecting device is in normal use, just press the flushing button, and all the subsequent flushing cycle actions are completely controlled by the system controller of the collecting device. Some fault systems in operation can be automatically detected and cleared by self-diagnosis and routine fault clearing of the health system.

The entire health system is compact, with all controls integrated on the master bathroom panel. Through the control board of the main bathroom can realize the system of antifreeze emptying, can detect the water tank and sewage tank level and heat tracing, can control the normal operation of the collection system and fault diagnosis.

参考文献

[1] Theodore Wildi. Electrical Machines, Drives, and Power Systems.北京：科学出版社，2002: 635-695.

[2] 李飞. 动车组专业英语.成都：西南交通大学出版社，2018：176-206.

[3] 李建国. 中国高速动车组. 北京：中国铁道出版社，2012：1-16.

[4] 刘建国. 高速铁路概论. 北京：中国铁道出版社，2009：116-160.